# Industry Research Using the Economic Census

# Industry Research Using the Economic Census
## How to Find It, How to Use It

Jennifer C. Boettcher and Leonard M. Gaines

GREENWOOD PRESS
Westport, Connecticut • London

**Library of Congress Cataloging-in-Publication Data**

Boettcher, Jennifer C.
   Industry research using the economic census : how to find it, how to use it / Jennifer C. Boettcher
   and Leonard M. Gaines.
     p. cm.
  Includes bibliographical references and index.
  ISBN 1–57356–351–X (alk. paper)
  1. Economic census—Handbooks, manuals, etc. 2. Industrial statistics—United States—Statistical
  services. 3. United States—Census—Handbooks, manuals, etc. I. Gaines, Leonard M. II. Title.
   HC101.B594 2004
338.0973'0072'7—dc22                 2004008607

British Library Cataloguing in Publication Data is available.

Library of Congress Catalog Card Number: 2004008607
ISBN: 1–57356–351–X

First published in 2004

Greenwood Press, 88 Post Road West, Westport, CT 06881
An imprint of Greenwood Publishing Group, Inc.
www.greenwood.com

Printed in the United States of America

The paper used in this book complies with the
Permanent Paper Standard issued by the National
Information Standards Organization (Z39.48–1984).

10  9  8  7  6  5  4  3  2

This book is dedicated with all our love to:
Hulbert and Clare Boettcher
and
Nancy and Julie Gaines

# Contents

*Preface*                                                                           ix

*Introduction*                                                                    xiii

**PART I: UNDERSTANDING THE ECONOMIC CENSUS**                                      1

Chapter 1: Overview and History                                                    3

Chapter 2: Economic Census Procedures                                             27

Chapter 3: Terminology                                                            39

Chapter 4: North American Industry Classification System (NAICS)                  51

Chapter 5: Reports and Special Publications                                       69

Chapter 6: Formats                                                               109

**PART II: SELECTED INDUSTRIES**                                                 127

Chapter 7: Agriculture                                                           129

Chapter 8: Transportation and Warehousing                                        153

Chapter 9: Manufacturing                                                         183

Chapter 10: Wholesale Trade                                                      199

Chapter 11: Retail Trade                                                         213

Chapter 12: Remaining Sectors                                                    233

*Appendixes*

A. Acronyms and Initials Used in This Book                                       245

B. Sample Questionnaires                                                         247

C. Regional Federal Depository Libraries                                         287

D. State Data Center/Business and Industry Data Center Lead Agencies             293

E. Census Bureau Regional Offices                                                299

Index                                                                            301

# Preface

## THE NEED FOR THIS BOOK

While most people in this country are familiar with the once-every-10-years U.S. Census of Population and Housing because they are a part of it, relatively few people even know about the census of businesses that occurs every 5 years. Yet, these U.S. Economic Censuses provide data essential to understanding the nation's economy.

In our respective jobs, we have found many people who were amazed to find out that the answers to their questions could be found in this hidden resource. Many of the people, far from novices at economic or business research, become frustrated because they don't know where to look in the deep piles of data that come from the Economic Census for the one or two pieces of information that they needed. Many of the people were far from novices at economic or business research.

Through these experiences, it became clear that the guides and other information about the Economic Census that have been provided by the Census Bureau and data intermediaries are good general introductions to this goldmine. But they are not the detailed maps and guides that many data users need to find their way through this labyrinth. Instead many of them feel like the old-time explorers working with a very sketchy set of information about where they need to go and how to get there.

Additionally, there have been a number of significant changes in the 1997 and 2002 Economic Censuses that have made many of those previous sketchy maps based on earlier Economic Censuses obsolete.

We also found that a number of good guides and other resource books exist about the decennial censuses, but none exists about the Economic Censuses. This is clearly a gap that needed to be filled.

## PURPOSE

The purpose of this book is twofold: to explain Census concepts, methods, terminology, and data sources in an understandable manner; and to assist Census users in locating needed Census data. The book is designed as a working handbook for Economic Census users.

The chapters are written so they can be read from start to finish, but because of the sheer amount of detail presented, a reader can take away some understanding by just reading parts of the chapters. Most of the chapters in this book are designed so they can be read independently of the other chapters, but reading the entire book will provide you with the greatest understanding of the Economic Census. It is hoped that Census users will also use this work as a reference book, consulting it to answer specific questions as the need arises.

This book does not duplicate the data from the census, but introduces you to the features, uses, and formats of the data. *Industry Research Using the Economic Census* is not meant as a blind apology for the Census Bureau and its methods. Although the United States Economic Census is widely regarded as the best business census in the world, it is not without its problems, as any Census Bureau official would readily admit. Wherever appropriate, the limitations of the data, publications, and software are discussed.

## ORGANIZATION

*Industry Research Using the Economic Census* is divided into three sections. The first part of this book (chapters 1 through 6) begins by providing an overview of the Census. Chapter 1 is an overview to the Economic Census, a review of what was not collected, and includes a history of the Economic Census. The differences between the 1997 and 2002 Economic Censuses are delineated within this historical context. Resources for more recent data and data not included in the Economic Census are also included in chapter 1. Chapter 2 describes, in some detail, the procedures used by the Census Bureau to collect and tabulate the data. Chapter 3 provides an overview of terminology and concepts used in the Census. Chapter 4 reviews the development and structure of the SIC and NAICS classification systems. Chapter 5 is dedicated to understanding the different reports produced by the Census Bureau as part of the Economic Census. Chapter 6 educates the reader about the distribution and access of the Census: print, CD-ROMs, and Internet. It is designed to assist the reader in efficiently accessing the needed data and it provides examples of how to cite the results in different styles.

The second part (chapters 7 through 12) contains examples of five different industry sectors (chapters 7 through 11 in order): Agriculture, Transportation and Warehousing, Manufacturing, Wholesale Trade, and Retail Trade. In each of these chapters you can find an overview of the sector and highlight specific Economic Census data products about the sector. At the end of these chapters you will find an SIC-NAICS comparison chart, which allows you to see how the industrial definitions changed in the transition between these two systems. The chapters also include information on other data sources that can be used to update information between the Census years. Chapter 12 discusses the remaining sectors covered by the Economic Census with an emphasis on the similarities and differences of the coverage and data products of these sectors with those covered in chapters 7 through 11.

The final part of this book contains the appendixes, consisting of a list of acronyms used in this book and sample Economic Census questionnaires. Also included in the appendixes are lists of the Government Printing Office Regional Depository Libraries, the State Data Center/Business-Industry Data Center Lead Agencies, and the Census Bureau Regional Offices—all of which can provide access to the Economic Census data and assistance in working with it.

## WHAT WE HOPE YOU GET OUT OF THIS BOOK

Librarians, students, faculty, and researchers looking for economic or business information should find this book useful. If an economic developer, for example, was interested in estimating the electricity used by a book printing plant employing 50 people or the total sales of stationery stores in a given country, the only place to find these answers is the Economic Census. We hope that users find this resource to be a useful map to finding your way through the Economic Census goldmine.

In particular, we hope that you will use this book as a reference tool when you have questions about whether or not some particular piece of information can be found in the Economic Census. Even if we don't answer that question directly, we hope we can guide you in the right direction to find the answer.

It is possible that you know that the answer to your question exists in the Economic Census, but you don't know which tool for accessing it is the best one for your needs. In that case, we hope that we have provided you with enough information about the various tools to choose among and to start using them.

If you find that the answers to your questions don't lie in the Economic Census, we hope that we have provided you with enough direction to find the answer elsewhere.

We also hope that by reading this book you will find out something interesting about the Economic Census that you would like to explore further.

## A WORD OF CAUTION

Because the Internet is an important means of disseminating statistical data and has been fully embraced by the Census Bureau for this purpose, we refer to many Web sites in this book. We also describe a number of specific Web pages here.

In addition to being a powerful, inexpensive, and efficient means to disseminate statistical data, the Internet is highly dynamic. Therefore, we caution you that some of our references and descriptions may have changed by the time you read this. Understanding that this may happen, we have tried to refer to Web sites that will be around for a while. We have also tried to keep our discussions of the specific Web pages more general in nature so that you will still be able to use them. We hope we have been successful in this effort.

## THE OTHERS WHO MADE THIS BOOK POSSIBLE

As with any undertaking of this scale, it would have been impossible to write this book without the support, understanding, and assistance of many other people. We would like to take this opportunity to acknowledge and thank them.

An effort like this also affects the lives of people around the authors in many ways, often preventing the authors from doing things they would like to do. This is all the more so when writing a book is an "extracurricular" activity. Having said that, we would like to thank our families, friends, and colleagues, whom we have often neglected while working on this task, for understanding when we said we couldn't do something because we were busy with writing a book. Special thanks goes to our immediate families and closest friends for their extra support throughout the writing process and understanding when working on this book really prevented us from having fun with them. Extremely special thanks go to Nancy and Julie for having to live with Leonard during this whole process. Ken and Jennifer's family has always been supportive, especially when they stopped asking, "How's the book?"

We also wish to thank our respective employers for allowing us to take off the time we needed to write this book.

As always, several people deserve individual recognition for their efforts in making this book a reality. Michael Lavin gets our thanks for suggesting that we team up on this project; Anne Thompson from the Greenwood Publishing Group for keeping us on the straight and narrow in bringing this book to completion.

Paul T. Zeisset from the U.S. Census Bureau's Economic Planning and Coordination Division gets our strongest thanks for reviewing what we wrote in a timely manner, finding and clarifying the details about the Economic Census that we missed, and suggesting better ways of saying things. We are greatly indebted to Paul for all his effort and assistance. Any errors in this book are strictly the result of our choosing not to follow Paul's expertise.

Any and all opinions stated in this book are strictly those of the authors and do not reflect or represent any position of Georgetown University, Empire State Development, of the State of New York, our respective employers.

Jennifer Boettcher
Arlington, VA
Leonard M. Gaines
Colonie, NY

# Introduction

We are in the midst of [a] great technological revolution which is accelerating change, hastening obsolescence, creating new industries and transforming old ones, remaking the industrial map of the country, and bringing within the range of the feasible great heights of production, productivity, and well-being...The need for the benchmark statistics provided by the Bureau of the Census is greater today than ever before, and promises to grow in intensity.

—*Watkins Commission Report, 1954*

The economy, industries, and companies are what business research is all about. The United States Economic Census is crucial to understanding all three. *Industry Research Using the Economic Census* is designed to increase your understanding of the Economic Census to help you in making decisions. It will aid you in learning how to use the Economic Census in order to recognize trends in your industry, provide marketing direction, reveal financial benchmarks, decide on business placement, and understand the foundations of key economic indicators.

Most people are familiar with the Census of Population and Housing conducted every 10 years. The Census Bureau has been collecting data on the nation's businesses in one form or another since the 1810 Census. Yet few people are aware of the amazing resource and potential of the "Other Census" conducted by the Census Bureau every 5 years. In fact, a mid-1990s study of census data use by agencies participating the Census Bureau's State Data Center/ Business and Industry Data Center program indicated that economic data accounted for less than 5 percent of the Census Bureau's data used by these agencies (Gaines 1997, 72).

Yet, the Census Bureau's economic data is extremely important to the nation's business community. The Economic Census is used to target sales, calculate Gross Domestic Product (GDP), measure market share, decide regional economic policy, and define the economic health of the United States and its territories. The importance of the Economic Census was highlighted in 1953 by the Watkins Commission Report, which contained unreserved testimonials supporting the Economic Census from business, financial, professional, and governmental groups. Many business leaders also supported the 1997 and 2002 Economic Censuses.

Why is this census so overlooked by the public? Primarily, because the people reaping these benefits do so indirectly without realizing that they are getting these benefits. Rather than using Economic Census products directly, they reap the benefits by using data products, which in turn rely on the Economic Census.

This book addresses the history of the Economic Census. It describes the processes of collecting, distributing, and using the data from the Census. Data products for selected industry sectors included in the Economic Census and closely related surveys are described in detail and the remaining sectors are summarized.

## IMPORTANCE OF THE ECONOMIC CENSUS DATA

The power of the Economic Census has been traditionally limited to such people as the marketing giants who can tease out data from the reports, real estate developers who can see trends emerge from detailed reports, investment analysts who can hire economists to draw out the necessary numbers to understand an industry, and bureaucrats who can call upon the network of government agencies to interpret the data. This book is your key to unlocking the true potential of the data provided in the reports and other data products.

Within this book you will read stories—stories that may sound familiar to small business owners, senior vice presidents, marketers, city officials, educators, or librarians. Reading this book should help you avoid making the common mistakes related to choosing wrong sales territory, misjudging your market share, investing in an infrastructure that is becoming obsolete, or realizing the importance of a process to your company after it gets spun off. The stories talk about the importance of using the data of the Economic Census when making decisions.

Since the Census is about data and the book is about information and the desired outcome is knowledge, it is best to quickly review the differences between data, information, and knowledge. Data, the plural form of datum, are items much like a group of numbers within a set. The context of data or the name of the set is information. For example, 76.1 books, 5.8 magazines, and 2.7 stationery are data. Knowing that these data are the shares of revenue of each item as a percent of total sales in bookstores in Virginia is information. Knowledge comes from being able to benchmark an independent bookstore by using industry norms from the Census to allocate stock in the store. The power of this book comes from recognizing the options the Census provides with its data, applying the information, and demonstrating knowledge. The more information you have, the lower your risk of making a bad decision.

The data collected by the Census Bureau portray the many dimensions of the economy. One data point can be used geographically at the national, state, county, metropolitan area, and ZIP code levels. That data point can also be used in broad industry sectors or specific industries, e.g., from the information sector or paging service. That data point can also be a part of a Census program looking at owners' educational background in the *Characteristics of Business Owners* report, an operating expense for a retailer in the *Business Expenses* report, or a part in describing the different transportation methods used in the *Vehicle Inventory and Use Survey.* This book provides a context for understanding the relationships among the data in all of its forms.

The Economic Census is released in print and computerized format. The book will help guide you through the options of the different formats. Most, but not all, of the data is free over the Internet. By giving you information about the availability of what you want, this publication can help you maximize your fiscal and time resources.

## SOME CHANGES IN THE ECONOMIC CENSUS

The 1997 Economic Census saw a number of very significant changes, such as the introduction of a new system for defining industries and much greater use of the Internet as a data dissemination tool. The 2002 Economic Census also saw some changes, but to a much lesser degree than 1997. These changes included new questions about e-commerce, further changes in the industrial classification system (and the conversion of some reports to the new system), and greater software capabilities on the CD-ROM products produced as part of the Economic Census.

The United States government created the Standard Industrial Classification (SIC) system in the 1930s for federal statistical agencies to use in describing the nation's economy. Most other governmental agencies and commercial data publishers have used this system as the main way to classify industrial activity. The business world, as we know it, is changing. In recognition of this fact the SIC system has been replaced by the North American Industry Classification System (NAICS).

With the release of the 1997 Economic Census in early 1999, the business community was introduced to the North American Industry Classification System. There was an additional minor revision of NACIS in 2002. As part of this change, there is no longer a single service sector. New industry sectors were created, such as the Information or Health Care and Social Assistance or Accommodation and Food Services sectors.

The 1997 Economic Census was the first government data series to use the new NAICS system. With the introduction of NAICS, all governmental, and many non-governmental, statistical series relating to commerce are changing. The change is a result of the United States, Mexican, and Canadian governments creating a system that will be compatible among the NAFTA counties and includes new industries like bioremediation, management consulting, Internet service providers, publishing plants, and other new industries. The clean-slate approach taken by the governments has resulted in 20 sectors, where before there were 10; six digits, where before there were four; and 36 percent of the new industries being defined in such a way that they effectively have no historical data.

The new system brings questions. A guide is needed to understand how the changes will affect the business world. This book goes beyond technical aspects of physically changing the codes. It also addresses the anxieties of people as they realize the different competitive, regulatory, and economic environments these changes may put upon their companies.

Another change with this Census is the greater use of the Internet to distribute the data. In fact, more data is now available on the Internet than in print—and the number of reports actually printed is decreasing with each new Census. Even more data will be available on CD-ROMs or DVDs than on the Internet. The CD-

ROMs and DVDs also come with new software to search, retrieve, and organize data, so the data can be used in a spreadsheet or a text document. This book describes the capabilities of the Internet and the software on the CD-ROMs.

The 2002 Economic Census program includes more information about e-commerce, women-owned businesses, minority-owned businesses, and business-owner characteristics than earlier censuses. It also includes the most recent changes in NAICS that affect the construction, wholesale, parts of retail, and other service industries. The software available with the 2002 Economic Census CD-ROMs will have mapping and time series analysis capabilities.

## BIBLIOGRAPHY

Gaines, Leonard M. 1997. *The Selection of Census Data in State Data Center/Business and Industry Data Center Program Organizations: A Gatekeeping-based Model.* Ann Arbor, MI: UMI Dissertation Information Service. (PhD. diss., Rensselaer Polytechnic Institute. UMI Number: 9807706.)

U.S. Bureau of the Census. 1997. *Business Leaders Speak Out about the Economic Census.* Washington, DC: The Bureau. http://www.census.gov/epcd/www/ec97quotes.html (accessed October 18, 2003).

U.S. Bureau of the Census. 1997. *Two Moments of Truth: 1954 and 1997 (EX97X-TMT).* Washington, DC: The Bureau, 1997. http://www.census.gov/epcd/www/img/ec97x-tm.pdf (accessed October 18, 2003).

U.S. Bureau of the Census. 2002. *What Others Are Saying about the 2002 Economic Census.* Washington, DC: The Bureau. http://www.census.gov/epcd/ec02/quotes.htm (accessed October 18, 2003).

# PART I
# Understanding the Economic Census

# CHAPTER 1
# Overview and History

*The Economic Census is indispensable to understanding America's economy. It insures the accuracy of the statistics we rely on for sound economic policy and for successful business planning.*

*—Alan Greenspan, Chairman of the Federal Reserve Board of Governors*

1. What Is the Economic Census?
2. History
3. New in 1997
4. New in 2002
5. Related Censuses
6. Other Exclusions and Limitations
7. Question: Test Your Knowledge
8. Data Availability
9. Data Reports

    A. Industry Series
    B. Geographic Area Series
    C. Subject Series
    D. Other Reports

10. Using Economic Census Data

    A. Government
    B. Private Sector and Other Users

11. Chronological History
12. Updated Sources

    A. From the Census Bureau
    B. Bureau of Labor Statistics
    C. Other Government Sources
    D. Commercial Sources

13. Answers: Test Your Knowledge
14. Bibliography

## WHAT IS THE ECONOMIC CENSUS?

The Economic Census is a major source of facts about the structure and functioning of the nation's economy. It provides essential information for government, business, researchers, and the general public. The Economic Census furnishes an important part of the framework for such composite measures as the gross domestic product estimates, input/output measures, production and price indexes, and other statistical series that measure short-term changes in economic conditions.

Remember this is a census not a survey. Unlike a survey that queries a section of a target group and then statistically projects the results to the rest of the group, a census defines the group and sends the questionnaires to everyone, so there is no need to statistically project a result. It this case, the target group is all economic activity in the United States, excluding the agriculture and government sectors and parts or all of some industries. The Economic Census provides details for most detailed industry and many geographic levels. Some annual reports like the *Annual Survey of Manufacturers* present only national and some state data. Other reports, like the *County Business Patterns,* provide limited industry details. The Economic Census is done every five years, because the amount of preparation, gathering, and presentation of data is immensely time consuming and expensive. So why don't they do it every ten years like the Census of Population and Housing? Because the country needs the data to recapitulate the economic assumptions being used in economic surveys and models. The Economic Census provides the benchmark data and tools *all* business, policy, and economic decisions are rooted in.

Using the Economic Census allows people to understand a geographic region, a business operation, and a whole industry. The array of uses are vast and this book is going to help you understand how to use the data to plug into that array and understand the economy better. It all starts with the business. The business can be a store, factory, warehouse, or home office. According to the Census Bureau a business at a specific location is called an establishment. The Economic Census is conducted on an establishment-level basis. A company operating at more than one location is required to file a separate report for each store, factory, and other locations. Each establishment is assigned a separate industry classification based on its primary activity and not that of its parent company.

A common mistake is getting a product, establishment, company, and industry confused. The Economic Census provides data on all four of these concepts. Products or revenue source, such as automobile tires or testing services, are given a product code and are reported in the Subject Series reports for specific sectors. Establishments are a specific business at a specific location. Establishments usually create profit by providing a variety of products or services. You can get a lot of establishment details from the Economic Census, including: What is the average revenue per business in a city? How much is a business in this industry paying for computer equipment and services? or What is the normal mix of services offered by other business in your industry? Note the Census Bureau is very strict in *never* revealing enough data to let a user figure out an individual establishment's identity. A company consists of one or more establishments under common ownership or control. Each company is required to give the Bureau separate data for each of their establishments, because frequently different establishments do different things, and typically different establishments are located in different geographic areas. So it is each establishment that gets a North American Industry Classification System (NAICS) code, not the company as a whole. An industry is a group of establishments using roughly the same process to produce similar goods or services. It could be defined narrowly like all paging services or defined broadly to broadcasting and telecommunications. NAICS provides the frame of reference for defining industries in the Economic Census.

Section 131 of the United States Code Title 13 establishes the timing of the Economic Census by stating:

> The Secretary [of Commerce] shall take, compile, and publish censuses of manufactures, of mineral industries, and of other businesses, including the distributive trades, service establishments, and transportation (exclusive of means of transportation for which statistics are required by law to be filed with, and are compiled and published by, a designated regulatory body), in the year 1964, then in the year 1968, and every

> fifth year thereafter, and each such census shall relate to the year immediately preceding the taking thereof.

Which means the Economic Census is taken every five years with the reference years being the years ending with two and seven.

## HISTORY

The Economic Census has been taken as an integrated program at 5-year intervals since 1967 and before that for 1954, 1958, and 1963. Prior to that time individual components of the Economic Census were taken separately at varying intervals. Figure 1.1 shows roughly when data started being collected in each of the industrial sectors. When looking at this figure, remember that some sectors were collected for a while, then were dropped for a while, and have returned.

The Economic Census traces its beginnings to the third Decennial Census in 1810, when questions on manufacturing and occupation were included with those for population. Coverage of economic activities was expanded for the 1840 Decennial Census and subsequent censuses to include mining and some commercial activities. The 1905 Manufactures Census was the first time a census was taken apart from the regular decennial population census. Censuses covering retail and wholesale trade and construction industries were added in 1930, as were some covering service trades in 1933. In 1939 the federal government created a standardized description of industries that became the Standard Industrial Classification (SIC) codes. Censuses of construction, manufacturing, and the other business services were suspended during World War II.

The 1954 Economic Census was the first census to be fully integrated: providing comparable census data across economic sectors, using consistent time periods, concepts, definitions, classifications, and reporting units. It was the first census to be taken by mail, using lists of firms provided by the administrative records of other federal agencies. Since 1963, administrative records also have been used to provide basic statistics for very small firms, reducing or eliminating the need to send them census questionnaires.

The range of industries covered in the Economic Censuses expanded between 1967 and 1992. The Census of Construction began on a regular basis in 1967, and the scope of service industries, introduced in 1933, was broadened in 1967, 1977, and 1987. While a few transportation industries were covered as early as

**Figure 1.1**
**Economic Census Coverage by Sector 1840 to 2002**

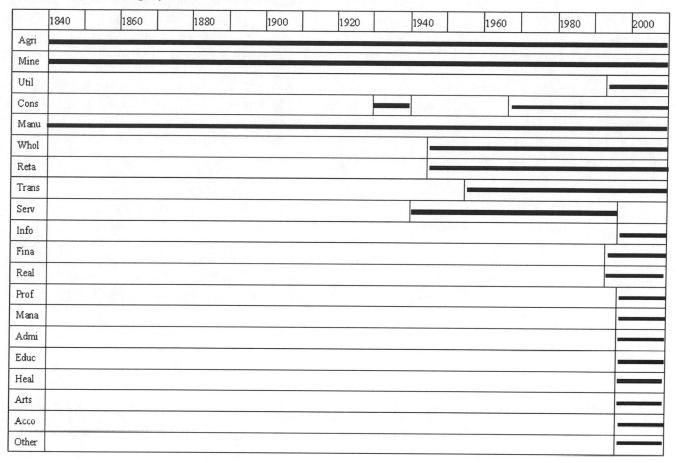

1963, it was not until 1992 that the census broadened to include most of transportation, communications, and utilities. Also, the finance, insurance, and real estate industries were added in 1992. With these additions, the Economic Census and the separate Census of Governments and Census of Agriculture collectively covered roughly 98 percent of all economic activity.

Printed statistical reports from the 1992 and earlier censuses provide historical figures for the study of long-term time series and are available in some large libraries. All of the census reports printed from 1967 through 1996 are still available for sale on microfiche from the Census Bureau. CD-ROMs issued from the 1987 and 1992 Economic Censuses contain databases with nearly all of the printed data plus additional statistics, such as ZIP Code statistics, found only on CD-ROM. More information on the history of the Economic Census can be found at the end of this chapter. All of the Economic Census reports starting with the 1992 Economic Census are available on-line through the Census Bureau's Web site.

## NEW IN 1997

What's in a name? Before 1997 each industry sector was identified as its own census: Census of Manufacturers, Census of Construction, and so on. The Census Bureau did some market research and decided that it could promote response better if the whole program was identified with a single recognizable name. An added benefit for the users is that the unified image of the Economic Census highlights the entire range of information that is available across the nation. All reports are titled as Economic Census reports and are no longer treated as if each sector had a separate census. Examples of how to cite reports are shown in chapter 6.

With the breakdown of mental barriers between industry sectors, there is a greater integration of data economy-wide. Data for all sectors are being integrated in the Core Business Statistics reports and key CD-ROM files. Those statistics that are published separately by sector have a more consistent look and feel across sectors than they did in the past.

However, "feel" is a subjective word. There are less physical outputs in 1997 and 2002 than in earlier censuses. Only highlights of the Economic Census are published in paper reports. Nonetheless, software on the Internet includes the ability to print out most of the detailed data using PDF documents. CD-ROMs have the most comprehensive collection of data. There are no microforms or magnetic tapes issued with these censuses.

The most significant technological change is the use of the Internet. The data are being released faster than before on the Census Bureau's Web site at http://www.census.gov/epcd/www/econ97.html. On the Economic Census Home Page, anyone can learn about the census, retrieve the data, and find general examples of how to use it. It also eliminates the need for preliminary reports in manufacturing, mining, and construction, since the data are put up as soon as they're calculated. The data can be retrieved through the Internet in different formats: portable document format (PDF) reports, ready-made tables in down-loadable ASCII, and customized tables using American FactFinder.

Gone are the days of the Go and Extract software programs on the CD-ROM—two separate but complementary DOS-based software programs used to access the electronic information from the 1987 and 1992 Economic Censuses. Now the Census Bureau is using new software on the CD-ROMs to retrieve commonly requested titles and to do more complicated search, retrieve, customized, and output functions than either of these programs was able to do alone. See chapter 6 for more details on how to use the new software.

The best and biggest change to the content of the Economic Census is the use of the North American Classification System (NAICS) codes in designing the framework for collecting the data. The 1997 Economic Census publishes data primarily on the basis of NAICS. Only limited data were published according to the old Standard Industrial Classification (SIC) system: a detailed "Bridge Table" showing the relationships between NAICS and SIC categories, state-level statistics based on SIC, a few programs based on administrative records or surveys (such as the Surveys of Minority- and Women-Owned Businesses), and preliminary national totals in the *Advance* report.

While many of the individual SIC industries correspond directly to industries as defined under the NAICS system, most of the higher-level groupings do not. Particular care should be taken in comparing data

for retail trade, wholesale trade, and manufacturing, which are sector titles used in both NAICS and SIC, but cover somewhat different groups of industries. At the end of most industry chapters, there is a list of the NAICS codes for a particular sector along with corresponding SIC codes. To see how the transition affected the SIC industry refer to the Bridge Tables. For example, from the NAICS manual it is possible to determine that gas stations, as defined by the SIC system were split into two NAICS industries: gas stations with convenience food, and gas stations without. The Bridge Tables will allow you to determine, for the first time, what portion of gas stations went into each new industry. This is an essential resource for anyone attempting to link time series on the old and new basis. The Census Bureau felt that the Bridge Tables are important enough to issue in print. Where changes are significant, it may be impossible to construct a time series that includes data for time periods crossing the 1997 threshold.

Individual changes within each industry are described in the industry chapters. One major change affecting all industries is the counting of auxiliary establishments (or those establishments supporting other establishments owned by the same company rather than selling to outsiders). Under the SIC rules, auxiliary establishments were classified according to the primary industry of the parent company. For example, warehouses of an auto manufacturer were classified under manufacturing of automobiles, not warehousing. The most important type of auxiliary is the central administrative office or company headquarters, but there are also company warehouses, trucking offices, R&D facilities, data processing offices, and so forth. If these entities operate out of separate establishments, the Bureau asks companies to report them separately. Under NAICS, auxiliaries are classified by their own primary activity. Warehouses are classified in the Warehousing and Storage industry and company headquarters have been placed in a brand new sector (55) for the Management of Companies and Enterprises.

For more information about the effects of changing from SIC to NAICS on the Economic Census and other statistical sources see chapter 4.

## NEW IN 2002

Unlike the 1997 Economic Census, which had significant changes due to the introduction of NAICS and a unified name, the 2002 Economic Census changes are generally smaller, incremental changes. However, there are a few significant changes in the 2002 Economic Census compared to the 1997. They can be summarized as:

1. NAICS 2002 is used to classify industries instead of NAICS 1997. This change only affects the construction, wholesale trade, retail trade, and information sectors to varying degrees.
2. There are changes in the CD-ROM software to support time series analysis, mapping, and charting of the data.
3. The Survey of Business Owners (formerly known as the Minority- and Women-Owned Business Surveys) has been expanded to include more information about the characteristics of business owners and about their company's origin.
4. The North American Product Classification System is used to report the sources of revenues in the few service industries where this classification system exists.
5. Industry Series reports have been added for the sectors where they didn't exist in the past, such as retail trade, and most summary reports have been eliminated.
6. Questions were added about sales through e-commerce or electronic methods (the Internet, electronic data interchange, etc.).
7. This is one of the first data products to use the Metropolitan and Micropolitan Statistical Areas that were defined by the Office of Management and Budget using data from Economic Census 2000.

Each of these changes is described in more detail in the appropriate chapters of this book.

## RELATED CENSUSES

Agriculture covers about two percent of Gross Domestic Product (GDP), however you will not see it on the Economic Census Web page. For the first time in U.S. history, the Census Bureau is not including agriculture in the Economic Census reports. It is no longer the Bureau's responsibility. It is now in the hands of the National Agriculture Statistical Service (NASS). Since this is a book for all industries, we have included an industry chapter on the Census of Agriculture.

Another industry not covered by the Economic Census is tax-support services. The government sec-

tor accounts for around 12 percent of economic activity. This sector includes data that might have been included in other sectors found in the Economic Census, for example city run road maintenance (is not aggregated in the construction sector); country run libraries (are not in the information reports); colleges, universities, and secondary and primary schools (are not in the education statistics); a regional agency that operates a power plant (is not counted in the utilities sector); supermarkets run by the military, called commissaries (are not in the retail data); and U.S. Post Offices (are not shown in the transportation sector). However, tax-exempt establishments not run by a government body are counted in the Economic Census, with the exception of government hospitals. All hospitals, including those run by government agencies, are counted in the health-care sector. Just be aware of these exclusions when you think you have the whole picture when using the Economic Census. The Census Bureau does conduct a Census of Governments that does not present data according to NAICS or SIC systems.

## OTHER EXCLUSIONS AND LIMITATIONS

There are some intrinsic limitations with any collection of data. These can be a result of groups outside of the framework, policy, budget, non-compliance, tradition, inputting errors, and other situations. It just means some establishments don't get counted. Most industry chapters indicate which industries are included in the table in the end of the chapter.

Additionally, the Economic Census is subject to a number of errors. These include both sampling and nonsampling errors. For more information about these errors, see chapter 3.

There are sections of the economy that are not measured by SIC or NAICS: illegal commerce such as narcotics manufacturing, distribution, and retail; underground economies such as barter and babysitting; non-employed housework that supports the economic development of the household; and other miscellaneous economic activities are not measured. This part of the economy has never been successfully counted and it is beyond the Census Bureau's responsibility to try. There are scholarly and government studies that have attempted to estimate the impact of these economic effects; ask your local librarian to help you find such studies. Also, the data were collected by establishments *in* the United States; income and employment for companies with operations outside of the measured geographic areas were not included.

There are a few industries not covered by any census due to policy reasons. This includes churches because of the constitutional separation of church and state. Labor, political, or religious organizations operations are also exempt, however by contacting the groups headquarters or using the Internet by going to http://www.guidestar.org/, you should be able to get a copy of the their annual report that should give you details. Trusts and funds are also not counted with the other financial industries. Another industry that blurs lines is domestic help. This means that households with privately employed help are not counted as an establishment; however, a business paying someone to do the same work in someone else's home is an establishment and counted in the Economic Census.

The Census Bureau has always included the agriculture sector in the Economic Census. Then for the 1997 Economic Census, tradition was broken. The National Agriculture Statistical Service of the Department of Agriculture was given the responsibility of reporting on the agriculture sector, which makes sense since the USDA is responsible for all other agricultural statistical counts (see the Agriculture Census, chapter 7, for more detail). The only problem was that the budget did not fund the other agricultural related industries that were moved out of the agriculture sector and placed into more appropriate sectors like those of landscape architecture, landscaping services, veterinary services, pet care, agricultural services, forestry, and fisheries, so they did not get counted in 1997, but were included in 2002.

Curiously, the railroad industry (NAICS 482 Rail Transportation sub-sector) is completely excluded from the Economic Census. It appears that the only operating statistics available for this sector from the federal government are from the Department of Transportation's *National Transportation Statistics Yearbook* at http://www.bts.gov/publications/nts/. Other than that, consult a trade association for more detail about the industry. Other transportation data missing from the Economic Census are the major large certificated passenger air transportation companies, but their information can also be found from the Department of Transportation.

During the preparation for the census, budget cuts took their toll by eliminating data one might expect to find in the Economic Census. There are fewer geographic details for certain industries. (In certain industrial areas, maintaining confidentiality was the main reason for limiting geographic coverage.) Consult Table 1.1 for the geographic levels at which industries are reported. State and metro area data will appear for fewer sectors in "miscellaneous subjects" reports, too. The ax also fell on the Characteristics of Business Owners survey and outputs for exports. And the outlying area of American Samoa was not included until the 2002 Economic Census.

There are also establishments and companies that refused to respond to the Census Bureau's requests for information. After repeated requests by mail, phone, and in some cases in-person visits by the Bureau's employees, the Census Bureau was unsuccessful in getting all the data directly from the company. In that case they had the option to impose section 224 of Title 13 of the United States Code, which states:

> Whoever, being the owner, official, agent, person in charge, or assistant to the person in charge, of any company, business, institution, establishment, religious body, or organization of any nature whatsoever, neglects or refuses, when requested by the Secretary or other authorized officer or employee of the Department of Commerce or bureau or agency thereof, to answer completely and correctly to the best of his knowledge all questions relating to his company,

## QUESTION: TEST YOUR KNOWLEDGE

**Are these establishments covered in the Economic Census? Answers can be found at the end of the chapter.**

Amazon.com
Barge operations on the Mississippi
Cook County Public Library
Consultants
Double D Horse Ranch
Forensic Laboratories
Ford Motor Company Headquarters
Hard Times Café
Hat Manufacturers in Guam
Riverside Post Office
Silver Dollar Mine
Newark Evening News
Personal Chefs
Singapore Hilton

**Table 1.1**
**Geographic and Format Coverage by Industry**

| Sector and Reports | Geography | Media |
|---|---|---|
| **Mining**   21 | | |
| Industry Series (29 reports) | U S | D V |
| Geographic Area Series | U S | D V |
| Subject Series: Product Summary | U | D V P |
| Subject Series: Materials and Fuels Consumed | U | D V P |
| Subject Series: General Summary | U S | D V P |
| Location of Mining | U S | D |
| **Utilities**   22 | | |
| Geographic Area Series | U S M | D V |
| Subject Series: Revenue Lines | U | D V |
| Subject Series: Establishment and Firm Size | U | D V |
| Subject Series: Miscellaneous Subjects | U S | D V |
| Summary | U | D V P |
| **Construction**   23 | | |
| Industry Series (28 reports) | U S | D V |
| Geographic Area Series | U S | D V |
| Subject Series: Industry Summary | U S | D V P |
| Subject Series: Geographic Area Summary | U S | D V P |
| **Manufacturing**   31-33 | | |
| Numerical List of Mfd/Mineral Products | (NA) | D V P |
| Industry Series (473 reports) | U S | D V |
| Geographic Area Series | U S M C P | D V |
| Subject Series: General Summary | U S M | D V P |
| Subject Series:  Product Summary | U | D V P |
| Subject Series:  Materials Consumed | U | D V P |
| Subject Series:  Concentration Ratios | U | D V |
| Subject Series:  Class of Customer | U | D V |
| Location of Manufacturing | U S M C P | D |
| ZIP Code Statistics | Z | D |
| **Wholesale Trade**   42 | | |
| Geographic Area Series | U S M C P | D V |
| Subject Series:  Commodity Line Sales | U S M | D V |
| Subject Series:  Establishment and Firm Size | U | D V |
| Subject Series:  Miscellaneous Subjects | U S | D V |
| Summary | U | D V P |

business, institution, establishment, religious body, or other organization, or to records or statistics in his official custody, contained on any census or other schedule or questionnaire prepared and submitted to him under the authority of this title, shall be fined not more than $500; and if he willfully gives a false answer to any such question, he shall be fined not more than $10,000.

However, this is something the Census Bureau has not done because doing so would ultimately make it more difficult to collect data in the future. Also, statistical methods for estimating missing data do exist, but

**Table 1.1 (Continued)**
**Geographic and Format Coverage by Industry**

| Sector and Reports | Geography | Media |
|---|---|---|
| **Retail Trade   44-45** | | |
| Geographic Area Series | U S M C P | D V |
| Subject Series:  Merchandise Line Sales | U S M | D V |
| Subject Series:  Establishment and Firm Size | U | D V |
| Subject Series:  Miscellaneous Subjects | U S | D V |
| Summary | U | D V P |
| ZIP Code Statistics | Z | D |
| **Transportation and Warehousing   48-49** | | |
| Geographic Area Series | U S M | D V |
| Subject Series: Revenue Lines | U | D V |
| Subject Series: Establishment and Firm Size | U | D V |
| Subject Series: Miscellaneous Subjects | U S | D V |
| Summary | U | D V P |
| Vehicle Inventory and Use Survey | U S | D V |
| Commodity Flow Survey | U S | D V |
| **Information   51** | | |
| Geographic Area Series | U S M C P | D V |
| Subject Series:  Sources of Receipts | U S | D V |
| Subject Series: Establishment and Firm Size | U | D V |
| Subject Series: Miscellaneous Subjects | U S | D V |
| Summary | U | D V P |
| ZIP Code Statistics | Z | D |
| **Finance and Insurance   52** | | |
| Geographic Area Series | U S M | D V |
| Subject Series:  Revenue Lines | U | D V |
| Subject Series:  Establishment and Firm Size | U | D V |
| Subject Series: Miscellaneous Subjects | U S | D V |
| Summary | U | D V P |
| **Real Estate and Rental and Leasing   53** | | |
| Geographic Area Series | U S M C P | D V |
| Subject Series:  Sources of Receipts | U | D V |
| Subject Series:  Establishment and Firm Size | U | D V |
| Subject Series:  Miscellaneous Subjects | U S | D V |
| Summary | U | D V P |

using the models to estimate too much data can also result in poor quality data.

## DATA AVAILABILITY

The wealth of data from the Economic Census is worth digging for. Like all mining operations it is important to know where to start your search. The industry, geographic location, subject matter, and the use of the data all give clues on where to start mining. This section of the chapter will be briefly going over the titles and contents of the series. Table 1.1 shows the industry sector coverage by geographic area and format. For more details about the reports see chapter 5.

With the advent of the Internet, the lines between data and publications are blurring. Most reports are published in PDF and very few are being sent out in print form from the Government Printing Office

Table 1.1 (Continued)
Geographic and Format Coverage by Industry

| Sector and Reports | Geography | Media |
|---|---|---|
| **Professional, Scientific, and Technical Services    54** | | |
| Geographic Area Series | U S M C P | D V |
| Subject Series:  Sources of Receipts | U S | D V |
| Subject Series: Establishment and Firm Size | U | D V |
| Subject Series: Miscellaneous Subjects | U S | D V |
| Summary | U | D V P |
| ZIP Code Statistics | Z | D |
| **Management of Companies and Enterprises    55** | | |
| Geographic Area Series | U S | D V |
| Auxiliary Establishments | U S | D V |
| Subject Series: Miscellaneous Subjects | U | D V |
| Summary | U | D V P |
| **Administrative and Support and Waste Management and Remediation Services    56** | | |
| Geographic Area Series | U S M C P | D V |
| Subject Series:  Sources of Receipts | U S | D V |
| Subject Series:  Establishment and Firm Size | U | D V |
| Subject Series:  Miscellaneous Subjects | U S | D V |
| Summary | U | D V P |
| ZIP Code Statistics | Z | D |
| **Educational Services    61** | | |
| Geographic Area Series | U S M C P | D V |
| Subject Series:  Sources of Receipts | U S | D V |
| Subject Series: Establishment and Firm Size | U | D V |
| Subject Series: Miscellaneous Subjects | U S | D V |
| Summary | U | D V P |
| ZIP Code Statistics | Z | D |
| **Health Care and Social Assistance    62** | | |
| Geographic Area Series | U S M C P | D V |
| Subject Series:  Sources of Receipts | U S | D V |
| Subject Series:  Establishment and Firm Size | U | D V |
| Subject Series: Miscellaneous Subjects | U S | D V |
| Summary | U | D V P |
| ZIP Code Statistics | Z | D |

(GPO). But not all data are available in the PDF files; the ZIP Code and metropolitan Merchandise Line Data are only found on the CD-ROM.

There may be other data that were collected but were not available in any report or in the format desired. If you are truly interested in an industry, seek out the questionnaire and see what data were collected but not published. In that case, you might want to consider a special tabulation. Special tabulations are delivered in electronic or tabular form of data collected in the Economic Census, depending on availability of time and personnel. These special tabulations are prepared on a cost basis. The data will be reported using the same rules prohibiting disclosure of confidential information (including name, address, kind of business, or other data for individual business establishments or companies) that govern the regular publications. However, even for hard-core users, most of

**Table 1.1 (Continued)**
**Geographic and Format Coverage by Industry**

| Sector and Reports | Geography | Media |
|---|---|---|
| **Arts, Entertainment, and Recreation   71** | | |
| Geographic Area Series | U S M | D V |
| Subject Series:  Sources of Receipts | U S | D V |
| Subject Series: Establishment and Firm Size | U | D V |
| Subject Series: Miscellaneous Subjects | U S | D V |
| Summary | U | D V P |
| ZIP Code Statistics | Z | D |
| **Accommodation and Food Services   72** | | |
| Geographic Area Series | U S M C P | D V |
| Subject Series:  Merchandise Line Sales | U S M | D V |
| Subject Series: Establishment and Firm Size | U | D V |
| Subject Series: Miscellaneous Subjects | U S | D V |
| Summary | U | D V P |
| ZIP Code Statistics | Z | D |
| **Other Services (Except Public Administration)   81** | | |
| Geographic Area Series | U S M C P | D V |
| Subject Series:  Sources of Receipts | U S | D V |
| Subject Series:  Establishment and Firm Size | U | D V |
| Subject Series: Miscellaneous Subjects | U S | D V |
| Summary | U | D V P |
| ZIP Code Statistics | Z | D |
| **Outlying Areas** | | |
| Puerto Rico: | | |
|   Geographic Area Series | PR C | D V P |
|   Subject Series | PR | D V P |
|   Construction | PR M C | D V P |
|   Manufactures | PR M C | D V P |
| Virgin Islands | VI C P | D V P |
| Guam | GU C | D V P |
| Northern Mariana Islands | NM C | D V P |
| **Economy-Wide** | | |
| Core Business Statistics: | | |
|   Advance Report | U | D V P |
|   Comparative Statistics | U S | D V |
|   Bridge Between NAICS and SIC | U | D V P |
|   Nonemployers Statistics | U S | D |
| Company Statistics, incl. Minority- & Women-Owned Bus. | U S M C P | D V P |
| Business Expenses | U | D V |

Geography Options: U = United States; S = states; M = MAs; C = counties; P = places; Z = Zip Codes. Media Options: D = database files (Internet and CD-ROM); V = viewable files (Internet and CD-ROM); P = printed reports.
Note: Summary Reports are only for the 1997 Economic Census.

the data needs will be met by one of the aforementioned reports or publicly available datasets.

While the classification system has changed, the reports still provide the same basic types of statistics available in previous censuses. The subject and geographic series cover the 18 industrial sectors, with the exclusion of agriculture and pubic administration. They all contain the number of establishments; employment; payroll; value of sales, receipts, revenue, or shipments; and special topics for each industry. Remember, what is covered are establishments with employees; to get a comprehensive number of all establishments you must add the non-employer data and also be aware of the other items not covered in the reports.

The educational, health care and social assistance, arts, entertainment, and recreation, and other services sectors all have many establishments that are exempt from federal income tax in addition to the taxable establishments. The Bureau takes this into account and provides data for both parts of the industry. Data for tax-exempt services are shown for states and metropolitan areas, but are not shown for counties, cities, or ZIP code areas.

Of course there are tax-exempt firms in many parts of the economy, such as thrift stores run by charitable institutions. In the five sectors mentioned above, tax-exempts are so prevalent in at least some industries that they are accounted separately. Tax-exempt hospitals dominate employment in health care and social assistance. The Economic Census covers all hospitals, whether they are run by governments, are for-profit, or are non-profit. Educational services show a surprisingly small fraction in the tax-exempt category, until one realizes that the Economic Census does *not* cover elementary or secondary schools, colleges, and professional schools. The remaining educational establishments that are covered in the Economic Census are the for-profit business, technical, and trade schools, private dance schools, etc. At the same time, tax-exempts account for only a small portion of the employment in professional, scientific, and technical services. Legal aid societies and tax-exempt R&D are aggregated with the other industries.

## DATA REPORTS

There are several general types of reports included in the Economic Census. These include subject series, industry series, core business statistics, and geographic area reports. Each of these series is described in moderate detail in this section. There can be some overlap in the data presented in different series. For example, the mining sector has a subject report on *Materials and Fuels Consumed* and each of the industry reports in that sector also contains a table on this topic.

## Industry Series

In the 1997 Economic Census there were 537 reports in the Industry Series. Historically, these reports were issued only for the manufacturing, mining, and construction sectors. These sectors represent the goods-producing part of the economy. However, starting with the 2002 Economic Census, they are being issued for all sectors. These reports provide data primarily at the national level, although there is some state data.

Operation researchers and others interested in detailed looks at specific industries will find these reports fascinating. Industry Series reports include a wider range of data items than most other reports. One of the unique features is the inclusion of data for specific products produced and materials consumed in manufacturing and mining. Having these data gives you a look at both the inputs and outputs of each industry. The detailed 10-digit product classifications give you some of the most detailed data in the Economic Census.

## Geographic Area Series

Even with all of the other wonderful reports mentioned in this section being available, the most common requests are for the Geographic Area Series report for a state. Geographic reports contain four key statistics: number of establishments, sales or receipts, number of employees, and annual payroll. None of these reports is issued in print through GPO. New to the 2002 Economic Census is the merger of the geographic area data into a single file on CD-ROM and on Internet databases, so that it is easier to retrieve all of the data for any one area.

Geographic Area reports are issued separately for each of the 18 NAICS sectors included in the Economic Censuses. These reports contain information for states, metropolitan areas, counties, and places with 2,500 or more inhabitants. Statistics for smaller areas are frequently withheld to avoid disclosing information about individual firms. There are ZIP code reports, but those report only for the number of establishments and a range for the number of employees.

The actual geographic detail reported varies according to the individual sector. Utilities, transportation and warehousing, and finance and insurance only provide data for states and metropolitan areas. Reports for the construction, mining, and management of enterprise sectors contain data only down to the state level.

The actual data reported also varies according to sector. Reports for the construction, mining, and management of enterprises sectors also show additional statistics, such as value-added and capital expenditures. The educational, health care and social assistance, arts, entertainment, and recreation, and other services sectors have tax-exempt establishments. To address the different priority of the charities, the reports will include tables for both tax-exempt and taxable establishments.

## Subject Series

Most of the industry sectors include four *Subject* reports: *Revenue Lines* (or something equivalent), *Establishment and Firm Size, Miscellaneous Subjects,* and *Summary.* (In 2002 only a few sectors have *Summary* reports.) As seen in Table 1.1, most of the reports are at the national level only. However some data are released at the state or metropolitan area level on CD-ROM or on the Internet. Only the *Summary* reports were published in print format in the 1997 Economic Census; however, they were not available in print in the 2002 Economic Census.

One of the more interesting subject series reports in the Retail Trade sector is the *Merchandise Line Sales* report, which shows the kinds of merchandise sold by the various kinds of businesses carrying each line. In most of the other sectors this report is called the *Source of Receipts/Source of Revenues.* The comparable report in the Wholesale Trade sector is the *Commodity Line Sales* report. In these reports a person can see the parts of a business that are most profitable. In many sectors there are only national data available. In the wholesale trade sector, line data are also presented for the 15 largest metropolitan areas and the 15 largest states. The most detail is reported in the retail and accommodation and food services sectors where this type of data is reported for all states and metropolitan areas. A corresponding classification of manufacturing and mining by products produced is included in the Industry Series reports and in the *Summary* reports for those sectors.

The *Merchandise Line Sales* for retail breaks down the sales of each type of retail store by 40 broad retail merchandise lines, such as men's and boy's clothing, major household appliances, or hardware. From one table you can learn what merchandise lines are sold by hardware stores and from another table, what kinds of stores sell hardware. If you're in the business of selling hardware to retailers, you will find that almost two-thirds of your potential market is not hardware stores but stores like lumber yards and department stores. These data are published in a PDF with national level data, but CD-ROM users are also able to get merchandise line sales data for states and metropolitan areas.

*Establishment and Firm Size* reports present data on the number of establishments, sales, payroll, and employment and are cross-tabulated by industry, by size of establishment, by size of firm, by concentration, and by legal form of organization for the United States. More will be covered in the Reports and Industry chapters.

The *Miscellaneous Subjects* reports are hard to describe here because they vary greatly from one sector to the next. For example in the wholesale trade sector, the report covers such topics as sales and commissions of agents, brokers, and commission merchants; petroleum bulk stations by type of state; and end-of-year inventories in a total of 13 tables. In the retail trade sector, only two subjects are shown—floor space for selected kinds of businesses and class of customer by kind of business. Then in the accommodations and food services sector, 10 subjects are presented including such topics as average cost per meal, seating capacity, and number of guestrooms.

After the publication of all industry, area, and subject reports for each sector, a single volume is published that summarizes the most widely used statistics about that sector from all of the previously issued reports.

## Other Reports

There is a wealth of other reports produced by the Census Bureau as part of the Economic Census. These include reports based on surveys that are taken along with the Economic Census, such as the Survey of Business Owners, the Vehicle Inventory and Use Survey, and the Commodity Flow Survey. These other reports also include reports on U.S. territories, and various aspects of the overall economy.

The *Core Business Statistics* are also referred to as the Economy-Wide Series because the reports in this series cover all economic sectors included in the Economic Census. The reports consist of the *Advance Report, Comparative Statistics, Bridge Between NAICS and SIC, Nonemployers Statistics, Business Expenses,* and, new in 2002, *E-Commerce Statistics.*

The *Advance Report* is the first published report that came out of the 1997 Economic Census in March 1999. It was issued in print using both SIC and NAICS. It became obsolete in short order as the more detailed reports were issued.

The *Comparative Statistics* report compares U.S. and state data between the census years. All dollar values presented are expressed in current dollars (e.g., 2002 data are represented in 2002 dollars and 1997 data are expressed in 1997 dollars). Consequently, when making comparisons with prior years, users of the data should consider the changes in prices that have occurred.

The *Bridge* report is an essential resource for anyone attempting to link time series on the old and new basis, and will serve as the basis for converting other data. Because these data will be so widely used, this report will be in print. In 2002 the *Bridge* report is much smaller, only covering the 2002 changes in NAICS. You will need both the 2002 and 1997 *Bridge* reports to calculate historical time series.

All of the reports discussed to this point provide data only for businesses with paid employees. The *Nonemployer Statistics* report is the one report to look at if you want information about self-employed individuals who do not have other people working for them. The 1997 Economic Census was the first time this report covered all industries. The data included in this report show the number of companies and their receipts. Nonemployers account for only about 3 percent or so of sales and other revenues. But if you are counting numbers of companies, nearly three-fourths are nonemployers. Data are available for states, counties, and metro areas, but not for places or ZIP Codes. It is important to note that these firms are counted by the address listed on their tax forms rather than their physical location.

New in the 2002 Economic Census is a report on e-commerce. The *E-Commerce Statistics* report shows data on sales through the Internet and other electronic networks. The data are presented by industry for the nation and each of the states.

The focus in the *Minority- and Women-Owned Business* program is on showing the total number of businesses owned by Blacks, Hispanics, and Asians and American Indians, along with overall totals for women. In the 1997 Economic Census the data in this

series are reported according to SIC sectors. In 2002, NAICS was used as the reporting basis.

Data on operating expenses of retailers; merchant wholesalers; and service firms and auxiliary establishments of manufacturing, mining, and construction firms (as classified under SIC for the 1997 Economic Census) are presented in the report *Business Expenses.* These operating expenses include supplemental labor costs, energy costs, taxes, and a variety of purchased services including advertising, legal and accounting services, repairs, and information technology.

*ZIP Code* statistics are published to about the same extent as they were in 1992 and 1997, for manufacturing, retail trade, and for various service industries. The data appear in the CD-ROM and on the HTML pages only. On the CD-ROM they include establishment counts by industry and employee by size. You can determine total sales by ZIP, but not many other aggregate statistics. Through the HTML pages you can find the number of establishments and ranges for the sales, annual payroll, and employment. These data are the only indicators of the geographic distribution of business within large cities, since the Economic Census includes no data for census tracts or the other small areas published in the population census. But users should be aware that ZIP Codes are constructs of the United States Postal Service and are redefined by them as needed to maintain the efficient delivery of the mail. Therefore, ZIP Code-based data should be used with caution.

The Bureau of the Census works very hard at finding all the businesses in U.S. controlled areas. According to section 191 of Title 13 of the United States Code:

> Each of the censuses authorized by this chapter [13 UCS §§ 131 et seq.] shall include each State, the District of Columbia, the Virgin Islands, Guam, the Commonwealth of the Northern Mariana Islands, and the Commonwealth of Puerto Rico, and as may be determined by the Secretary, such other possessions and areas over which the United States exercises jurisdiction, control, or sovereignty. Inclusion of other areas over which the United States exercises jurisdiction or control shall be subject to the concurrence of the Secretary of State.

The Economic Census does not include the *Census of Outlying Areas* as part of the Geographic Area Series, but as it own series. If you are looking to do business in Guam, the Northern Mariana Islands, or the

U.S. Virgin Islands, you might not know where else to look. Industry detail for these areas appears in printed reports. In 1997 it was based on SICs, while in 2002 NAICS was the reporting basis.

The *Vehicle Inventory and Use Survey* reports on the physical characteristics and operational use of the Nation's 60-million private and commercial trucks. The *Commodity Flow Survey* reflects the origin and destination of commodities shipped from selected industries. These surveys have their own geographic area data series, but they are not considered part of the Geographic Area Series described above.

## USING ECONOMIC CENSUS DATA

Throughout the book you will be learning ways of using the Economic Census. Businesses, governments, industry analysts, and others already use these data. It's about time that students and other researchers learn to unlock the potential. This book can also be a refresher for the people who think they know it all.

Most researchers will lament the passing of a good clean time series. Gone are the days of tracing back or projecting forward the service sector. It's gone. The service sector was divided up into more relevant sectors. Some industries were created, some moved to other sectors, and still some more were divided into a variety of sectors, like a dropped plate braking on a hard floor. How does one glue the old data to the new numbers? By using the *Bridge Between NAICS and SIC*—this will be explained in more detail later in the Reports chapter (chapter 5).

Only the *Comparative Statistics* report in each census contains a substantial amount of data from the previous census. Even then, the data reported from the last census are somewhat limited and users may need to access the reports from the earlier census in order to find historically comparable data. Printed reports might be available as a source of data from the 1992 and earlier censuses. However, depending on the amount of data being sought and the particular subjects being looked at, the printed reports might not be the most desirable means of getting the data. The other way of accessing the older data is to use the Extract or Go software on the CD-ROMs issued from the 1987 and 1992 Economic Censuses. Both databases include nearly all data published in print, plus additional statistics, such as ZIP Code statistics (published only on CD-ROM). To learn how to use the Go and Extract programs, search the GODORT Handout Exchange at

http://www.lib.umich.edu/govdocs/godort/cdrom. htm. All of the census reports printed since 1967 are still available for sale on microfiche from the Census Bureau. Before 1967, consult the Government Printing Office Regional Depository Library in your area, see appendix C. To learn how to retrieve the data from the current census review the Formats chapter (chapter 6).

Using the Economic Census in your professional life is only limited by knowing the potential of the source and your active imagination. Here are some examples of how governments and business use the data.

## Government

Policymaking agencies of federal, state, and local governments use the data to monitor economic activity and to assess the effectiveness of policies. Monitoring business activity is the major reason why the data were collected. Important measures of economic activity, including Monthly Retail Sales and the Gross Domestic Product (GDP), are based, at least in part, on census data. Trade associations and news media study census data to find key business facts and to project trends. The Economic Census furnishes an important part of the framework for such composite measures as the gross domestic product estimates, input/output measures, production and price indexes, and other statistical series that measure short-term changes in economic conditions.

Legislatures use census data in the preparation and evaluation of new laws. Legislatures and other federal and state agencies look to Economic Census data to measure the effectiveness of programs such as minority contracting guidelines, trade policies, and job retraining. Similarly, a local government might use the data to assess business activities and tax bases within their jurisdictions and to develop programs to attract business.

Economic development agencies attempt to attract new business to the city, and retain the ones they already have, by talking to individual companies about their real estate and labor force needs. They use Economic Census data to identify industries growing nationally but not doing as well locally. Other economic development agencies use Economic Census data in their attempt to attract or retain businesses by comparing the cost of doing business in different locations. Or a state economic development agency identifies industries with the highest employee growth using CD-ROM and gives those industries top priority as it launches a program to assist companies in trade leads to continue the economic growth of the community.

Small Business Development Centers in many states help business owners assess their marketing and management challenges. In working with their clients these centers often turn to the Economic Census for information about the client's industry both nationally and locally.

## Private Sector and Other Users

Even if they aren't always aware of it, businesses and related users (such as not-for-profit organizations, trade associations, academics, and the general public) are heavy users of Economic Census data. When looking at new ventures, businesses and other organizations providing financing to them frequently compare a business to the norms for its industry. Individual businesses use the data to locate potential markets and to analyze their own production and sales performance relative to industry or area averages. Trade associations use the data to look at relationships between their industry and others. Consultants, students, and researchers use census data to analyze changes in industrial structure and location.

Businesses compare their sales to census totals for their industry or area to make plans and evaluate performance. Totals from 1997 don't mean much to establishments in 2003. So businesses don't look at the numbers; instead the business calculates ratios such as revenue per employee and adjusts a target if their ratio is out of line with the norm. Almost any data item can be made into a ratio by dividing the number of establishment or revenue by that item.

Firms supplying goods and services to other businesses use census data to target industries for marketing. Manufacturers look at statistics on materials consumed to learn about industries that use their products. A manufacturer of wooden pallets opens a new factory when she finds the city with the most warehouses in a ratio to other pallet manufacturers.

Companies use census data to design sales territories, allocate advertising, locate new stores or offices, and find new customers. For example, a wine distributor of New Zealand table wine might use the merchandise line data from the retail and food and accommodations sectors to learn what areas in Massachusetts sell the most wine through which venues. Armed with this knowledge, the distributor can help their salespeople increase their sales by targeting new customers more effectively. They might also find that

there are enough potential customers in the area that they need to hire additional sales people.

Trade associations study trends in their own and competing industries, which allows them to keep their members informed of market changes. Trade associations and industry trade press can take the census data, combine them with data of their own and generate whatever numbers it wants. Often, trade associations have access to specialized and unique data about their industry that they can add to the Economic Census to develop some interesting analyses. Partially because census data is not copyrighted, these associations will sometimes report on their analysis to their members or the general public without giving the Census Bureau any credit as an underlying source of data. As a result people are using Economic Census data without realizing it.

An entrepreneur used census data to pitch her idea for a new business to a venture capitalist specializing in supporting minority-owned business in nontraditional industries. She used data from the *Surveys of Minority- and Women-Owned Business Enterprises* on her line of business in conjunction with data on women in managerial occupations from the Census of Population to make her case.

Recently, a computer programmer examined census data about the industries where he thought his skills could be used by looking at the expenses for the cost of purchased software and other data processing services. After exploring the statistics, he concentrated his job search on the industries that had grown substantially in recent years. He also studied statistics about those industries in preparing for job interviews.

## CHRONOLOGICAL HISTORY

As with any data collection effort that has been around for nearly 200 years, the Economic Census has seen many changes. This section gives you the more detailed history mentioned earlier. In this history you are introduced to some of the key events in the development of this census.

### 1810

By stating, "that it shall be the duty of the several marshals, secretaries, and their assistants aforesaid, to take, under the direction of the Secretary of the Treasury, and according to such instructions as he shall give, an account of the several manufacturing establishments and manufactures within their several districts, territories, and divisions" (Census Bureau,

2000, B-2), Congress ordered the first census relating to the nation's economy in an act they passed on May 1, 1810, but the effort was limited to commerce related to occupations, manufacturing, and farming.

The data on manufacturing were limited to general information about the quantity and value of more than 220 kinds of goods including those produced in households. Federal marshals and their staffs collected the manufacturing data while they collected the population data required as part of the third Decennial Census of the population.

## 1850–1870

While economic data were collected in 1810, 1820, and 1840, these data are considered to be of little value, except as general indicators of manufacturing development during this period. Probably, due to a perception of slow economic growth during the 1820s, no economic data were collected as part of the 1830 Census. Recognizing the need to improve the quality of the data collected during the 1850 Census, Congress passed an act on March 3, 1849, creating a Census Board: Act to Make Arrangements for the Taking of the Seventh Census. The act gave the power to a group under the Secretary of State, Attorney General, and Postmaster General, with a budget of $10,000. In planning the 1850 Census, this board consulted with prominent statisticians on how to conduct the census—this type of consultation is a practice that has continued to this day.

Other major changes to the census that occurred at this time were the inclusion of mining and fishing industries (commerce was added in 1840). Some telegraph facilities were also included. Another significant change was that the federal marshals supervised the data collection in the field, but unlike earlier censuses, a central office in Washington compiled and published the results. Finally, the actual field workers were provided with detailed instructions and training for the first time.

The major changes during the 1860 and 1870 Censuses were limited to changes in industry coverage and the information requested from businesses. The duties fell to the Secretary of Interior to compile and release the data. During the Civil War, the census was taken and both sides participated in the collection. 1870 Census saw the first statistical atlas produced as part of the census. It was called the *Statistical Atlas of the United States Based on the Results of the Ninth Census 1870: With Contributions From Many Eminent*

*Men of Science and Several Departments of the Government,* compiled by Francis Amasa Walker (New York: Julius Bien, 1874.)

## 1880

The 1880 Census saw several significant changes from the earlier censuses. The first change was that census supervisors and "experts" handled data collection instead of federal marshals. The second change to the census was that administrative policies now allowed the imposition of penalties for census workers who falsified records, did not perform their duties, or breached the confidentiality of responses.

## 1890

The 1890 Census saw the use of administrative records for the first time. Administrative records are records collected by the government for non-statistical purposes. In this case, mortgage records were used as the source of information describing the property, mortgage provisions, and addresses of the parties involved in the mortgage for mortgages made between 1880 and 1890. Additional information about the mortgage was obtained by from the mortgagors or, if they did not respond, the mortgagees.

## 1902

The world of the economic census changed in March 1902 when Congress passed the Permanent Census Act. This act created the Census Office, which became the Bureau of the Census in 1903, as a permanent agency. Additionally, as part of this act, Congress required the "collection of the statistics of manufacturing establishments..." (Census Bureau 2000, B-7) in 1905 and every 10 years after that. However, due to World War I, the 1915 Census was not taken.

## 1905

This year was the first time that a census of any part of the economy was collected independently of the population and housing censuses. It was also the first time that the entire census was collected by mailing questionnaires to the respondents, having them return the questionnaires by mail, and having enumerators visit those respondents who did not return the questionnaires in a timely manner. This type of mailout/mail-back data collection would not be used again to collect population data until the 1970 Census. Finally, the Bureau of Census retabulated the data on manufacturing from the 1900 Census based on the definition of manufacturing used in 1905.

## 1910

The 1910 Census Act specified that the responses of business, mining, and manufacturing establishments would be confidential. While this confidentiality had been promised through administrative policies since 1880, it was now guaranteed by law.

## 1917–1918

As part of the nation's war effort, several special economic censuses were conducted. This was the first time that a special effort was made to collect data related to a national emergency. These special focus censuses are probably the conceptual foundation for many of the specialized current industrial surveys that the Census Bureau would do during World War II and the second half of the twentieth century.

## 1920

This was the first time field enumerators corrected schedules/questionnaires containing inconsistent or incomplete responses. Technology entered into the tabulation of the economic censuses as punch cards were used along with a new integrating tabulator machine which did more sophisticated tabulation work than the tabulators used for the population and housing data since 1890.

Finally, Congress required that data on manufacturing be collected every two years starting in 1920. Except for the World War II years, this was done until 1947.

## 1940

Due to many detailed changes in coverage between the 1935 and 1940 Censuses, the Census Bureau recommended against comparing the aggregate figures from the two years with each other. This is not unlike the 1992 and 1997 Censuses that require great care in doing comparisons as a result of the introduction of NAICS.

## 1942–1945

Due to World War II, the periodic censuses were suspended in favor of a series of current surveys. These surveys collected data about selected targeted

industries more frequently than would have been possible with a full census.

## 1947

The Census of Manufactures was resumed with data collection being conducted almost entirely by mail-out/mail-back procedures. Information about manufacturing establishments from the Social Security Administration was used to help ensure that the mailing list used in this census provided complete coverage of these establishments. A major change from earlier censuses was the introduction of the Standard Industrial Classification (SIC) system. This system of grouping establishments into industries would be used through the 1997 Economic Census.

## 1948

This was a year of great change in the economic census system. First, Public Law 80–671, introduced by Senator Albert W. Hawkes,

- Made the Censuses of Manufactures and Businesses every five years (instead of every 2 and 10 years respectively). The Census of Manufactures would cover years ending in 2 and 7. The Censuses of the other business sectors would cover years ending in 3 and 8.
- Allowed the Census Bureau to make responding to the Economic Censuses mandatory.
- Authorized the use of surveys to be used for annual and other interim data. (The Annual Survey of Manufactures started in 1949 under this provision.)

Another change occurring at this time was that field office staff coded and edited questionnaires while workers in the field did any necessary follow-up work directly with the establishments. A third change introduced this year was the use of sampling to collect data from small, single-establishment firms. Finally, a post-enumeration survey was introduced to measure how well the Census Bureau did at collecting data from all establishments. This post-enumeration survey indicated an undercoverage of 8.2 percent of service establishments and 3.6 percent of retail establishments. This procedure would be introduced into the Population and Housing Censuses starting in 1950.

## 1953–1955

This was another critical period in the Economic Census's development. Initially, during 1953 Congress denied funds for the data collection phase of the Censuses of Business and Manufactures. This denial led the Commerce Secretary to appoint an independent "Intensive Review Committee." Dr. Ralph J. Watkins, Director of Research for Dun and Bradstreet, Inc., chaired this committee. His committee found that "We are in the midst of great technological revolution which is accelerating change, hastening obsolescence, creating new industries and transforming old ones, remaking the industrial map of the country, and bringing within the range of the feasible great heights of production, productivity, and well-being…The need for the benchmark statistics provided by the Bureau of the Census is greater today than ever before, and promises to grow in intensity" (Census Bureau 2000, 37). As a result of this committee's March 1954 recommendations, Congress provided funds for a 1954 census covering businesses, manufacturing, mineral trades, construction, and services to be taken during 1955. Congress also provided for a census to be taken every five years starting in 1958.

This was the first time that the economic censuses were taken as an integrated census. This census was the first to use consistent definitions, classifications, time periods, and reporting units across all economic sectors. As a result, comparisons could now be made between economic sectors.

It was also the first time since 1890 that data were collected from administrative records. This time, administrative records were limited to collecting data on establishments without employees. All information not collected from administrative records was collected entirely by mail, something that had not been done before. The Annual Survey of Manufactures mailing list served as the core mailing list for the Economic Census.

With the introduction of modern electronic computing (using the UNIVAC I computer), the Census Bureau was able to combine information from different establishments into companies. This allowed the publication of the first enterprise statistics data series.

In many ways the 1954 Economic Censuses can be considered the first modern economic census. While there have been changes since these censuses, the fundamentals have stayed essentially the same.

## 1967

This is when Congress modified Title 13 of the United States Code (the part of law governing most Census Bureau activities) to have the Economic Cen-

suses refer to years ending in 2 and 7 instead of 3 and 8. This new timing allowed more even use of the Census Bureau's permanent resources over a decade.

Also, the 1967 Economic Censuses saw the introduction of complementary disclosure analysis. The purpose of this analysis is to prevent people from finding confidential information about an establishment by calculating suppressed data from other pieces of reported data.

## 1992

The industry coverage of the Economic Censuses was expanded to include the Finance, Insurance, and Real Estate (F.I.R.E.) sector. Additionally, most portions of the Transportation, Communications and Utilities sector not previously covered were added.

## 1997

As detailed in other sections of this book, there were a number of major changes introduced with this census. These include

- The first use of the North American Industry Classification System (NAICS)
- The use of the Internet as the primary means of data dissemination
- The use of computerized self-administered questionnaires (CSAQ), a Windows-based electronic questionnaire
- The use of DocuPrint technology to more efficiently produce the questionnaire packets mailed to respondents

## 2002

Not as revolutionary as the 1997 Economic Census, the 2002 Economic Census implements a number of changes to make the data more relevant, to reduce the company's reporting burden, and to make the final product more useful. The long forms include additional questions on e-commerce sales, leased employees, and supply chain (including outsourcing). All respondents have the option of electronic reporting via downloadable spreadsheet forms. The electronic distribution continues with the additional software that supports time series analysis, charting, and mapping for Geographic Information Systems (GIS). NAICS was revised in 2002 to include new industries in construction, wholesale, parts of retail, and parts of information sectors. New product classifications and expansion of e-commerce augment the reports.

## Summary

As can be seen from this section, the Economic Censuses have gone through many changes over the nearly two centuries of their existence. While we have highlighted the major changes that have taken place and shaped the Economic Census as we know it today, each time that a census related to the nation's economy has been taken, there have been some changes from the ones that have come before. Many factors such as the changing economy, changing technology, national events, and politics have influenced these changes.

If you are interested in finding out more about the history of the Economic Censuses, the Census Bureau has included a detailed background piece in the 1997 Economic Census's history report and William F. Micarelli has written an in-depth history for *Government Information Quarterly's* (1998) symposium issue on the 1997 Economic Census.

## UPDATED SOURCES

Keeping updated on the most recent census is as easy as bookmarking the Economic Web site from the Census Bureau, http://www.census.gov/econ/www/index.html. Getting current data means turning to other sources that use the Economic Census as a benchmark but are based on surveys or statistical projections to adjust for the time since the census. In general, you will never see the industrial and geographic detail you see in the years when the Economic Census is released. Meanwhile, you will have to settle for fewer geographic and operational figures.

The Economic Census presents statistics for the nation, states, metropolitan areas, counties, places, and ZIP Codes, but that coverage varies from sector to sector. The greatest variety of statistics and the most detailed industry classifications and subject detail area usually published at the national level. There are fewer statistics and less detailed classifications for states, and fewer still for smaller areas, to avoid disclosing information about individual firms and to reduce publishing costs. By comparison, most current economic surveys provide very little geographic detail. *The Annual Survey of Manufactures* publishes national and state data, but only a few of the *Current Industrial Reports* have state data. The *Survey of Retail Trade* previously published data for the largest states and metropolitan areas, but is now confined to national totals. Among the current programs, only those based on governmental administrative records provide information for counties or places, like *County Business Pat-*

*terns* and some of the *current construction reports.* Below are some general sources on updating some of the census data.

## From the Census Bureau

*Annual Capital Expenditures Survey*
Department of Commerce. Bureau of the Census.
Print: C 3.289:
http://www.census.gov/csd/ace/

This annual survey provides information on capital investment in structures and equipment by nonfarm businesses. The data also provide facts about trends in capital expenditures useful for identifying business opportunities, product development, and business planning.

*Census Product Update*
Department of Commerce. Bureau of the Census.
Web: C 3.163/7:
http://www.census.gov/mp/www/cpu.html

A biweekly newsletter from the Census Bureau with timely information on recently released and key upcoming data products.

*County Business Patterns*
Department of Commerce, Bureau of the Census
Print: C 3.204/3–1:
CD-ROM: C 3.204/4:
http://www.census.gov/epcd/cbp/view/cbpview.html

A series of annual reports providing data on detailed economic activity at national, state, and county levels. Arranged by the North American Industry Classification System (NAICS) within a geographic area, it reflects the employment, payroll, and number of establishments. Excludes data on self-employed persons and government, farm, and household workers.

*ZIP Code Business Patterns*
U.S. Department of Commerce. Bureau of the Census.
CD-ROM: C 3.294:
http://censtats.census.gov/cbpnaic/cbpnaic.shtml

Like *County Business Patterns* this report includes the number of employees, annual payroll, first quarter payroll, and number of establishments by ZIP code. It also includes the number of employees and establishments for each industry within a ZIP code.

*Historical Statistics of the United States: Colonial
    Times to 1970*
U.S. Department of Commerce. Bureau of the Census.
Published 1975. Parts 1–2.
Print: C 3.134/2: H62/970

Found in most libraries, this is an invaluable resource for historical coverage of population, labor, prices, agriculture, economy, and business. The emphasis is on national information with some state and metropolitan area coverage.

*Quarterly Financial Report for Manufacturing, Mining, and Trade Corporations*
Commerce Department, Census Bureau
Print: C 3.267:
http://www.census.gov/csd/qfr/

Presents current aggregate statistics on the financial position of U.S. corporations. The report presents estimated statements of income and retained earnings, balance sheets, and related financial and operating ratios for the domestic operations of all manufacturing corporations with assets over $250,000 and corporations in the mining and trade areas with assets over $50 million. Data are classified by industry and by asset size.

*Statistical Abstract of the United States*
Commerce Department, Census Bureau
Print: C 3.134:
CD-ROM: C 3.134/7:
http://www.census.gov/statab/www/

The Statistical Abstract has been published since 1878, and is a succinct statistical profile of life in the United States. It is one of the very best publications of the U.S. government, and one of the best reference books available. Each section is logically arranged by major topic (e.g. Population, Banking, Finance, and Insurance, Construction and Housing, Manufactures) and there is an excellent index.

## Bureau of Labor Statistics

*Compensation & Working Conditions*
U.S. Department of Labor. Bureau of Labor Statistics.
Print: L 2.44/4:
http://www.bls.gov/opub/cwc/home.htm

Contains analytical articles on wages, benefits, employer costs, and work-related accidents and illnesses. Covers all sectors, public, private, business, and government. Tables include "Employment Cost Index," major work stoppages, and data from the *Occupation Compensation Survey.*

*Employment and Earnings*
U.S. Department of Labor. Bureau of Labor Statistics.
Print: L 2.41/2:
http://www.bls.gov/ces/cesee.htm

Composed almost entirely of tables of statistics. Includes characteristics of the employed and unemployed such as age, sex, and occupation, employment by major industry, average weekly hours and average hourly and weekly earnings for production workers by major industry or manufacturing group, and unemployment rates. Data are given for U.S., states, and more than 200 metropolitan areas.

*Employment, Hours, & Earnings, United States*
U.S. Department of Labor. Bureau of Labor Statistics.
Print: L 2.3: 2481
http://www.bls.gov/ces/home.htm

Monthly and annual average data for employment, hours, and earnings by industry using 2-, 3-, and 4-digit SIC codes. Published on a rotating basis.

*Occupational Outlook*
U.S. Department of Labor. Bureau of Labor Statistics.
Print: L 2.3: 2472

Excellent publication with charts showing projected growth by employment, industry, and occupation. Emphasis is on occupations and industries that have the greatest projected job growth. Graphs and charts illustrate the role of education and training as well as declining industries. Tables list employment by industry and also by occupation with statistics and projections. Factors affecting the changes in each industry and each occupation are also detailed.

*Employment Situation*
U.S. Department of Labor. Bureau of Labor Statistics.
Print: L 2.53/2:
http://stats.bls.gov:80/news.release/empsit.toc.htm

This is one of the most current print publications for employment statistics. These are news releases that contain a monthly summary of employment and unemployment and tables of data from the *Current Population Survey* and the *Current Employment Statistics* survey. Contents include monthly figures for employment status, sex, age, race, unemployment indicators, average weekly hours worked, and earnings by industry. Not as comprehensive as *Employment and Earnings* but more current.

*Monthly Labor Review*
U.S. Department of Labor. Bureau of Labor Statistics.
Print: L 2.6:
http://www.bls.gov/opub/mlr/mlrhome.htm

This is an important resource containing articles and tables of current labor statistics. It covers employment and unemployment, earnings and hours, wages and collective bargaining, and productivity. Three years of labor market indicators are provided. Also includes tables of international comparisons.

*Occupational Compensation Survey*
U.S. Department of Labor. Bureau of Labor Statistics.
Print: L 2.121/:
http://www.bls.gov/ncs/ocs/home.htm

Formerly entitled *Area Wage Surveys.* Each of the 70 metropolitan areas in the series has a separate report giving earnings data by occupation. Jobs are categorized by professional and administrative, technical and protective services, clerical, maintenance and tool room, material movement, and custodial occupations. The *National Summary* (L 2.3:) provides data such as the number of workers by occupation, weekly earnings (mean and median), weekly earnings by pay range and occupation, average weekly pay by company size and occupation, and pay by selected cities. Approximately one-third of the reports contain information on benefits.

*PPI Detailed Report*
Labor Department, Labor Statistics Bureau
Print: L 2.61:
http://www.bls.gov/ppi/home.htm

These reports give the producer price indexes for industries, products, and commodities. Each report contains tables, text, and technical notes. Tracks producer prices for finished goods, intermediate goods, crude goods, mining, and manufacturing. The *Annual Supplement* (L 2.61/11:) contains annual averages and monthly compilations for the preceding year.

## Other Government Sources

*Federal Register*
National Archives and Records Administration, Federal Register Office
Print, Microform: AE 2.106:
http://www.access.gpo.gov/su_docs/aces/fr-cont.html

Daily (Monday through Friday, excluding federal holidays) publication listing public regulations and legal notices issued by federal agencies. The *Federal Register* and the *Code of Federal Regulations* (CFR) must be used together to determine the latest regulation in force. Use the *Federal Register* to keep informed about changes in NAICS.

*Economic Indicators*
Congress, Joint Economic Committee
Print: Y4.Ec7: Ec7
http://www.access.gpo.gov/congress/eibrowse/broecind.html

Statistical summary published by the Council of Economic Advisors. Monthly, quarterly, annual, and historical GDP data, as well as personal income, corporate profits, unemployment, wages, productivity, producer prices, and summary consumer price data are all summarized here. International trade statistics are also included.

*Economic Report of the President*
President of the United States
Print: PR 42.9:
http://w3.access.gpo.gov/usbudget

Council of Economic Advisors report to the President. This is essentially the executive office's plan for the economy. It is also a good source for historical economic tables.

*SOI (Statistics of Income) Bulletin*
Treasury Department, Internal Revenue Service
Print: T 22.35/4:
http://www.irs.gov/taxstats/content/0,,id = 97507,00.html

The SOI Bulletin publishes the earliest annual financial statistics obtained from the various types of tax returns filed. Also included are state, historical, and personal income data. Along with the statistics, each issue includes a "Featured Articles" section with articles about some aspect of U.S. or international taxation.

*Statistics of Income, Corporation Income Tax Returns*
Treasury Department, Internal Revenue Service
Print: T 22.35/5:
http://www.irs.gov/taxstats/article/0,,id =
    96249,00.html

This is an annual compilation of corporate tax returns with detailed tables and analysis. It includes corporate income tax forms and instructions for that year.

*Summary of Commentary on Current Economic Conditions (Beige Book)*
Federal Reserve System, Federal Reserve District
http://www.federalreserve.gov/FOMC/
    BeigeBook/2003/

This is a summary from each Federal Reserve Bank district. It contains anecdotal information on current economic conditions in each district obtained through reports from bank and branch directors and interviews with key business people, economists, market reports, and other sources.

*Survey of Current Business*
Commerce Department, Economic Analysis Bureau
Print: C 59.11:
CD-ROM: C 59.11/1: (annual only)
http://www.bea.gov/bea/pubs.htm

This title features special reports and tables of key economic events that are surveyed once per year. Each monthly issue includes national income and product accounts, business cycle indicators, and annual and quarterly historical data.

*STAT-USA*
Commerce Department

C 1.91: (subscription service via Internet)
http://www.stat-usa.gov

STAT-USA provides access to a variety of statistics and reports produced by the U.S. government for a fee. Domestic economic indicators include statistics on construction, retail and wholesale trade, manufacturing, price and productivity (including the consumer price index and the producer price index), employment, business cycle indicators, fiscal and monetary policy, and national income and product accounts. Also included are regional economic series, featuring gross state product, personal income, and regional economic series projections.

## Commercial Sources

*Annual Statement Studies*
Robert Morris Associates
Print: HG 5681 .B2 R6

This provides composite financial data for approximately 300 lines of business. Information for each industry is broken down by company size. Figures cover the previous year or two. Note: Compiles statistics for companies with less than $100 million in assets.

*Industry Surveys*
Standard & Poors
Print: HG 4905 .S7

This contains basic analyses of 30 to 40 major industries with many subject breakdowns within each industry. Statistical information includes sales, profit margin, P/E ratios, and capital expenditures.

*Statistical Service*
Standard and Poors
Print: HG4921 .S76

This source comes in two parts, Current Statistics and Basic Statistics (historical data). Along with the S&P stock market index data it also aggregates most of the government economic data. No analysis, just the numbers.

## ANSWERS: TEST YOUR KNOWLEDGE

Amazon.com—Yes, the industry would be NAICS 454110 Electronic Shopping and Mail-Order Houses; they would be counted with all the businesses that use the electronic commerce as their method of selling. Use the merchandise line data to see what products are sold online or by mail order. Amazon.com's auxiliaries like their warehouses and call centers would be counted in other industries.

Barge operations on the Mississippi—Yes, the industry would be NAICS 483211 Inland Water Freight Transportation, but it would limit the data to Mississippi River. To see what products are transported using shallow draft ships use the *Commodity Flow Survey.*

Cook County Public Library—No, even through there is a code for libraries. A government-run library is *not* counted in the Economic Census, but it would be counted in Census of Governments.

Consultant—Yes and no, if the consultant works in a company then the consultant is an occupation, however if the consultant runs his or her own business and generates income, then she would be counted in a NAICS industry based on the subject area he or she consulted in. Be aware that consulting is one of those fields where nonemployers and the regular reports should be combined since a large percentage of consultants don't have employees.

Double D Horse Ranch—No, since this industry falls in the Agriculture Sector, NAICS 112920 Horse and Other Equine Production, it will not be reported in the Economic Census, but in the Census of Agriculture.

Forensic Laboratories—Yes and no, if the laboratory is part of a government agency it's not counted, but if it is independent, then it would be in NAICS 621511 Medical Laboratories

Ford Motor Company Headquarters—Yes, the industry would be NAICS 551114 Corporate, Subsidiary, and Regional Managing Offices, not automobile manufacturing. Ford Motor Company Head office has more in common with Kraft Foods Headquarters, than a manufacturing plant, so they would be grouped together.

Hard Times Café—Yes, the industry would be NAICS 72211 Full-Service Restaurants. Restaurants are no longer being counted in the retail sector, but in its own Accommodation and Food services sector.

Hat Manufacturers in Guam—Yes, since Guam is a U.S. territory the establishment would be included in the *Census of Outlying Areas.* The industry details only goes down to the sub-sector level, using the SIC system.

Silver Dollar Mine—Yes, the industry would be NAICS 212222 Silver Ore Mining. Mining is the sector least affected by the NAICS code conversion.

Newark Evening News—Yes, it depends on the activity which industry it would fall into. If it was the newspaper's office, it would be NAICS 511110 Newspaper Publishers. If it was the place where the paper is printed, it would be in NAICS 32311 Printing.

Personal Chefs—Yes and no, if the personal chef is employed in a household it would not be counted. If multiple households hire the chef then they would fall into NAICS 722320 Caterers. Most likely he or she would be included in nonemployer statistics and not food service reports.

Singapore Hilton—No, even if the parent is an American company, if the economic activity is generated outside U.S. it will not be reflected anywhere in the Economic Census.

## BIBLIOGRAPHY

Hernon, Peter, and Kathy V. Friedman, eds. 1998. "Symposium on the 1997 Economic Census, U.S. Bureau of the Census." Special Issue, *Government Information Quarterly* 15 (3): 243–377. http://www.census.gov/epcd/www/giq97.html

U.S. Bureau of the Census. 1999. *Guide to the 1997 Economic Census.* Washington, DC: The Bureau. Available on the Census Bureau's Web site at http://www.census.gov/epcd/www/guide.html (retrieved October 16, 2003).

U.S. Bureau of the Census. 2003. *Guide to the 2002 Economic Census.* Washington, DC: The Bureau. Available on the Census Bureau's Web site at http://www.census.gov/epcd/ec02/guide.html (retrieved October 16, 2003).

U.S. Bureau of the Census. 2000. *History of the 1997 Economic Census.* Washington, DC: The Bureau. Available on the Census Bureau's Web site at http://www.census.gov/crod/ed97/pol00-hec.pdf (retrieved October 16, 2003).

# CHAPTER 2
# Economic Census Procedures

The term "productive industry" must be understood, in the largest significances, to include all manufacturing, mechanical, and mining operations, and also all coast, lake, and river fisheries. The smallest shop must not be omitted, provided the production reaches $500 annually, including the *cost of materials.*

*(Instructions to Assistant Marshals—Census of 1870)*

1. How the 1997 Economic Census Was Conducted

    A. Content Determination
    B. Questionnaire Development
    C. Data Collection
    D. Publication

2. Conducting the 2002 Economic Census
3. Bibliography

## HOW THE 1997 ECONOMIC CENSUS WAS CONDUCTED

Every statistical data collection effort like the Economic Census is a process with several distinct stages. These are

1. Overall content identification
2. Development of the questionnaires
3. The actual data collection process including

    A. Promoting awareness
    B. Distributing the questionnaires
    C. Receiving the completed questionnaires
    D. Following up on questionnaires that are not returned promptly
    E. Recording the responses

4. Determining the data tabulations and products to be produced
5. Tabulating the data
6. Producing and promoting the products
7. Getting ready for the next census

This chapter summarizes how and when the Census Bureau implemented each of these activities for the major components of the census. Key players at each step of the process are also mentioned.

At the end of every Economic Census a detailed report is written describing how that particular census was conducted. These are the *History Reports* for each census.

## Content Determination

While Title 13 of the United States Code specifies that an Economic Census is to be taken in years ending in a 3 or an 8 covering years ending in 2 and 7, it does not specify what should be asked in the census. That decision has been left to the Census Bureau's director. In practice, staff in the Bureau's economic subject divisions makes these decisions, namely: the Manufacturing and Construction Division, the Company Statistics Division, and the Service Sector Statistics Division.

These divisions, along with the Economic Planning and Coordination Division, asked key constituencies for input on the content of the census. These constituencies included professional, industry, and business associations. They also included the other federal government agencies that are heavy users of the economic census data for programmatic or benchmarking purposes. Programmatic purposes include policy, decision-making, and program administration uses. Benchmarking is the adjustment of other statistical data to be consistent with the findings of the census. The Bureau's advisory committees also had the opportunity for input into the census's content. The Census Bureau has several committees of outside experts in areas related to the Bureau's activities who advise the Bureau on significant issues.

Finally, the Office of Management and Budget (OMB) had final authority on approving the content and design of all Economic Census forms. In its review OMB had to determine that the information requested

- Was necessary
- Was not available from other sources
- Could be easily provided (or reasonably estimated) by the respondents
- Maintains historical continuity

This process of content determination ran from January 1994 through early 1997 for the 1997 Economic Census, with a comparable time period for the 2002 Economic Census. It resulted in the following information being requested from all respondents:

- Kind-of-business activity (economic sector)
- Physical location of the establishment
- Form of ownership (corporation, etc.)
- Dollar volume of business in 1997 (sales, etc.)
- Number of employees
- Dollar amount of payroll

Additionally, many industry-specific questions were asked, such as electricity used in the manufacturing industries or quantity and value of milk sold by grocery stores. These industry-specific questions are detailed in the industry chapters on each industry sector.

## Questionnaire Development

Because of the necessarily close relationship between determining the content and designing the questionnaire, these two activities were handled by many of the same people at the same time. Government officials consulted associations, regular users, and other interested parties to create the questionnaire.

Given the number of different industry-specific questions that were needed and the many variations on some of these, 479 different questionnaires were developed for the 1997 Economic Census, and more than 650 forms for the 2002 Economic Census. Table 2.1 shows the number of questionnaires developed for each part of the Economic Census. Within a sector the primary differences between the questionnaires were generally in the industry-specific questions on common production inputs, products or services, and the information needed to verify the establishment's industry (complicated in 1997 by the need to convert from the SIC system to NAICS).

In addition to determining the questions and their wordings, many other decisions had to be made regarding the questionnaires. It is important to note that many of these details can affect the tendency of respondents to actually complete and return the questionnaires. These decisions included

- Size and format of the questionnaires
- Means of identifying each of the questionnaires (form numbers and titles)
- The sequence of standard questions
- File copy requirements
- How the design process, itself, would be conducted
- Color schemes for the paper and ink
- Shading of the questionnaires
- The processing equipment to be used in printing, mailing, receiving, and reading the questionnaires
- Microfilming requirements

In addition to the questionnaires, envelopes and instruction sheets needed to be designed. Since each new census tends to be very similar to the last Economic Census in content, much of this design work was limited to changes required by new processing equipment, identification codes and titles, and lessons learned from the earlier effort. In the 1997 Economic Census the need for additional information to reclassify establishments based on NAICS was also included as a design consideration.

Details about the changes from the 1992 Economic Census can be found in chapter 4 of the *History of the 1997 Economic Census*.

Several sample questionnaires can be found in Appendix B of this book.

## Data Collection

Actually collecting the data is a relatively short part of the Economic Census cycle. It is also the hardest part of the census since the Census Bureau has little direct control over what happens at this time. In order to help ease the data collection phase, the Census Bureau ran a promotional campaign. However, in spite of this promotional campaign some establishments did not return their questionnaire in a timely manner, so follow-up activities were needed. Finally, when the questionnaires were returned to the Bureau, they needed to be checked in, read, and potentially edited.

This section describes each of these activities.

### Promotion Issues

The Census Bureau had two underlying and interrelated objectives in their Economic Census promotion efforts. First and foremost, they wanted to get estab-

**Table 2.1**
**Number of 1997 Economic Census Questionnaires by Sector or Type**

| Type | Questionnaires |
|---|---|
| Manufacturing | 253 |
| Mining | 12 |
| Construction | 11 |
| Retail Trade and Accommodations and Food Services | 44 |
| Wholesale Trade | 48 |
| Service Industries | 54 |
| Finance, Insurance, and Real Estate | 24 |
| Utilities (utilities, transportation, and communications) | 8 |
| Vehicle Inventory and Use Survey | 4 |
| Business Owners and Self-Employed Persons | 2 |
| Business Expenditure Survey | 9 |
| Economic Census of Outlying Areas (including Spanish and English questionnaires for Puerto Rico and the Virgin Islands of the United States) | 6 |
| General Schedules | 4 |
| **TOTAL** | **479** |

lishments to complete and return their questionnaires by February 12, 1998, for the 1997 Economic Census and February 12, 2003, for the 2002 Economic Census. As John P. Govoni, Chief of Economic Planning and Coordination Division at the Census Bureau stated, "Every census—whether of people or of business establishments—must persuade those from whom they would collect the data to *provide the information*. No data response, no census results" (Census Bureau 2000, 37).

The second objective was to increase awareness of the products and uses of economic census data. These objectives are related in that getting a faster response means that the data could be released sooner—making it more useful. Also, it was hoped, the more useful the respondents saw the data to be, the more likely they were to respond to the Economic Census in a timely manner. It is important to remember that in many

businesses one unit may complete the questionnaire—such as the accounting department, while another unit—maybe marketing—actually uses the results. So, in many cases, the accounting department had to be informed of the ways that the marketing and other divisions of their company could use the information that they were being asked to provide.

The results from the 1992 Economic Census suggested several things that the Census Bureau needed to do in order to improve the response to the 1997 Economic Census. These included

- Making it clear to the respondents, especially large multi-establishment firms, that the entire Economic Census is a unified event.
- Remind respondents that their answers were required by federal law.
- Target large companies for a better and faster response.

## The Unity of the Census

As can be seen in the chapter on the history of the Economic Census, the 1997 Economic Census was the first census that was truly an integrated Economic Census, with the exclusion of the agriculture sector. The 2002 Economic Census, in some ways, was even more unified than the 1997 one.

Prior to 1997 there were a number of sector-specific censuses with some level of integration. As a result, the accounting department of a multi-establishment business might receive a questionnaire for the Census of Retail Trade for several establishments, the Census of Wholesale Trade for another, and the Census of Services for yet another establishment. Because there was no nominal connection between these censuses and "the economic censuses" being promoted in the media, it was very possible that the director of the accounting department would not recognize these questionnaires as being the economic censuses being advertised and would be more likely to set the questionnaires aside.

In response to this lesson from 1992, the Census Bureau developed a unified image for the entire Economic Census. This included adopting the formal name of "1997 Economic Census," using this name on everything related to this census, keeping the sector titles in relatively smaller type on all census materials adopting the single unified logo shown in Figure 2.1, and giving the message that this was the single major event in measuring the nation's economy. Only the date changed in the logo for 2002.

## "Your Response Is Required by Law"

The single most effective piece of the 1992 Economic Census's efforts to improve response might have been placing a message reminding the respondents that their response was required by law on the envelopes used to mail the questionnaires to single-establishment companies. Based on this experience, the Census Bureau included this message on the outside of *all* form packages mailed as part of the 1997 Economic Census.

## Large Companies

A group of very large companies is singled out for special outreach procedures, either because of their size (typically with more than 5,000 employees) or history of poor response in past censuses. While these companies represent just seven percent of all estab-

**Figure 2.1**
**Unified 1997 Economic Census Logo**

lishments that the Census Bureau mailed questionnaires to, they account for over 30 percent of the Nation's economic activity. Because of the importance of these companies to getting accurate data about the economy, the Census Bureau used special procedures to reach out to them. These procedures are described under "Targeting Large Companies" below.

## Actual Promotional Activities

There were a number of key players involved in promoting the Economic Census. Each player worked in their area of expertise and supported the efforts of other players. The following is a description of the 1997 Economic Census promotional activities. The 2002 Economic Census promotion effort was very similar in nature, but some details differed. If you are interested in these details, they will be included in the *History of the 2002 Economic Census* when it is released.

The Economic Census Staff in the Economic Planning and Coordination Division (EPCD) provided overall planning and direction for promotional activities.

Lisboa Associates (New York, NY) is the advertising agency that was contracted to support most of the major promotional activities for the Census Bureau. They conducted and interpreted the research necessary to design and implement the Economic Census promotional plan. Based on the research findings, they proposed the marketing strategy for the census. This firm did the creative work involved in developing artwork. Media kits and public service announcements were developed and distributed by Lisboa Associates. This company also distributed over 50,000 copies of the *Accountant's Guide to the 1997 Economic Census.* Lisboa also provided the Census Bureau with ongoing information about the performance of the promotion efforts through a newspaper clipping service and a statistical analysis of the clips, response cards received, etc.

The Census Bureau's Public Information Office was responsible for working with EPCD and Lisboa Associates on the details of their projects, developing press releases and other publicity materials needed to support the items. Lisboa Associates was responsible for developing and distributing—through existing channels—video and radio materials, and promoting and/or assisting in interviews related to the Economic Census.

The Bureau's Congressional Affairs Office was responsible for keeping Congress informed about the development and progress of the Economic Census. Given the Congressional oversight and funding role of all Census Bureau activities, this was a particularly important function. Unlike the decennial censuses where Congress is extremely interested in every aspect of the census, Congress tends to let the Census Bureau's experts work on the Economic Census without too much interference by emphasizing the budget issues, general methods, and schedules.

The Bureau's Marketing Services Office provided guidance for the product marketing activities.

Many data users view the organizations participating in the State Data Center (SDC) and Business and Industry Data Center (BIDC) programs as extensions of the Census Bureau. As such, these organizations are frequently looked to for information about the Bureau's activities. Historically, these organizations have reported responding to about 166,000 requests for data from the business community every year. Given the methods of recording requests used by these organizations, this number misses many individual contacts with the business community and understates the number of different businesses these organizations contact in a given year. However, it is possible to see that these programs were a source of

contact with Economic Census respondents that could not be ignored. Given these roles as a data and information provider having a significant outreach to the business community, it was only natural for the Census Bureau to look to the organizations participating in these programs for assistance in promoting the Economic Census. The Census Bureau's Customer Liaison Office coordinated contacts with the SDC/BIDC organizations. While they varied greatly from organization to organization, SDC/BIDC agencies provided a variety of promotional services to the Census Bureau such as including articles in their own newsletters, speaking about the Economic Census at conferences (both to promote responses and to describe the data products), and speaking to the media about the Economic Census.

## Materials

A number of materials were developed by the Census Bureau for use in promoting Economic Census responses. There were two primary audiences for these materials. The first was the print and broadcast media. The second audience was the accountants who would actually complete the questionnaires for many businesses.

Materials aimed at the first audience included press releases, sample editorials, fact sheets, a brochure describing NAICS, clip art, response dates, information on how to get assistance, a set of frequently asked questions about the Economic Census and their answers, information on how the Economic Census data have been used in the past, summary findings from the 1992 Economic Census, and text for three Public Service Announcements (PSAs). The three PSAs each had a different message and time frame for when they should have been used. The first message, for use between September and December 1997, was "the questionnaires are coming." The second message, which was targeted for January and February 1998, contained the message "the questionnaires are here." The final message was "the questionnaire responses are past due" and was used during March 1998.

These materials were combined into press kits that were distributed by the contractor as follows:

- General business publications—1,021 kits
- Industry associations—2,112 kits
- Newspapers—905 kits
- Regional business publications—823 kits
- Chambers of Commerce—3,027 kits

- State Data Center/Business and Industry Data Center organizations—2,189 kits

Additionally, these materials were made available on the Census Bureau's Web site in formats that could be easily downloaded and used as desired. Finally, the Congressional Affairs Office modified these kits for distribution to Congressional offices.

Since many businesses, especially smaller ones, have all of their forms, including the Economic Census questionnaires, completed by their accountants, the Census Bureau needed to make certain that these respondents knew how to complete the questionnaires accurately. This became even more important because any one accountant would be likely to complete the questionnaires for a number of establishments, thus multiplying the problems caused by any misunderstanding of the directions. Therefore, the Census Bureau developed the *Accountant's Guide to the 1997 Economic Census.* Over 50,000 copies of this guide were distributed to independent accountants. The list of accountants came from the membership rolls of the National Accounting Association and the American Society of Certified Public Accountants. This guide contained answers to many of the questions commonly asked by respondents, sample questionnaires, reminders about the February 12, 1998, deadline for responding, instructions on how to request an extension, and directions for getting more information.

## Mailing the Questionnaires

Mailing the questionnaires requires the Census Bureau to have an accurate list of the business establishments throughout the entire country. This list needs to contain the physical location, mailing address, industry, and organizational information about each establishment in the country. The Standard Statistical Establishment List (SSEL), currently called the Business Register, maintained on an ongoing basis by the Census Bureau was just such a list. It contains information on about 6.5 million businesses throughout the nation. The SSEL is based on information that the Census Bureau receives from (and by law cannot give back to) the Internal Revenue Service, the Social Security Administration, and the Census Bureau's own surveys. From this list, the Census Bureau has mailing addresses for all businesses covered in the Economic Censuses.

The Census Bureau used the SSEL information for multi-establishment companies to

- Identify all active companies and establishments.
- Identify those headquarters to be multi-establishment companies that were sent a single consolidated questionnaire requesting summary data for all of their establishments. These companies were selected because of their relatively small size or the economic operations of their individual establishments.
- Assign the proper questionnaire types to: (1) establishments that might have been beyond the scope of the Economic Census, (2) finance, insurance, and real estate, and communications establishments—usually, consolidated questionnaires, (3) auxiliary establishments, and (4) all other establishments based on their industrial classification.

For single-establishment companies the SSEL was used to: (1) select those establishments with payroll in 1997, (2) assign the questionnaires to these companies based on NAICS and other information, and (3) sample these companies in order to reduce total respondent burden.

While some of the information collected in the census can be found in various administrative records, such as the Security and Exchange Commission filings required of many publicly traded companies (these have been suggested as an alternate source for the data), these sources are inadequate for the purposes of the Economic Census. Often these filings lack key information needed for the census, such as information about the value of specific products sold. Another problem is that the administrative records do not define variables the same way as they are defined in the census. One example of this problem is that many wholesale agents and brokers typically report commissions as their gross receipts, not the aggregate sale price of the goods sold, as would typically be reported by a merchant wholesaler. A third major problem with these administrative records, including those from the Internal Revenue Service, is that they report data on the company as a whole, and not on an establishment-by-establishment basis.

## Sampling

In order to reduce the aggregate time needed for respondents to answer the census, many small single-establishment companies were exempted from the census. Sampling only a small portion of these companies accomplished this goal. The definition of small varied between each four-digit SIC or five-digit NAICS industry. However, the definition was set at the level where the companies selected not to get a questionnaire accounted for only about ten percent of the total value of shipments or sales for that industry. Limited information for companies that were excluded from the census sample was collected from administrative records obtained from the Internal Revenue Service. Some industrial classification information was obtained from the U.S. Bureau of Labor Statistics. Many tables in the various data products contain information about the level of sampling and administrative records used in any particular industry or geographic area.

Additionally, for certain industries, the Economic Census included both a short and long version of the questionnaire. These forms differed in the level of detail included in the questions—especially about revenue sources and expense categories. In affected industries, all multi-establishment companies and the largest single-establishment companies received a long form. Only a stratified sample of smaller, single-establishment companies were selected to receive a long form, while the remainder received short forms.

## DocuPrint

Prior to the 1997 Economic Census, all questionnaires were printed by private-sector printers. For multi-unit companies, which were to receive separate forms for each of their establishments, the Census Bureau needed to assemble the appropriate forms into mailing packages by hand. Starting in 1997, the Bureau used a DocuPrint 4890 Highlight Color Laser Printing System to print questionnaires, other forms, instructions, and cover letters for the Economic Census, where it was more cost-effective to do so.

The DocuPrint 4890 was programmed to print the entire questionnaire package sent to multi-unit companies. This process included selecting the appropriate questionnaires (out of the 460 questionnaires used in this Economic Census), labeling, and printing in the sequence required to form the mailing package. By using this technology, the Census Bureau eliminated the need to assemble and inspect the packages by hand before mailing them.

## Nonresponse Follow-Up Activities

As with any data collection effort, there are a number of respondents who don't respond in a timely manner. All high quality data collection operations attempt to minimize the number of nonrespondents. The Economic Census is no exception in this regard. Only about one-half of single-establishment businesses re-

turned their forms by the deadline; by the time the follow-up activities are complete, around 90 percent of all single-establishment business have responded. The Census Bureau used several methods to collect data from as many respondents as possible. In general, all census follow-up activities can be divided into mail and telephone work.

Additionally, the Census Bureau re-mailed questionnaires and reminder mailings to all respondents who did not respond in a timely manner. Businesses that were granted time extensions for responding were sent reminder mailings but not more questionnaires.

## Single-Establishment Companies

Companies with only one establishment were divided into four categories for follow-up purposes:

1. Those included in the Annual Survey of Manufactures,
2. Those needing to supply more information in order to be classified into the correct industry,
3. Those that came into existence during the third quarter of 1997 (i.e., births), and
4. All other companies.

Depending on which group a company was in and how many follow-up attempts were already made, the company might receive just a reminder letter or an entirely new questionnaire package (with a more strongly worded cover letter). Table 2.2 summarizes the follow-up schedule. In looking at this table, you should note that the "closeout date" is the date that a questionnaire had to be recorded as being received to avoid getting a follow-up package.

## Multi-establishment Companies

For follow-up purposes, companies with more than one establishment were grouped together based on three criteria. The first of these was the company size. Depending on the standards for a company's industry sector, it was classified into one of four categories: large (L), medium (M), or small (N or S). These categories were only used within the Census Bureau to group companies for the amount of follow-up effort that they would receive.

The second criterion was whether the company was totally or only partially delinquent in their response. A company was classified as totally delinquent if the Census Bureau received no response from the company by the cutoff date following each mailing. If at

**Table 2.2**
**1997 Economic Census Single Establishment Follow-up Activity Schedule**

| Close Out Date | Company Categories | Follow-up Number | Package Type |
|---|---|---|---|
| February 23, 1998 | 1 | First | Letter |
| February 28, 1998 | 2 | First | Questionnaire |
| March 4, 1998 | 4 | First | Questionnaire |
| April 15, 1998 | 1, 2, 4 | Second | Questionnaire |
| April 29, 1998 | 3 | First | Questionnaire |
| May 22, 1998 | 1, 2, 4 | Third | Questionnaire |
| May 22, 1998 | 3 | Second | Questionnaire |
| July 9, 1998 | 1, 2, 3, 4 with an estimated payroll over $200,000 | Fourth (except third for births) | Questionnaire |

Notes: Company Categories are: 1. Companies in the *Annual Survey of Manufactures*; 2. Companies needing more information to be classified; 3. Third-quarter 1997 births; and 4. All others.

least one questionnaire, but not all of them, was received from a company, it was classified as partially delinquent.

Whether or not the company requested an extension was the Census Bureau's third classification criterion. Follow-up activities for companies with extensions were less intense than those for companies without extensions.

Table 2.3 summarizes the follow-up activities for each type of multi-establishment company.

After the April, May, and June closeout dates, selected large- and medium-sized multi-establishment delinquent companies were selected for telephone follow-up. This follow-up activity was conducted by Census Bureau staff located at the Bureau's headquarters in Suitland, Maryland, as their workload of incoming calls permitted. The companies were called in order of descending payroll, so that the largest companies were called first. These telephone calls had three purposes: (1) to remind the company's contact person to file their census reports, (2) to determine when they would be filing the reports, and (3) to assist the respondent in completing the forms if that was necessary.

**Targeting Large Companies**

Historically, the Census Bureau has had problems getting timely responses from large companies. In

order to improve the speed with which the largest companies responded to the Economic Census, the Bureau made a special effort to reach out to the 1,000 largest companies. An additional 9,000 medium-sized companies were included in a scaled-back version of this program in which they received a mailing with a contact number for help with the Economic Census. Additionally, they received several telephone follow-ups from June through August 1998. The heart of this program was the idea that each of these companies would have an account manager assigned to them and any single account manager would work with between 5 and 25 companies.

The companies were notified of their selection for this program with a mailing in November 1996. This mailing included a customized cover letter, lists of the census forms that the company would receive, information about how to contact their account managers, a form allowing them to update the contact information for the contact person at the company, information about filing electronically, and a general information booklet about the Economic Census.

Account managers were scheduled to make a minimum of five, and as many as eight, phone calls to each company. These calls would be made beginning in December 1996 or January 1997 to verify receipt of the advance information and could last until June 1998 or later with offers of assistance or a "thank you" for completing the form.

Table 2.3
1997 Economic Census Multi-Establishment Company Nonreponse Follow-up Activities

| Criteria | | | Closeout Date | Follow-up Activity | |
|---|---|---|---|---|---|
| Company Size | Delinquency Status | Extension Status | | Number | Mailing Type |
| All | Totally | No | 2/2/98 | 1 | Letter |
| All | Totally | No | 4/1/98 | 2 | Letter |
| All | Partially | No | 5/7/98 | 1 | Letter |
| All | Totally | No | 5/7/98 | 3 | Letter |
| All | Totally | Unexpired | 5/7/98 | 1 | Letter |
| All | Partially | No | 6/10/98 | 2 | Letter |
| All | Partially | Unexpired | 6/10/98 | 1 | Letter |
| Large | Totally | No | 6/11/98 | 4 | Letter |
| Small | Totally | No | 6/25/98 | 4 | Questionnaire |
| All | Totally | Unexpired | 6/11/98 | 2 | Letter |

## Receiving and Processing the Questionnaires

There were three ways that data could be collected from individual companies. One way was to complete a questionnaire and return it to the Census Bureau by mail. Most companies receiving questionnaires used this method.

The second method was to file electronically. This method was available to selected large- and medium-sized companies. Ultimately, 671 companies responded by submitting either Computerized Self-Administered Questionnaires on diskettes or by electronic data interchange files on computer tape. These represented almost 317,600 establishments.

The final method of collecting data was through administrative records from other federal agencies, such as the Internal Revenue Service. Administrative records were used to collect information on industrial classification, number of employees, and payroll for the majority of small single-establishment and non-employer companies.

## Mail Responses—Check-in Procedures

The first step of receiving and checking the questionnaires in at the Census Bureau was to sort them for handling by the appropriate unit or individual. All correspondence was initially presorted by the post office based on mail box numbers—eight different mailboxes were used to provide group correspondence into general categories. Upon receipt at the Census Bureau's National Processing Center in Jeffersonville, Indiana, the mail from each mailbox was further divided into five major categories as follows:

- Materials addressed to a specific analyst were forwarded to that person.
- Correspondence that was undeliverable as addressed or follow-up letters related to these were referred to the Directory Analyst Unit where additional work to locate the company was conducted.
- Questionnaire return envelopes were sent to the Register Batch Unit for check-in.
- All other Economic Census related mail was sent to the Open and Sort Unit.
- Mail obviously not related to the Economic Census was referred to the appropriate subject area.

After the returned questionnaires (and other barcoded material) were separated from the other mail—either by being sent directly to the Register Batch Unit or being sent there from the Open and Sort Unit—the questionnaire was checked into the system as being returned. This was done by having its barcode read by a sorter/reader. If the sorter/reader couldn't read the barcode, it separated the document out from the others. These other documents were sorted by the questionnaire type or other types of documents. An attempt was then made to read the barcodes on the rejected items with a hand laser-wand. If this didn't work, a clerk manually keyed the barcode identification number into the check-in file.

After they were checked in as being returned, questionnaires from single-establishment companies were microfilmed for reference until the next census is completed and for permanent storage.

The path from check-in to keying was slightly different for questionnaires from multi-establishment companies. Between these two processing steps, these questionnaires went through a completeness and coverage check. During this check sufficient information was keyed into the computer to allow a comparison of key information included on the census questionnaires with that contained in the SSEL. This included information about the company's organization, new establishments, mergers, sales of plants, etc. If there were discrepancies between the two files, the file with "weaker" data was modified. For example, if there was a difference in the information about a company's organizational structure, the census questionnaires were considered to be more accurate (since they were more recent) and the SSEL was corrected. However, if the differences involved unusual employment or payroll data relationships, such as an unusually high or low payroll per employee in the census compared to the company's historic pattern, the administrative data was considered more accurate because of the longer time series for which it existed and the census responses would be adjusted. Finally, in the situation where a company reported data for the company as a whole rather than by establishment, the SSEL data was used to allocate the data to individual establishments. After this completeness and coverage check was completed, the forms for the multi-establishment companies, like those for the single-establishment companies, were microfilmed.

## Keying

After the forms were microfilmed, they were sent to another unit for keying into the computer. During this data entry process, clerks entered the data contained on the questionnaires. While they were entering the data, the clerks also provided a basic clerical review of the questions involving an attempt to be made by a supervisor to read illegible entries, calculating of midpoints of ranges reported by respondents, and the notation of other problems with the responses. At this same time, the computer performed several data validity checks.

## Quality Assurance Procedures—Data Quality

Following the data entry process, the data records were matched with the data contained in the SSEL. This allowed an establishment's responses to be compared with historical data about that establishment. This comparison was used to flag changes in company structure and affiliates, duplicate records, potential new establishments, address changes, and unusual responses.

Clerks handled records that were flagged due to missing data by either sending another questionnaire to the respondent, calling the respondent for the information, or inserting data derived from other information on the questionnaire. Records that were flagged because of other problems were sent to industry analysts for their review and resolution of the problem.

## Post-Collection Processing

After they were entered into the computer, and the data entry verification and editing were completed, the records were sent to the industry analysts for further data checks and for tabulation. The data records were subjected to a variety of data verification procedures. In particular, these procedures verified the kind-of-business, industry, geographic, and ZIP codes. They also checked payroll, sales, and employment data for reasonableness. These procedures were designed to catch major errors in the data, not minor ones. For example, if the correct value was a 200, these procedures catch a 2 being entered, but would not catch a value of 190. Generally, these procedures worked in several specific ways:

1. By comparing data within the questionnaire to other data within the questionnaire
2. Comparing the data to historic data for the establishment
3. Comparing data for the establishment with industry norms

If an establishment's response was outside of preset limits, the record was flagged for further research and verification. Correcting the problems might involve sending a customized letter to the respondent requesting additional information or verifying that write-in entries were coded correctly.

## Tabulation Procedures

Following the completion of the "complex edit" procedures by the subject analyst, the process of tabulating and publishing the data started. This process started with a macro-level analysis of the data. During this analysis the subject analyst ran preliminary tabulations of the data. These preliminary tables were compared with similar tables from other sources, such as the *County Business Patterns, Annual Survey of Manufactures,* and the 1992 Economic Census. The use of SIC-NAICS Bridge Codes allowed the analyst to produce the preliminary tables on an SIC basis. This allowed comparison of the results with the other sources. If any unusual results were found, the analyst did additional, more detailed research to identify and correct the problem or verify that the result was correct.

Finally, after all identified problems had been corrected to the best of their ability, the subject analysts reran the tables in final form and prepared them for publication.

## Publication

There are actually three major components to the publication process. The first of these is making decisions about the publication plans. The second is the actual publishing of the data. The final component is making the public aware of the data availability. The discussion here emphasizes the first and third components because the increased use of electronic media de-emphasizes the second.

## Product Planning

The final phase of any statistical undertaking is the release of the data and analysis. While this is considered to be the final stage in the census process, many of the decisions about the final products (at least in a general form) must be made early in the planning process in order to assure that the data will be collected properly. Two of these early decisions involve the primary release medium and the general content of the tables.

In making these decisions, the Census Bureau conducted a survey of known users of the 1992 Economic Census. The results of this survey indicated that users were very interested in receiving data in an electronic format with software to access the data. The reasons for this interest in electronic data revolved around speed and ease of manipulation. The ability to increase the amount of data released at the same, or lower, cost was also a factor.

Based on this survey and general trends in technology, the Census Bureau decided to use electronic formats as the primary data release method and de-emphasize printed formats. There were several electronic formats available to data users. These included CD-ROMs and the Internet. The decision was made to print very few reports. Reports comparable to the 1992 Economic Census's printed reports—and not printed as part of the 1997 Economic Census—were made available as printable (PDF) documents that could be downloaded from the Census Bureau's Web site. If a user wished, the Census Bureau was willing to print these documents on demand. The cost of this service was about 10 cents per page plus a $20 handling and delivery charge. These documents would be produced with a heavy stock cover and a rudimentary binding. Details about working with these media are presented elsewhere in this book.

The decision to make electronic media the primary data access method increased the need for standardization of tables across sectors. This increased standardization allowed easier programming of the software provided by the Census Bureau for access to the data. It also made it easier for users to combine data from various sectors for further manipulation.

## Publicity

As mentioned earlier in this chapter, one goal of the Census Bureau's promotional plans was to increase awareness of the products' usefulness to respondents. This was done by providing respondents with examples of the data produced from the 1992 Economic Census and ways it was used.

Another aspect of product promotion was to make the public aware of 1997 Economic Census data as they became available. To this end, the Census Bureau engaged in three major activities:

1. A notice was displayed on the Census Bureau's Web site.
2. A press release was issued with the release of the first report in each of the Geographic Area Series and the economy-wide reports.

3. A user conference was held in 25 major cities, typically shortly following the release of the retail trade report for the state, usually with the assistance of the State Data Center agencies, to introduce these products to data users. In some cases more than one meeting was held in a state.

Additionally, announcements appeared in the Census Bureau's periodic listing of new products.

## CONDUCTING THE 2002 ECONOMIC CENSUS

In most ways, the 2002 Economic Census was planned and conducted the same way as the 1997 Economic Census. Some of the particular individuals and groups involved in the planning may have been different between the two censuses.

However, several changes of note did occur between the two censuses. The first of these affected data collection. The second change involved several new topics being included on the questionnaires. A third change involved the introduction of new product classifications in selected service industries. Finally, several changes affecting the data products were introduced in 2002.

For more than three decades, the Census Bureau has allowed companies in selected industries to report electronically, and the practice gradually expanded up through the 1992 Economic Census. Initially, the reporting was only on computer tape. For 1992, Electronic Data Interchange was tried. For 1997, the objective was to make electronic reporting available to virtually all companies. Electronic versions of every form were available for downloading and submission via the Internet. Initially, the software only allowed the user to fill out forms one by one, but, several weeks into the data collection period, capabilities were added to allow multi-unit companies to download a list of their establishments, fill in a spreadsheet, typically by copying and pasting from other company spreadsheets, and uploading the result into the electronic questionnaire instrument. It should be noted that many businesses, especially smaller ones, continued to report their data on the paper forms sim-

ply because it was easier for them to do so. Additionally, the Census Bureau maintained an automated Help Desk to provide answers to common questions on a 24/7 basis.

Three new topics were included in the 2002 Economic Census. The first of these related to sales through e-commerce or sales over computer networks. Secondly, information was collected on leased employees—employees reported on another company's payroll, but working for the establishment in question and hired with input from both companies. Finally, there were more questions about the establishment's supply chain, including the outsourcing of services.

One outgrowth of the work involved with developing NAICS was a recognition by the United States, Mexico, and Canada of the advantages of having a common product classification scheme extending beyond the physical products used for foreign trade. To this end, the three countries have been developing such a system. As of the 2002 Economic Census, the system was ready to be introduced for the Information; Finance and Insurance; Professional, Scientific, and Technical Services; and Administrative and Support and Waste and Remediation Services Sectors.

Several major changes affected the products being released from the 2002 Economic Census. The first was a decision to issue industry reports for all sectors, not just manufacturing, construction, and mining. The second change was to eliminate most of the summary reports printed in the 1997 Economic Census. Lastly, the decision was made to have the CD-ROM software support time series comparisons (where supported by the data), mapping, and charting the data.

## BIBLIOGRAPHY

Hernon, Peter, and Kathy V. Friedman, eds. 1998. "Symposium on the 1997 Economic Census, U.S. Bureau of the Census." Special Issue, *Government Information Quarterly* 15 (3): 243–377. Also available on the Census Bureau's Web site at http://www.census.gov/epcd/www/giq97.html

U.S. Bureau of the Census. 2000. *History of the 1997 Economic Census*. Washington, DC: The Bureau.

# CHAPTER 3
# Terminology

A lady is nothing very specific. One man's lady is another man's woman; sometimes, one man's lady is another man's wife. Definitions overlap but they almost never coincide.

—*Russell Lynes, "Is There a Lady in the House?" Look (July 22, 1958)*

1. General Concepts

   A. Economic vs. Demographic data
   B. Data Collection Methods, Censuses, and Current Programs

2. What Is a Business?
3. What Does a Business Do?

   A. Industrial Classification Systems
   B. Product Classification Systems

4. Other Ways to Classify Businesses

   A. Employer and Nonemployer Businesses
   B. Taxable and Tax-Exempt Businesses
   C. Auxiliary Establishments
   D. Small, Medium, and Large Businesses

5. Core Data

   A. Employment
   B. Payroll
   C. Sales

6. What Else Do We Know about Businesses in an Industry?

   A. Capital Expenditures
   B. Other Expenditures
   C. Materials Consumed
   D. Class of Customer
   E. Company and Enterprise Statistics

7. Geography

   A. United States
   B. States
   C. Counties and County Equivalents
   D. Economic Places
   E. Consolidated Cities
   F. Metropolitan and Core Based Statistical Areas
   G. ZIP Codes

8. Data Quality Measures

   A. Missing Data Measures
   B. Sampling Error

9. Data Intermediaries

Now that you understand the procedures used to retrieve the data, this chapter will introduce you to common terminology used throughout the Economic Census.

As with any research area, the Economic Census uses some precisely defined terms. Some of these are common to all areas of the census while others are used in only one or two areas. In this chapter, we will describe the meaning of the terms used in the Economic Census.

## GENERAL CONCEPTS

There are several basic concepts that many data users confuse when looking for data produced by the Census Bureau. Understanding the differences between these concepts is essential to knowing where to look for the data.

### Economic vs. Demographic Data

The Census Bureau focuses on data from two different sources. When the data come from or is about businesses, they are referred to as *economic* data. *Demographic* data are collected from or about people. This can be particularly confusing when looking for data about the amount of money received by people living in a particular area. Since that is data about people, it would be found in the Census Bureau's demographic products such as Census 2000. Many data users would think that since this is a question of money, it is an economic topic and would try to find it in the Census Bureau's economic data products. Occupation, industry, and employment status are other demographic items that many people feel they can find in the economic data.

## Data Collection Methods, Censuses, and Current Programs

There are several ways to collect data about a population. One method, a *census*, involves asking everyone in the population a set of questions or collecting information about every member of the population. Another method is to ask a representative group of individuals from the population key questions; this is a *sample*. The third major data collection method, *administrative records*, involves using data collected for some other purpose, such as income tax records, instead of asking members of the population the questions that you want answered.

As described in the procedures section, the Economic Census actually uses a combination of the sampling and administrative records methods. However, since it involves an attempt to collect information about every business in the nation, it still qualifies as a census.

One weakness of censuses is that they take a relatively long time to collect, process, and produce results—up to 4 years. Many data users need information that is much more up to date, but not necessarily as detailed as that provided through a census. For this reason, the Census Bureau has many programs aimed at producing current data. Some of these programs, such as the *Annual Survey of Manufactures* or *Monthly Retail Trade Statistics,* rely on surveys of a relatively small number of businesses. Other programs, like *County Business Patterns,* depend on administrative records for their information.

## WHAT IS A BUSINESS?

The way we define a business has a significant impact on the statistics about businesses and what those statistics tell us. Because of this, there are two primary ways of defining businesses that are used in the Economic Census: establishments and enterprises.

An *establishment* is a specific business at a specific location. An *enterprise*, on the other hand, is all of the establishments under a common ownership or organizational structure, regardless of where they are located. An establishment can only be a part of one enterprise. But one enterprise can be made up of one or many establishments, as in a parent company and

its subsidiaries. Most Economic Census data are reported on an *establishment basis*.

To the Census Bureau a *firm* or *company* is a group of establishments under common ownership that are reported in a given category. An example should help clarify the difference between these two concepts. Wal-Mart is a major retailer operating under two names, Wal-Mart and Sam's Club. Each Wal-Mart store, Sam's Club store, distribution center, and headquarters facility would be a different establishment. However, these would all be grouped together into a single enterprise. Wal-Mart is a single firm in national tabulations of all retailers, but it is also one firm in tallies of discount department stores and one firm in tallies of warehouse clubs and superstores. Similarly, Wal-Mart is one retail firm in each of the states in which it has stores. Thus, a sum of all firms across industry or geography categories overcounts the actual number of enterprises at the national level, unlike the number of establishments, which is cleanly additive.

You should note that in *some* circumstances, several locations of one business might be grouped together as one establishment. Frequently, this is done because the business does not differentiate between the individual locations for payroll and other reporting reasons. Bank branches where employees are frequently assigned to several branches in the same county based on any given day's need and where payroll records are all handled through a common payroll office are a common example of several locations being reported as one establishment. Activity at ATMs is included in the totals for the branch bank that runs them.

## WHAT DOES A BUSINESS DO?

There are two basic ways to look at what a business does. The primary one that is used by the Census Bureau is the business's process or industry. The other way to look at businesses, which is also used in the Economic Census, is by what they are producing.

### Industrial Classification Systems

While it is important to know how many establishments there are in an area, data users are usually more interested in knowing what is happening in a given type of business or what types of businesses there are in a given area. In order to do this, we need to identify the types of businesses active in an area. This is done through a system for classifying establishments by what they do.

## The SIC System and NAICS

Actually, the 1997 Economic Census employed two different systems. One of these systems is the *Standard Industrial Classification* (SIC) system that has been used since the late 1930s with occasional minor changes. The other system is the *North American Industry Classification System* (NAICS) that was introduced in the United States in 1997. While the 2002 Economic Census is totally based on NAICS, it actually uses two modestly different versions of NAICS— NAICS 1997 and NAICS 2002. Chapter 4 has more information about these classification systems.

Both of NAICS and SIC rely on grouping similar systems together. However, they use different rules for these groupings. With the SIC system, establishments were grouped according to the product they sold, the customers they served, or some other reason. Under NAICS, the process that establishments use in producing their product or service is the primary basis for grouping establishments into industries.

An example of how these two systems differ is the area of printing and publishing. Under the SIC system, any establishment involved with the printing or publishing process is classified as a manufacturing establishment. However, with NAICS those establishments that put ink on paper or some similar physical process like that are considered to be manufacturing establishments. On the other hand, the establishments primarily involved with getting the publication written, edited, and sold (like Greenwood Press, Inc.) are classified as information establishments.

There are other industrial classification systems used throughout the world. For example, the European Union has their own system as does the Australian government. One important industrial classification system is the United Nations' International Standard Industrial Classification (ISIC) system Revision 3. There are ongoing efforts to reduce the differences among these various industrial classification systems.

## Types of Sectors

The sectors within NAICS can be grouped together into several types based on generally common types of activities.

One of these groups is made up of the *goods producing* sectors. These are the sectors that produce physical goods—mining; construction; manufacturing; and agriculture, forestry, fishing, and hunting. These sectors—except for agriculture, etc., which is covered in the Census of Agriculture—have similar types of products from the Economic Census.

All remaining sectors are considered to be *service producing*. This category is much broader than the Services Industries division of the SIC. It could be argued that the Utilities sector should be part of the goods-producing group, but since Economic Census reports for this sector follow the pattern of those for other service producing sectors, they are included in the latter group.

There are other ways to group sectors, but the ones listed above are commonly used groupings.

## Product Classification Systems

While many data users are interested in the activities and processes an establishment uses, many data users are just as interested in what the establishment is selling. These are an establishment's physical goods or services. There are several ways to describe and classify the products being sold by various industries. These are described below.

### Products Sold

The goods producing industries make products that they sell to other manufacturers or wholesalers. Under NAICS each industry has a set of products that are considered the major products of that industry. For example, the creamery butter industry (NAICS code 311512) produces three products—bulk creamery butter (packaged in quantities larger than 3 pounds), creamery butter shipped for consumers (packaged in containers 3 pounds or smaller), and anhydrous milk-fat creamery butter (butter oil). The shipped amount and value of each product are reported in the Industry Series reports. In working with these statistics, it is important to pay attention to the units used for the amount of production or shipments because they can vary by product.

These are collected by asking each establishment what they produce. This is done on the census questionnaires. As shown in Appendix B, the questionnaires ask about specific products that are commonly produced in that industry along with the ability to write in products that are not listed.

### Merchandise, Commodity, and Revenue Lines

In the service-producing sectors businesses tend to offer a far greater variety of goods and services than those in the goods producing sectors. For example, while an establishment in the creamery butter industry might produce and sell the three types of products described above, a dairy wholesaler will sell butter, margarine, butter spreads, different types of cheese, liquid milk, evaporated milk, powdered milk, eggs, etc. A grocery store will sell an even greater variety of goods. Similarly, most establishments in the service sectors provide a wide variety of services.

Since it is not practical to ask respondents in these sectors to identify the sales of hundreds or thousands of products, the Census Bureau groups these products and services together into broader categories and asks respondents to report sales in those categories. Using the grocery store example listed above, the Census Bureau asks about sales of dairy products and related foods, including milk, cheese, butter, etc. This is actually reported in the merchandise line sales report as part of the broader category of "Groceries and Other Food Items for Human Consumption Off the Premises."

In the retail trade sector, this concept is referred to as *merchandise lines*. *Commodity lines* represent the same concept in the wholesale trade sector. Finally, in the service sectors the comparable concept is *revenue lines* or *sources of receipts*.

## North American Product Classification System

Recognizing the need for a uniform classification of products and services across the three NAICS countries, in February 1999 their statistical agencies launched an effort to develop a standardized product classification system, called the *North American Product Classification System* (NAPCS). They decided to start this effort for the products produced by the NAICS service sectors. This effort is designed to occur in three phases. As these product lists are developed, they are replacing the traditional revenue line categories in the Economic Census.

The first phase covers the Information; Finance and Insurance; Professional, Scientific, and Technical Services; and Administrative and Support and Waste Management and Remediation Services sectors. By the end of 2002, this phase had generated 36 product lists with 26 of these being incorporated into the 2002 Economic Census instead of the revenue lines. The remaining product lists will be used in the 2007 Economic Census.

The second phase started in July 2001 and is scheduled for completion at the end of 2003. It covers the

Transportation and Warehousing; Educational Services; Health Care and Social Assistance; Arts, Entertainment, and Recreation; and Accommodation and Food Services sectors.

Phase III, scheduled to start in early 2004, will complete the development of product lists for the NAICS service industries and the Public Administration sector. Please note that the Funds, Trusts, and Other Financial Vehicles sub-sector will be excluded. As part of this phase, the three countries will also explore extending the scope of NAPCS to the goods producing industries.

## Harmonized System

Many data users, especially those interested in foreign trade, are familiar with the *Harmonized Tariff Schedule of the United States Annotated* (HTSA) used for tariff purposes and published by the U.S. Office of Tariff Affairs and Trade Agreements. This is based on the *Harmonized System*, a global classification used to describe most goods traded throughout the world.

Since this system is based around the needs to administer foreign trade agreements and tariffs, it provides a much more detailed classification of products than would be feasible in the Economic Census. For example, the butter described above is divided into three different categories depending on such factors as the butterfat content, where it is traded, and how it falls under various U.S. Department of Agriculture regulations.

The Census Bureau uses this system to report foreign trade data. It is not used in the Economic Census.

## OTHER WAYS TO CLASSIFY BUSINESSES

There are several other characteristics that the Census Bureau uses to classify businesses in the Economic Census. These are important to understand because they determine where the data are to be found.

### Employer and Nonemployer Businesses

Most data reported in the Economic Census are based on businesses with paid employees. These businesses are referred to as *employers*. The Census Bureau asks businesses to count the number of employees the same way they do when they report employees' wages and earnings to the IRS for payroll tax purposes. These businesses account for most of the nation's business revenues.

However, most businesses in the country, especially in selected industries, have no employees and are called *nonemployer* businesses. Common examples of these businesses include individual consultants, writers, barbers, and people selling crafts at crafts fairs. (Please remember that many other people in these fields either work for someone else or have people working for them and would be included in the employer business counts.) While there are many nonemployer businesses, their overall contribution to the nation's economy is relatively small. However, they play a major role in some industries and geographic areas.

## Taxable and Tax-Exempt Businesses

Most businesses in this country are subject to paying income taxes and classified as *taxable*. A business which does not pay income taxes simply because their taxable income is below a threshold set by law is still considered a taxable business.

Some businesses, however, are *tax-exempt*. That is, they are not required to pay income taxes because they meet various legal criteria about their purpose. Examples of these tax-exempt businesses include charitable organizations and not-for-profit hospitals.

Both taxable and tax-exempt businesses are counted in the Economic Census, provided they are in industries that are covered by the census. For example, colleges and universities are out of scope of the Economic Census, whether taxable or tax-exempt.

Taxable and tax-exempt businesses are differentiated only in five service sectors. Because retail trade is not one of these, for example, the statistics do not differentiate tax-exempt thrift stores from other used-merchandise retailers.

## Auxiliary Establishments

Many large multi-establishment enterprises have specialized establishments intended to primarily serve other establishments within the enterprise rather than serve external customers. Examples of these would be centralized accounting offices, a corporate research and development facility, a company warehouse, or a headquarters facility.

Under the SIC system's classification rules, *auxiliary establishments* were grouped into the division representing the primary source of income for the enterprise. The rules for NAICS changed this, so the auxiliary is classified according to its own activities. Thus, an oil company's corporate headquarters located in New York City would be classified as a min-

ing establishment under the SIC rules, but as a corporate headquarters establishment under NAICS.

Please note, however, that due to the schedule for introducing NAICS and the amount of information needed to properly classify auxiliary establishments, the 1997 Economic Census segregated non-headquarters auxiliary establishments in separate reports. Thus, for example, the reports on warehousing and storage industries exclude corporate warehouses for 1997. This treatment will change for 2002.

## Small, Medium, and Large Businesses

Many data users are interested in looking at businesses in groups like small or large businesses. However, these are not standardized terms. For example, New York State defines a small business as an independently owned business, with operations in New York State, and having 100 or fewer employees in total (not just within New York State). The U.S. Small Business Administration's (SBA) advocacy office views a small business as a domestically owned enterprise with 500 or fewer employees. Clearly, New York State and the SBA will say that there are different numbers of small businesses within New York State.

To complicate this issue even more, one organization could use different definitions for different purposes. The SBA definition described above is used for tracking statistics on the number of and trends in small businesses. SBA uses this information for advocacy purposes. However, if you were to apply for SBA assistance, a different definition would be used. This assistance definition sets a different threshold based on the primary industry of the enterprise. These thresholds are a combination of the NAICS industry and either employment or revenues. For assistance purposes SBA might define a small business in one industry as having 500 employees or fewer, in another industry the threshold might be $3,500,000 in revenue or 1,500 employees or fewer.

The Census Bureau does *not* report on the number of small, medium, or large businesses. It does report on the number of establishments, companies, and enterprises by employment and revenue or sales size classes. Typical employment categories reported by the Census Bureau are 1 to 4 employees, 5 to 9 employees, 500 or more employees, etc. Data are more widely available on the size of establishments than on the size of companies. The user should recognize the difference, since reference to small business most often refers to the size of the company.

## CORE DATA

There is a basic core of data reported for all industries by the Census Bureau. These data items include the number of employees, what they are paid, and the value of the product that goes out of the establishment. Additionally, the number of establishments, as described above, is reported with the other core data.

## Employment

The number of people working at an establishment is called its *employment*. In the Census, each establishment is asked about the number of people working there during the pay period containing March 12. This date was chosen because it allows for comparisons with other sources of employment numbers, such as the *County Business Patterns* reports. It is also directly comparable to the employment figures reported by the Bureau of Labor Statistics in its *Current Employment Survey* and its monthly estimates of the labor force. All of these use a common reference point of the 12th of the month.

Another reason for picking the March 12 reference date is that there are relatively few *seasonal jobs* during this month. A seasonal job would be something like lifeguarding on a beach during the summer or working in a department store during October, November, and December. By not including this type of seasonal employment because of the March 12 reference date, the Economic Census provides a better picture of the underlying number of jobs year round in an area.

In the goods-producing sectors (manufacturing, mining, and construction) establishments are asked to differentiate between production workers and other employees. The number of production workers is requested for the payroll periods containing March 12, May 12, August 12, and November 12. This allows researchers to look at seasonal employment changes in these industries.

## Payroll

Another way of measuring the size of a business is by knowing what it pays its employees. This is known as its *payroll*. Total payroll includes the gross pay for all workers in the establishment. This means that all salaries, wages, commissions, dismissal pay, bonuses, vacation and sick-leave pay, contributions to qualified pension plans (such as 401(k) and Keogh plans) by the employees, and tips and gratuities—if they are re-

ported to the employer—are all included. This is figured before any deductions.

However, it does not include payrolls of departments or concessions operated by another company at the establishment. This means that if IBM has a manufacturing plant with a cafeteria run by ARA, the cafeteria employees are not included in IBM's payroll. Also not included are the profits or other compensation received by the owners.

Payroll is reported on both an annual and first quarter (January through March) basis. By comparing these two figures, it is possible to get a general sense of the stability of an industry's payroll during the year.

It is important to remember that payroll is reported by the Census Bureau in thousands of dollars—shown in the reports as "($1,000)." This means that a reported payroll of $123,532 is *not* $124,000, but is really $124,000,000. If you attempt to calculate payroll per employee (or average compensation) and forget about this, your numbers will not seem logical because they are off by a factor of 1,000.

In reports for the goods-producing sectors (manufacturing, mining, and construction) the Census Bureau provides the wages for employees involved with producing the actual product. This is in addition to the total payroll, which includes managers and sales people. Having the production workers' payroll broken out is useful when attempting to compare production worker wages across geographic areas or industries.

## Sales

The value of *sales* is the third measure of business size that is used. This includes the receipts from a physical product that leaves the establishment, payments for services rendered, and membership dues and assessments. Sales excludes credit charges, sales taxes, etc.

Unfortunately, due to a variety of historical reasons, different sectors refer to this one concept by different names. For example, in the manufacturing sector this is called the "value of shipments" and in the services sector it is called "receipts."

You should note that the manufacturing sector reports also show a closely related set of data called "value added by manufacturing." This measure represents the amount of work done in the establishment by transforming the materials coming in so that there is a more useful product going out. This can only be done when the Bureau knows the cost of inputs. An example of this transformation would be a steel mill getting the raw iron ore, coke, etc. as inputs and producing bars of steel. The work done in making the steel, and related activities, is the value added by this plant. Then another mill might buy the steel bars and roll it into railroad tracks. The work done by this second mill is the transformation of the steel bars into the railroad track. This value added is really the difference in the value of the railroad track and the steel bars and other inputs. However, the value of shipments for the second mill will include the cost of the steel bars. This is explained in more detail in the section on the manufacturing sector.

## WHAT ELSE DO WE KNOW ABOUT BUSINESSES IN AN INDUSTRY?

While the items that were just discussed are included in almost all of the Economic Census reports, there are a number of additional topics that are presented in selected reports. These include capital expenditures, expenditures, products sold, materials purchased, ownership, and organization type. In some sectors there is information about the products sold by the type of business and about the types of businesses selling particular kinds of products, called merchandise line or source of revenue.

### Capital Expenditures

As part of their normal operations, businesses need to invest in new equipment and facilities. These represent major expenses for a business. Since these are frequently paid for by reducing the owners' equity or by issuing new stock (both components of the owners' capital in the company) in either the short-term or long-term (if they are initially paid for through a loan of some type) they are called *capital expenditures*. They are also expenses that can have substantial impacts in the economy, such as generating construction jobs or jobs in other goods producing sectors. So, there is a great interest in these expenditures.

Specifically, these costs include money spent on purchasing permanent additions to or major alterations of company facilities involved with producing their products (such as the manufacturing plant). Also included as capital expenditures is the purchase of machinery and equipment used to replace existing equipment or to expand capacity if this equipment is subject to depreciation. For example, if a manufacturing company purchases a personal computer to help control their manufacturing process and they depreciate its cost over time, then they would report this as a capital expenditure. However, if they purchase the same computer for the accounting department or do not depreciate its cost, then it would not qualify as a capital expenditure.

There are a few additional rules that come into play in determining what is a capital expenditure:

- Assets leased from nonmanufacturing companies through a capital lease are counted as capital expenditures.
- Facilities owned by the federal government, but operated by a private company under a federal contract are not counted. An example of this type of facility is the Knolls Atomic Power Lab in Schenectady, NY.
- Plants and equipment provided by communities and nonprofit organizations are excluded from capital expenditures. These types of deals are often used as incentives to get a company to locate in a particular community.
- Land is not a capital expenditure.
- The cost of maintenance and repairs are not included. They are reported as current operating expenditures.

Capital expenditures are most commonly an expense reported for the goods producing sectors, like manufacturing, etc.

### Other Expenditures

All businesses have a wide variety of expenditures that are part of their normal day-to-day operations. Included in these expenses are such things as rent, repair of buildings, repairs to machinery, advertising, computer software and services, refuse removal, and many other items. As you can see from this short list, businesses use many types of goods and services in their routine operations. Individually, these purchases tend to be smaller than the capital expenditures, but over the long run, they can be much larger.

### Materials Consumed

This is a large group of variables. It includes all of the materials used by a manufacturing or mining establishment that actually produces goods. Examples of materials used by the creamery butter industry are

- Whole milk
- Cream
- Butter
- Condensed and evaporated milk

- Packaging paper and plastics film, coated and laminated
- Plastics containers
- Paperboard containers, boxes, and corrugated paperboard

The specific materials asked about on the questionnaires vary from industry to industry. Question 16 of these questionnaires lists the types of materials that are commonly used in that industry. This is designed to make it easier for the person completing the questionnaire. As with the products question, there is an option to write in other materials. Appendix B contains a sample questionnaire that would be sent to the creamery butter industry.

## Class of Customer

Many of the tables in the *Miscellaneous Subjects* reports refer to class of customer or client. These are groups of customers with potentially different characteristics or buying patterns. For example, government agencies tend to contract for different types of research and development activities than corporations would contract for. So a table might break out the receipts from government and corporations by industry.

The exact customer classes reported in the Economic Census vary from industry to industry.

## Company and Enterprise Statistics

While most of the reports in the Economic Census are based on statistics about establishments, there are a few reports that provide information based on companies or enterprises. In addition to the number of firms, their sales, employment, and payroll, there is information about the legal form of organization and the race, ethnicity, and gender of the owners.

Businesses can be organized according to several different legal types. These include sole-proprietorships, partnerships of various types, and corporations of various types. Also, a company can be organized as a parent with subsidiaries, although the Census Bureau does not publish data for subsidiaries—only enterprises and establishments.

Extreme care is needed when looking at the reports about businesses owned by women and minorities across multiple years. Starting in 1997, these reports covered all enterprises, but there is a lack of minority data about publicly traded corporations, foreign-owned businesses, and not-for-profit businesses. Prior to 1997, these reports were limited to businesses readily linked to individuals: sole proprietorships, partner-

ships, and SubChapter S corporations. Regular corporations, typically including the largest companies, were excluded from the survey prior to 1997. This change in coverage reduces the ability to look at trends between 1992 and 1997.

It is worth noting that in the 1982, 1987, and 1992 Economic Censuses, the Characteristics of Business Owners Survey detailed the age, education, work experience, etc. of the business owners. These reports also gave details about financing and before-tax incomes of businesses. However, the reports on the Characteristics of Business Owners Survey were not funded for the 1997 Economic Census. Some of these same data have returned as part of the 2002 Economic Census Survey of Business Owners.

## GEOGRAPHY

All data reported by the Census Bureau represent some geographic area. It doesn't make sense to talk about an industry's sales being $5 billion without telling the reader where the establishments making these sales are located. Even if you are looking at a derived ratio, such as sales per employee, you need to specify the area covered by that statistic. It could theoretically represent one state, with another state having a very different ratio, or it could be the ratio for the entire United States.

All of the reports included in the Economic Census include some reference to geographic areas. Often the references are to easily understood geographic areas such as the United States or the individual states. However, the geographic area reports generally include other geographic areas that are not so clear-cut. These types of areas include the outlying areas, counties, economic places, ZIP Codes, and metropolitan areas. Each of these geographic areas is described below.

## United States

In the Economic Census, this represents the 50 fifty states plus the District of Columbia. All of the report series in the Economic Census contain national data. It does not include U.S. territories or foreign subsidiaries of U.S. based enterprises or the operations of U.S. companies outside of the United States.

## States

These are the individual states plus the District of Columbia. This is as detailed as some of the reports show geographic data.

Nearly all report series include at least some data by state. The industry reports show data for states that have some activity in that industry but do not have one company that is so large that showing data for that industry in that state would essentially tell you details about that one company. For example, you won't find data for the photographic equipment manufacturing industry for New York State because having that level of detail would effectively be telling you what Kodak is doing.

## Counties and County Equivalents

Counties, and their equivalents, are major subdivisions of states that fully divide up the area of a state. Most states are divided into counties. However, some states have other equivalent areas. Several examples of these are that Louisiana is divided into parishes instead of counties, Virginia is divided into counties and independent cities, and Alaska is divided into boroughs and unincorporated areas (the Census Bureau divides the unincorporated areas into county-like areas).

## Economic Places

There are two types of economic places—places of 2,500 inhabitants or more—and in Michigan, New Jersey, Pennsylvania, New York, Wisconsin, and the six New England states—major subdivisions of counties (towns or townships, depending on the state) with a minimum population of 10,000 people. Data are also reported for the remainder of a town or county if it meets the 10,000-population rule. The population used for determining whether to include these areas comes from the most recent census for the area (either the 2000 Census for the 2002 Economic Census, the 1990 Census, or a special census that was conducted after 1990 for the 1997 Economic Census).

Places are centers of population. Depending on the state these might be called cities, towns, townships, or villages. These are incorporated areas that are smaller than counties. The exact names of these areas and their structure vary from state to state.

In working with these areas you will need to be familiar with the geographic structure in the states that you are analyzing. For example, in New York State, cities, towns, and Indian reservations divide up the entire area of a county. Villages are overlays on top of towns. So, here if you are looking at the data for a village and a town, you need to remember that the number of establishments in the village is included in the number of establishments in the town. Unlike the Census of Population and Housing, the Economic Census does not recognize census designated places (CDPs).

## Consolidated Cities

In some states, separately incorporated municipalities, or places, can consolidate their governmental operations into a single government. Legally, both areas still exist, but they effectively have one functioning government. The Economic Census provides data for these combined areas. The seven consolidated cities recognized by the Census Bureau for the 1997 Economic Census were

- Athens-Clarke County, Georgia
- Butte-Silver Bow, Montana
- Columbus, Georgia
- Indianapolis, Indiana
- Jacksonville, Florida
- Milford, Connecticut
- Nashville-Davidson, Tennessee

## Metropolitan and Core Based Statistical Areas

While municipalities are very important for governmental operations, they do not really describe the current way that people are actually settling down to live and conduct their business. In order to respond to this problem, the federal government during the 1940s developed statistical areas representing where people are gathering to live. These statistical areas represent socially and economically integrated areas identified on the basis of commuting patterns.

Over the years since they were first defined, the exact criteria used to define these statistical areas have changed but the basic idea has stayed the same. Every 10 years, the U.S. Office of Management and Budget reviews the criteria used to define these areas and has always made changes to the criteria. Also, in 1990 the name for this concept changed from *Standard Metropolitan Statistical Areas* (SMSAs) to *Metropolitan Areas* (MAs).

There were three types of metropolitan areas recognized for the 1997 Economic Census. The basic type is the *Metropolitan Statistical Area* or MSA. This is a county or group of counties around a population center of 50,000 residents forming an integrated economic and social unit. The level of integration is based on commuting patterns as reported in the 1990 Census of Population and Housing. It is important to note that MSAs contain complete counties. (In the six New England states, where county governments have very little function, cities and towns are used as the building blocks of the metropolitan area and county-based areas are a secondary type of area.) It is very possible to have large areas of counties where the major economic activity is agriculture being considered metropolitan because a portion of the county is densely populated and is economically and socially integrated with a population center, or this area might be the population center on its own.

The second type of MA is the *Primary Metropolitan Statistical Area* (PMSA). These areas look like MSAs, except that they are economically and socially integrated with another metropolitan area.

Several PMSAs combine to form a *Consolidated Metropolitan Statistical Area* (CMSA). Generally, CMSAs represent what most of us consider the metropolitan area around a major city, such as Boston, New York, Washington, or Los Angeles. An example of these relationships is that the New York, NY PMSA consists of the five counties (boroughs) of New York City, Westchester, Rockland, and Putnam Counties to the north of New York City. Nassau and Suffolk Counties (or Long Island) combine to form the Nassau-Suffolk, NY PMSA. These two PMSAs along with about a dozen more combine to form the New York City–Northern New Jersey–Long Island, NY-NJ-CT CMSA. This CMSA covers the southwestern portion of Connecticut, twelve counties in New York State, a large portion of northern New Jersey, and one county in Pennsylvania.

Many of the Economic Census geographic series reports contain data by metropolitan area. These reports show the data for all of the metropolitan areas in a state. They also show data for the combined area in the state that is outside of any the state's metropolitan area. In the Geographic Area Series reports on the web and through American FactFinder, these non-metro state remainder data are not shown.

This concept changed again after Census 2000. The areas defined under the new criteria are called *Core Based Statistical Areas* (CBSAs). The criteria for CBSAs were formally issued on March 31, 2000, and implemented on June 30, 2003. The 2002 Economic Census is the first census to use these areas. The building blocks for CBSAs are counties throughout the nation. In the six New England states an alternative type of area, the *New England City and Town Areas* (NECTAs), also exist, but are considered to be secondary types of areas. NECTAs are built up from towns and cities instead of counties, but NECTAs are not published in the 2002 Economic Census.

There are two primary types of CBSAs—Metropolitan Statistical Areas (MeSAs) and Micropolitan Statistical Areas (MiSAs). Both types of areas are designated by OMB and are built from counties around an urban core defined by the Census Bureau using data from Census 2000. A *Metropolitan Statistical Area* is a county or group of socio-economically integrated counties, based on commuting patterns, around an urbanized core of 50,000 or more residents. A *Micropolitan Statistical Area* is also a county or group of socio-economically integrated counties around an urban core or cluster of 10,000 to 49,999 residents.

If a Metropolitan Statistical Area has a single urbanized core of at least 2.5 million residents, it may be divided into *Metropolitan Divisions* (MDs). Again, a Metropolitan Division is a county or group of counties containing an employment center.

If two or more adjacent CBSAs have a moderate level of commuting between them, they can be combined into a larger *Combined Statistical Area*. The individual Metropolitan and Micropolitan Statistical areas within the combined area retain their individual identities, but data are reported for the larger area.

The Census Bureau provides maps and lists of these areas.

In looking at these areas over time it is critical to review which counties were included in the areas of interest. Since the names used for any given area are based on the primary cities in the area, changes in the component counties are not always obvious. For example, the Albany-Schenectady-Troy, NY Metropolitan Statistical Area of the 1990s included Albany, Montgomery, Rensselaer, Saratoga, Schenectady, and Schoharie counties. An area with the same name was designated in 2003. This new area is comprised of Albany, Rensselaer, Saratoga, Schenectady, and Schoharie counties (note that Montgomery County was removed from this area). Depending on issues related to confidentiality, it may or may not be possible to build data for consistent geographic areas from the data available for the individual counties.

## ZIP Codes

The United States Postal Service's *Zoned Improvement Plan* areas (ZIP Codes) are commonly used by businesses primarily to identify where their customers are located. Because these areas are so commonly used, the Census Bureau reports a large amount of data for them. However, there are a number of issues that the data user must be aware of when deciding to use these data.

Second, ZIP codes were originally created to allow the post office to make mail delivery more efficient. That remains the primary purpose of this system. As a result, the Postal Service changes the exact area covered by a ZIP code whenever it needs to in order to maintain, or improve, the efficiency of mail delivery. In practice, this means that in areas experiencing either rapid growth or decline in population or business (actually mail volume), the post office is likely to make significant changes in ZIP code boundaries from one year to the next. Even in areas of stability, the post office makes changes to ZIP code boundaries from time to time—though these tend to be smaller changes than in areas experiencing growth or decline. Year to year changes in ZIP Code boundaries make these areas not particularly useful in looking at data over time.

Third, since ZIP codes exist for the efficient delivery of the mail, they routinely cross governmental unit boundaries. Thus a business in Massachusetts might be located in a ZIP code normally thought of as a New York State ZIP code—or the other way around.

The Census Bureau created areas known as *ZIP Code Tabulation Areas* (ZCTAs) for Census 2000. These areas are approximations of the true ZIP Codes that are used by the USPS or the Bureau's economic programs. One reason that ZCTAs were create is that given the purpose of ZIP codes, it is common for a single census block (the smallest area of land bounded by streets or other permanent features—and used extensively in the Population and Housing Census) to be served by more than one ZIP code. Since Census 2000 data are actually tabulated from census blocks, the Census Bureau must assign one ZIP code to a particular block. Additionally, there are areas where overlapping ZIP codes exist. Because the Census Bureau needs to assign just one ZIP code for each block, data for the ZIP code not identified will be incorrect.

For the Economic Census, and other economic data, the Census Bureau uses the ZIP code reported by the business. The list of ZIP codes identified in the Census Bureau's economic programs differs from that produced by the Bureau's demographic programs.

Given these caveats, you are cautioned to consider usefulness of ZIP codes as a meaningful geographic

level in any given use of Economic Census data. In some cases, these problems will not have an impact on the usefulness of the data. However, in other cases, they may make the data essentially meaningless. There are service providers that match geographic areas using government and commercial definitions of geography: Clartias, CACI, and geographic information system (GIS) software.

## DATA QUALITY MEASURES

For a variety of reasons the Census Bureau does not actually collect information from every business establishment in the country. When it is not possible to get data from an establishment, the Census Bureau uses one of two methods to fill in the missing data. A few Economic Census products are actually based on samples and are subject to sampling error.

### Missing Data Measures

The first method, and the more accurate one, is to get the missing information from administrative records. Administrative records are records that are collected for administrative rather than statistical purposes, such as income tax returns. While the information taken from administrative records is generally considered good data, it comes with several problems. One is that there may be differences in how a concept is defined between the Census and the program collecting the data. Another problem is that there may be some incentive, such as lowering taxes, encouraging people to misstate the information on the administrative records. So, data taken from administrative records is definitely subject to being less accurate than data collected for statistical purposes. An even bigger problem with administrative records is that they don't give the Census Bureau everything they need, like establishment detail. However, some data about the specific establishment is better than something more general. Additionally, income tax data are on a fiscal year, which, in periods of growth or decline, might be very different than calendar year figures. Since the Census Bureau gets payroll tax data on a calendar year basis, there may be inconsistency between various pieces of information about the establishment.

The second method estimates the data based on mathematical models related to information from the administrative records and other sources, such as industry averages. Because these are based on mathematical models that rely on information that is not establishment specific, this is considered the weaker of the two data collection methods.

Fortunately, the Census Bureau gives us an indication of the quality of the data by reporting the percent of sales, etc. from the two sources mentioned above. The more information that you can get from the actual establishment the better off you are. That is why it is better to have low percentages in these measures of data quality. For example, data for an industry that has only 9 percent of the data from the above sources has more reliable data than an industry with 35 percent or more coming form these less reliable sources.

## Sampling Error

When the data are collected from a sample such as from some of the construction data or Survey of Business Owners, the Economic Census reports provide one of two statistical measures of data accuracy. These are the *standard error* and *relative standard error*. Both of these are related to the size of the sample used and give an indication of the statistical quality of the data. As the sample size increases, the smaller these measures become. Again, the larger these values are, the less reliable the data is. Further details on these measures can be found in nearly any introductory statistics textbook.

## DATA INTERMEDIARIES

The Census Bureau relies on several different groups to assist in distributing its data and technical support to the public. These groups can be thought of as wholesalers or retailers of census data. All of these groups provide a variety of services to the public and will refer data users to another intermediary who can provide better assistance if appropriate.

One group of intermediaries is the *Government Printing Office's Federal Depository Library Program*. The libraries participating in this program receive federal government publications and other data free of charge with the understanding that they will provide the information to the public. Each state con-

tains one or two regional depository libraries and a number of selective depositories. The regional depositories are required to maintain as complete a collection of federal documents as possible. As a rule, because of their general nature, they are not familiar with the subtleties of the data themselves. However, they can find that information out and are very good at locating the data itself. Appendix C provides a list of the Regional Depository Libraries.

The *State Data Center/Business-Industry Data Center* (SDC/BIDC) and *Census Information Center* (CIC) programs are various programs administered through the Census Bureau. Many participants in these programs are regular users of census data and know the ins-and-outs of it very well. Their level of knowledge is often controlled by their own research or work responsibilities. The participants in the SDC/BIDC program are usually state, regional, or local government agencies; academic research institutes; chambers of commerce; or libraries. They usually work with data from all areas of the Census Bureau, with the BIDC participants emphasizing the economic data a bit more than the demographic data. CIC participants tend to be regional or national advocacy groups with interests in more specialized areas—such as data on Hispanics or Latinos. The exact services provided by the participants in these programs vary between the individual organizations. Appendix D provides a list of the SDC/BIDC lead agencies in each of the states. (The CIC organizations are not included since most of them do not work with the economic data to any extent.)

The final group of intermediaries, according to some people at the Census Bureau (others would argue that, technically, these are not intermediaries), is the *Census Bureau's Regional Offices*. The information specialists working in the Bureau's 12 regional offices are truly experts on the Census Bureau's data products. And, if they don't know the answer, they can usually place one or two phone calls to get it. The largest drawback in working with these information specialists is that there are usually only two of them in any regional office, so they can be spread rather thin. Appendix E is a list of these offices.

# CHAPTER 4
# North American Industry Classification System (NAICS)

Order is Heaven's first law; and this confessed,
Some are, and must be, greater than the rest,
More rich, more wise; but who infers from hence
That such are happier, shocks all common sense.
—*Alexander Pope (*An Essay on Man, *Epistle IV, 1753)*

1. What Is NAICS?
   A. Industry Classification Problems
2. Understanding the NAICS Sectors
   A. Agriculture, Forestry, Fishing, and Hunting
   B. Mining
   C. Utilities
   D. Construction
   E. Manufacturing
   F. Wholesale Trade
   G. Retail Trade
   H. Transportation and Warehousing
   I. Information
   J. Finance and Insurance
   K. Real Estate and Rental and Leasing
   L. Professional, Scientific, and Technical Services
   M. Management of Companies and Enterprises
   N. Administrative and Support and Waste Management and Remediation Services
   O. Educational Services
   P. Health Care and Social Assistance
   Q. Arts, Entertainment, and Recreation
   R. Accommodations and Food Services
   S. Other Services (except Public Administration)
   T. Public Administration
   U. Auxiliary Establishments
3. NAICS Implementation
4. Building Time Series
   A. Census Bureau Bridge Tables
   B. Bureau of Labor Statistics's Current Employment Survey
5. Other Impacts of Moving from the SIC System to NAICS
6. Summary
7. Bibliography

The federal government effectively discontinued using the Standard Industrial Classification (SIC) to measure the nature of business over a number of years starting with the release of the 1997 Economic Census in 1999 and ending with the release of several wage-related series from the Bureau of Labor Statistics in 2005. The North American Industry Classification System (NAICS, pronounced nakes) is taking its place. In many ways NAICS is a vast improvement over the SIC; allowing for greater detail, logical groupings of industries, and international compatibility with NAFTA partners. However, the transition from the SIC system to NAICS provided challenges and opportunities for everyone: government agencies, publishers, and researchers.

## WHAT IS NAICS?

A quick glance at Table 4.1 seems to indicate that NAICS is simply an extension of the SIC four-digit hierarchical system to a six-digit hierarchical system. However, a closer inspection of these two systems shows that they are very different.

NAICS was created using a clean-slate approach by representatives of the U.S. Economic Classification Policy Committee, Statistics Canada, and Mexico's Instituto Nacional de Estadistica, Geografia e Informatica. This tri-national committee developed NAICS using four—sometimes competing—guidelines to direct their work. These guidelines were

- Use of production-oriented conceptual frameworks—that is, establishments using similar processes for their production activities would be grouped together. (For example, corn farming had two SIC codes, one for regular corn (0115) and one

Table 4.1
Comparison of SIC and NAICS Structures

| Standard Industrial Classification | | North American Industry Classification System | |
|---|---|---|---|
| Number of Digits and Description | Example | Number of Digits and Description | Example |
| 1- Division | I- Service Industries | 2 – Sector | 71- Arts, Entertainment and Recreation |
| 2 - Major Group | 79- Amusement and recreational services | 3 - Subsector | 711-Performing Arts, Spectator Sports, and Related Industries |
| 3 - Industry Group | 794- Commercial Sports | 4 - Industry Group | 7112- Spectator Sports |
| 4 - Industry | 7948- Racing, Including Track Operations | 5 - Industry | 71121- Spectator Sports |
| | | 6 - U.S. Industry | 711212 -Racetracks |

for cash crops (popcorn) (0119), but in NAICS there is just one industry for corn (111150), since the types of corn covered in the two SIC industries are grown the same way.)

- Special attention is given to emerging industries (such as credit card issuing), service industries (such as barber schools), and advanced technologies (such as remediation of land).
- Continuity of time-series between the systems should be maintained.
- Compatibility with the United Nations International Standard Industrial Classification (ISIC, Revision 3).

It was also understood that NAICS would have to be reviewed and revised more often than the SIC system was. While the SIC system was created in 1939 it was revised only six times in its history: 1945, 1957, 1967, 1972, 1977, and 1987. While NAICS was introduced in 1997, it has already been revised in 2002, with the creation of new industries in the sectors of construction, wholesale, retail, and information. Additionally, revisions for 2007 are already being developed.

Where the SIC system had 10 broad industry sectors or divisions, NAICS expands this to 20 sectors. The new sectors created in NAICS predominantly cover the service and technology areas of the economy. Existing and newly identified industries were combined to create new sectors. Several old divisions,

such as the Service Division, were dissolved. Using Census Bureau and other data the U.S. Economic Classification Policy Committee realized that services made up most of the country's economic activities but only 40 percent of the SIC categories (Zeisset 1998). The old SIC Services Division was distributed into new sectors such as the Information Sector or the Health Care and Social Assistance Sector. Even SIC Divisions that kept their names do not reflect the original classification concepts. For example, Retail Trade division in the SIC system would seem to correspond directly to the Retail Trade sector in NAICS, but there are significant differences. The biggest is that Food Services, including restaurants and drinking places, was moved from the Retail division under the SIC system to the new Accommodation and Food Services sector in NAICS. That removed about 10 percent of retail sales and about one-third of retail employment.

Some of the new industries existed in the SIC system, but were divided into many different industries. For example, Help Supply Services (SIC 7363) has been divided into Temporary Help (NAICS 56132) and Employee Leasing (NAICS 56133), and Business Services, NEC (not elsewhere classified) (SIC 7389) was divided into 36 different NAICS industries in nine different NAICS sectors in the 1997 version of NAICS. Some industries, such as Truck and Utility Vehicle Manufacturing (NAICS 336112), were not

Table 4.2
NAICS Sectors, U.S. Industries, and Number of Industries Not Identified in the SIC System

| NAICS Sector | Description | U.S. Industries | Industries Not Identified in the SIC System |
|---|---|---|---|
| 11 | Agriculture, Forestry, Fishing, and Hunting | 64 | 20 |
| 21 | Mining | 29 | 0 |
| 23 | Utilities | 10 | 6 |
| 23 | Construction | 31 | 6 |
| 31-33 | Manufacturing | 474 | 79 |
| 42 | Wholesale Trade | 71 | 2 |
| 44-49 | Retail Trade | 75 | 20 |
| 48-49 | Transportation and Warehousing | 57 | 28 |
| 51 | Information | 36 | 22 |
| 52 | Finance and Insurance | 42 | 23 |
| 53 | Real Estate and Rental and Leasing | 24 | 15 |
| 54 | Professional, Scientific, and Technical Services | 47 | 28 |
| 55 | Management of Companies and Enterprises | 3 | 1 |
| 56 | Administrative, Support, Waste Management, and Remediation Services | 43 | 29 |
| 61 | Education Services | 17 | 12 |
| 62 | Health Care and Social Assistance | 39 | 27 |
| 71 | Arts, Entertainment, and Recreation | 25 | 19 |
| 72 | Accommodation and Foodservices | 15 | 10 |
| 81 | Other Services (except Public Administration) | 49 | 19 |
| 92 | Public Administration | 24 | 2 |
| TOTAL | | 1,180 | 368 |

identified before. Other industries are not affected at all. It has been estimated that 58 percent of the SIC industries can be easily converted into NAICS 1997, when time series need to be continued forward (Gaines, Cole, Haver, and Murphy 1998).

Table 4.2 shows the number of U.S. industries in each NAICS sector. It also shows what portion of these industries were not identified in the SIC system.

## Industry Classification Problems

Historically, SIC coding was slow in keeping up with changing industries. By building a periodic review of the NAICS industry structure into the NAICS agreement, Canada, Mexico, and the United States are committed to keeping NAICS more current. However, there are, and always will be, lags between the development of a new industry and its inclusion in any formal classification scheme. By having a periodic review of its structure built into the system, NAICS attempts to shorten this lag time compared to the SIC system.

Some other sections of the economy are not explicitly included in either the SIC system or NAICS, but could be classified in it if there was a desire to do so. These include illegal commerce, such as narcotics manufacturing (3254—Pharmaceutical and Medicine Manufacturing), distribution (424210—Drugs and Druggists' Sundries Merchant Wholesalers), and retailing (45439—Other Direct Selling Establishments). The underground economy such as some bartering activities and babysitting; housework done by members of a household; and other miscellaneous economic activities that are not measured in any government numbers also could be classified in these systems, but generally aren't included in statistical programs because direct measurement is not possible. Until such time as these can be measured or there is sufficient pressure to recognize them as a part of the economy, it is unlikely they will be classified according to any industrial classification system by statistical programs.

Historically, different organizations assigned different SIC codes to the same establishments. This was especially true when an establishment's activities were unclear on the forms used to classify them or they had more than one type of activity at the single establishment (for example, in the Catskill region of New York State there was once a single establishment that sold sandwiches and provided on-site facilities for washing clothing). At the narrowest level (the fourth digit) of SIC codes, 71 percent of the codes were not compatible between Standard and Poor's Compustat and Center for Research in Security Prices (CRSP) databases (Guenther and Rosman 1994); another article found a 79 percent disagreement, primarily because CRSP was using a firm's historical SIC (Kahle and Walking 1996). With NAICS, the assignment may even be worse, since there are 369 "new industries" codes to consider when assigning a code. Two other factors that might cause different codes to be assigned to a single establishment are changes in the establishment's activity over time (especially if the codes are assigned at different times) and how detailed the information used to assign the industry is.

Much of the confusion with SIC codes comes from the fact that the system measures the activity of a single establishment, and this continues with NAICS. However, many regulators and publishers use the classification system to identify a company's activities rather than the establishment-level activity. For companies that manufacture only one product in a single place and provide all auxiliary services from that one establishment, this is not a problem. The struggle comes when the company has more than one establishment engaged in many different activities. For example, what industry is a multi-dimensional company like General Electric properly classified in? Is it a credit card issuer, a manufacturer, a leasing company, or something else? The government used SIC codes when deciding what was a small business or which company got audited because its financial statements were different from industry norms. When it is left to a commercial publisher or a government agency to assign industry codes to the companies, the task of defining a company's primary activity was not as easy as it appeared on the surface. Assuming that publishers assign codes based on the largest revenue sector generated by the company, then the code assigned by different publishers or agencies should be the same. That is not the case.

A final problem with the move from the SIC system to NAICS is the move itself. As described in detail later in this chapter, there has been a period where different agencies were reporting their data using different classification systems. This has created problems for some data users.

## UNDERSTANDING THE NAICS SECTORS

As previously stated, NAICS industries are designed to group establishments using similar processes together. The establishments using the most similar processes are grouped into a single industry and the industries using the most similar processes are grouped together into industry groups, on up to the sector level. In this section you will find general descriptions of the NAICS sectors, descriptions of how they relate to the SIC divisions (sectors), and a summary of the level of agreement on the destinations of the industries within the sector across the three nations using NAICS.

### Agriculture, Forestry, Fishing, and Hunting

The Agriculture, Forestry, Fishing, and Hunting Sector (11) contains establishments that are primarily engaged in growing crops, raising animals, harvesting timber, and harvesting fish or other animals from farms, ranches, or the wild.

This sector differs from the SIC Agriculture, Forestry, and Fishing Division in that veterinary and horticultural consulting services have been moved out to Scientific, Technical, and Professional Services; establishments preparing crops for marketing or slaughtering animals are now considered manufacturing establishments; pet care services are now included in Other Services; and landscaping establishments have been moved to the Administrative and Support and Waste Management and Remediation Services sector. Additionally, some of the industries have been redefined to better represent the similarities in their production processes. For example, shellfish farms were taken from the SIC Animal Aquaculture industry and combined with cultured pearl production from the SIC Miscellaneous Marine Products industry to form the new NAICS Shellfish Farming industry because these establishments essentially use the same techniques to grow and harvest the shellfish. Logging and farriers are the two activities that moved into this sector from other areas.

Generally, there is agreement among all three countries using NAICS at the 5-digit (NAICS industry) level.

## Mining

The establishments in the Mining sector (21) are primarily involved with extracting materials from the earth.

The only real changes between the NAICS Mining sector and the SIC Mineral Industries division are that establishments primarily involved with geophysical surveying and mapping were moved into the Professional, Scientific, and Technical Services, and some supporting activities such as grinding and washing stones and recovering sulfur from natural gas moved into this sector. Additionally, those establishments involved with preparing mining sites or constructing buildings and other structures related to mining were moved into the Construction sector out of the different SIC mining industries they support.

Throughout this sector there is agreement among the United States, Canada, and Mexico at the 5-digit (NAICS industry) level.

## Utilities

The Utilities sector (22) covers the establishments involved with providing electricity, natural gas, steam, water, and removing sewage. The provision of these

products and services is done through a permanent infrastructure.

Under the SIC system these industries were part of the Transportation, Communications, and Utilities Division. In addition to moving these industries into their own sector, the specific industries were organized to better reflect the production process orientation of NAICS by putting nuclear power plants together in one industry and coal-fired power plants in another industry.

Below the sector level there is only agreement between the United States and Canada on this sector's structure.

## Construction

Establishments within the Construction sector (23) are involved with erecting, alterations, repairs, maintenance, installation, or reconstruction of buildings and other structures. Establishments involved with heavy construction other than buildings (such as roads) are also included in this sector.

The only activities moved out of construction in the move from SIC to NAICS were power washing building exteriors and asbestos abatement and lead paint removal. Construction management, non-cemetery related land subdivision, heavy construction equipment renting and leasing, boiler cleaning, and household antenna and satellite antenna installation activities moved into the Construction sector from other areas.

Outside of the 4-digit Foundation, Structure, and Building Exterior Contractors Industry Group, there is generally agreement among all three countries at the industry level (5-digit) and, in many cases, at the national industry level (6-digit). In most of the cases where the three nations did not reach agreement, including the one industry group, there is agreement between the United States and Canada. The United States defines the national industries differently than the other nations only within the Residential Building Construction industry. It is important to note that agreement among the three countries on the structure within this sector did not occur until NAICS 2002. Thus, the 1997 and 2002 data *within* the sector cannot be compared with each other, however sector-level data is consistent over the two versions of NAICS.

## Manufacturing

The activities included in the Manufacturing Sector (31–33) are the transformation of material, substances, or components through mechanical, physical, or chemical means into new products.

Besides the movement of logging and treating stone and minerals from the SIC Manufacturing division into the NAICS Agriculture and Mining sectors, the largest movement out of the SIC Manufacturing division was that publishing activities have moved to the new NAICS Information Sector. Additionally, some research and development activities were moved to the NAICS Professional, Scientific, and Technical Services Sector. On the other hand, a number of activities moved from the SIC Retail and Services Divisions into the NAICS Manufacturing Sector. The SIC retail establishments moving into manufacturing were those that primarily made a product on-site and sold it to the general public, such as a bakery that did the baking in the back of the store or a clothing store mainly selling clothing they made from fabric in the store. The former service establishments were those with activities most similar to manufacturing, such as establishments involved with the bulk reproduction of computer programs or armature rewrapping services. Finally, there was substantial realignment of many, but not all, of the industries that were kept in manufacturing.

Agreement among all three countries involved with NAICS is the norm down to the 5-digit, NAICS industry level. In many cases, there is agreement between United States and at least one of the other two countries at the 6-digit, national industry level.

## Wholesale Trade

Establishments in the NAICS Wholesale Trade Sector (42) are intermediaries in the distribution of merchandise who sell or arrange for the sale of goods for resale. Or they might sell or arrange the sale of capital or durable nonconsumer goods, such as manufacturing equipment or farming equipment. Finally, wholesalers may be involved in the sale of raw and intermediate materials and supplies used in the production of other goods. Wholesalers are distinguished from retailers in that they normally operate from a warehouse or office providing them with little or no space to display merchandise. Additionally, wholesalers typically have strong, long-term relationships with their clients.

With the exception of parts of a very few SIC Wholesale industries, the main movement out of this SIC division was into the NAICS Retail Sector. On the in-bound side of the changes, only parts of a couple of SIC Service industries moved.

One of the most significant changes from NAICS 1997 to NAICS 2002 is that within this sector the United States structured it in a way that is different from Canada and Mexico. Thus, the three countries agree only at the sector level. The NAICS2002 United States structure recognizes the differences between merchant wholesalers (who take legal ownership of the goods they are selling) and wholesale electronic markets and agents and brokers (who arrange the sales without taking legal ownership).

## Retail Trade

The NAICS Retail Trade Sector (44–45) includes establishments involved in selling merchandise to the general public, usually in small quantities. There are two general types of retailers—store and nonstore retailers. Store retailers operate out of fixed point-of-sale locations that are sited and designed to attract a high volume of walk-in customer traffic. Nonstore retailers use other methods of attracting business, such as broadcasting "infomercials," issuing catalogs, door-to-door selling, vending machines, or portable stalls.

In addition to movement of some establishments into Retail Trade from the Wholesale trade sector in the move from the SIC system to NAICS, several other changes took place. First, as mentioned in the description of the Manufacturing Sector, parts of some SIC Retail Trade industries were moved into manufacturing. Second, eating and drinking establishments where moved from the SIC Retail Trade division to the NAICS Accommodations and Food Services Sector. Going into the NAICS Retail Trade Sector were establishments providing services for products they sold, even if these services provided the major source of revenues for the establishment.

Within the NAICS Retail Trade Sector only Canada divides the Sub-sectors (3-digit level) and finer industrial classifications the same way as the United States. This limits comparability with Mexican data to the sector level.

## Transportation and Warehousing

The Transportation and Warehousing Sector (48–49) contains establishments involved with moving people or goods from one place to another. It also contains establishments primarily involved with storing goods. Sightseeing transportation is also included in this sector. Finally, establishments primarily doing work supporting the main activities of this sector are also included. Examples of this include air traffic control and other airport operations, harbor-based tugboat operations, truck weighing operations, and stockyards that are not designed for fattening or selling livestock.

This sector includes the SIC Transportation, Communication, and Public Utilities division industries except for those involving public utilities (moved to the NAICS Utilities Sector) and communication services (moved to the NAICS Information Sector). Ambulances were moved out of transportation and into the Health Care and Social Assistance Sector. Moving into this sector from other SIC divisions were establishments involved with scenic transportation (such as some aerial tramways and sightseeing boats) and some transportation-related services.

There is agreement with Canada and Mexico down to the 5-digit industry level. In many cases, there is also agreement with at least one of the two countries at the 6-digit national industry level.

## Information

The NAICS Information Sector (51) includes establishments distributing information and cultural products, processing data, or providing the means to transmit or distribute these products and data.

This sector brings together activities from a number of SIC divisions. As mentioned above, publishers came here from the SIC Manufacturing division. Communications services, such as the broadcast media and telephone services, used to be in the SIC Transportation, Communication, and Public Utilities division. Various computer data services and libraries are examples of activities moving here from the SIC Services division. Additionally, many of the computer-related activities, such as Internet Service Providers or Internet Publishing and Broadcasting, have been recognized as industries rather than being grouped together as they were under the SIC system.

In recognition of the increasing importance of Internet services after the early 1990s, when NAICS 1997 was designed, this sector was substantially restructured for NAICS 2002. However, this restructuring was internal to the sector, so sector totals are consistent over time.

The three NAICS countries have reached agreement on the structure of this sector down to the 5-digit industry level. In several areas the United States has further divided these industries into individual 6-digit national industries.

## Finance and Insurance

The Finance and Insurance Sector includes those establishments creating, liquidating, or changing ownership of financial assets. Establishments facilitating these financial transactions are also included here.

In order to maintain the process orientation of NAICS and realizing the inherent differences between financial and real estate activities, the designers of NAICS identified the NAICS Finance and Insurance Sector (52) and the Real Estate and Rental and Leasing Sector as two distinct sectors instead of the combined Finance, Insurance, and Real Estate (F.I.R.E.) division of the SIC system. The only industries moving into this sector other than the finance and insurance activities of the SIC F.I.R.E. division were pawnshops, from the SIC Retail division, and credit card and check validation services, from the SIC Services division.

Due to differences in the structure of Mexico's financial activities, the three countries generally agree only to the sub-sector (3-digit) level. However, the Funds, Trusts, and Other Financial Vehicles sub-sector is unique to the United States. Agreement between NAICS 2002 in the United States and NAICS 2002 in Canada generally occurs down to the industry (5-digit) level and in some cases down to the national industry (6-digit) level.

## Real Estate and Rental and Leasing

The activities included in the NAICS Real Estate and Rental and Leasing Sector (53) are renting, leasing, or otherwise allowing the use of tangible or intangible assets. Related support activities, such as real estate sales and real estate appraisals, are also included in this sector. One notable exception to this definition is real estate investment trusts (R.E.I.T.), which are included in the Finance and Insurance Sector as investment instruments. Leasing of equipment with an operator is another exception to this definition and is included in a variety of other sectors, depending on the type of equipment, because the operator's expertise and services are also included.

Except for the cemeteries, which moved to the Other Services (except Public Administration) Sector, and land subdivision and development, which moved to the Construction Sector, all of the real estate activities from the SIC Finance, Insurance, and Real Estate division are included in this sector. The non–real estate rental and leasing activities come from the SIC Services and Transportation, Communications, and Public Utilities divisions.

Generally, there is agreement down to the industry (5-digit) level between all three NAICS countries. The most notable exceptions are in the real estate leasing, real estate property management, and real estate appraisal areas where there is agreement between the United States and Canada.

## Professional, Scientific, and Technical Services

As the name implies, establishments in the NAICS Professional, Scientific, and Technical Services Sector (54) are involved with performing professional, scientific, and technical services for the operations of other organizations. Selected examples of these activities are legal services, accounting and related services, architectural services, engineering services, computer programming services, management consulting services, interior design services, and research ad development services.

This sector is one of the areas without a clearly comparable SIC division. While most of the establishments in this sector were included in the SIC Services division, many had come from other divisions. These other areas include agriculture, mining, manufacturing, transportation, and wholesale trade.

The industries (5-digit) within this sector are the same in all three countries.

## Management of Companies and Enterprises

Establishments included in the NAICS Management of Companies and Enterprises Sector (55) are primarily responsible for overseeing, administering, and managing other establishments of the same business. Usually, they are responsible for strategic or organizational planning and decision making for the entire business. Additionally, establishments responsible for holding securities of companies or enterprises for the purpose of owning a controlling interest in them (e.g., holding companies or the headquarters of conglomerates) are included in this sector.

This is another sector that is new with NAICS. Many of the establishments in this sector would have been classified as auxiliaries in the SIC system. However, the offices of holding companies are two specific industries that moved from the SIC Finance, Insurance, and Real Estate division into this new sector.

Due to the simple structure of this sector, it is comparable down to the 5-digit (industry) level.

## Administrative and Support and Waste Management and Remediation Services

While the name of the NAICS Administrative and Support and Waste Management and Remediation Services Sector (56) seems like it covers very disparate activities, the establishments within this sector are united by the performance of routine support activities for the day-to-day operations of other organizations.

Again, this sector is new to NAICS. The component industries come from a combination of SIC divisions. Most industries come from the SIC Services or Transportation, Communication, and Public Utilities divisions. However, some industries also come from the agricultural or construction areas.

There is agreement among the three NAICS countries down to the 5-digit industry level within the Administrative and Support Services sub-sector. Agreement on the structure of the Waste Management and Remediation Services sub-sector is limited to the United States and Canada.

## Educational Services

The NAICS Educational Services Sector (61) establishments are involved in providing instruction and training about a wide variety of subjects. This sector includes elementary schools through colleges and universities. It also includes a wide variety of specialized training schools and establishments.

All of the industries within this sector were part of the SIC Services division.

Within this sector, the three NAICS countries have agreed to be consistent down to the industry (5-digit) level.

## Health Care and Social Assistance

Establishments providing health care and social assistance to individuals are included in the NAICS Health Care and Social Assistance Sector (62). Examples of specific services included in this sector include physicians' offices, home health services, nursing care facilities, vocational rehabilitation services, community food services, and child day care services.

Nearly all of the industries included in this sector were included in the SIC Services division. The only exception is ambulance services, which were included in the SIC transportation area.

This is another of the sectors where Mexico, Canada, and the United States define the 5-digit industries the same way.

## Arts, Entertainment, and Recreation

The NAICS Arts, Entertainment, and Recreation Sector (71) includes establishments operating or providing services to meet various cultural, entertainment, and recreational desires. Examples of these establishments include performing arts companies, spectator sports, cultural and sports events promoters, agents, independent performers, museums, amusement and theme parks, casinos (without hotels), and marinas.

Nearly all of these industries were included in the SIC Services division. The exceptions to this are dinner theatres, which were included in the SIC Retail Trade division, marinas had been in the transportation area under the SIC system, and stadium and arena owners were included in the real estate area.

The three NAICS countries agree on the structure of this sector down to the industry (5-digit) level.

## Accommodations and Food Services

Establishments providing lodging and/or preparing meals, snacks, and beverages for immediate consumption are included in the NAICS Accommodations and Food Services Sector (72). Casinos with hotels are included in this sector.

With the exception of some contracted food service providers coming from the SIC transportation area, this sector is a combination of parts of the SIC Retail Trade and Services divisions.

This is another sector that the three nations involved with NAICS agree on the structure down to the 5-digit industry level.

## Other Services (except Public Administration)

The NAICS Other Services (except Public Administration) Sector (81) captures all of the services not included somewhere else in the NAICS structure. This includes such services as repairs, religious activities, grant making, advocacy, laundry, personal care, death care, and other personal services. Also included here are private households employing people as maids, nannies, butlers, gardeners, etc. to help run the household.

While there are a few scattered services that were included in other SIC divisions, nearly this entire sector was part of the SIC Services division.

The cross-national comparability of this sector varies greatly below the sub-sector (3-digit) level. In some areas, there is agreement among all three nations down to the 6-digit national industries. However, in other areas there is agreement between only Canada and the United States below the sub-sector level.

## Public Administration

Federal, state, and local government establishments involved with administering, managing, and overseeing public programs are included in the NAICS Public Administration Sector (92). Where possible, depending on the quality of record keeping, establishments owned by governments but performing functions classified in other sectors are placed in those other sectors. Just one example of this is a hospital owned by a county government; this hospital would be classified in the Health Care and Social Services Sector.

Historically, this sector is very much like the SIC Public Administration division.

Due to the structural differences among the governments of the three countries, there is agreement on the structure of this sector only at the sector level.

## Auxiliary Establishments

While auxiliary establishments aren't a sector within either NAICS or the SIC system, they do deserve special mention because they are handled very differently in the two systems and this can have a substantial impact on the data. An auxiliary establishment is one that is owned by a company and exists to serve other establishments in the same company rather than customers outside the company. Some examples of auxiliary establishments are corporate headquarters, research and development facilities, and corporate accounting offices.

Under the rules of the SIC system, auxiliary establishments were counted in the sector that was the main revenue source for the company. This means that the corporate headquarters, located in New York City, of a major oil company, possibly with a thousand or more employees, would be classified as a mining establishment, even though there is no significant mining activity within New York City. It also means that as a major corporation, such as General Electric, expanded and changed its focus from manufacturing to financial services, all of its auxiliary establishments would move from the manufacturing sector to the F.I.R.E. division regardless of the work that was performed at each one. It also means that you would underestimate the importance of scientific and technical services in an area containing a corporate research and development facility employing hundreds of people. But if this same facility did its work for other companies, the employees would be counted in the scientific and technical services area.

NAICS changes all of this by classifying auxiliary establishments according to the work being done at the establishment. This means that the oil company headquarters is now classified along with other corporate headquarters and the research and development facility is classified in Professional, Scientific, and Technical services.

## NAICS IMPLEMENTATION

Unlike Canada and Mexico, which have relatively strong central statistical agencies, the United States has a number of specialized statistical agencies located in different parts of the federal government. Each one of these agencies operates relatively independently of each other with general coordination of statistical policy handled by the Office of Management and Budget. Due to this relative independence, each agency collects and processes its data in different ways. This results in each agency implementing NAICS on their own timetable.

For example, the Census Bureau, within the U.S. Department of Commerce, collects and processes the data itself. Thus, it was able to make the necessary changes to its computer programs and operations relatively quickly and then start implementing NAICS with the 1997 Economic Census.

The U.S. Department of Labor's Bureau of Labor Statistics (BLS), on the other hand, contracts with each state's employment security agency for them to collect most data and to classify each establishment into the appropriate industry. Therefore, BLS was dependent on each state's employment security agency to reclassify each establishment before BLS could change to NAICS. Further slowing down BLS's conversion to NAICS was the fact that under the contract between BLS and the states, the states normally verify each establishment's classification on a three-year cycle. Since the least disruptive method of converting to NAICS for BLS was to build the reclassification into the normal workload for the states, that is what they did. Given the time needed to write, test, and distribute the appropriate programs, BLS waited until the 2002 version of NAICS was finalized before they started converting their programs. This means for a couple of years the Federal Departments of Labor and

Commerce and researchers were using different systems to define industry data.

The Department of Commerce's Bureau of Economic Analysis (BEA) relies on industry data from both the Census Bureau and the Bureau of Labor Statistics as inputs to its economic models. Because of this, BEA could not start producing its data on a NAICS basis until both Census and BLS converted their data.

Table 4.3 shows when each agency's specific programs were (or in some cases, will be) converted to NAICS.

While the negotiators who created NAICS tried to retain time series, they were not always successful, but in many cases they were. The clean-slate approach completely broke up some industries that had been identified in NAICS.

In some cases, it is relatively easy to work back from NAICS and either rebuild the SIC industry from the components now identified as individual NAICS industries or, at least, get a reasonably close approximation. For example, as shown in Table 4.4, the SIC Cash Crops Industry was divided into new industries for each crop. Since each of the new NAICS industries, except corn, came from this single SIC industry, it is possible to approximate its current data reasonably accurately and maintain a time series.

In other cases, one SIC industry was split into several NAICS industries, but unlike the cash grains example above, some of the NAICS industries were built from pieces of several SIC industries. In this situation, it is often difficult or impossible to estimate the SIC industry accurately. A good example is the SIC Real Estate Agents and Managers industry shown in Table 4.5. The real estate broker condominium associations were combined with other homeowner associations and athletic associations to create a new NAICS Industry—Other Similar Organizations (except Business, Professional, Labor, and Political Organizations)—this along with the movement of cemetery management to a combined industry makes it almost impossible to accurately estimate the data for the SIC Real Estate Agents and Brokers industry using NAICS-based data.

The new system also created industries that were never officially identified before. This was done by taking parts of various SIC industries and combining them into a single industry. In some cases it might be possible to work back to the old industry, but in others it is not. In the Music Publishers example shown in

**Table 4.3**
**NAICS Implementation Schedule**

| Publications | Reference year(s) of data | Year of release |
|---|---|---|
| **Census Bureau** | | |
| *Economic Census* | 1997 | 1999-2001 |
| *Annual Survey of Manufactures* | 1998 | 2000 |
| *Service Annual Survey* | 1998-1999 | 2001 |
| *Annual Wholesale and Retail Trade Surveys* | 1992-1999 | 2001 |
| *Monthly Manufacturer's Shipments, Inventories, and Orders* | 1992-2001 | 2001 |
| *Monthly Wholesale and Retail Trade* | 1992-2001 | 2001 |
| *Annual Capital Expenditures Survey* | 1998-1999 | 2001 |
| **Internal Revenue Service** | | |
| *Statistics of Income* | 1998 | 2000 |
| **Bureau of Labor Statistics** | | |
| *Unemployment Insurance-Covered Employment and Wages (ES 202)* | 2001 | 2002 |
| *Current Employment Statistics (BLS 790)* | 2003 | 2003 |
| *Producer Price Indexes* | 2004 | 2004 |
| *Mass Layoff Statistics* | 2002 | 2002 |
| *Current Populations Survey* | 2003 | 2003 |
| *Job Openings and Labor Turnover Survey* | Data going back to 2000 | 2003 |
| *Employment Projections* | 2002-2012 | 2003 |
| *Productivity Measures for Selected Industries* | 2001 | 2003 |
| *Occupational Employment Statistics* | 2002 | 2004 |
| *Census of Fatal Occupational Injuries* | 2003 | 2004 |
| *Survey of Occupational Injuries and illnesses* | 2003 | 2004 |
| *Foreign Labor Force Statistics* | 2003 | 2004 |
| *Employment Cost Index* | 2005 | 2006 |
| *Employer Costs for Employee Compensation* | 2004 | 2004 |
| *National Compensation Survey – Wages* | 2006 | 2006 |
| *National Compensation Survey – Benefits* | 2006 | 2006 |

**Table 4.3 (Continued)**
**NAICS Implementation Schedule**

| Publications | Reference year(s) of data | Year of release |
|---|---|---|
| **Bureau of Economics Analysis** | | |
| *Foreign Direct Investment in the U.S. (FDIUS) U.S. Business Enterprises Acquired or Established by Foreign Direct Investors* | 1997 | 1999 |
| *Inventories and Sales for Manufacturing and Trade* | 1997-2000 | 2001 |
| *State Personal Income and Earnings by Industry* | 2001 | 2002 |
| *Benchmark Input-Output Accounts* | 1997 | 2002 |
| *FDIUS Balance of Payments Data* | 1997-2001 | 2002 |
| *U.S. Direct Investment Aboard (USDIA) Operations Data* | 1999 | 2002 |
| *National Income and Product Accounts* | 2000-2002 | 2003 |
| *Fixed Assets* | 1997-2002 | 2004 |
| *Gross Domestic Product by Industry* | 2000-2002 | 2004 |
| *Gross State Product* | 2000-2002 | 2004 |
| *Annual Input-Output Accounts* | 2000-2001 | 2004 |
| *USDIA Balance of Payments* | 1999-2003 | 2004 |

Table 4.6, Music Publishers, NAICS 51223, was created by taking parts of SIC industry 2731 (Books: publishing), SIC 2741 (Miscellaneous Publishing), and SIC 8999 (Services, NEC). It is worth noting that other parts of these SIC industries were assigned to other NAICS industries.

## BUILDING TIME SERIES

Looking at economic data for just a single point is often of limited use. Most economic data take on greater meaning when a trend over time is looked at. By looking at a time series you can gain a sense of how things are developing or changing.

With the creation of NAICS and its continuous revisions, analyzing a time series can be difficult. In looking at data over time, even for an industry that has the same name over time, it is critical to know if it was defined the same way over the entire period you are looking at. This means looking at the exact definition used in the 2002 NAICS, 1997 NAICS, 1987 SIC, and possibly earlier versions of the SIC system. Because of movement of entire industries, this actually is more of a problem as you move to higher levels (fewer digits) in the hierarchy of NAICS. In the transition from the SIC system to the 1997 version of NAICS, 422 industries were moved as complete industries into the new system. Another 38 SIC industries are directly derivable where they were simply divided into multiple NAICS industries without contributions from other SIC industries.

If your time series goes back to SIC-based data, you can find out how the industry was translated into NAICS from a tool on the Census Bureau's Web site at http://www.census.gov/epcd/naics/frames3.htm. Figure 4.1 is a sample of this tool showing part of the transportation area. In looking at this page on the Census Bureau's site, the top half is sorted by the NAICS

**Table 4.4**
**A Reasonable Time-Series Industry Conversion**

| SIC | Description | NAICS | Description |
|---|---|---|---|
| 0119 | Cash Grains, NEC | 1111 | Oilseed and Grain Farming (pt.) |
| 0119 (pt.) | Dry Pea and Bean | 11113 | Dry Pea and Bean |
| 0119 (pt.) | Oilseed | 11112 | Oilseed |
| 0119 (pt.) | Popcorn | 11115 | Corn (pt) |
| 0119 (pt.) | Other Farms | 111199 | All Other Grain Farming |

**Table 4.5**
**Industry with Splits into Parts of Industries**

| SIC | SIC Description | NAICS | NAICS Description |
|---|---|---|---|
| 6531 (pt.) | Real Estate Agents and Brokers | 53121 | Offices of Real Estate Agents and Brokers |
| 6531 (pt.) | Condominium Associations | 81399 | Other Similar Organizations (except Business, Professional, Labor, and Political Organizations) (pt) |
| 6531 (pt.) | Residential Property Managers | 531311 | Residential Property Managers |
| 6531 (pt.) | Nonresidential Property Managers | 531312 | Nonresidential Property Managers |
| 6531 (pt.) | Real Estate Appraisers | 53132 | Offices of Real Estate Appraisers |
| 6531 (pt.) | Cemetery Management | 81222 | Cemeteries and Crematories (pt) |
| 6531 (pt.) | Real Estate Agents and Managers, NEC | 53139 | Other Activities Related to Real Estate |

**Table 4.6**
**A Newly Identified Industry**

| SIC | Description | NAICS | Description |
|---|---|---|---|
| 2731 (pt.)<br>2741 (pt.)<br>8999 (pt.) | Books: publishing<br>Miscellaneous Publishing Services, NEC | 51223 | Music Publishers |

codes and shows which SIC industries the NAICS industry was constructed from. The bottom half of this page is sorted by SIC code and shows which NAICS industry the SIC industry (or parts of it) went to. It should be noted that the tables on this Web page also appear as appendixes in the NAICS 1997 manual, but you might have to flip back and forth between pages to learn what can be seen on a single Web page. It is also important to note that this tool and the appendixes in the NAICS 1997 manual are based on relationships between SIC and NAICS industries as they were expected to occur prior to the information from the 1997 Economic Census—a better source for these relationships is the 1997 Economic Census Bridge Tables described below. The NAICS 1997 to NAICS 2002 relationships can be found in the 2002 Economic Census Bridge Tables.

From the piece of the table shown, it can be seen that intercity and rural business transportation (NAICS 48521) is the same as SIC 4131 and the table includes an E code (existing industry) to tell you that this is simply an existing industry. In that case, creating a time series is as easy as gathering all the information from 1997 forward using the one NAICS 48521 and to represent the industry back to 1963 when the Census of Transportation started using SIC 4131.

Taxi Service has an R code (revised industry) as shown in the top half of Figure 4.1. This entry in the table tells you that this NAICS industry was created by combining taxicabs with taxicab dispatch services, which was part of communications services, NEC under the SIC system. According to the bottom half of Figure 4.1 the old taxi service industry is just part of the NAICS Taxi Service industry. In the 1997 transition 388 of the NAICS industries were created from multiple SIC industries or parts of them.

For new industries marked with an N, such as limousines, no time series should even be attempted. Notice that in the top of Figure 4.1 the limousine industry is marked as a new industry even though it was part of local passenger transportation. Then according to table 2, illustrated in the bottom half of Figure 4.1, limousine service is just one of many components broken out from SIC 4119 (Local Passenger Transportation, NEC). The @ next to the 4119 code, as shown in the head note, "indicates time series breaks >3% of 1992." In other words, NAICS based data cannot be combined to estimate the SIC 4119 total. That is confirmed by reading the Bridge Tables.

The relationship between SIC and NAICS is often not that simple, as illustrated by ambulances, as part of SIC 4119. Ambulance service was removed from transporting and was parked in the ambulatory health care services sub-sector, NAICS 621. From an economist's perspective, this exemplifies one of the major improvements in NAICS: Industries have been reclassified based not on the service offered (transportation of patients), but on the nature of the need (other ambulatory health care services).

The 2002 correspondence tables replace the @ symbol with a drawbridge, described in the next section. Also, due to Web site policy changes at the Census Bureau, the 2002 tables do not provide an option for two-tables-at-once viewing. If you wish to see both directions of the correspondence at once, clicking a link in one table launches a second window showing the other table. You can then resize both windows to view them the way you wish on the screen.

## Census Bureau Bridge Tables

While the NAICS/SIC correspondence tables discussed above are very useful in understanding the potential relationships among the industries included in the various NAICS and SIC systems, they are not based on any actual data. The Census Bureau's Bridge Tables are based on actual data collected in the Economic Census. These were produced for both the 1997 and 2002 Economic Censuses. But it is important to note that the 1997 Bridge Tables cover the SIC to NAICS 1997 change while the 2002 tables cover only the NAICS 1997 to NAICS 2002 changes. Thus the 2002 tables are much shorter than the 1997 version.

When deciding if it is reasonable to develop a time series for any given industry, it is useful to know how comparable the new industry is to the old one(s). To know if a time series can be maintained you will have to use the 2002 and 1997 Bridge Tables. However, these are only available for the nation. Using the proportions reported here for a local area requires assuming that the makeup of the industry in the local area is the same as at the national level. Also, using these proportions for years other than 1997 or 2002 (as appropriate) requires assuming that the makeup of the industry stays the same over time. These may or may not be safe assumptions—that is a decision each data user needs to make on his/her own.

As a quick indicator of the ability to build a time series, the Census Bureau has included a drawbridge to help the user. How closed or open the drawbridge is is a quick indicator of the ability to build a time series spanning the transition.

Figure 4.2 is a part of the 1997 bridge table. This sample shows a closed bridge for the taxi service industry, indicating that adding taxi cab dispatch services to the taxi cabs has such a small impact that there is no reason to not build a time series crossing over the 1997 switch from the SIC system to NAICS.

By showing an open bridge for the school and employee bus transportation industry, the bridge table indicates that it is probably unwise to build a time series spanning this transition. The reason for caution with this industry is that there is too much of a mix between

**Figure 4.1**
**Sample SIC-NAICS 1997 Correspondence Table**

NAICS and SIC: Tables 1 and 2 Compared with Frames – Netscape

File  Edit  View  Go  Communicator  Help

Bookmarks   Location: http://www.census.gov/epcd/naics/frames3.htm      What's Related

Codes: u--U.S. only; c--U.S. and Canada; E--existing industry; N--new; R--revised; *--part

**Table 1**

Search   Top Menu   Help   Exit

| 1997 NAICS | 1997 NAICS--U.S. Description | Codes | 1987 SIC | 1987 U.S. SIC Description |
|---|---|---|---|---|
| 4852 | Interurban and Rural Bus Transportation | | | |
| 48521 | Interurban and Rural Bus Transportation | E | 4131 | Intercity and Rural Bus Transportation |
| 4853 | Taxi and Limousine Service | | | |
| 48531 | Taxi Service | R | 4121 | Taxicabs |
| | | | *4899 | Communications Services, NEC (taxi cab dispatch services) |
| 48532 | Limousine Service | N | *4119 | Local Passenger Transportation, NEC (limousine rental with driver and automobile rental with driver) |
| 4854 | School and Employee Bus Transportation | | | |
| 48541 | School and Employee Bus Transportation | R | 4151 | School Buses |
| | | | *4119 | Local Passenger Transportation, NEC (employee transportation) |

**Table 2**

Top Menu   Exit

@ indicates time series break >3% of 1992 value of shipments

| 1987 SIC | 1987 U.S. SIC Description | 1997 NAICS | 1997 NAICS--U.S. Description |
|---|---|---|---|
| | . Airport Limousine Transportation | 485999 | All Other Transit and Ground Passenger Transportation (pt) |
| 4119@ | Local Passenger Transportation, NEC | | |
| | . Ambulances | 62191 | Ambulance Service (pt) |
| | . Employee Transportation | 48541 | School and Employee Bus Transportation (pt) |
| | . Sightseeing Buses and Cable and Cog Railways, Except Scenic | 48711 | Scenic and Sightseeing Transportation, Land (pt) |
| | . Special Needs Transportation | 485991 | Special Needs Transportation |
| | . Hearse Rental with Driver and Carpool and Vanpool Operations | 485999 | All Other Transit and Ground Passenger Transportation (pt) |
| | . Automobile Rental with Driver and Limousine Rental with Driver | 48532 | Limousine Service |
| 4121 | Taxicabs | 48531 | Taxi Service (pt) |
| 4131 | Intercity and Rural Bus Transportation | 48521 | Interurban and Rural Bus Transportation |

Document: Done

Figure 4.2
1997 Economic Census Bridge Table Sample

| NAICS | SIC | Pt | Description | Estab-lish-ments | Revenue ($1,000) | Paid employees | Annual payroll ($1,000) |
|---|---|---|---|---|---|---|---|
| 4853 | | | Taxi & limousine service | 6,418 | 3,154,521 | 57,282 | 880,626 |
| 48531 | | | Taxi service | 3,184 | 1,280,597 | 27,850 | 392,759 |
| 485310 | 4121 | 9/92 | Taxi service | 3,184 | 1,280,597 | 27,850 | 392,759 |
| | | | Taxicab service | 3,184 | 1,280,597 | 27,850 | 392,759 |
| 48532 | | | Limousine service | 3,234 | 1,873,924 | 29,432 | 487,867 |
| 485320 | | | Limousine service | 3,234 | 1,873,924 | 29,432 | 487,867 |
| 23¾of | 4119 | 20 | Limousine or auto rental with driver | 3,234 | 1,873,924 | 29,432 | 487,867 |

| NAICS | SIC | Pt | Description | Estab-lish-ments | Revenue ($1,000) | Paid employees | Annual payroll ($1,000) |
|---|---|---|---|---|---|---|---|
| 4854 | | | School & employee bus transportation | 4,484 | 4,392,783 | 151,664 | 1,877,956 |
| 48541 | | | School & employee bus transportation | 4,484 | 4,392,783 | 151,664 | 1,877,956 |
| 485410 | | | School & employee bus transportation | 4,484 | 4,392,783 | 151,664 | 1,877,956 |
| 2⅓of | 4119 | 91 | Employee bus service | 158 | 158,947 | 4,223 | 67,261 |
| | 4151 | 9/92 | School bus service | 4,326 | 4,233,836 | 147,441 | 1,810,695 |

| NAICS | SIC | Pt | Description | Estab-lish-ments | Revenue ($1,000) | Paid employees | Annual payroll ($1,000) |
|---|---|---|---|---|---|---|---|
| 4855 | | | Charter bus industry | 1,531 | 1,768,199 | 31,483 | 548,026 |
| 48551 | | | Charter bus industry | 1,531 | 1,768,199 | 31,483 | 548,026 |
| 485510 | | | Charter bus industry | 1,531 | 1,768,199 | 31,483 | 548,026 |
| 14¾of | 4141 | 9/92 | Charter bus, service-local | 482 | 459,953 | 8,694 | 143,572 |
| | 4142 | 9/92 | Charter bus service, interstate/interurban | 1,049 | 1,308,246 | 22,789 | 404,454 |

| NAICS | SIC | Pt | Description | Estab-lish-ments | Revenue ($1,000) | Paid employees | Annual payroll ($1,000) |
|---|---|---|---|---|---|---|---|
| 4859 | | | Other transit & ground passenger transportation | 2,555 | 1,810,796 | 46,304 | 719,866 |
| 48599 | | | Other transit & ground passenger transportation | 2,555 | 1,810,796 | 46,304 | 719,866 |
| 485991 | | | Special needs transportation | 1,789 | 1,141,413 | 31,791 | 486,676 |
| 14¾of | 4119 | 92 | Special needs transportation | 1,789 | 1,141,413 | 31,791 | 486,676 |
| 485999 | | | All other transit & ground passenger transportation | 766 | 669,383 | 14,513 | 233,190 |
| 1¾of D | 4111 | 04 | Scheduled airport shuttle service | 534 | 601,988 | 13,435 | 217,633 |
| 1¾of | 4119 | 99 | Other passenger transportation, n.e.c. | 232 | 67,395 | 1,078 | 15,557 |

the SIC industries going into this NAICS industry and some other NAICS industries.

To learn more about how to read the Bridge Tables go to chapter 5 (Reports).

## Bureau of Labor Statistics's Current Employment Survey

Since the Bureau of Labor Statistics needs time series data in order to develop seasonal adjustment factors, it converted the Current Employment Survey (CES) data to a NAICS basis back to 1990. The actual work was performed by the individual states. This is probably one of the most reliable historical series that could be produced when moving from the SIC system to NAICS because it was generally done on an establishment-by-establishment basis. But even working at this level, there are limitations. The basic methods available for converting establishment-based historical files from the SIC system to NAICS are described by Klimek and Merrell (2000) and Mikkelson, Morisi, and Stamas (2000). Gaines (2000) describes some of the limitations of these methods.

## OTHER IMPACTS OF MOVING FROM THE SIC SYSTEM TO NAICS

While NAICS was officially created for statistical purposes only and this is clearly stated by OMB, you can be sure that it is being used for other purposes. Some of the purposes will be official in nature; others will be more strategic uses by businesses.

On the official side, many government agencies involved with regulating, monitoring, or assisting businesses do so on the basis of industrial classifications. For example, the U.S. Small Businesses Administration (SBA) identifies small business according to criteria that vary according to their industry. This had been done on the basis of the SIC-based industries. The Small Business Administration has revised its regulations to use NAICS industries. As a result, a business that had been classified as small using the SIC industries may no longer qualify for SBA assistance or vice versa.

On the strategic management side, many businesses compare themselves against industry norms. Often these norms have been developed from official industry statistics. These statistics might come from the Census Bureau, the Bureau of Labor Statistics, or the Internal Revenue Service. In any of these cases, the industries are now defined using NAICS. Because the industries businesses use to compare themselves against might have been redefined, the norms they compare themselves to might be based on a different set of businesses. Businesses might start making a different set of strategic decisions since the information leading to those decisions has changed.

The conversion from the SIC system to NAICS doesn't just affect official statistics, but many private data vendors are also changing. One group of private data vendors that are being forced to change their products because of the industrial classification changes is the consultants involved with economic modeling. These consultants rely heavily on the official statistics produced by the federal government. Thus, they need to rebuild all of their models to reflect the new system.

Companies providing information about individual businesses, such as Dun and Bradstreet, aren't under as much pressure to convert to NAICS as the economic consultants. However, many of them are changing over to either reporting just the NAICS industry (or industries) for the businesses they describe or reporting both NAICS and SIC codes.

## SUMMARY

We are living in a changing economic world. In order to describe the current world, the framework used to describe it has changed. The new system, NAICS, is a system based much more on the production processes businesses use than the old SIC system was. NAICS has taken a clean slate approach to identifying industries and in the process has interrupted the ability to look at long-term trends in many industries.

However, NAICS does provide a structure that is more reflective of today's economy rather than the 1930s economy, which formed the basis for the SIC system. NAICS also recognizes the importance of being able to compare economic data with other countries like Canada and Mexico.

While changing the structure used to describe the nation's economy presents a number of challenges, in the long run we will have a much clearer picture of that economy.

You can learn more about the North American Industry Classification System by visiting the unofficial clearinghouse for NAICS at http://www.library. georgetown.edu/bic/naics.htm. To learn about how to use NAICS in the Economic Census read on.

# BIBLIOGRAPHY

Ambler, Carol. 1998. "NAICS and U.S. Statistics." Paper presented at the annual meeting of the American Statistical Association, Dallas, Texas, August 9–13, 1998 http://www.census.gov/epcd/www/asambler.htm (accessed October 22, 1998).

Ambler, Carol, and James Kristoff. 1998. "Introducing the North American Industry Classification System." *Government Information Quarterly* 15 (3): 363–73.

Boettcher, Jennifer. 1996. "NAFTA Prompts a New Code System for Industry—The Death of SIC and Birth of NAICS." *Database* 19 (2): 42–45.

Executive Office of the President, Office of Management and Budget, Economic Classification Policy Committee. 1998. *North American Industry Classification System (NAICS)—United States, 1997.* Springfield, VA: NTIS.

*First International NAICS Users Conference: Conference Proceedings.* 1998. NAICS Association, Rockaway, NJ: Utah State University, September 30, 1998.

Gaines, Leonard M. 2000. "The Transition from SIC to NAICS—A Discussion." *Proceedings of the Second International Conference on Establishment Surveys Proceedings,* 1321–23. Alexandria, VA: American Statistical Association.

Gaines, Leonard, Jonathan Cole, Maurine Haver, and John Murphy. 1998. "Moving from SIC to NAICS: What Does It Mean for Data Users?" *Proceedings of the Joint Statistical Meetings, Dallas, Texas, August 9–13, 1998,* 227–28. Alexandria, VA: American Statistical Association.

Guenther, David, and Andrew Rosman. 1994. "Differences between COMPUSTAT and CRISP SIC Code and Related Effects on Research." *Journal of Accounting and Economics* 18 (1): 115–28.

Kahle, Kathleen M., and Ralph A. Walkling. 1996. "The Impact of Industry Classifications on Financial Research." *Journal of Financial and Quantitative Analysis* 31 (3): 309–35.

Klimek, Shawn D., and David R. Merrell. 2000. "On Reclassifying Industries from the Standard Industrial Classification System to the North American Industry Classification System." *Proceedings of the Second International Conference on Establishment Surveys Proceedings,* 1305–10. Alexandria, VA: American Statistical Association.

Kort, John R. 2001. "North American Industry Classification System in BEA's Economic Accounts." *Survey of Current Business* 81 (5): 7–13.

Mikkelson, Gordon, Teresa L. Morisi, and George Stamas. 2000. "Implementing the NAICS for Business Surveys at BLS." *Proceedings of the Second International Conference on Establishment Surveys Proceedings,* 1315–20. Alexandria, VA: American Statistical Association.

Murphy, John B. 1998. "Introducing the North American Industry Classification System." *Monthly Labor Review* 121 (7): 43–47.

Parker, Robert. 2001. "Impact of the North American Industry Classification System on U.S. Economic Data." *Business Economics* 36 (2): 56–59.

U.S. Census Bureau. 1998. "Implications of Implementing NAICS in the Current Services Program." www.census.gov/epcd/www/naicssvc.html (accessed December 1, 1998).

Walker, James, and John Murphy. 2001. "Implementing the North American Industry Classification System at BLS." *Monthly Labor Review* 124 (2): 15–21.

Zeisset, Paul, and Mark Wallace. 1998. "How NAICS Will Affect Data Users." Economic Planning and Coordination Division, Bureau of the Census. http:\\www.census.gov/epcd/www/naicsusr.html (accessed December 6, 1998).

# CHAPTER 5
# Reports and Special Publications

It is a capital mistake to theorize before one has data.
—*Sherlock Holmes (Sir Arthur Conan Doyle [1859–1930])*

1. Background for This Chapter
2. Report Availability
3. Advance Report
4. Industry Reports
5. Geographic Area Series
6. ZIP Codes
7. Subject Series

    A. Source of Revenue/Merchandise Line Sales/ Commodity Line Sales
    B. Establishment/Firm Size
    C. Miscellaneous Subjects
    D. Summary

8. Location of Manufacturing Plants/Location of Mining
9. Economy-wide Statistics Series

    A. Comparative Statistics
    B. Bridge Reports
    C. Business Expenses
    D. Nonemployer Statistics
    E. Survey of Business Owners
    F. Outlying Areas

10. Transportation

    A. Commodity Flow Survey
    B. Vehicle Inventory and Use Survey

11. Special Requests

    A. Special Tabulations
    B. Center for Economic Studies Resources

The power of information is limited only by the quality of the data collected and your imagination. This chapter will introduce you to the reports found throughout the Economic Census program. It will also describe some ways to use the data and information included in the Economic Census reports, hopefully prompting you to think about other ways you can use the data. By understanding the reports, your time spent gathering the data will be shorter, thus allowing you more time to use the information.

## BACKGROUND FOR THIS CHAPTER

Before we begin it is helpful to have a clear idea of the definitions we are using when we talk about data, information, and knowledge. *Data,* the plural form of *datum,* are a group of numbers within a set. Usually, these numbers have no clear meaning by themselves. That meaning is provided, in part, by the context of the data or name of the set. When this meaning is understood, the numbers change from data to information. For example, the numbers 52—18,588—3,892— 317 are data; knowing that these numbers are how many catering establishments there are in Kentucky, their total sales and annual payroll in thousands of dollars, and how many paid employees in 1997 provides information. Understanding how that information relates to other data/information or how it can be used to answer a question is knowledge. If you know how many catering business are in each county of Kentucky, you can divide up your sales force to focus on the most profitable areas.

When you look at the Economic Census the data are almost certain to be over two years old. Yet, even in the fast paced business world the information can still be useful. One way that you can use the data even though it might seem outdated is to create ratios showing relationships between relevant variables. (Generally, these ratios are fairly stable over time.) For example, in Figure 5.1 you can see the data on the number of establishments and number of employees in the Jewelry, precious metal industry (SIC 3911) in each of the two census years. You might be looking at these data in the year 2000 and are interested in know-

Figure 5.1
Comparative Statistics Sample from HTML Tables

| Com-para-bit | SIC | 1987 SIC Description | Establishments | | | Value of Shipments ($1,000) | | | Paid employees | | | Annual payroll ($1,000) | | |
|---|---|---|---|---|---|---|---|---|---|---|---|---|---|---|
| | | | 1997 | 1992 | % chg | 1997 | 1992 | % chg | 1997 | 1992 | % chg | 1997 | 1992 | % chg |
| | 39 | Miscellaneous manufacturing industries | 18,043 | 17,035 | 5.9 | 50,997,838 | 39,498,319 | 29.1 | 393,972 | 365,465 | 7.8 | 10,563,481 | 8,417,045 | 25.5 |
| | 391 | Jewelry, silverware, and plated ware | 2,828 | 2,838 | -0.4 | 7,243,618 | 5,730,865 | 26.4 | 46,547 | 45,500 | 2.3 | 1,208,070 | 1,068,386 | 13.1 |
| | 3911 | Jewelry, precious metal | 2,272 | 2,204 | 3.1 | 5,416,836 | 4,190,081 | 29.3 | 34,694 | 32,525 | 6.7 | 884,942 | 757,959 | 16.8 |
| | 3914 | Silverware and plated ware | 162 | 213 | -23.9 | 907,716 | 685,461 | 32.4 | 6,457 | 6,710 | -3.8 | 187,774 | 157,313 | 19.4 |
| | 3915 | Jewelers' materials and lapidary work | 394 | 421 | -6.4 | 919,066 | 855,323 | 7.5 | 5,396 | 6,265 | -13.9 | 135,354 | 153,114 | -11.6 |
| | 393 | Musical instruments | 576 | 461 | 24.9 | 1,356,651 | 982,087 | 38.1 | 13,411 | 12,215 | 9.8 | 363,022 | 272,653 | 33.1 |
| | 3931 | Musical instruments | 576 | 461 | 24.9 | 1,356,651 | 982,087 | 38.1 | 13,411 | 12,215 | 9.8 | 363,022 | 272,653 | 33.1 |
| | 394 | Toys and sporting goods | 3,600 | 3,242 | 11.0 | D | 12,122,567 | N | (100,000+) | 97,503 | N | D | 2,133,046 | N |
| | 3942 | Dolls | 240 | 209 | 14.8 | 299,821 | 250,952 | 19.5 | 3,393 | 3,649 | -7.0 | 63,722 | 64,105 | -0.6 |
| | 3944 | Games, toys, and children's vehicles | 789 | 919 | -14.1 | D | 4,290,955 | N | (25k-49999) | 31,883 | N | D | 702,907 | N |
| | 3949 | Sporting and athletic goods, n.e.c. | 2,571 | 2,114 | 21.6 | 10,591,160 | 7,580,660 | 39.7 | 69,664 | 61,971 | 12.4 | 1,831,218 | 1,366,034 | 34.1 |

ing how many people are currently employed in this industry. You can estimate this number using the ratio of employees per establishment in 1997 (it was 15.3 employees/establishment in 1997 and 16.1 in 1992—a relatively stable ratio over a 5-year period) and a count of establishments from 2000 to estimate the number of employees in 2000. Depending on the question that you are trying to answer, you might be interested in a variety of other ratios, such as the portion of employees in a sub-sector working in a specific industry, value of shipments per establishment, value of shipments per employee, or payroll per establishment.

The quality of the data in the reports depends on quality of the data entered by each of the establishments included in the census (and whether or not they actually responded). Each piece of information recorded on the census form finds its way into a variety of reports. This chapter will be exploring the implications in the different reports of data entered onto the Economic Census questionnaires by a company we are calling Pamina's Flutes, describing the limitations and uses of the reports.

Let say the owner and manager of Pamina's Flutes, a small manufacturer of Musical Instruments (NAICS 339992), fills out the census form. In the past years only the owner made the flutes and did all of the work in running the business, but recently business has been so good that extra people were hired. In previous years, the owner would never have seen an Economic Census form, because the data would have been pulled from their income tax form, schedule C. So the business' information would only be included in the *Nonemployer Reports*. There is also a chance that it might have been included in the Survey of Business Owners.

However, once the owner started to file quarterly withholding taxes for the employees on IRS Form 941, the business would be identified as having employees and could be included in all of the other censuses and surveys conducted by the Census Bureau. Then its responses to the questionnaires it receives would be included in the appropriate reports mentioned below. It should also be noted that most very small businesses are not actually sent questionnaires, but their data are derived from the forms they submit to the Internal Revenue Service and Social Security Administration for various administrative purposes. (This is referred to as the administrative records data collection method.) If Pamina's Flutes did get an Economic Census form (other than the one used to classify establishments into the correct industry), one of the questions

would ask for the value of its shipments. The response to that one question would be reflected in the aggregate value of an industry for manufacturers; then that aggregate value will be compared with the last census in the comparative tables, used in geographic strength in geographic areas, and included in the numbers concerning women-owned business. Using the various reports, anyone can understand the operations of an industry. With a little thought, anyone can see the strengths, weaknesses, threats, and opportunities for an establishment connected to that industry.

As the owner of Pamina's Flutes, it was Pamina's responsibility to fill out the questionnaire accurately, completely, and in a timely manner. If the form was not done with those criteria in mind, it may lead to nonsampling errors. Nonsampling errors can arise in any data collection, including a census. Being a census means the Bureau doesn't have to worry about sampling errors, but it does have to be aware of nonresponse and incorrect responses entered by the company or being incorrectly entered into the computer by the Census Bureau. Responses on the form clearly not reflecting the true nature of the business (such as extremely high payrolls for the number of employees), or missing responses are corrected or supplied by the Census Bureau's staff using a variety of procedures and the results are called imputed answers.

## REPORT AVAILABILITY

Most of the data we will be showing in this chapter comes from the Portable Data Format (PDF) reports. Please note there are substantially more data that can be found on the Census Bureau's Web site as drill-down hypertext tables, in American FactFinder, and on the CD-ROMs for the Economic Censuses. Tables 1.1, for the major reports, and 5.1, for the other reports, show which formats are used to report the data, at what geographic details, and their expected 2002 release date. Quick instructions about the scope, coverage, classification system, data items, and publications about the Economic Census and related surveys are published in the Guide to the Economic Census and Related Statistics at http://www.census.gov/epcd/ec02/guide.html.

All of the data from the census will be available in database format in the CD-ROMs and most of the data will be posted on the Internet. Most of the variables use the same units in each sector where they occur, so you can compare sales in the retail trade reports with

Table 5.1
Other 2002 Economic Census Reports Issuance Programs

| Sector and Title | Geography | Media | Date |
|---|---|---|---|
| **Economy-Wide** | | | |
| Core Business Statistics: | | | |
| Advance Report | U | A C D P Pr | 2004q1 |
| Comparative Statistics | U S | A C D P | 2005q2 |
| Bridge Between NAICS and SIC | U | A C D P Pr | 2005q2 |
| Nonemployer Statistics | U S M C | . C D P | 2004q4 |
| Survey of Business Owners (including minority- and | | | |
| women-owned businesses) | U S M C P | . C D P Pr | 2005q3-06q1 |
| Business Expenses | U | . C D P Pr | 2005q2 |
| Puerto Rico and Island Areas | area | . C D P Pr | 2005q1-06q1 |
| **Mining** | | | |
| Numerical List of Mfd/Mineral Products | (NA) | A C . P Pr | 2004q1 |
| Subject Series: Product Summary | U | A C D P Pr | 2006q2 |
| Subject Series: General Summary | U S | A C D P Pr | 2006q1 |
| Subject Series: Materials Consumed Summary | U | A C D P Pr | 2006q1 |
| Location of Mining | U S | A C | 2006q2 |
| **Construction** | | | |
| Industry Series Summary | U S | A C D P Pr | 2004q4 |
| Geographic Area Summary | U S | A C D P Pr | 2005q1 |
| **Manufacturing** | | | |
| Numerical List of Mfd/Mineral Products | (NA) | A C . P Pr | 2004q1 |
| Subject Series: General Summary | U S M | A C D P Pr | 2006q1 |
| Subject Series: Product Summary | U | A C D P Pr | 2006q1 |
| Subject Series: Materials Consumed Summary | U | A C D P Pr | 2006q1 |
| Subject Series: Concentration Ratios | U | A C D P | 2006q1 |
| Location of Manufacturing | U S  C P | A C | 2006q2 |
| **Transportation and Warehousing** | | | |
| Vehicle Inventory and Use Survey | U S | . C . P Pr | 2003q3-04q4 |
| Commodity Flow Survey | U S | . C . P Pr | 2003q4-04q4 |

Geographic options: U = United States; S = States; M = MAs; C = Counties; P = Places; Z = Zip Codes.
Media options: A = American FactFinder (Internet); C = CD-ROM; D = Drill-down hyptertext; P = PDF; Pr = Printed report reports.

value of shipments reported in manufacturing reports since sales and the equivalent variables are always reported in thousands of dollars.

Most reports mentioned in this chapter include only establishments with paid employees. In terms of sales, that omits the roughly 3 percent of all sales coming from establishments without any employees. But if you are counting numbers of companies, nearly three-fourths of businesses are nonemployer businesses. Statistics about nonemployers are available for all sec-

tors of the economy for 1992, 1997, and all years after 1997.

It is important to remember that the definitions of all industry sectors changed in 1997 with the introduction of NAICS. This was not a bad thing. For example, under the SIC system all gas stations were lumped together; in NAICS they are split into gas stations with convenience stores and gas stations without convenience stores. The bridge tables allow you to determine how the SIC industry was divided into the

NAICS industries. All of the 2002 Economic Census reports used NAICS, while the 1997 Economic Census still had some reports showing data using the SIC system. It should be noted that the NAICS 2002 system differs from NAICS 1997, but the changes were internal to each of the affected sectors.

We'll begin our look at the reports with the *Advance* report.

## ADVANCE REPORT

The *Advance* report provides a preliminary look at data for the whole economy. It is the first report to be released, generally within fifteen months after the end of the reference year. The data are preliminary and will be superseded as more detailed geographic area and industry reports are published. A major reason for revising data between the *Advance* report and the later reports is that review of the data at the detailed industry or area level sometimes reveals errors of classification, omission, or double-counting not initially apparent. Once additional reports are released for a specific industry, they should be used instead of the *Advance* report. Thus, there is no point in referring now to the 1997 *Advance* report.

The 2002 *Advance* report contains only national level data, and shows just the sectors and sub-sectors, not detailed industries. Nonemployer businesses are excluded from this report.

The 2002 *Advance* report contains two tables: Table 1, Advance Summary Statistics for the United States: 2002, and Table 2, Advance Comparative Statistics for the United States: 2002 and 1997. The data in the tables are preliminary and Table 2 is updated in the *Comparative Statistics* report the following year. While Table 1 is limited to current data, Table 2 shows figures for the current and past census, making possible calculations of percent change over the five-year period. Both tables give figures on number of establishments, value of sale, receipts, revenue, or shipments in thousands of dollars, annual payroll in thousands of dollars, and number of paid employees.

## INDUSTRY REPORTS

This series of reports presents the most subject detail about any specific industry. There is a separate report for each industry. While these reports include very specific information about each industry, most of this information is at the national level—with some state-level data also being presented.

The information from these reports is the data that goes into making the Bureau of Economic Analysis's Input/Output tables. Researchers looking at specific industries also use this information.

In the past these reports have only been prepared for the goods producing industries, namely the mining, construction, and manufacturing sectors. Starting with the 2002 Economic Census, this series covers all sectors, however since those reports were not available to the authors at the time of the writing, you will see the information presented in the three sectors that did release industry reports in 1997: mining, construction, and manufacturing. Due to the differing nature of the various sectors, there may be differences in the reports produced for each sector. It is important to note that the industry reports for the service producing sectors will not contain any state data or data about the materials used by these industries.

Industry reports generally include three types of statistics:

- **Industry Statistics**—general and detailed statistics for the NAICS industry with basic data by state, and separately by employment size of establishment.
- **Product Statistics** (manufacturing and mining)—Shipments for 2002 and 1997 classified by seven-digit product class and ten-digit North American Product Classification System (NAPCS). While the seven- and ten-digit product codes are extensions of the six-digit NAICS codes, these tables include shipments of producers of these products who are not classified in this industry, and exclude those shipments of establishments in this industry that are primarily classified outside this industry. For example dog food manufacturing would be further divided into canned as well as dry and semi-moist shipped in packages less than 25 pounds and those shipped in more than 25 pound packages. It is reasonable to expect the Census Bureau to also include product statistics in the service sectors where products have been defined under NAPCS.
- **Materials Consumed** (manufacturing and mining)—As shown in Figure 5.2, you can see the amount and value of the materials used by a specific industry. The materials consumed table is the best place for wholesalers looking to market their product. Searching the CD-ROM version by product code, you can see which industries use particular materials, how much they use, and what they spend on those materials.

Figure 5.2
Materials Consumed by Kind: 1997 and 1992

| NAICS material code | Material consumed | 1997 | | 1992 | |
|---|---|---|---|---|---|
| | | Quantity | Delivered cost ($1,000) | Quantity | Delivered cost ($1,000) |
| **311111** | **DOG & CAT FOOD MFG** | | | | |
| 11114001 | Wheat ......1,000 s tons.. | 260.8 | 37 755 | 238.3 | 27 245 |
| 11115001 | Field corn, whole grain ......mil lb.. | 5 485.9 | 337 791 | S | 168 736 |
| 11119901 | Oats ......1,000 s tons.. | 13.8 | 2 630 | D | D |
| 11119903 | Barley ......1,000 s tons.. | 11.1 | 3 064 | 4.7 | 1 209 |
| 11119905 | Sorghum ......1,000 s tons.. | D | D | 36.7 | 5 390 |
| 31121101 | Wheat flour ......1,000 cwt.. | S | 60 013 | 3 375.5 | 27 421 |
| 31121115 | Wheat millfeed and screenings ......1,000 s tons.. | S | 57 355 | F360.4 | 34 770 |
| 31122207 | Soybean millfeed and screenings ......1,000 s tons.. | 51.6 | 10 125 | 37.7 | 7 720 |
| 31121135 | Other millfeed and screenings ......1,000 s tons.. | F29.9 | 5 711 | D | D |
| 31121137 | Hominy feed and corn meal ......1,000 s tons.. | 21.1 | 5 343 | N | N |
| 31122109 | Corn gluten feed and meal ......1,000 s tons.. | 489.1 | 136 512 | F334.3 | 80 521 |
| 31121900 | Alfalfa meal, excluding alfalfa hay ......1,000 s tons.. | D | D | 10.5 | 1 590 |
| 31131003 | Sugar, cane and beet (in terms of sugar solids) ......1,000 s tons.. | S | 9 752 | | 5 762 |
| 31131007 | Molasses ......1,000 s tons.. | S | 503 | 2.6 | 302 |
| 31122307 | Cottonseed cake and meal ......1,000 s tons.. | D | D | D | D |
| 31100017 | Fats and oils ......1,000 s tons.. | 463.9 | 174 202 | F272.1 | 92 840 |
| 31161303 | Meat meal and tankage ......1,000 s tons.. | P1 075.7 | 318 622 | F941.3 | 194 778 |
| 31161305 | Poultry leather and byproducts meal ......1,000 s tons.. | 469.5 | 205 682 | 320.0 | 118 422 |
| 31170000 | Fish meal and solubles (dry weight equivalent) ......1,000 s tons.. | 225.7 | 101 058 | 116.8 | 50 626 |
| 31212000 | Brewers' and distillers' grains ......1,000 s tons.. | 233.3 | 70 877 | 111.7 | 21 515 |
| 31122205 | Soybean cake and meal ......1,000 s tons.. | 627.1 | 154 191 | S | 150 272 |
| 32518827 | Calcium ......1,000 s tons.. | F71.2 | 3 029 | 4 | 4 625 |
| 32518837 | Phosphorus, elemental (technical) ......1,000 s tons.. | S | 17 882 | 915.2 | 11 936 |
| 31194205 | Salt ......1,000 s tons.. | S | 2 767 | 49.0 | 4 787 |
| 32518841 | Other minerals, except trace minerals ......1,000 s tons.. | 20.9 | 13 663 | 920.2 | 8 744 |
| 32541109 | Vitamins ...... | X | 44 219 | X | 24 593 |
| 32541111 | Drugs and antibiotics ...... | X | D | X | 406 |
| 32541105 | Other microingredients, including trace minerals ...... | X | 65 670 | X | 47 562 |
| 32221001 | Paperboard containers, boxes, and corrugated paperboard ...... | X | 83 603 | X | 117 451 |
| 001900A1 | Packaging paper and plastics film, coated and laminated ...... | X | 94 159 | X | 36 281 |
| 31491101 | Bags, textile (burlap, cotton, polypropylene, etc.) ...... | X | D | X | D |
| 001900A3 | Bags, plastics, foil, and coated paper ...... | X | 138 999 | X | 88 754 |
| 32222401 | Bags, uncoated paper and multiwall ...... | X | 102 370 | X | 90 834 |
| 33243101 | Metal cans, can lids and ends ...... | X | 386 978 | X | 291 774 |
| 00970099 | All other materials and components, parts, containers, and supplies ...... | X | 629 322 | X | 564 013 |
| 00971000 | Materials, ingredients, containers, and supplies, n.s.k. ...... | X | 434 742 | X | 122 289 |

**Table 5.2**
**Geographic Areas in the Economic Census by Sector**

| Sector | States | MA | Counties | Places 2500+ | ZIP Codes |
|---|---|---|---|---|---|
| Mining | X | | | | |
| Utilities | X | X | | | |
| Construction | X | | | | |
| Manufacturing | X | X | X | X | X |
| Wholesale Trade | X | X | X | X | |
| Retail Trade | X | X | X | X | X |
| Transportation and Warehousing | X | X | | | |
| Information | X | X | X | X | |
| Finance and Insurance | X | X | | | |
| Real Estate and Rental and Leasing | X | X | X | X | |
| Professional, Scientific, and Technical Services | X | X | T | T | T |
| Management of Companies and Enterprises | X | | | | |
| Administrative and Support and Waste Management and Remediation Services | X | X | X | X | X |
| Educational Services | X | X | T | T | T |
| Health Care and Social Assistance | X | X | T | T | T |
| Arts, Entertainment and Recreation | X | X | T | T | T |
| Accommodation and Food Services | X | X | X | X | X |
| Other Services (Except Public Administration) | X | X | T | T | T |

X = Reported in 1997 and 2002 Economic Censuses
T = Only taxable businesses reported in 1997; both taxable and tax-exempt businesses reported in 2002.

Much of the data in the Industry Series are superseded by later reports. Key statistics in the Geographic Area Series and Subject Series eventually replace the most widely used data in the Industry Series. The differences are usually not large, but, in general, now that all reports are available, national numbers from the 1997 Economic Census should first be sought in the "Summary" reports for manufacturing, mining, and construction, and the Industry Series should be used primarily for those data not shown in other reports.

## GEOGRAPHIC AREA SERIES

*Geographic Area* reports feature the number of establishments, the number of employees, annual payroll, employment, and sales or other measures of revenue—classified by NAICS industry for each state.

In goods producing sectors additional variables are shown, for example the number of production workers, value added, cost of materials, etc. Goods producing sector reports also include information on the operating characteristics (selected types of expenses, etc.) but only for the sector as a whole and just for the state as a whole.

Depending on the sector, these may also show data for the metropolitan areas, counties, and places within a state. Area reports for mining also include additional industry statistics and offshore areas. Table 5.2 shows the specific types of geographic areas covered for each sector.

Except for the broadest sector totals, each industry category must meet some threshold in order to be shown for a particular area. Thresholds vary from sector to sector, or even industry to industry. The most stringent are in manufacturing, where industry categories, including manufacturing as a whole, must have at least 500 employees in order to be shown for cities or counties. In general, the larger the area, the more industry detail that is available. Thus, a county with many manufacturing establishments is likely to have more industry detail in the manufacturing report than a county with fewer manufacturing establishments. Because there are more retail establishments than establishments in other sectors, retail trade reports generally have more industries shown for smaller counties and cities than do other sectors.

Within a report the types of geographic areas that might be reported are

- **States**—States are the primary governmental divisions of the United States. The District of Columbia is treated as a statistical equivalent of a state for census purposes.
- **Metropolitan Areas/Core Based Statistical Areas**—These two types of areas are groups of socio-economically integrated counties around an urban center. They are defined by the Office of Management and Budget (OMB) based on commuting data from the most recent population and housing census. Metropolitan Areas, which include Metropolitan Statistical Areas (MSA), Primary Metropolitan Statistical Areas (PMSA), and Consolidated Metropolitan Statistical Areas (CMSA) were used in the 1997 Economic Census. After the 2000 Census, OMB changed the whole concept to Core Based Statistical Areas, which include Metropolitan Statistical Areas, Micropolitan Statistical Areas, Combined Statistical Areas, and Metropolitan Divisions. The 2002 Economic Census is one of the first statistical data series to use the Core Based Statistical Areas.
- **Counties**—Counties and their equivalents, 3,141 in all, are the primary political and administrative divisions of states. These areas are called parishes in Louisiana. In Alaska, 23 boroughs and "census areas" are treated as county equivalents for census purposes. Several cities (Baltimore, MD, St. Louis, MO, Carson City, NV, and 41 cities in Virginia) are independent of any county organization and, because they constitute primary divisions of their states, are accorded the same treatment as counties in census tabulations. The part of Yellowstone National Park in Montana is treated as a county equivalent. The District of Columbia has no primary divisions, and the entire area is considered equivalent to a county for statistical purposes. Kalawao County, HI, is combined with Maui County for statistical purposes.

- **Economic Places**—The Economic Census provides information for legally defined, incorporated municipalities (cities, towns, villages, and boroughs) with 2,500 or more inhabitants as of the most recent population census. Hawaii does not have incorporated places that are recognized for census purposes, so data there are provided for census designated places (CDP's) with 2,500 or more inhabitants. All told, data are presented for 6,920 places in the United States. Additionally, county subdivisions (usually towns or townships) with a population of 10,000 or more are recognized as economic places in the twelve states with strong minor civil divisions—Michigan, Minnesota, the six New England states, New Jersey, New York, Pennsylvania, and Wisconsin. These 669 towns and townships are presented in the same tables as places.
- **Regions**—These are groups of states and are shown only in the U.S. data for the construction sector. There are four regions:

  - *Northeast Region:* Maine, New Hampshire, Vermont, Massachusetts, Rhode Island, Connecticut, New York, New Jersey, Pennsylvania
  - *Midwest Region:* Ohio, Indiana, Illinois, Michigan, Wisconsin, Minnesota, Iowa, Missouri, North Dakota, South Dakota, Nebraska, Kansas
  - *South Region:* Delaware, Maryland, District of Columbia, Virginia, West Virginia, North Carolina, South Carolina, Georgia, Florida, Kentucky, Tennessee, Alabama, Mississippi, Arkansas, Louisiana, Oklahoma, Texas
  - *West Region:* Montana, Idaho, Wyoming, Colorado, New Mexico, Arizona, Utah, Nevada, Washington, Oregon, California, Alaska, Hawaii

Geographic area reports are issued state-by-state for all 18 sectors (except Sector 55, Management of Companies and Enterprises). While that adds up to nearly 900 individual reports in page-image (PDF) format, there is generally only one data file of geographic area series statistics for each sector on the CD-ROM and in American FactFinder. Further, the CD-ROM and AFF consolidate the four core statistics for all industries and all areas for ease in generating statistics that cross sector lines in the Economy-Wide Key Statistics file.

## ZIP CODES

Since they are heavily used in marketing and in administrative records, there has been a strong demand for the Census Bureau to produce data by ZIP Code. Additionally, in larger cities this is one way to identify what is happening within the city. To meet these demands, the Census Bureau produces Economic Census data by ZIP Codes.

It is important to remember that ZIP Codes are administrative entities of the U.S. Postal Service. ZIP Codes generally do not coincide with the Census Bureau's geographic or political areas (they cross all types of boundaries—even state borders), and they change according to postal requirements. Most ZIP Codes do not have specific boundaries, and their implied boundaries do not necessarily follow clearly identifiable physical features. At the time of the Economic Censuses, there were about 40,000 ZIP Codes, although several thousand had no business activity and are not included in files. When looking at these data, it is best to view it as a rough sketch of the area, rather than a high quality photograph.

Limited statistics are summarized for individual five-digit ZIP Codes in manufacturing, retail trade, and several of the service sectors. These statistics are generally limited to a count of the establishments in each industry or kind of business, further classified by size. In addition, statistics on employment, payrolls, and sales or receipts are presented in ranges for nonmanufacturing businesses by sector within a ZIP Code, not by individual kind of business. Because business activity in many ZIP codes is dominated by a very small number of establishments, these aggregates are shown only in ranges. *ZIP Code Statistics* (CD-ROM database) presents counts of establishments by employee size range for five-digit ZIP Codes in 9 of the 18 sectors covered in the Economic Census:

- Manufacturing
- Retail Trade
- Professional, Scientific, and Technical Services
- Administrative and Support and Waste Management and Remediation Services
- Educational Services
- Health Care and Social Assistance
- Arts, Entertainment, and Recreation
- Accommodation and Food service
- Other Services (except Public Administration)

These sectors include roughly 70 percent of employees counted in the economic census.

The statistics shown for all of these sectors include the count of establishments in several employment-size categories, typically establishments with fewer than 5 employees, 5 to 9 employees, 10 to 19 employees, 20 to 49 employees, 50 to 99 employees, and 100

employees or more. For eight of the sectors there are also counts of establishments by size of sales or receipts.

## SUBJECT SERIES

In addition to the industry reports, in each industry there are one or more reports in most sectors that allow users to look at additional dimensions when analyzing a specific industry. The data in these reports are primarily shown at the national level, but some state data are available for some topics. Common to most sectors are statistics on the sources of revenues or sales, establishment and firm size (e.g., for differentiating big and small businesses), and capital expenditures and assets. Other topics include information on legal form of organization (corporations, partnerships, and individual proprietorships), and measures that are unique to a particular sector—such as the number of hotel rooms in the accommodations and food services sector. Finally, *Summary* reports for manufacturing, mining, and construction supersede key statistics in the Industry Series reports published much earlier.

### Source of Revenue/Merchandise Line Sales/Commodity Line Sales

The *Merchandise Line Sales, Commodity Line Sales,* and *Source of Receipts or Revenue* reports show what types of merchandise or services are being sold by the businesses in a specific industry. These reports also show which industries are selling specific types of products. While the PDF versions of wholesale, retail, and accommodation and food services reports show only national data, state and metropolitan area data are available in the various electronic formats.

The *Merchandise Line Sales* reports cover the retail trade and accommodations and food service sectors. The *Commodity Line Sales* reports cover the wholesale trade sector. And the *Sources of Revenues* or *Sources of Receipts* reports cover the various service, utilities, and finance and insurance sectors.

While there are no Line Sales reports for manufacturing, mining, and construction, Industry Series reports for manufacturing and mining include detailed data by product class and product. The construction industry reports include data classified by type of construction.

An example of merchandise line data is shown in Figure 5.3. In the retail report one can examine what merchandise lines are sold in pet stores. It is interest-

Figure 5.3
Merchandise Lines Sold with a Pet Store

[Includes only establishments with payroll. For meaning of abbreviations and symbols, see introductory text. For explanation of terms, see Appendix A]

| NAICS code and ML code | Kind of business and merchandise line | Establishments handling merchandise line — Number | Establishments handling merchandise line — Total sales ($1,000) | Merchandise line sales — Amount ($1,000) | As percent of total sales of — Establishments handling line | As percent of total sales of — All establishments[1] | Sales of establishments reporting merchandise line sales as percent of total sales |
|---|---|---|---|---|---|---|---|
| 4539 | Other miscellaneous store retailers—Con. | | | | | | |
| 0460 | Toys, hobby goods, & games (including video & electronic games & wheel goods, except bicycles) | 1 473 | 820 878 | 73 331 | 8.9 | .2 | X |
| 0490 | Optical goods (including eyeglasses, contact lenses, sunglasses, etc) | 75 | 35 390 | 699 | 1.7 | Z | X |
| 0500 | Sporting goods (including boats, bicycles, parts & accessories, etc) | 2 408 | 950 336 | 490 436 | 51.6 | 1.4 | Z |
| 0590 | Recreational vehicles, parts & accessories | 152 | 351 816 | 44 065 | 12.5 | .1 | X |
| 0600 | Hardware, tools, & plumbing & electrical supplies | 308 | 155 944 | 17 293 | 11.1 | .1 | X |
| 0620 | Lawn, garden, & farm equipment & supplies, cut flowers, plants & shrubs, fertilizers, etc. | 799 | 429 824 | 96 534 | 20.1 | .3 | X |
| 0640 | Dimensional lumber & other building/structural materials & supplies | 901 | 1 008 012 | 347 489 | 34.5 | 1.0 | X |
| 0670 | Paint & sundries | 91 | 46 826 | 4 606 | 9.8 | Z | X |
| 0680 | Manufactured (mobile) homes | 5 485 | 13 347 491 | 12 945 967 | 97.0 | 38.1 | X |
| 0690 | Wallpaper & other flexible wallcoverings | 13 | 2 950 | 197 | 6.7 | Z | X |
| 0700 | Automobiles, vans, trucks, & other powered transportation vehicles (motorcycles, motor scooters, motorbikes) | 137 | 230 339 | 21 842 | 9.5 | .1 | X |
| 0720 | Automotive fuels | 123 | 166 940 | 28 550 | 17.1 | .1 | X |
| 0730 | Automotive lubricants (oil, greases, etc) | 165 | 152 189 | 1 556 | 1.0 | Z | X |
| 0740 | Automotive tires, tubes, batteries, parts, & accessories | 46 | 50 242 | 3 209 | 6.4 | Z | X |
| 0790 | Household fuels (oil, LP gas, wood, & coal) | 73 | 55 081 | 3 419 | 6.2 | Z | X |
| 0800 | Pets, pet foods, & pet supplies | 8 450 | 5 565 643 | 5 237 477 | 94.1 | 15.4 | X |
| 0850 | All other merchandise | 22 786 | 12 355 872 | 9 726 718 | 78.7 | 28.7 | X |
| 9810 | Unclassified merchandise | 2 855 | 3 174 982 | 332 900 | 10.5 | 1.0 | X |
| 9900 | Nonmerchandise receipts, excluding sales & other taxes | 6 633 | 7 729 323 | 627 592 | 8.1 | 1.8 | X |
| 45331 | Pet & pet supplies stores | 8 318 | X | 5 492 749 | X | 100.0 | 82.2 |
| 0100 | Groceries & other foods for human consumption off the premises | 23 | 17 334 | 1 972 | 11.4 | Z | X |
| 0200 | Men's wear | 36 | 20 018 | 1 206 | 6.0 | Z | X |
| 0220 | Women's, juniors', & misses' wear | 21 | 6 893 | 148 | 2.1 | Z | X |
| 0290 | Footwear (including accessories) | 38 | 18 963 | 761 | 4.0 | Z | X |
| 0330 | Audio equipment & musical instruments & supplies (including radios, stereos, CDs, sheet music, etc) | 23 | 7 011 | 127 | 1.8 | Z | X |
| 0380 | Kitchenware & home furnishings (incl cookware, cooking access, dinnerware, giftware, decorative access, mirrors, closet & bathroom access, etc) | 12 | 6 671 | 267 | 4.0 | Z | X |
| 0400 | Jewelry (including watches & watch attachments, novelty jewelry, etc) | 98 | 24 369 | 2 197 | 9.0 | Z | X |
| 0420 | Books | 1 887 | 2 206 212 | 90 757 | 1.4 | .6 | X |
| 0460 | Toys, hobby goods, & games (including video & electronic games & wheel goods, except bicycles) | 31 | 8 749 | 709 | 8.1 | Z | X |
| 0490 | Optical goods (including eyeglasses, contact lenses, sunglasses, etc) | 20 | 3 869 | 67 | 1.7 | Z | X |
| 0500 | Sporting goods (including boats, bicycles, parts & accessories, etc) | 78 | 38 996 | 2 261 | 5.8 | Z | X |
| 0600 | Hardware, tools, & plumbing & electrical supplies | 89 | 46 172 | 2 586 | 5.6 | Z | X |
| 0620 | Lawn, garden, & farm equipment & supplies, cut flowers, plants & shrubs, fertilizers, etc. | 540 | 298 829 | 51 662 | 17.3 | .9 | X |
| 0640 | Dimensional lumber & other building/structural materials & supplies | 12 | 8 219 | 403 | 4.9 | Z | X |
| 0670 | Paint & sundries | 14 | 7 115 | 225 | 3.2 | Z | X |
| 0730 | Automotive lubricants (oil, greases, etc) | 24 | 14 855 | 408 | 2.7 | Z | X |
| 0790 | Household fuels (oil, LP gas, wood, & coal) | 30 | 19 594 | 989 | 5.0 | Z | X |
| 0900 | Pets, pet foods, & pet supplies | 8 318 | 5 492 749 | 5 232 209 | 95.3 | 95.3 | 63.7 |
| 0901 | Pets | 6 990 | 4 414 056 | 351 732 | 8.0 | 6.4 | X |
| 0902 | Pet foods | 7 965 | 5 221 996 | 2 035 434 | 39.0 | 37.1 | X |
| 0903 | Pet supplies | 7 504 | 5 245 833 | 2 061 702 | 39.3 | 37.5 | X |
| 0904 | Aquarium products & fish | 7 165 | 4 960 118 | 783 341 | 15.8 | 14.3 | X |
| 0850 | All other merchandise | 256 | 103 238 | 10 881 | 10.5 | .2 | X |
| 0883 | All other merchandise | 256 | 103 238 | 10 881 | 10.5 | .2 | X |
| 9810 | Unclassified merchandise | 468 | 217 705 | 90 901 | 13.9 | .6 | X |
| 9900 | Nonmerchandise receipts, excluding sales & other taxes | 2 183 | 2 645 339 | 120 768 | 4.6 | 2.2 | 76.6 |
| 9942 | Pet care services (including pet boarding, grooming, & other pet care services) | 2 047 | 2 584 545 | 114 924 | 4.4 | 2.1 | X |
| 9965 | All other nonmerchandise receipts | 223 | 109 564 | 5 844 | 5.3 | .1 | X |

ing to note that pets account for just $352 million worth of sales out of total industry sales of nearly $5.5 billion. Also, groceries and other foods for human consumption off the premises represent another $2 million in sales for these types of stores.

Figure 5.4 illustrates the percent of the broad line of pets and pet supplies sales accounted for by various kinds of businesses (i.e., pet store or supermarket).

Someone in the business of selling pet food to retailers would find this information very interesting. No surprise that most pet supplies are sold in pet stores across the United States, except for Washington, D.C. (line 8), where 65.5 percent of all pet supplies are sold in supermarkets. If this table had been sorted by total sales totals, it would have shown a different story.

*Source of Receipts* or *Revenue* reports focus primarily at the national level, but include selected data by state in both PDF and in database files. The lines or sources of receipts or revenue shown vary greatly industry to industry, unlike retail and wholesale trade, where certain broad lines are shown for all types of stores.

## Establishment/Firm Size

The *Establishment and Firm Size (including Legal Form of Organization)* reports present data on the number of establishments, sales, payroll, and employment, cross-tabulated by size of establishment, by size of company, by concentration, and by legal form of organization, for the United States in each industry. Legal forms of organizations include corporations, individual proprietorships, partnerships, cooperative associations, and other legal forms of organization. This sounds confusing until you realize that these tables are used to show concentration for firms in an industry from various perspectives. This report slices and dices the data so you can see if there are firms that can monopolize an industry.

In the case of direct mail advertising (as shown in Figure 5.5), there are 3,454 establishments. Of those, 501 were not operating for the entire year, probably because the establishment came into being or closed during the year. Of the 2,953 who were operating all year, 186 of them made over $10 million in revenue and three establishments made less than $10,000. There were 1,266 establishments that made over $1 million. This bit of knowledge is wonderful when looking for industries with high revenue generation.

Of course you should also look at their expenses, the employee per establishment ratio, and their diversity of revenue line from other census reports before you invest too much in the industry.

National level details are covered in the five columns: number of establishments, receipts ($1,000), annual payroll ($1,000), first-quarter payroll ($1,000), and number of paid employees for pay period including March 12. The tables cover employment and revenue sizes for establishments, employment and revenue sizes of firms, single units and multi-units, and concentration by largest firms. For the table grouped by largest firms you can see by the top four, eight, twenty, and fifty firms. In five sectors, data for firms subject to federal income tax are shown separate from data for tax-exempt firms.

The last table in the report shows the legal forms of organization of firms. Note that individual proprietorships are *not* the same as nonemployers. Nonemployers are not represented in any of these tables. Figure 5.6 show that corporations dominate direct mail advertising, accounting for 84 percent of all establishments and 96 percent of all receipts.

In the cases of manufacturing, mining, and construction, establishment size statistics are found in the Industry Series and general summary since there are no *Establishment and Firm Size* reports for these sectors. The Economic Census does not produce any firm size statistics for these three sectors.

For manufacturing there is a Subject Series called the *Concentration Ratios in Manufacturing*. It contains three tables: share of industry statistics for companies ranked by value added; share of value of shipments accounted for by the four, eight, twenty, and fifty largest companies in each of the three-, four-, five-, and six-digit NAICS industries; and share of value added accounted for by the four, eight, twenty, and fifty largest companies in each of the three-, four-, five-, and six-digit NAICS industries. The tables have common column headers plus the Herfindahl-Hirschmann index.

The Herfindahl-Hirschmann index is calculated by summing the squares of the individual company percentages for the fifty largest companies or the universe if there are fewer than 50 companies, whichever accounts for fewer companies. It is used when judging if an industry is too concentrated and might be appropriate for antitrust action. An industry with an index reading of 1,000 is considered highly concentrated and is closely monitored.

Figure 5.4
Sample CD-ROM Merchandise Line Table Showing Type of Store and Geography

| ROW # | Geography | 1997 NAICS code | NAICS Industry | Merchandise line (ML) code | Merchandise line (ML) | Number of establishments | Sales ($1,000) | Broad ln sls for this NAICS(%) |
|---|---|---|---|---|---|---|---|---|
| | | | Pets and pet supplies line of sales by geography | | | | | |
| 1 | Omaha, NE--IA MSA | 453910 | Pet and pet supplies stores | 0800 | Pets, pet foods, & | 19 | 47,622 | 78.8 |
| 2 | Stamford-Norwalk, CT PMSA | | | | | 19 | 23,285 | 70.4 |
| 3 | Fargo-Moorhead, ND--MN MSA | | | | | 8 | 4,291 | 69.4 |
| 4 | Ventura, CA PMSA | | | | | 34 | 27,723 | 67.8 |
| 5 | Reading, PA MSA | | | | | 16 | 7,143 | 65.6 |
| 6 | Burlington, VT MSA | | | | | 11 | 6,431 | 65.5 |
| 7 | Phoenix-Mesa, AZ MSA | | | | | 81 | 104,794 | 65.5 |
| 8 | District of Columbia | 445110 | Supermarkets and other grocery (except convenience) | | | 50 | 9,744 | 63.9 |
| 9 | Boulder--Longmont, CO PMSA | 453910 | Pet and pet supplies stores | | | 20 | 13,317 | 63.8 |
| 10 | Madison, WI MSA | | | | | 15 | 16,698 | 63.2 |
| 11 | Danbury, CT PMSA | | | | | 15 | 8,160 | 63.2 |
| 12 | Springfield, MA MSA | | | | | 28 | 20,080 | 63.0 |
| 13 | Denver, CO PMSA | | | | | 97 | 83,780 | 62.9 |
| 14 | Rochester, MN MSA | | | | | 6 | 5,302 | 62.5 |
| 15 | San Diego, CA MSA | | | | | 121 | 95,461 | 62.3 |
| 16 | Manchester, NH PMSA | | | | | 9 | 7,025 | 62.0 |
| 17 | Denver-Boulder-Greeley, CO CMSA | | | | | 124 | 98,451 | 62.0 |
| 18 | Nassau-Suffolk, NY PMSA | | | | | 133 | 75,879 | 61.9 |
| 19 | Cleveland-Lorain-Elyria, OH PMSA | | | | | 64 | 49,291 | 61.3 |
| 20 | Champaign--Urbana, IL MSA | | | | | 7 | 5,765 | 61.2 |
| 21 | Newark, NJ PMSA | | | | | 73 | 45,341 | 61.1 |
| 22 | Des Moines, IA MSA | | | | | 19 | 11,609 | 61.0 |
| 23 | Minneapolis--St. Paul, MN--WI MSA | | | | | 128 | 99,538 | 60.9 |
| 24 | Kenosha, WI PMSA | | | | | 8 | 4,043 | 60.7 |
| 25 | Orange County, CA PMSA | | | | | 120 | 85,030 | 60.6 |
| 26 | La Crosse, WI-MN MSA | | | | | 6 | 3,827 | 60.3 |
| 27 | Detroit, MI PMSA | | | | | 174 | 152,016 | 59.5 |
| 28 | Nashua, NH PMSA | | | | | 11 | 10,647 | 59.5 |
| 29 | Lafayette, IN MSA | | | | | 9 | 5,293 | 59.2 |
| 30 | New Haven--Meriden, CT PMSA | | | | | 14 | 11,182 | 59.0 |
| 31 | Trenton, NJ PMSA | | | | | 17 | 10,968 | 59.0 |
| 32 | Jersey City, NJ PMSA | | | | | 13 | 4,843 | 58.8 |
| 33 | Los Angeles--Riverside--Orange County, CA CMSA | | | | | 505 | 384,878 | 58.6 |
| 34 | Los Angeles--Long Beach, CA PMSA | | | | | 266 | 201,120 | 58.6 |
| 35 | Baltimore, MD PMSA | | | | | 94 | 77,540 | 58.2 |
| 36 | Sacramento, CA PMSA | | | | | 61 | 53,222 | 58.1 |
| 37 | Detroit--Ann Arbor-Flint, MI CMSA | | | | | 213 | 178,962 | 58.0 |

Figure 5.5
Establishment and Firm Size Sample Table

[Includes only establishments with payroll. For meaning of abbreviations and symbols, see introductory text. For explanation of terms, see Appendix A. For method of assignment to categories shown, see Appendix C]

| NAICS code | Kind of business or operation and receipts size of establishment | Establishments (number) | Receipts ($1,000) | Annual payroll ($1,000) | First-quarter payroll ($1,000) | Paid employees for pay period including March 12 (number) |
|---|---|---|---|---|---|---|
| 54 | PROFESSIONAL, SCIENTIFIC, & TECHNICAL SERVICES—Con. | | | | | |
| 541 | Professional, scientific, & technical services—Con. | | | | | |
| 54186 | Direct mail advertising | | | | | |
| | All establishments ................. | 3 454 | 8 672 214 | 2 426 572 | 560 921 | 85 669 |
| | Establishments operated for the entire year ...... | 2 953 | 8 466 985 | 2 382 517 | 549 143 | 83 295 |
| | Establishments with receipts less than $10,000 ........... | 3 | 20 | 16 | 4 | 3 |
| | Establishments with receipts of $10,000 to $24,999 ......... | 16 | 283 | 127 | 29 | 26 |
| | Establishments with receipts of $25,000 to $49,999 ......... | 46 | 1 781 | 745 | 191 | 94 |
| | Establishments with receipts of $50,000 to $99,999 ......... | 131 | 9 677 | 2 886 | 741 | 291 |
| | Establishments with receipts of $100,000 to $249,999 ......... | 398 | 69 350 | 18 182 | 4 260 | 1 267 |
| | Establishments with receipts of $250,000 to $499,999 ......... | 525 | 189 987 | 52 666 | 12 265 | 2 847 |
| | Establishments with receipts of $500,000 to $999,999 ......... | 568 | 406 431 | 118 410 | 27 434 | 5 746 |
| | Establishments with receipts of $1,000,000 to $2,499,999 ... | 603 | 957 259 | 283 608 | 63 717 | 12 272 |
| | Establishments with receipts of $2,500,000 to $4,999,999 ... | 308 | 1 095 366 | 341 408 | 75 202 | 12 587 |
| | Establishments with receipts of $5,000,000 to $9,999,999 ... | 169 | 1 144 350 | 349 971 | 81 375 | 12 258 |
| | Establishments with receipts of $10,000,000 or more ......... | 186 | 4 592 481 | 1 214 498 | 283 925 | 35 904 |
| | Establishments not operated for the entire year............ | 501 | 205 229 | 44 055 | 11 778 | 2 374 |

Figure 5.6
Legal Form of Organization—Sample Taken from the CD-ROM

| | | | | E9754S7 - Professional, Scientific, and Technical Services: Establishment and Firm Size:  Legal Form of Organization:1997 | | | | |
|---|---|---|---|---|---|---|---|---|
| 1997 NAICS code | NAICS Industry | Tax Status | Legal Form of Org of Estabs | Number of establishments | Receipts ($1,000) | Annual payroll ($1,000) | First quarter payroll ($1,000) | Number of employees |
| | | | All establishments | 3,454 | 8,672,214 | 2,426,572 | 560,921 | 85,669 |
| | | | Corporations | 2,898 | 8,312,893 | 2,365,644 | 546,935 | 82,154 |
| 54186 | Direct mail advertising | Taxable establishments | Individual proprietorships | 430 | 202,098 | 35,814 | 8,431 | 2,438 |
| | | | Partnerships | 122 | D | D | D | 1,000 to 2,499 employees |
| | | | Other legal forms of organization | 4 | D | D | D | 20 to 99 employees |

## Miscellaneous Subjects

The *Miscellaneous Subjects* reports are hard to describe because they vary greatly from one sector to the next. Even within a single sector, some data might be shown for some industries, not others. Knowing what can be found in a report is a boon to any researcher. In Table 5.3 you can see the tables available for each industry sectors. The 1997 Economic Census even contains a *Miscellaneous Subject* report for Auxiliaries.

The auxiliaries sector includes establishments with payroll mainly engaged in providing services to one or more establishments of the same enterprise, excluding corporate, subsidiary, and regional managing offices. These establishments generally do not produce any products nor do they provide services for customers outside the enterprise, but may do so as a secondary activity.

Generally, the data are shown only at the national level.

## Summary

After the publication of all industry, area, and subject reports for each sector, a single volume is published that summarizes the most widely used tables about that sector from all of the previously issued reports. These *Summary* reports are not published until about four years after the reference year. Nearly all of the tables are at the national level; sometimes the reports may have core statistics for states. Additional summary reports consolidate product data and materials consumed by kind for the manufacturing and mining sectors. If you need a quick way to learn an industry sector, this is the source to read. These reports are part of the 1997 Economic Census, but they are being produced as part of the 2002 Economic Census only for manufacturing, mining, and construction.

## LOCATION OF MANUFACTURING PLANTS/LOCATION OF MINING

The *Location of Manufacturing Plants* and the *Location of Mining* reports presents counts of establishments by employment-size class by detailed NAICS for the U.S., states, counties, and places. The statistics shown for each industry-area combination are the counts of establishments in several employment-size categories: establishments with 1 to 19 employees, 20 to 49, 50 to 99, 100 to 249, 250 to 499, 500 to 999, and 1,000 employees or more. These establishment counts by size class are not considered to be a disclo-

sure of confidential information, so a data line is present for every 6-digit industry with one or more establishments within an area. Thus, this report is a useful complement to the manufacturing Geographic Area Series, where no data are shown for industries or industry groups with fewer than 500 employees in a county or city.

The *Location of Mining Operations* data files include statistics on the number of establishments for three- and six-digit NAICS industry by state and offshore area by employment size of the establishment. The state reports for the mining industries include data at the state level and some offshore areas. Data are not available below the state level.

Data for offshore areas that are part of Alaska, California, Louisiana, and Texas are included in their respective state area reports and represent offshore operations on all these state offshore leases and all federal offshore leases defined by their state plane coordinate systems. State offshore areas include the areas extending from the coastline up to three geographical miles distance except for Texas and Florida where they extend three marine leagues from the coastline in the Gulf of Mexico. Data for offshore areas not associated with a state are in an Offshore Areas geographic report, which includes the following areas:

- Northern Gulf of Mexico Offshore
- Northern Gulf of Mexico Federal Areas defined by the Universal Transverse Mercator Coordinate System (including areas generally south of the state plane coordinate systems of Louisiana and Texas)
- Pacific Offshore
- Pacific Federal Areas defined by the Universal Transverse Mercator Coordinate System

The *Location of Manufacturing* data files contain statistics on the number of establishments for the three- and six-digit NAICS industry by state, county, place, and ZIP Code by employment-size of the establishment.

## ECONOMY-WIDE STATISTICS SERIES

Economic Census reports have traditionally been published sector by sector. (Indeed, prior to 1954, the Census of Manufactures wasn't even collected for the same time period as the other economic censuses.) The *Economy-Wide Statistics* titles present information across all (or at least most) sectors. Some of these titles allow data users to examine changes over time,

**Table 5.3**
**Miscellaneous Subject Topics by Sector**

| Sector | Miscellaneous Subject Topics |
|---|---|
| Utilities | Utility revenue by class of customer, Exported energy to Canada and Mexico, Cost of purchased electricity for resale by utilities, Construction activity by utilities |
| Wholesale | Sales by class of customer; Employment by principal activity; End-of-year inventories; Detailed type of operation; Sales and commissions of agents, brokers, and commission merchants; Gross margin and its components for merchant wholesalers; Gross profit and its components for merchant wholesalers; Petroleum bulk stations by type of station; Bulk storage capacity by type of facility and type of product; Bulk storage capacity by type of product; Bulk storage capacity by type of product and storage capacity size; and Primary method of receiving petroleum bulk liquid products |
| Retail | Floor space by selected kind of business and Class of customer by kind of business |
| Transportation and Wholesaling | Purchased transportation by motor freight carrier; Revenue-generating equipment for passenger transportation; Cost of arranged transportation by mode of shipping; and Construction activity by pipelines |
| Information | Exported services by selected kind of business; Receipts by class of customer for telecommunications and online information services; Receipts by class of customer for cable and other program distribution services; Construction activity by selected kind of business; and Total operating expenses for libraries and archives |
| Finance and Insurance | Insurance agents and brokers; Administrative expenses; Insurance benefits paid to policyholders; and Exported services by selected kinds of business |
| Real Estate and Rental and Leasing | Real estate agents and brokers; Commissions and fees paid to co-brokerage companies; Construction expenditures; Construction expenditures by type of building; Construction expenditures by type of construction; Revenue by class of client; and Exported services by selected kinds of business |
| Professional, Scientific, and Technical Services | Exported service by selected kind of business; Receipts by class of client for selected professional, scientific, and technical services; Fees by class of client for architectural, engineering, and related services; Gross billings for advertising agencies; Personnel and payroll by occupation and legal form of organization for legal services firms subject to federal income tax; Personnel and payroll by occupation for legal services firms exempt from federal income tax; Personnel and payroll by occupation and legal form of organization for accounting, tax preparation, bookkeeping, and payroll services; Personnel by occupation and legal form of organization for engineering services; Personnel by occupation and legal form of organization for architectural services; Personnel by occupation and legal form of organization for surveying and mapping (except geophysical) services; Personnel by occupation and legal form of organization for geophysical surveying and mapping services; and Personnel by occupation and legal form of organization for computer systems design and related services |

**Table 5.3 (Continued)**
**Miscellaneous Subject Topics by Sector**

| Sector | Miscellaneous Subject Topics |
|---|---|
| Management of Companies and Enterprises | Exported services; Research and development; Establishments reporting sales; Value of inventories; Value of billings to other establishments of the same company; Sales by type; Billings by type; and Employment by function |
| Administrative and Support and Waste and Remediation Services | Exported services by selected kind of business; Leased employees by industry category and client; Fees by class of client; Fees by class of client for administrative and other support services; and Fees by class of client for travel arrangement and reservation services |
| Health and Social Services | Personnel by occupation and legal form of organization for firms subject to federal income tax; Personnel by occupation and legal form of organization for firms subject to federal income tax; Personnel by occupation and legal form of organization for firms subject to federal income tax; Personnel by occupation and legal form of organization for firms subject to federal income tax; Personnel by occupation and legal form of organization for firms exempt from federal income tax; Personnel by occupation and legal form of organization for firms subject to federal income tax; and Transferred contributions for firms exempt from federal income tax |
| Arts, Entertainment, and Recreation Services | Exported services by selected kind of business and Other sources of receipts by selected kind of business |
| Accommodations and Food Services | Primary type of foodservice; Average cost per meal; Seating capacity; Principal menu type or specialty; Sales by day-part; Concession operators; Establishments using a trade name authorized by franchiser; Distribution of contract feeding sales by facility serviced; Number of guestrooms; and Guestroom size of establishments |
| Other Services | Exported services by selected kind of business; Receipts by class of client for selected other services; Receipts from labor charges and parts installed for repair and maintenance services; and Transferred contributions for religious/grantmaking/civic/professional and similar organizations exempt from federal income tax |
| Auxiliaries | Exported services; Research and development; Establishments reporting sales; Value of inventories; Value of billings to other establishments of the same company; Sales by type; and Employment by function. |

where businesses are spending their money, or the characteristics of business owners. These reports include multiple industry sectors and are often overlooked by data users doing industry-based research using the subject, industry, and geographic series. Each of the *Economy-Wide Statistics* reports is available in PDF and on CD-ROM, but none were included in American Fact Finder (AFF) for 1997.

The Economic Census of 2002 is based on the 2002 NAICS codes and, to a limited extent, NAICS 1997. However in 1997, many of these reports classified establishments using the Standard Industrial Classification System (SIC) allowing for some comparisons between 1992 and 1997.

Most of these reports present data only at the national level, but a few report the data for smaller areas.

This is done largely to maintain confidentiality of individual businesses. For sample surveys, like Business Expenses Survey, producing national data costs far less than producing estimates for states or smaller areas.

All dollar values presented are expressed in current dollars; i.e., 2002 data are expressed in 2002 dollars. Consequently, when making comparisons with prior or current years, users of the data should consider the changes in prices and inflation that have occurred. All dollar values are shown in thousands of dollars.

## Comparative Statistics

The *Comparative Statistics* report compares data between the current and last Economic Censuses. This report presents the four core data items: the number of establishments; employment; payroll; and value of sales, receipts, revenue, or shipments for establishments with paid employees.

The 1997 report presents data down to the four-digit SIC levels for the U.S. and states. Selected subdivisions of four-digit SICs (assigned six-digit codes) are also included in the U.S. data. No data are given for MA, county, or places. The *Comparative Statistics* report supersedes the preliminary 2-digit SIC statistics included in the *Advance* report.

The 2002 report presents the data using the 1997 version of NAICS. In most industries there is no difference between the 1997 and 2002 versions of NAICS, but there are differences in the construction, retail, wholesale, and information sectors.

Why would you use this report? This is the report you would need to see the changes between census periods. This report is great for looking at historical trends in an industry and getting historical core data items such as number of establishments, how many employees, total payroll, and amount of sales, receipts, revenue, or shipments. As you can see in Figure 5.1, the musical instruments manufacturing industry has grown in number of businesses, value of shipments, payroll, and number of employees. However, if you look at average pay per employee, you see a very different trend. In 1992 the payroll was $27,069 per employee ($272,653,000/12,215), while in 1997 it was $22,321 per employee ($363,022,000/13,4111), a decrease of 17.5 percent.

The 1997 report is particularly useful if you wish to look at long-term trends in industries—provided you don't want to look at something more recent than 1997. If you do want to look at a trend crossing the 1997 industry classification system threshold, you should use the *Bridge* reports (described below) to link the SIC and NAICS industries. But due to changes in each industry's structure, extreme care needs to be taken when looking at long-term trends. When looking at selected industries, you will also need to look at the *2002 Bridge Between NAICS 2002 and NAICS 1997*.

## Bridge Reports

Many users are more interested in looking at how an industry has changed over time than what it looks like now. Usually this is not a problem, however, whenever there is a change in the way industries are defined, looking at time series becomes problematic. While there have been a number of changes in industrial classifications over the years, they have been relatively rare (every 10 to 15 years or so) and generally affected only a portion of the industries. But a whole new industrial classification system (NAICS) started being introduced with the 1997 Economic Census. This new system represents a complete overhaul of the nation's industrial classification system. As a result of this change, it is difficult to create time series for many industries.

The Census Bureau is well aware of the need to look at industrial changes over time (this is something that Census Bureau staff needs just as much as the rest of us). In an attempt to respond to this need, the Census Bureau has developed a set of tables showing the relationships between SIC and NAICS industries for 1997. Because there were revisions to NAICS in 2002, the Census Bureau also produced a set of bridge tables showing the relationships between the NAICS 1997 and NAICS 2002 industries, but only for those industries affected by that revision.

While we show you how to work with the bridge reports using the 1997 version as an example, the same ideas are used for the 2002 version. The 1997 *Bridge Between NAICS and SIC* presents data cross-tabulated by both the old and new classification systems, identifying the lowest common denominators between the two systems. The bridge tables define how much of each SIC category is going to each NAICS and—vice versa—thus users can identify comparability issues much more readily than any other source.

Conceptually, the bridge tables complement the correspondence tables at the end of many industry chapters of this book and in the NAICS manuals, i.e. which NAICS replaces which SIC codes. One major difference between the correspondence tables and the bridge tables is that the correspondence tables are based on the theoretical relationships between industries in the two classification systems while the bridge tables rely on the relationships shown to exist in the data actually collected in the census. In the *Bridge* report each line is extended to show core data items associated with both NAICS and SIC combinations. From that, users will be able to calculate percentages for allocation strategies and assemble time series. This is the essential resource for anyone attempting to link time series on the old and new basis or between the 1997 and 2002 versions of NAICS. Because it presents the same information classified in more than one way, the *Bridge* report has been termed the "Rosetta Stone" of industry codes.

Since the *Bridge Between NAICS and SIC* and most of the other reports using SIC are at the national level, researchers are going to have to make some assumptions when looking at time series at local levels. One assumption that needs to be made is that the mix of establishments in the specific industry being looked at is the same locally as it is nationally. Another assumption that is necessary to use the bridge tables is that the establishment mix between the two industries in the two systems has been constant over time. In many cases these assumptions may be reasonable, but in many other cases they may not be. That is a decision each individual data user needs to make. It is also possible that users will decide that the breaks and combinations of some series are simply too complicated to allow reasonable bridges between the two systems.

Most people studying economic trends will confine themselves to looking at the nation, states, and counties. County boundaries are very stable with changes being few and far between, while many places, metropolitan areas, and ZIP Codes change boundaries more frequently. Geographic comparability of sub-state areas may be a moot issue, because there are no plans to publish data for counties, places, and metropolitan areas on a basis allowing for comparison with other data (that is, SIC-based data) and researchers may be uncomfortable making the assumptions required for this type of trend analysis. Thus, questions as seemingly routine as "Did manufacturing employment in my city go up or down?" remained unanswered for the 1992 to 1997 period.

Because these data are so widely used, the *Bridge* reports are issued in print as well as in PDF form. The Web site version of the *Bridge Between NAICS and SIC* (see Figure 5.7) graphically illustrates the compa-

rability with three drawbridge symbols that show the general level of comparability between the two systems. On the Web site this symbol is also used as a link to the 1992 figures shown in *Comparative Statistics*. The graphics and percentages shown below are not included in the PDF or CD-ROM versions of *Comparative Statistics*.

Here are some clues on how to read the online version of the bridge table. All data shown vertically are hierarchal—that is some rows are nested under higher-level rows. Special food service (7223) is the industry group totals, while the food contractors (722310), caterers (722320), and mobile food services (722330) are industries. A common mistake is to try to add up the column, in this case is would lead to at least doubling the totals. In the case of drinking places (alcoholic beverages) only one industry is in the whole group. To read across, 722410 shows the NAICS code and that there is complete comparability, since the bridge is closed; then totals for the number of establishments, sales in thousands, paid employees, and annual payroll in thousands of dollars are displayed. The line below shows the SIC code, and the 97/92 symbol is used as a link to the 1992 figures shown in Comparative Statistics, similar to Figure 5.1. In the case of 2002 bridge tables, the symbol reads 02/97. Note that there are 97/92 links only for SICs, not for NAICS codes since NAICS-based data are not available for 1992. If you read across the line for mobile food service, you are informed that the data on this line represent only 6 percent of SIC 5963. The 20 in the Pt column is an arbitrary code for this part of SIC 5963 (Direct selling establishments)—the Census Bureau assigned an additional two digits to many SIC industries in order to identify subdivisions of the industry.

The bridge illustrations in Figure 5.7 show confidence in matching older classification with the newer system. Where there is complete comparability between NAICS and SIC for the 1997 Census or between 2002 and 1997 NAICS for the 2002 Census, the bridge is complete with a superstructure. When you can estimate sales or receipts data from one year to the next within 3 percent, then the drawbridge is shown as only slightly open, and if you can imagine yourself taking a little risk, you can get across. Then when the conversion between the two systems substantially disrupts comparability, a drawbridge is shown open. The time series is broken by more than 3 percent of estimated sales or receipts and probably cannot be calculated back very safely.

Figure 5.7
Sample NAICS to SIC Bridge

| NAICS | SIC | Pt | Description | Estab-lish-ments | Sales ($1,000) | Paid employees | Annual payroll ($1,000) |
|---|---|---|---|---|---|---|---|
| **7223** | | | **Special foodservices** | **28,062** | **19,407,810** | **464,870** | **5,765,977** |
| **7231** | | | **Foodservice contractors** | **18,991** | **15,159,590** | **361,996** | **4,617,362** |
| 722310 | | | Foodservice contractors | 18,991 | 15,159,590 | 361,996 | 4,617,362 |
| D | 5812 | 50 | Foodservice contractors | 18,991 | 15,159,590 | 361,996 | 4,617,362 |
| **72232** | | | **Caterers** | **6,478** | **3,368,823** | **91,191** | **978,105** |
| 722320 | | | Caterers | 6,478 | 3,368,823 | 91,191 | 978,105 |
| D | 5812 | 20 | Caterers | 6,478 | 3,368,823 | 91,191 | 978,105 |
| **72233** | | | **Mobile foodservices** | **2,593** | **879,397** | **11,683** | **170,510** |
| 722330 | | | Mobile foodservices | 2,593 | 879,397 | 11,683 | 170,510 |
| 6% of | 5963 | 20 | Mobile foodservices | 2,593 | 879,397 | 11,683 | 170,510 |

| NAICS | SIC | Pt | Description | Estab-lish-ments | Sales ($1,000) | Paid employees | Annual payroll ($1,000) |
|---|---|---|---|---|---|---|---|
| **7224** | | | **Drinking places (alcoholic beverages)** | **52,825** | **12,295,709** | **321,294** | **2,649,481** |
| **7241** | | | **Drinking places (alcoholic beverages)** | **52,825** | **12,295,709** | **321,294** | **2,649,481** |
| 722410 | | | Drinking places (alcoholic beverages) | 52,825 | 12,295,709 | 321,294 | 2,649,481 |
| | 5813 | 97/92 | Drinking places (alcoholic beverages) | 52,825 | 12,295,709 | 321,294 | 2,649,481 |

N=Not available D=Withheld to avoid disclosure

While Figure 5.7 shows that NAICS 722410 represented only 6 percent of the sales of SIC 5963, another table shows the data from the SIC perspective, and the "6% of" can be used to link directly there. Figure 5.8 shows $879,397,000 in revenue from mobile food service is the only part of SIC 5963 to be separated out, and that the remainder is now NAICS 454390 Other direct selling establishments.

## Linking the Systems for Continuous Analysis

One of the preeminent virtues of the Economic Census program is that comparable data have been collected at relatively fixed intervals and with consistent definitions across decades. Nonetheless, census reports typically included very little historical data. Comparative statistics, covering the current and most recent census, have generally been included for the United States and, in some sectors go down to the state level, in census reports prior to 1997.

One source for getting data from selected previous Economic Census is volume 1j of the 1992 Economic Censuses CD-ROM series, which includes a national time series from the *Annual Survey of Manufactures* from 1958 to 1995, and monthly retail sales from 1967 to 1994. Volume 4 of the 1992 Economic Censuses CD-ROM series, entitled Non-employer Statistics, includes the 1987 Economic Censuses Geographic Area Series files for retail trade, wholesale trade, service industries, and manufacturing in a format that mirrors their 1992 counterparts. More comprehensive data for 1987, and a few data sets for 1982 and 1977, are included on the final 1987 Economic Census CD-ROM (1e). Selected tape files from Economic Censuses 1972 to 1982 may be obtained from the National Archives and Records Administration.

Printed reports from 1992 and earlier economic censuses are no longer available for sale. Many libraries and State Data Center/Business and Industry Data Center Program participants keep historical copies of the Economic Census reports for their state. Regional Federal Depository Libraries (one or two major libraries in each state) are required to maintain as complete a collection of federal government documents, including the Economic Censuses, as they possibly can, and individual reports may be borrowed through interlibrary loan. If no other source is available, photocopies of historical census volumes can be ordered from Census Customer Services.

The introduction of NAICS with the 1997 Economic Census caused major disruptions in the availability of comparable information across time periods. From 1967 to 1987, the SIC system was updated three times (and each time a significant number of new industries was introduced into the existing framework). What was different for 1997 was that the whole framework changed. Additionally, instead of occasional revisions to the system (as occurred under the SIC system) NAICS will be reviewed and tweaked every five years. For more discussion on NAICS, see chapter 4.

It is generally easy to build a time series starting in 1997 using NAICS, but going backwards in time before 1997 can be problematic because many NAICS categories require information that was not collected in 1992 and earlier censuses. For instance, NAICS 45321, Office Supplies and Stationery Stores, differs from SIC 5943, Stationery Stores, primarily by the addition of certain office supply stores that were previously classified in wholesale trade. Census questionnaires prior to 1997 did not separately differentiate office supply stores from other kinds of office supply wholesalers, so NAICS 45321 cannot be estimated for prior periods. However, the bridge report and various assumptions allow users to estimate the true data in the past, but the validity of these assumptions needs to be considered very carefully.

While data for nearly half of the SIC industries in use in 1992 can be converted to 1997 NAICS industries easily, a substantial number of industries can only be estimated. That makes the 1997 Economic Census particularly important, because the census questionnaires gathered enough information to identify each establishment's industry using both the NAICS and SIC classification systems. The Comparative Statistics report, described above, shows the number of establishments, sales, employment, and payroll for each SIC for the nation and each state, for both 1997 and 1992. By looking at the earlier censuses, basic SIC-by-state time series can be carried backward from 1997 to 1987, and farther to the extent that particular industries are not affected by SIC changes in 1987, 1972, and 1967.

The Census Bureau had to estimate some national-level NAICS time series back to 1992 after the publication of 1997 census results. That project, intended to support time series for monthly surveys, is limited to broad industry categories within manufacturing, retail trade, and wholesale trade. The level of industry detail

Figure 5.8
Sample SIC to NAICS Bridge Table

| SIC | NAICS | Pt | Description | Establish-ments | Sales ($1,000) | Paid employees | Annual payroll ($1,000) |
|---|---|---|---|---|---|---|---|
| 596 | 97/92 | | **Nonstore retailers** | 34,308 | 86,372,426 | 399,414 | 9,199,476 |
| 5961 | | | Catalog & mail-order houses | 9,943 | 64,312,338 | 206,098 | 5,247,810 |
| N | 454110 | Σ | Electronic shopping & mail-order houses | 9,943 | N | 10,609 | N |
| | 454110 | 10 | Mail-order houses, department store merchandise | 316 | 1,306,895 | 10,609 | 200,531 |
| | 454110 | 20 | Mail-order houses, other general merchandise | 778 | D | D (10k-24999) | D |
| | 454110 | 30 | Mail-order houses, specialized merchandise | 8,778 | 53,493,615 | 167,636 | 4,342,850 |
| | 454110 | 40 | Television order, home shopping | 71 | D | D (5000-9999) | D |
| 5962 | | | Automatic merchandising machine operators | 7,070 | 6,884,497 | 66,348 | 1,333,428 |
| | 454210 | | Vending machine operators | 7,070 | 6,884,497 | 66,348 | 1,333,428 |
| 5963 | | | Direct selling establishments | 17,295 | 15,175,591 | 126,968 | 2,618,238 |
| 98% of | 454390 | Σ | Other direct selling establishments | 14,702 | 14,296,194 | 29,355 | 2,447,728 |
| | 454390 | 11 | Direct selling, furniture, home furnishings, electronics, & appl | 4,248 | 3,593,747 | 29,355 | 547,845 |
| | 454390 | 12 | Direct selling, cameras & photographic equipment | 36 | 23,546 | 148 | 3,209 |
| | 454390 | 21 | Direct selling, videos, tapes, compact discs, & records | 210 | 265,527 | 2,242 | 47,826 |
| | 454390 | 22 | Direct selling, books & magazines | 513 | 1,241,091 | 11,826 | 224,026 |
| | 454390 | 23 | Direct selling, newspapers | 540 | 245,266 | 5,407 | 52,373 |
| | 454390 | 31 | Direct selling, stationery | 137 | 105,558 | 740 | 16,573 |

published can be quite limited if the census has limited confidence in the estimates.

Anyone attempting to estimate NAICS categories prior to 1997 should recognize that many new industries reflected in NAICS did not exist to a significant extent in prior periods. The bridge tables provide information that is necessary to know about the ability to develop a time series and how to develop one, if the data user wishes to.

If you are interested in estimating a time series between NAICS and SIC industries, the following steps are one way of doing so:

1. Identify your NAICS industry.
2. Use Bridge Tables to find the closest SIC industry
   - If the bridge is complete, you will have no problems constructing time series.
   - If the draw bridge is partially open, learn the percentage that is compatible with your SIC and calculate that percentage from the 1992 numbers and make a footnote about the differences.
   - If the drawbridge is completely open, then the industry is incompatible with older SIC data, your time series will have to start with 1997. However, there *might* be enough information available by combining data on various pieces of it or building ratios between the one piece that you are interested in and the complete industry from another source, such as the 1997 County Business Patterns. It is important to remember that there are a number of critical assumptions involved with procedure and extreme caution is needed when doing this.
3. Decide how far back you want to go or can go. In doing this consider
   - Historical changes in the SIC industry definition.
   - Major changes in the industry—for example, it doesn't make sense to estimate computer retailers before the early to mid-1980s since the products they sell (personal computers, software, etc.) did not really constitute enough of a market for many retailers to specialize in at that time.
   - Some NAICS industries cannot be traced back to before 1997.
4. Build your time series
   - If data are only needed starting from 1992 use the 1997 Comparative Report.
   - If data are needed from before 1992, gather the SIC data from the sources mentioned above.

- Please note the changes in SIC code from 1987, 1972, and 1967.

5. If data are needed from 1997 forward, use the most current report and note changes in NAICS.

When reporting a time series spanning the transition year of 1997, it helps readers if you create a footnote explaining that some of the data has been estimated due to the conversion from SIC to NAICS. What you say should vary according to the amount of estimation you had to do. Including the information from the bridge tables about the relationship of the industries in the two classification systems can be very helpful. For example, the *Bridge* report will show the number and sales of those music publishers that were transferred out of publishing, along with other components of the new publishing category.

At broader levels of classification, the changes between SIC and NAICS are further confounded by the rearrangement of the industry sectors. For example, the subdivision of the SIC Services Division into five NAICS sectors and parts of four others and the addition of parts of other divisions into these same NAICS sectors means that there is no easy way to compare the SIC divisions to the NAICS sectors. Less noticeable, but perhaps more troublesome, are shifts affecting such SIC divisions—like manufacturing, wholesale trade, and retail trade—that retain their name as a sector in NAICS, but are being affected by changes in scope. Retail trade is smaller under NAICS than under SIC just because eating and drinking places, which accounted for roughly ten percent of SIC-based retail sales, were transferred to the new Accommodation and Food Services sector. Retail losses are offset partially by transfers between retail and wholesale trade, such as the office supply stores mentioned above. Manufacturing also shrinks somewhat under NAICS because significant components have been reclassified elsewhere. See chapter 4 on NAICS for more information about these changes.

## Business Expenses

This report, also called the *Business Expenditures Survey,* was prepared as part of the Company Statistics Series. It provides aggregate data on the operating expenses of businesses. Table 5.4 lists the subject covered by the industries they represent by SIC sectors. The 1997 data were classified by SIC because, at the time the sample was drawn, a sampling frame was not yet available based on NAICS. The same data are expanded and collected in the 2002 Census for the NAICS sectors.

Reports go down to the industry level for most of the report. Not all industries are represented. Data for businesses without paid employees are included for only the retail and service industries. Data on service industries include tax-exempt organizations with paid employees.

Regular economic census questionnaires for manufacturing, mining, and construction include a variety of business expenses. Those sectors were not canvassed in this survey, but data from Industry Series reports were republished in *Business Expenses*. A consequence is that the manufacturing, mining, and construction statistics in *Business Expenses* are summarized by kind of business based on the NAICS, while the business expenses for other sectors are based on SIC.

A few industries changed sectors when reclassified to a NAICS basis. For example, retail bakeries with baking on the premises moved from the retail sector on an SIC basis to manufacturing on a NAICS basis. Consult the bridge tables for SIC comparisons. In this case, expenses data for retail bakeries are tabulated in both retail (SIC-based) and manufacturing (NAICS-based). In all cases the amount of this duplication is insignificant at SIC division and NAICS sector industrial classification levels.

The federal government is the primary user of the *Business Expenditures Survey*. In particular, the Bureau of Economic Analysis (BEA), the federal agency that produces gross domestic product estimates and maintains the national economic accounts, uses Census Bureau information on expenses as an important part of the framework for the national income and product accounts, input-output tables, and economic indexes, and to fill previously identified critical gaps in underlying data in these accounts.

## Nonemployer Statistics

The *Nonemployer Statistics* report is the only source for information about the 16 million or three-quarters of the nation's companies with no paid employees. The series is useful for studying the economic activity of small businesses at various geographic levels.

*Nonemployer Statistics* summarizes the number of establishments and revenue of these companies. These nonemployers are typically self-employed individuals,

family business, or partnerships operating businesses that have chosen not to incorporate. These businesses may or may not be the owner's principal source of income. But it should be noted that in order to qualify as a business, the firm must report revenues of at least $1,000. Overall as shown in Table 5.5 these businesses accounted for about three percent of the country's business receipts in 1997.

Payroll tax records are at the heart of the Census Bureau's system for keeping its business register up to date. Since nonemployers are not included in the Bureau's business register they do not get census questionnaires and are not reflected in any of the detailed sector-specific reports. Nonemployers are, however, included in "all firms" totals in reports on minority- and women-owned business. In contrast, self-employed owners of incorporated businesses typically pay themselves wages or salary, so that the business is an employer and is counted in all of the Economic Census series.

Since there are so many nonemployer firms and establishments with such a low portion of receipts, it is necessary to consider whether you should include the information about nonemployer businesses or not. While we think about nonemployers as individual consultants and small retailers, they exist in all sections of the economy. In addition to the examples listed above you can find nonemployers in manufacturing as artisans, construction as independent contractors, health care as doctors, etc.

Nonemployer Statistics are shown for the U.S., states, metropolitan areas, and counties, but not for places. The first time the Nonemployer Statistics report covered all sectors of the economy was in 1997. Also, starting in 1997 the Census Bureau began issuing data on nonemployer businesses every year. Prior to this, limited data were issued only for the years of the Economic Censuses.

The *Nonemployer Statistics* series data are available electronically in CD-ROM and hypertext table (html) formats for the U.S., states, counties, and metropolitan statistical areas and in Portable Document Format (PDF) for the national and state levels only. No printed publications of *Nonemployer Statistics* are available. Two tabulations are presented in PDF. The national-level tabulation presents data by legal form of organization, number of establishments, and receipts by NAICS industry. The state-level tabulation only presents number of establishments and receipts by NAICS industry. The nonemployer report is updated annually by *Nonemployer Statistics,* http://www.census.

**Table 5.4**
**Business Expenditure Survey Subjects by Sector**

| Business Expenses (SIC sectors) | Wholesale | Retail | Services | Commun- ications | Truck- ing | Stor- age | Airlines |
|---|---|---|---|---|---|---|---|
| Operating Expenses by Type | | | | | | | |
| operating expenses | X | X | X | | | | |
| Payroll | X | X | X | | | | |
| payroll, as a percentage of operating expenses | X | X | X | | | | |
| employer costs for fringe | X | X | X | | | | |
| employer costs for fringe, as a percentage of operating expenses | X | X | X | | | | |
| Benefits | X | X | X | | | | |
| benefits, as a percentage of operating expenses | X | X | X | | | | |
| cost of contract labor | X | X | X | | | | |
| cost of contract labor, as a percentage of operating expenses | X | X | X | | | | |
| taxes and license fees | X | X | X | | | | |
| taxes and license fees, as a percentage of operating expenses | X | X | X | | | | |
| depreciation and amortization charges | X | X | X | | | | |
| depreciation and amortization charges, as a percentage of operating expenses | X | X | X | | | | |
| lease and rental payments | X | X | X | | | | |
| lease and rental payments, as a percentage of operating expenses | X | X | X | | | | |
| telephone and other | X | X | X | | | | |
| telephone and other, as a percentage of operating expenses | X | X | X | | | | |
| purchased communications | X | X | X | | | | |
| purchased communications, as a percentage of operating expenses | X | X | X | | | | |
| purchased utilities | X | X | X | | | | |
| purchased utilities, as a percentage of operating expenses | X | X | X | | | | |
| purchased office supplies | X | X | X | | | | |
| purchased office supplies, as a percentage of operating expenses | X | X | X | | | | |
| purchased packaging and other materials | X | X | X | | | | |
| purchased packaging and other materials, as a percentage of operating expenses | X | X | X | | | | |
| advertising services | X | X | X | | | | |
| advertising services, as a percentage of operating expenses | X | X | X | | | | |
| commissions paid | X | X | X | | | | |

**Table 5.4 (Continued)**
**Business Expenditure Survey Subjects by Sector**

| Business Expenses (SIC sectors) | Wholesale | Retail | Services | Commun- ications | Truck- ing | Stor- age | Airlines |
|---|---|---|---|---|---|---|---|
| commissions paid, as a percentage of operating expenses | x | x | x | | | | |
| contract work | x | x | x | | | | |
| contract work, as a percentage of operating expenses | x | x | x | | | | |
| purchased repair and maintenance services | x | x | x | | | | |
| purchased repair and maintenance services, as a percentage of operating expenses | x | x | x | | | | |
| cost of purchased legal services | x | x | x | | | | |
| cost of purchased legal services, as a percentage of operating expenses | x | x | x | | | | |
| cost of purchased accounting, auditing, and bookkeeping services | x | x | x | | | | |
| cost of purchased accounting, auditing, and bookkeeping services, as a percentage of operating expenses | x | x | x | | | | |
| cost of data processing and other computer-related services | x | x | x | | | | |
| cost of data processing and other computer-related services, as a percentage of operating expenses | x | x | x | | | | |
| other operating expenses payroll | x | x | x | | | | |
| other operating expenses payroll, as a percentage of operating expenses | x | x | x | | | | |
| Detailed Lease and Rental Payments and Costs of Repair Services | | | | | | | |
| lease and rental payments | x | x | x | | | | |
|    Buildings, offices, and structures | x | x | x | | | | |
|    Machinery and equipment | x | x | x | | | | |
| purchased repair and maintenance services | x | x | x | | | | |
|    Buildings, offices, and structures | x | x | x | | | | |
|    Machinery and equipment | x | x | x | | | | |
| Detailed Purchased Utilities (This is also sometimes included in lease payments) | | | | | | | |
| all utilities except purchased fuels and electricity | x | x | x | | | | |
| cost of purchased electricity | x | x | x | | | | |
| fuels for heating, power, or generation of electricity | x | x | x | | | | |
| water, sewage, trash, and other utilities. | x | x | x | | | | |
| Detailed Costs for Data Processing and Other Computer-Related Services | | | | | | | |
| cost of purchased software and other data processing services | x | x | x | | | | |
|    purchases of prepackaged | x | x | x | | | | |

**Table 5.4 (Continued)**
**Business Expenditure Survey Subjects by Sector**

| Business Expenses (SIC sectors) | Wholesale | Retail | Services | Communications | Trucking | Storage | Airlines |
|---|---|---|---|---|---|---|---|
| purchases of custom | x | x | x | | | | |
| purchases of all other software | x | x | x | | | | |
| Sales, Annual Payroll, Employer Costs for Fringe Benefits, and Contract Labor | | | | | | | |
| Sales | x | x | x | | | | |
| annual payroll | | x | x | | | | |
| employer cost for fringe benefits | | x | x | | | | |
| employer cost for fringe benefits, as a percentage of annual payroll | | x | x | | | | |
| legally required fringe benefits | | x | x | | | | |
| voluntary fringe benefits | | x | x | | | | |
| contract labor costs | | x | x | | | | |
| Sales, Cost of Goods Sold, Measures of Value Produced | | | | | | | |
| sales, receipts and revenue | x | x | | | | | |
| purchases of merchandise for resale | x | x | | | | | |
| end of year inventory | x | x | | | | | |
| end of last year inventory | x | x | | | | | |
| cost of goods sold | x | x | | | | | |
| gross margin, total | x | x | | | | | |
| gross margin, as percentage of sales | x | x | | | | | |
| value added, total | x | x | | | | | |
| value added, as percentage of sales | x | x | | | | | |
| net income produced at market prices | x | x | | | | | |
| net income produced at market prices, as percentage of sales | x | x | | | | | |
| net income produced at factor cost | x | x | | | | | |
| net income produced at factor cost, as percentage of sales | x | x | | | | | |
| Estimated Operating Revenue and Expenses | | | | | | | |
| operating revenue, total | | | | x | x | x | x |
| operating expenses, amount | | | | x | x | x | x |
| annual payroll | | | | x | x | x | x |
| employer cost for fringe benefits | | | | x | x | x | x |
| access charges (telephone only) | | | | x | | | |
| Depreciation | | | | x | x | x | x |
| lease and rental | | | | x | x | x | x |
| cost of purchased repair services | | | | x | | x | x |
| Insurance | | | | x | x | x | |
| costs for communication services | | | | x | | | |

**Table 5.4 (Continued)**
**Business Expenditure Survey Subjects by Sector**

| Business Expenses (SIC sectors) | Wholesale | Retail | Services | Commun-ications | Truck-ing | Stor-age | Airlines |
|---|---|---|---|---|---|---|---|
| cost of purchased utilities | | | | x | | | x |
| cost of purchased advertising services | | | | x | | | x |
| taxes and licenses | | | | x | x | x | x |
| broadcast rights | | | | x | | | |
| music license fees | | | | x | | | |
| program and production costs, (cable only) | | | | x | | | |
| other operating expenses | | | | x | x | x | x |
| purchased fuels | | | | | x | | |
| purchased transportation (trucking only) | | | | | x | | |
| drug and alcohol testing and rehabilitation programs | | | | | x | | |
| purchased office supplies | | | | | | | x |
| Estimated Relative Standard Error for All Topics | x | x | x | x | x | x | |

gov/prod/www/abs/nonemp.html, generally issued two years after the reference year since the data are based on the income tax forms businesses file with the IRS.

*Nonemployer Statistics* were published as part of Area Series reports for 1982 and earlier censuses of retail trade, service industries, and construction. Separate reports were published in 1987 and 1992 for retail trade and service industries. Nonetheless, comparability of data over time may be affected by definition changes for establishments, activity status, industrial classifications, and processing methodology.

*Nonemployer Statistics* data originate chiefly from administrative records of the Internal Revenue Service (IRS). The data are primarily derived from IRS Form 1040 Schedule C filings by sole proprietorship businesses, although some partnerships and corporations qualify as nonemployer businesses where their tax returns indicate they have no paid employees. These data undergo complex processing, editing, and analytical review at the Census Bureau to distinguish nonemployers from employers, correct and complete data items, and form the final nonemployer universe.

**Table 5.5**
**National Comparison of Employers and Nonemployers, 1997**

| | Firms | Establishments | Sales or Receipts ($1,000) |
|---|---|---|---|
| All firms | 20,981,527 | 22,334,478 | 18,828,948,443 |
| Nonemployers (firms with no payroll) | 15,439,609 | 15,439,609 | 586,315,756 |
| Employers (firms with payroll) | 5,541,918 | 6,894,869 | 18,242,632,687 |

The industry scope of *Nonemployer Statistics* is slightly broader than that of the economic census, primarily by the inclusion the non-farming part of the Agriculture, Forestry, Fishing, and Hunting Sector. Tax-exempt nonemployer businesses are excluded. Investment Funds, Trusts, and Other Financial Vehicles (NAICS sub-sector 525) are excluded from nonemployer statistics. Management of Companies and Enterprises (NAICS sector 55)—which by definition must have employees—is excluded from nonemployer statistics too.

The industry detail for nonemployers is limited by the inability to gather certain kinds of detailed information on administrative forms. Thus, while the 1997 Economic Census published over 1,000 unique NAICS codes, *Nonemployer Statistics* was limited to less than 300.

The *Nonemployer Statistics* data series provides summary tabulations for Metropolitan Statistical Areas (MSA), each county (and county equivalent), each state, the District of Columbia, and the United States. The independent cities in Virginia and the cities of Baltimore, MD; Carson City, NV; and St. Louis, MO, are treated as separate counties. Puerto Rico and Outlying Areas are not included in the nonemployer tabulations.

It is important to note that in the *Nonemployer Statistics* reports, businesses are reported according to the address included on their income tax filings—these may or may not be their physical location. Generally, an establishment is a single physical location at which business is conducted or services or industrial operations are performed. However, the Bureau counts each distinct business income tax return filed by a nonemployer business as an establishment. Nonemployer businesses may operate from a home address or a separate business location. Most geography codes are derived from the business owner's mailing address, which may not be the same as the physical location of the business. A person operating more than one company from one mailing address is counted at that one address, but the number of tax returns that are filed determine the number of businesses that get counted. So it is possible for an entrepreneurial property manager with sole contracts and partnership agreements with various locations to be counted as many establishments—but if the properties were located in different counties, they would be counted in the one county where the tax forms filed from.

## Editing and Imputation

Editing is the process of correcting obvious errors, such as businesses being classified in an industry that is extremely unlikely to have businesses without employees, such as hospitals. This is done according to a set of logical rules.

The Census Bureau makes the assumption that certain kinds of businesses cannot really be carried on by firms without employees, and it edits the kind of business to a more likely code. Nonemployer establishments coded to Department Stores are reclassified to General Merchandise Stores; Hospitals are reclassified as Other Ambulatory Health Care Services; New Car Dealers are classified as Used Car Dealers; and nonemployers engaged in Rail Transportation are reclassified Support Activities for Transportation. Similarly, nonemployer establishments classified in Oil and Gas Extraction that are located in areas without oil and gas production are reclassified as Other Financial Investment Activities.

Imputation is a means of filling in information that was left blank on the appropriate form by the respondent.

For those nonemployer businesses that were lacking an industry classification, a NAICS industry code was copied from another nonemployer business with comparable receipts located in the same county. Less than three percent of the nonemployer businesses have imputed NAICS values.

## Comparability with Economic Census Data

Comparability of nonemployer statistics data with economic census employer data may be affected by definitional differences between administrative-record data and data collected directly from businesses on the Economic Census Bureau questionnaires. The nonemployer revenue data include gross receipts, sales, commissions, and income from trades and businesses, as reported on annual business income tax returns. Business income consists of all payments for services rendered by nonemployer businesses, such as payments received as independent agents and contractors. The composition of nonemployer receipts may differ from that of the related data item that is published for employer establishments. For example, for wholesale agents and brokers *without* payroll, the receipts item contains commissions received or earnings. In contrast, for wholesale agents and brokers *with* payroll, the sales item published in the Economic Census represents the value of the goods involved in the transactions.

Even at the state level, nonemployer numbers many not match. The U.S. Census Bureau counts as a business any entity with over $1,000 in business income. However, each state has its own definition on what would classify as business income. For example, a housewife in Utica, New York, making Fourth of July lawn decorations for "pin-money," generates $2,000 dollars a year. As long as she files a schedule C, her business would be counted and incorporated into the Census Bureau nonemployer statistics. The state of New York would not count her operation as a business, but as a hobby, because the state's threshold for business income is higher at $10,000. Thus, when looking at numbers relating to small business or entrepreneurs you should check their source and understand the definitions used when the data were produced. If data are based on federal numbers, make sure they include nonemployers and if data are based on state calculations, then check what their definitions are to include a business.

## Protecting Confidentiality

In accordance with U.S. Code, Title 13, Section 9, no data are published that would disclose the operations of an individual business. Because the preponderance of nonemployer statistics data items originate with the IRS, the Bureau adheres to both Census Bureau and IRS disclosure guidelines. For U.S.- and state-level data, the Bureau publishes the receipts in a data cell only if it contains three or more nonemployer businesses. For county- and MSA-level data, they publish the receipts only if it contains ten or more nonemployer businesses. According to Census Bureau disclosure rules, when a small number of nonemployer businesses have a dominant share of receipts, then receipts are suppressed to protect the dominant businesses. These suppressions are indicated with a flag of "D" in the report. If more than 40 percent of receipts in a published row are estimated, the Bureau suppresses the data because the data do not meet publication standards. A flag of "S" in the reports indicates these suppressions. The "D" and "S" flags indicate that there are establishments engaged in economic activity for that industry level, but that the receipts cannot be shown. Data cells that fail both conditions are assigned a flag of "D." Unlike the rule for the Economic Census, where establishment counts are not suppressed, Nonemployer Statistics

suppresses both establishment counts and revenue when there are fewer than 10 establishments represented.

## Survey of Business Owners

The *Survey of Business Owners and Self-Employed Persons* (SBO) measures the output of industries and geographic areas by gender, race, and ethnicity of business owners. Economic policymakers in federal, state, and local governments use the SBO data to understand conditions of business success and failure by comparing changes in business performances and by comparing minority-/nonminority- and women-/men-owned businesses.

The SBO corresponds to what were previously known as three surveys, the *Survey of Minority-Owned Business Enterprises* (SMOBE), *Survey of Women-Owned Business Enterprises* (SWOBE), and the *Characteristics of Business Owners Survey,* last done in 1997, 1997, and 1992 respectively.

### Coverage and Definitions

SBO includes all nonfarm businesses filing 2002 tax forms as individual proprietorships, partnerships, and any type of corporation, and with receipts of $1,000 or more. These reports present data for the U.S, each state, and the District of Columbia; metropolitan areas, which include metropolitan statistical areas, primary metropolitan statistical areas (PMSAs), and consolidated metropolitan statistical areas (CMSAs) in 1997, and metropolitan and micropolitan areas in 2002; counties; and places with 100 or more women- or minority-owned firms. Nonprofit and foreign-owned companies, as well as those with publicly held stock whose ownership was indeterminate, are covered in the *Survey of Business Owners.*

For this survey a company or business is defined as all operations under the same ownership, irrespective of the number of the company's employer tax identification numbers (EINs). This definition eliminated the likelihood of surveying the same business owner more than once. This definition has no effect on the employment and payroll data for these surveys, but slightly reduced the count for the number of businesses and the total receipts compared to other data from the Economic Census.

All locations under a common ownership within a geographic area are reported as a single firm. Thus, if a business has three operations in New York State, five in Virginia, and one in California, it would be counted as one firm in each state and one firm in the United States. Therefore, you cannot add smaller geographic areas together and expect to get the same number of firms as is reported at a larger geographic area. A similar situation arises when looking at data by industry.

## Content

The tables in each publication that show data for all U.S. firms are comparable to and include the minority-/women-owned firm data. Caution should be exercised in comparing data presented in this report with published or unpublished data from other reports of the Economic Census because the tables here count companies and most other reports count establishments. Other factors affecting the comparability of data between these reports and other reports from the same census are industrial scope or coverage, the minimum receipts required to be counted in the report, and the inclusion or exclusion of nonemployers.

The survey collects data on the gender, ethnicity, and race for up to three persons owning the largest share of the business—defined as having a majority of rights, equity, or interest in the business. Additional demographic and economic characteristics of the business owners and their businesses are also collected, such as owner's age; education level; veteran status; primary function in the business; family- and home-based businesses; types of customers and workers; and sources of financing for expansion, capital improvements, or start-up.

## Procedures

Unlike the other Economic Census questionnaires, the 2002 surveys were sent out in the summer of 2003 to a sample of the companies with employers, with two mail follow-ups at one-month intervals. Then in the spring of 2004, surveys were sent out to a sample of the nonemployer businesses. Some of the resulting tables do have separate columns for the larger and smaller businesses.

All firms, including nonemployers, operating during 2002, except those classified as agricultural, are represented in these surveys. The lists to identify possible firms (or universe) are compiled from a combination of business tax returns and data collected on other economic census reports. The Census Bureau obtains electronic files from the IRS for all companies filing Internal Revenue Service (IRS) Form 1040,

Schedule C (individual proprietorship or self-employed person); 1065 (partnership); or any one of the 1,120 corporation tax forms; and 941 (Employer's Quarterly Federal Tax Return). For businesses filing those forms, the IRS provided the Census Bureau with the following information: Name and address of the firm; principal industrial activity code, dollar receipts, annual payroll, legal form of organization, employer identification number of the firm, and Social Security numbers (SSNs) of the owners for filers of Form 1040 Schedule C and electronic filers of Forms 1065 and 1120S (subchapter S corporations);

There were six sampling frames (groups to be surveyed) used and every case was assigned to one of the following frames: American Indian, Asian/Pacific Islander, black, Hispanic, non-Hispanic, white male, and woman. To design the sample of firms, several sources of information were used to identify the probability that a business was minority- or woman-owned.

For all sole proprietorships and partnerships and corporations that filed an electronic tax return, IRS provided the SSN of the owner(s) to the Census Bureau. These SSNs were sent to Social Security Administration (SSA), which provided the race and sex indicated by the individuals on their applications for a social security number. Persons applying for SSNs prior to 1981 could categorize their race as (a) White, (b) Black, or (c) Other. In 1981, the racial descriptions on social security applications were expanded to (a) Asian, Asian-American, or Pacific Islander, (b) Hispanic, (c) Black, (d) Northern American Indian or Alaskan Native, and (e) White. Most persons who currently own businesses applied for their SSNs prior to 1981. Therefore, the majority of owners could be classified only as "White," "Black," or "Other" by use of SSA race codes.

For each SSN, the SSA also provided the Census Bureau with the individual's country of birth, current surname, original surname, mother's maiden surname, and father's surname. The Census Bureau has developed lists of American Indian, Asian, and Hispanic surnames based on research using prior survey data. In addition to SSA data, several other sources were used to pre-identify businesses by race, ethnicity, and gender of owner(s) as potentially minority-owned and include lists of minority- and women-owned businesses published in syndicated magazines, located on the Internet, or disseminated by trade or special interest groups and word strings in the company name indicating possible minority ownership (derived from earlier survey responses).

A firm selected into the sample was mailed one of two questionnaires. The Census Bureau sent one questionnaire to partnerships and corporations, or to sole proprietorships that submitted joint tax returns where, based on the administrative records, it was probable that the husband and wife were of different races. This questionnaire asked for the portion of the business controlled by each of the three largest owners. It also asked about each of these owners' disability status, sex, age, Hispanic origin, race, education, and role in the business.

A different questionnaire was used for nonemployers, sole proprietors, and self-employed individuals who were "single filers" or who filed joint tax returns where, based on administrative records, there was a low probability that the husband and wife were of different races. The businesses were asked to report the gender, race, and ethnicity of the primary owner(s) of the business. The form included an equal male/female ownership option for the collection of business owners by gender.

## Uses

Government program officials, industry organization leaders, economic and social analysts, and business entrepreneurs routinely use SBO statistics. For example, the Small Business Administration (SBA) and the Minority Business Development Agency (MBDA) assess business assistance needs and allocate available program resources. Local government commissions on small and disadvantaged businesses establish and evaluate contract procurement practices. A national women-owned business trade association assesses women-owned businesses by industry and area. Consultants and researchers analyze long-term economic and demographic shifts (but can only do this in general terms due to historical comparability problems with the data), and differences in ownership and performance among geographic areas.

## Reports

The Bureau releases publications on a flow basis— one group at a time: American Indians and Alaska Natives; Asians, Native Hawaiians, and Other Pacific Islanders; Blacks or African Americans; Hispanics; Minority Business Enterprise Summary; Women Business Enterprises; and a Company Summary. Data are available via the Internet, on CD-ROM, and printed reports. Users can easily see the number of minority-owned businesses, woman-owned businesses, and all total businesses for an area since the tables published on the Web organize the data by geographic area.

## Characteristics of Business Owners Survey

This report showed the demographics of small business owners: age, education, hours worked, and disability. It also provided a picture of the business characteristics, such as source of seed money, home-based, family-owned, franchising, year started, and sources of non-borrowed capital. The survey was conducted for 1992 and 1987.

Users of this report can develop an understanding of home-based business operations. You can investigate the start-up capital access, operational capital sources, and if the business is the only source of personal income. The report also states the source of income: government procurement, exports, retail, or wholesale. Each table is cross-tabulated by industry sub-sector, receipt size of firm, employment size of firm, and legal form of organization. With the right table you can see which industry is losing business, educational background by legal form of organization, or receipts size by when and how the owner acquired the business.

## Survey of Minority-Owned Business Enterprises/Survey of Women-Owned Business Enterprises

The *Survey of Minority-Owned Business Enterprises* (SMOBE) is conducted in conjunction with the *Survey of Women-Owned Business Enterprises* (SWOBE). The surveys provide basic economic data on businesses owned by women and by Blacks; persons of Alaska Native, American Indian, Asian, or Pacific Islander descent; and persons of Hispanic or Latin American ancestry. These surveys are based on the entire firm rather than on establishment level. The published data cover the number of firms, gross receipts, number of paid employees, and annual payroll. The data are presented by geographic area, size of firm, legal form of organization of firm, and (due to sampling design reasons) industry (using SIC codes for 1997 and the 1997 version of NAICS for the 2002 surveys).

In the SMOBE and SWOBE, minority/women ownership of a firm was based on the race/ethnicity/gender of the person(s) owning a 50 percent or greater interest in the business. If at least people from a single minority group control one-half of the ownership interests in a company, it is classified in that group. If the company can be classified into more than one minority group this way, it is—but in the summary report it is counted only once. For example, a firm could be included in both the Asian and Pacific Islander report and the Hispanic report if it were owned equally by two people, one of Japanese ancestry and one of Mexican ancestry. However, such a firm is counted only once at total levels in the SBO reports. If a business's ownership is divided so that no single group accounts for 50 percent or more of the ownership but the combination of minority ownership accounts for one-half or more of the ownership, then the business is counted as minority owned in the summary report, but is not counted in the individual reports.

Because of the fewer options available, ownership by sex is much more straightforward. The only real complication is where a firm is equally male-/female-owned. These were counted and tabulated as a separate category.

Figure 5.9 shows an example of the summary data for Ohio. Please note that if you add together the number of firms owned by each of the minority groups you end up with 49,940 firms, but the total number of minority-owned firms in the state is just 49,430 firms—a difference of 510 firms.

## Errors

The figures shown in these reports are, in part, estimated from a sample and will differ from the figures that would have been obtained from a complete census. Two types of possible errors are associated with estimates based on data from sample surveys: sampling errors and nonsampling errors.

The sample estimate can be used to gauge the standard error and then construct interval estimates with a prescribed level of confidence that the interval includes the average results of all samples. Suppose the estimated number of employer minority-owned firms in transportation services is 7,139 and the estimated relative standard error is 2 percent. The estimated standard error is 7,139 x .02 = 143. An approximate 90-percent confidence interval is 7,139 plus or minus (1.6 x 143) or 7,139 plus or minus 228.8 or 6,910.2 to 7,367.8.

All surveys and censuses are subject to nonsampling errors. Nonsampling errors are attributable to many sources: inability to obtain information for all cases in the universe, adjustments to the weights of respondents to compensate for non-respondents, imputation for missing data, data errors and biases, mistakes in recording or keying data, errors in collection or processing, and coverage problems.

Explicit measures of the effects of these nonsampling errors are not available. However, it is believed that most of the important operational and data errors were detected and corrected through an automated data edit designed to review the data for reasonableness and consistency.

## Historical Comparability

Many users are very interested in how things have changed over time. However, this is difficult to look at for minority- and women-owned businesses for several reasons. One major reason for this difficulty is that prior to 1997 most corporations were excluded from the survey, while starting in 1997 they were included. Additionally, prior to 1997 a firm was considered to be minority- or women-owned if 50 percent or more of the ownership was controlled by people from these groups, while starting in 1997, this threshold was raised slightly to 51 percent or more.

While the general coverage has remained the same between the 1997 and 2002 surveys, the industry classification has changed from an SIC basis to NAICS. Additionally, in 1997 respondents had to choose only one racial category to identify themselves, but in 2002, due to a change in racial reporting standards required by the U.S. Office of Management and Budget, respondents could choose more than one racial category. This limits historical comparability to the total number of firms for each geographic area and to the Hispanic and sex totals—and only with the 1997 surveys.

## Outlying Areas

The Economic Census does not include the *Economic Census of Puerto Rico and the Island Areas* as part of the Geographic Area Series, but as its own series. Statistics for Puerto Rico, the U.S. Virgin Islands, Guam, and the Northern Mariana Islands are published only in the separate *Economic Census of Puerto Rico and the Island Areas,* and are not included in any United States totals. In 1997, the Census Bureau did not collect economic census data for American

Figure 5.9
## Statistics for Minority-Owned Firms by Minority for States Sample

[Detail may not add to total because of rounding and because a Hispanic firm may be of any race and, therefore, may be included in more than one minority group (see Survey Methodology in the introductory text). For meaning of abbreviations and symbols, see introductory text. For explanation of terms, see Appendix A]

| Geographic area and minority | All firms[1] | | Firms with paid employees | | | | Relative standard error of estimate (percent)[2] for column— | | | | | |
| | Firms (number) | Sales and receipts ($1,000) | Firms (number) | Sales and receipts ($1,000) | Employees (number) | Annual payroll ($1,000) | A | B | C | D | E | F |
| | A | B | C | D | E | F | | | | | | |
|---|---|---|---|---|---|---|---|---|---|---|---|---|
| Ohio | 49 430 | 11 115 306 | 10 111 | 9 947 903 | 92 710 | 2 265 827 | 1 | 6 | 3 | 7 | 6 | 6 |
| Minority women | 16 462 | 1 431 790 | 2 260 | 1 127 256 | 15 218 | 364 863 | 4 | 17 | 9 | 22 | 18 | 35 |
| Minority men | 26 850 | 8 582 255 | 6 380 | 7 886 818 | 67 215 | 1 736 696 | 2 | 6 | 4 | 7 | 7 | 6 |
| Minority equally owned | 6 118 | 1 101 261 | 1 471 | 933 830 | 10 277 | 164 269 | 5 | 18 | 10 | 21 | 18 | 16 |
| Black | 26 970 | 3 946 848 | 3 486 | 3 499 457 | 32 719 | 788 525 | 1 | 9 | 6 | 10 | 14 | 18 |
| Women | 10 592 | 673 571 | 761 | 542 183 | 6 886 | 211 498 | 4 | 35 | 14 | 43 | 29 | 62 |
| Men | 14 298 | 2 992 152 | 2 347 | 2 712 359 | 23 232 | 513 628 | 3 | 11 | 8 | 12 | 16 | 14 |
| Equally owned | 2 080 | 281 125 | 378 | 244 915 | 2 601 | 63 398 | 12 | 15 | 17 | 18 | 25 | 27 |
| Hispanic | 6 448 | 1 512 809 | 1 199 | 1 283 564 | 11 353 | 310 617 | 5 | 12 | 11 | 12 | 10 | 14 |
| Women | 1 805 | 170 329 | 317 | 93 026 | 1 768 | 38 886 | 10 | 31 | 24 | 31 | 37 | 49 |
| Men | 3 683 | 1 135 349 | 709 | 1 011 942 | 8 543 | 253 473 | 5 | 10 | 11 | 11 | 12 | 14 |
| Equally owned | 960 | 207 131 | 174 | 178 596 | 1 042 | 18 258 | 10 | 33 | 31 | 36 | 26 | 13 |
| American Indian and Alaska Native | 5 124 | 1 074 343 | 682 | 932 874 | 9 357 | 204 934 | 5 | 13 | 12 | 15 | 38 | 30 |
| Women | 1 207 | 50 528 | 93 | 30 539 | 848 | 12 674 | 18 | 24 | 47 | 32 | 34 | 33 |
| Men | 3 018 | 851 092 | 527 | 769 242 | 7 976 | 179 224 | 8 | 18 | 12 | 20 | 46 | 35 |
| Equally owned | 898 | 172 722 | 62 | 133 094 | 533 | 13 036 | 14 | 39 | 33 | 51 | 38 | 41 |
| Asian and Pacific Islander | 11 398 | 4 603 153 | 4 767 | 4 235 973 | 39 392 | 962 918 | 4 | 6 | 5 | 7 | 7 | 8 |
| Women | 3 016 | 541 984 | 1 092 | 463 858 | 5 794 | 102 326 | 7 | 16 | 13 | 20 | 20 | 18 |
| Men | 6 132 | 3 617 873 | 2 818 | 3 394 890 | 27 497 | 791 016 | 4 | 7 | 5 | 8 | 11 | 10 |
| Equally owned | 2 250 | 443 296 | 858 | 377 225 | 6 101 | 69 577 | 12 | 22 | 19 | 25 | 28 | 24 |

Samoa. In 2002, The *Economic Census of Puerto Rico and the Island Areas* provides data for all island territories. Also starting with the 2002 Census, the reports also include all industries. Prior to 2002, this program was referred to as the Economic Census of Outlying Areas.

## Puerto Rico

The *Economic Census of Puerto Rico and the Island Areas: Puerto Rico* provides the most information of all of the outlying areas. It provides data on total sales, receipts, or value of shipments, kind of business, legal form of organization, employment, annual and first quarter payroll, sources of sales, and other industry specific measures such as number of hotel rooms or manufacturing export shipments, for all contacted establishments.

The Puerto Rico census is done by a mail-out/mail-back census of employer establishments. All known employers report data on one form and no information is collected for establishments without payroll. A memorandum of understanding designates the Census Bureau's and the Puerto Rico Planning Board's responsibilities for conducting the censuses. The Planning Board is consulted during the design stage, provides data on lottery and horse racing from their administrative records, and helps in publicizing the census.

This census results are four reports published for 1997 under the title *Economic Census of Outlying Areas: Puerto Rico:*

• The *Manufactures* report contains general employer statistics for industry groups by legal form of organization, sales and receipts by size, employment by size, and value of shipments exported. Statistics on industry groups are presented by the municipio and metropolitan statistical area (MSA).
• The *Construction* report contains general employer statistics for industry groups by legal form of organization, and employment by size. Statistics on industry groups are presented by the municipio and MSA level.
• The *Wholesale Trade, Retail Trade, and Service Industries* report is published in two books. Book one, the *Geographic Area Statistics*, contains general statistics for industry groups by the municipio and commercial region level. The island as a whole, metropolitan areas, commercial regions, municipios (county equivalents), and barrios and pueblos (place equivalents). The commercial regions are groups of municipios that collectively cover Puerto Rico. They are used in the reports for retail trade and service in-

dustries in lieu of MSAs, but are not used in other sectors.
• Book two, the *Subject Series,* contains data on commodity line sales by kind of business, and merchandise line sales by kind of business.

## Guam

The *Economic Census of Puerto Rico and the Island Areas: Guam* may sound like a strange title since Puerto Rico is in the Caribbean Sea and Guam is in the Philippine Sea, but the information is about the same. All establishments provide data on total sales, kind of business, legal form of organization, employment, annual and first quarter payroll, and sources of sales. Summary data covering hotels and other lodging places have reported additional data on sources of receipts and number of accommodations.

A memorandum of understanding outlines the responsibilities of the Census Bureau and the Government of Guam in conducting the censuses. The Bureau provides the necessary funds, enumerating procedures, forms, manuals, and training. The Governor of Guam appoints a project manager who is responsible for overseeing the census operation, hiring the enumerators, and collecting the data. The Guam government provides input to the questionnaire content and helps with publicity.

The data collection was more elaborate for Guam than for other areas. The mail-out/mail-back census of employer establishments was supplemented by personal enumeration of mail nonrespondents and nonemployer establishments. To enumerate establishments, Guam is divided into enumeration districts with each one assigned an interviewer. Interviewers systematically canvass their districts. A register book is used to screen out establishments that are not in the scope of the economic census, not in operation during the census year, or not a mail respondent. For each establishment determined to be in the scope of the census, enumerators fill out a questionnaire. Peddlers and other itinerant vendors without established places of business were not canvassed.

The *Economic Censuses of Outlying Areas: Guam* provides industry statistics at the industry sector level, by legal form of organization, sales and receipts by size, and employment by size for the island as a whole and election districts. Statistics on selected industry groups are presented at the district level. Data are also provided at the industry group and industry level when disclosure permits.

## U.S. Virgin Islands

The *Economic Census of Puerto Rico and the Island Areas: U.S. Virgin Islands* covers the territory as a whole; the islands of St. Thomas and St. John combined, and St. Croix; and three towns. All establishments provide data on total sales or receipts, kind of business, legal form of organization, employment, annual and first quarter payroll, and sources of sales. Cooperation, support, and methods are similar to those in Guam.

The report provides industry statistics at sector level, by legal form of organization, sales and receipts by size, and employment by size. Statistics on selected industry groups are presented for the islands and the three towns, located in the Caribbean Sea. Additional data are given for hotels, and other lodging places report additional data on sources of receipts and number of accommodations.

## The Commonwealth of the Northern Mariana Islands

The *Economic Census of Puerto Rico and the Island Areas: Commonwealth of the Northern Mariana Islands* also provides industry statistics at the major group level and, if disclosure rules permit, at the industry sub-sector and the industry level. General statistics are provided by legal form of organization, sales and receipts size, and employment size. Employment by industry group is presented for the territory as a whole and four municipalities. The islands, which are located in the Philippine Sea, also use the information from the census in the same manner as the other reports mentioned above.

## Uses

As with the remainder of the Economic Census, there are many uses of these data. A few examples are:

- The Virgin Island government uses Economic Census data to benchmark indexes of industrial production and productivity.
- Local governments use census data to assess business activities within their jurisdiction and to estimate the size and composition of industrial sectors, such as the tourist trade.
- The Department of Interior uses data to assess economic policy for Guam. Federal Emergency Management Agency uses data to help in assessment of damages due to natural disasters.

- The private sector uses the data to forecast general economic conditions; analyze sales performance; design sales territories; and measure potential markets. In a few industries, like pharmaceutical manufacturing, Puerto Rico accounts for a significant fraction of production associated with the United States.

## TRANSPORTATION

Since the way goods move around the country is critical to understanding the economy and planning our transportation system, the Census Bureau collects information about the vehicles used to transport these goods and where they are being moved. The *Vehicle Inventory and Use Survey* reports on the physical characteristics and operational use of the nation's 60 million private and commercial trucks. The *Commodity Flow Survey* reflects the origin and destination of commodities shipped from selected industries. Both have a Geographic Area Series covering 52 reports: United States as a whole, each state, and District of Columbia. More information about both of these surveys can be found in chapter 8, Transportation.

Some of the data reported in these surveys become the benchmarks used in the *Transportation Annual Survey.* The annual survey covers firms with paid employees that provide commercial motor freight transportation and public warehousing services. Data collected include operating revenue and operating revenue by source, total expenses percentage of motor carrier freight revenue by commodity type, size of shipments handled, length of haul, and vehicle fleet inventory.

## Commodity Flow Survey (CFS)

The *Commodity Flow Survey* (CFS) is undertaken through a partnership between the Bureau of the Census, U.S. Department of Commerce, and the Bureau of Transportation Statistics, U.S. Department of Transportation. This survey produces data on the movement of goods in the United States from large and small businesses. It provides information on commodities shipped, their value, weight, mode of transportation, hazardous materials, exports, as well as the origin and destination of shipments. The 2002 CFS is a sample survey of 50,000 businesses from the mining, manufacturing, wholesale, and selected retail establishments. Certain auxiliary establishments, such as warehouses are also included. The CFS produces summary statistics on the uses of our transportation system at the national, regional, division, state, MA, and the remainder of the state outside of MA.

This is a yearlong survey. Companies received one questionnaire during each quarter of 2002: a total of 4 reports. Each report covers about the same one-week period within the quarter, asking for information on a sample of a company's shipments for the week. (That is, a company whose first report covers the third week of the first quarter will also receive questionnaires covering the third week of quarters 2, 3, and 4.) The definition of shipments includes deliveries and other movements of goods that some respondents don't always relate to shipments. Respondents were encouraged to provide estimates if the specific data were not available.

The results of this survey are in great demand by transportation policy planners and decision makers at the U.S. Department of Transportation, and at state DOTs as well. The CFS data help these agencies make better decisions on how to allocate the billions of dollars needed to maintain and improve the transportation system in this country.

## Vehicle Inventory and Use Survey (VIUS)

The *Vehicle Inventory and Use Survey* (VIUS) is a periodic survey of private and commercial trucks registered (or licensed) in the United States. It is a sample survey taken every five years as part of the Economic Census. It provides information about the physical and operational characteristics of the Nation's truck population. VIUS, formerly known as the *Truck Inventory and Use Survey* (TIUS), covers state and U.S. level statistics on the physical and operational characteristics of the nation's truck, van, minivan, and sport utility vehicle (SUV) population. Some of the types of data collected includes the number of vehicles, major use, body type, annual miles, model year, vehicle size, fuel type, operator classification, engine size, range of operation, weeks operated, products carried, and hazardous materials carried. This survey shows comparative statistics reflecting percent changes in number of vehicles between census years for most characteristics.

VIUS forms were mailed to owners of a sample of more than 135,000 trucks registered in every state. Trucks were selected for the VIUS sample randomly, and to represent trucks registered to businesses and individuals in every industry. Van, minivan, and SUV owners received a short form; hence minimal data

were collected because they are relatively homogenous in design and use. No make or model data are reported.

The information in the survey is the only source of complete statistics about the physical and operational characteristics for our nation's truck population. While selected truck registration information is available in each state, these data typically do not include truck operational characteristics, do not include complete physical characteristics information, and are not readily available or comparable for all states.

Private and commercial trucks registered (or licensed) in the United States as of July 1 of the survey year are covered. The survey excludes vehicles owned by federal, state, or local governments; buses; ambulances; motor homes; farm tractors; unpowered trailer units; and trucks reported to have been sold, junked, or wrecked prior to July 1 of the year preceding the survey.

Data on physical characteristics include date of purchase, weight, number of axles, type of engine, overall length, and body type. Operational characteristics data include type of use, lease characteristics, operator classification, base of operation, gas mileage, annual and lifetime miles driven, weeks operated, commodities hauled by type, and hazardous materials carried.

VIUS is a mail-out/mail-back survey of selected trucks; large truck owners receive a standard form, and small truck owners (pickups, vans, minivans, and sport utility vehicles) receive a short form. A stratified random sample of registered trucks is selected from all 50 states and the District of Columbia. Samples are selected by state and stratified mainly by body type. Data collection is staggered over the year as state records become available. Owners report data only for the vehicles selected for the sample.

Survey results are used to estimate future transportation growth and fuel demands, calculate highway use costs and fees, evaluate highway traveler safety risks, assess truck energy efficiency and environmental impacts, develop and evaluate market strategies, assess equipment uses and costs, and calculate product longevity. Tire manufacturers use the data to calculate the longevity of products and to determine the usage, vocation, and applications of their products. Heavy machinery manufacturers use the data to track the importance of various parts distribution and service networks. Truck manufacturers use the data to determine the impact of certain types of equipment on fuel efficiency.

The Department of Transportation uses the data for analysis of cost allocation, safety issues, proposed investments in new roads and technology, and user fees. The Environmental Protection Agency uses the data to determine per mile vehicle emission estimates, vehicle performance and fuel economy, and fuel conservation practices of the trucking industry. The Bureau of Economic Analysis uses the data as a part of the framework for the national investment and personal consumption expenditures component of the Gross Domestic Product.

## SPECIAL REQUESTS

While the data routinely released from the Economic Census answers nearly all of the questions that are asked, there is the possibility that you might have a question that could be answered from the census but is not. If none of the reports of datasets contains the cross tabulation that you need to answer your question, there is still the possibility that you might be able to get the answer from the Economic Census. There are two additional possible ways that might allow you to get the data—special tabulations and the Longitudinal Research Database (LRD) or other databases maintained by the Center for Economic Studies (CES).

### Special Tabulations

Census Bureau staff can run special tabulations from the Economic Census's raw data, untabulated responses to the questionnaire. This allows you to get the customized data that you need to answer a unique question. While on the surface, this seems like a great option for getting any data from the Economic Census, there are several issues limiting the desirability of this option.

One of these issues is the cost, since the Census Bureau requires reimbursement of all costs related to a special tabulation. Depending on the complexity of the tabulation and the disclosure analysis required, a special tabulation could get expensive.

Another issue is the time the request takes. These requests are generally given lower priority by the Census Bureau compared to preparing scheduled publications. Therefore, you can expect that it will take several months to get the tabulation you want.

A third issue is the Census Bureau's disclosure analysis. The Bureau is responsible for ensuring that the tabulations do not violate the Census Bureau's confidentiality requirements. If they feel that the tabulations might violate these requirements, they can require that they be modified in order to maintain the confidentiality of the respondents. These modifications can include suppressing individual cells, rounding data in individual cells, or aggregating cells together. In the extreme, the Bureau can refuse to release the data.

For more information about special tabulations, contact the Chief of the Service Sector Statistics Division, or the Chief of Manufacturing and Construction Division at the Census Bureau.

### Center for Economic Studies Resources

The Census Bureau's Center for Economic Studies (CES) has developed the Longitudinal Research Database, a database containing every questionnaire response from the Economic Census since 1963 and the Annual Survey of Manufactures since 1972 for individual manufacturing establishments. Additional data sources are also included if their information can be linked to the individual establishments and other requirements are met. The LRD and other databases maintained by the CES are another way to get customized data from the Economic Census.

The data can only be accessed either at the Census Bureau Headquarters or at one of seven Research Data Centers (RDCs) around the country. Again, there are a number of issues limiting the desirability of using this resource:

- Your project must provide a benefit to Census Bureau programs. It may not merely satisfy a proprietary interest.
- You need to do the tabulations yourself. In order to do this you need to pass a security check and obtain Special Sworn Status, which subjects you to the same legal penalties (a fine of up to $250,000, up to five years in prison, or both) as regular Census Bureau employees for disclosing confidential information.
- The RDC *and* the Census Bureau must approve your proposal. If data from other agencies are also being used, those agencies must also approve your research proposal.
- All materials you wish to remove from the site must be submitted to Census Bureau personnel for disclosure review before it can be taken from the RDC.

The Census Bureau must be reimbursed for all of their costs associated with the research. Typical projects at CES are funded by grants from other federal agencies, but a limited number of fellowships are sponsored by other organizations, such as the American Statistical Association and National Science Foundation.

Additional information about this option is located on the Census Bureau's Web site at www.census.gov. Look for either the Longitudinal Research Database or the Center for Economic Studies under "Subjects A to Z."

# CHAPTER 6
# Formats

One evening at Dr B's [Billings] tea table he said to me "There ought to be a machine
for doing the purely mechanical work of tabulating population and similar statistics."
—*Herman Hollerith, (Letter to friend, c.1930)*

1. Print
2. Portable Document Format (PDF)

    A. Working with PDF Files
    B. Advantages and Disadvantages of PDF

3. Internet

    A. Economic Census Page
    B. American FactFinder

4. Compact Disc—Read Only Memory (CD-ROM)
5. How to Read a Table
6. Symbols and Abbreviations
7. Citing the Economic Census

    A. Printed Materials
    B. PDF Documents
    C. Hypertext Drill-Down Tables
    D. American FactFinder
    E. CD-ROM
    F. Maps
    G. Secondary Sources

8. Bibliography

The Census Bureau has been on the cutting edge of collecting, calculating, distributing, and storing data since before its creation as a permanent agency in 1902. The sciences of statistics and technology grew in concert with the censuses. In fact, computers owe a big debt to the Census Bureau for their early development. By the late 1800s, the census questions had been expanded and the population had grown to the point that the 1880 Census took nine years to compile. The Bureau needed a solution to the problems of tabulating large amounts of data in a short time. They turned to Herman Hollerith, who combined punch cards used in looms, tickets punched by railroad conductors, and machines used in banks. The result was the tabulator machine and a tally of the 1890 Census was completed within six weeks. Punch cards would be used until 1963. As technology advanced, demands for more storage of data and faster distribution of data products kept pace with its evolution.

Old technology like print has its limitations: it's bulky, expensive to reproduce, flammable, and not dynamic. For many years, microforms seemed an ideal storage solution: they're compact, easy to reproduce, archival for at least 150 years, and require low technology to access. Until recently, the Census Bureau was using microforms as its primary storage format for original materials, questionnaires submitted by establishments, and similar primary items. Since more information is being submitted electronically and digital storage is more affordable, the Bureau is now using imaging technology to store its original materials and keeping the digital answers in their original format.

The nature of microforms is not user friendly, and print is not an option for a dynamic electronic environment. The Census Bureau prefers electronic media for calculating data and formatting tabulations for output. In the past, they used magnetic tape and now use CD-ROMs, DVDs, and Internet as the media for distributing large amounts of data. Currently, the Bureau is minimizing the amount of information they actually print and has discontinued issuing data on microforms in favor of electronic publications on the Internet or CD-ROM/DVD. This chapter reviews the various formats the Economic Census uses to present data, describes how to use them, discusses the advantages and disadvantages of each, and suggests how to cite the various formats.

How do you know which medium to use? Factors that need to be considered in choosing a medium include which ones that have data that you want and what output format will be most useful to you. Secondary considerations are cost and storage space and time. Table 1.1 shows what media the different reports are distributed in; notice that some data are only available on CD-ROM.

## PRINT

Many data users like the printed reports because they allow for easy and fairly quick access to the data, especially if they are interested in just one or two simple numbers. This format also allows users to quickly browse through a large amount of information. However, the printed reports contain only a small fraction of the data available from the Economic Census. Due to cost considerations most of the titles are *not* distributed in print. The items issued in print either have an overarching importance, like the *Bridge Between NAICS and SIC* or because the reports received special funding for wider distribution, like the *Survey of Minority-owned Business Enterprises* or the *Economic Census of Outlying Areas.*

This does not mean that the printed medium—with the nicely formatted tables with support materials and appendixes—will no longer be seen. Most of the data previously given out in printed reports can now be accessed in a printable format (PDF) and downloaded for free from the Internet using Adobe Acrobat Reader. The Census Web site also offers the option for the reports to be "printed on demand."

The "print on demand" option is something the Census Bureau charges for. The only difference from your printing out the PDF and the Bureau printing out the report is your cost, time for shipping, and the plastic spine binding. If you want it shipped internationally, an additional cost of $25.00 will be added to each shipment. Generally, print on demand is not worth it. For instance, if you wanted every *Geographic Area Report* for the state of Alabama with a map of the metro areas in the state, it would cost you $550 using print on demand. Your cost to print out the PDF documents for the same series would be the time and the cost of paper for 1,642 pages and binding folders for 17 reports. At $0.10 a page and $2.00 dollars a binder, it would cost you about $200 dollars, verses the $550 for the print on demand version.

The advantages of printed reports are the familiarity of the medium and very low learning curve to using them, all the supporting reference information is bundled into the report, it's very portable, it is a static record that cannot be changed, and it's a good medium for archiving (printed pages last longer than software

application versions do). The disadvantages are the output is static, it cannot be manipulated or formatted, one copy can be used only at one time, and it takes up space.

## PORTABLE DOCUMENT FORMAT (PDF)

Closely related to print medium is the PDF, as created and maintained by Adobe Acrobat, a private-sector software program. A description of the software used to read these files follows a description of how the Census Bureau is using this medium to distribute data from the Economic Census.

The Census Bureau is using this format to replace most printed documents. On the other hand, some data, like ZIP Code Statistics, were never published in print, and thus they have not been published in PDF. This allows for the data to be released faster, because there is no delay between finalizing the report format and its release to allow for it to be physically printed. This format also allows the Census Bureau to release the data for free.

For our convenience, the Bureau has adopted a document layout that will allow the researcher to consistently move around in the report. It is best to refer to the pagination used by the Adobe tool bar at the bottom of the page when referencing a PDF document and only use the page number printed on the image when the document is a print format. For example, if you wanted to get the Table of Contents page for nearly all Economic Census PDF reports, you can move right to page 5 in the PDF viewer. Page 5 is the key to learning what is in a report.

The structures of all of the reports are the same for the Subject and Geographic Series. The Core Business Statistics and Industry Series follow similar structures as the other series; however, the pagination may change because of a longer Table of Contents. Because these reports are designed for printing, they follow the same structure as the actual printed reports and are based on an 8-1/2 by 11 inch page. The page numbers referred to here are those used by Adobe Acrobat and differ from those referred to in each report's Table of Contents. The standard Acrobat pagination of the PDF reports is

Page 1—Cover
Page 2—Acknowledgments
Page 3—Title Page
Page 4—Title verso page (reverse side of the title page)
Page 5—Table of Contents

Pages 6 to 8—Introduction to the Economic Census
Page 9—blank
Pages 10 and 11—description of report content
Pages 12 until Appendixes—Data Tables

The description of the report's content includes the industry sector's scope, general content, geographic area covered, comparability between the earlier census and most recent, disclosure, and availability of more frequent data. Those six topics are covered in all of the Subject and Geographic Area Series.

## Working with PDF files

Unlike print however, PDF allows users to search the document, change the way they view the documents, and allows for copying data or images for use in other software programs. When using the free Adobe Acrobat Reader, the contents of the document cannot be changed. However, if the full Adobe Acrobat is used, it is possible to change the contents of the document, or even to save it in rich text format (RTF) for use in other programs such as word processors.

Most computers already have the Reader installed; however, if you have to install the Reader, it is provided free from Adobe Acrobat at http://www.adobe.com/products/acrobat/readstep.html. Expanded versions allowing you to do more are available for a fee.

Figure 6.1 shows the tools associated with viewing, moving, searching for words, and capturing text and images within the document, along with saving options using Adobe Acrobat Reader 6 for Windows. Being familiar with this program's capabilities can in-

crease the usefulness of the Economic Census. If the options shown below are not available in your Reader, move your mouse to the top gray toolbar of the Reader, then click on the right side of mouse button to select. Select all options.

### Viewing

Acrobat Reader software will open an image file when you click on a link to a PDF file. Please note that the PDF image file is sent to your computer as a temporary file. It will be deleted when you exit your browser unless you choose to save it. However, when you exit the document or the program, you will not be asked if you wish to save the document.

### Moving

To move between pages use the scroll bars on the right side of the image or use the arrow icons. If you are showing the thumbnails of the left, you can also scroll down to the page you want to see there. If you know the page number that you want to go to, you can also enter it in the rectangle at the bottom of the page showing which page you are currently on (e.g., "5 of 117"). If you get a page number from the table of contents (generally on page 5), add 5 to get a PDF page number to enter at the bottom.

### Searching for Words

It is possible to search for words and numbers in PDF files. Type your terms or numbers in the "Acrobat Find" box (symbolized by the binoculars icon). If you

**Figure 6.1**
**Adobe Acrobat Reader Tools**

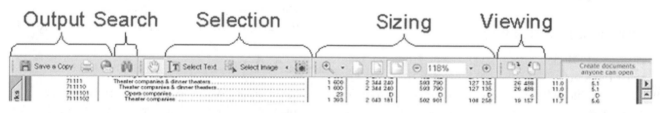

turn off the option to "Match Whole Word Only," Acrobat Reader will search for parts of words or numbers instead of just the whole word. For example, if you are looking for NAICS code 711, it will also retrieve 37112, unless you choose "Match Whole Word Only."

Once you know how a report is organized, it may be more efficient to search for a geographic area name or a NAICS code than to use the very limited table of contents.

## Copying and Capturing

There are no marking or highlighting capabilities in the Acrobat Reader (these features are available in the fee-based Reader); however, you can copy text and capture images to cut and paste into a word processing program. To copy or capture, select the appropriate tool (select text or select graphic buttons), highlight the section by dragging the mouse across the needed section, and click the right mouse button to get copy command or use the copy button (do not use the browser's cut or copy commands).

The copy image function works really well with the tables. The structure of the image is retained and should be used in capturing the look of the table. The copy text function only captures the words on the page, but not the structure and should only be used if you need the data and you can't access corresponding data in American FactFinder or on CD-ROM. To copy a column of numbers into a spreadsheet program, use the "Copy selected text" option. Once the spreadsheet program is open, paste the text into the program (you may have to realign numbers and delete the commas or spaces between hundreds and thousands—a tedious process). Do one column at a time so each number will be in one cell.

## Printing and Downloading

Printing a PDF document is very easy. However, because of the size of the file, some printers may not be able to print the whole document at once. Acrobat's print command allows you to print the entire document, the current page, or any specific range of pages.

Downloading is also an option; however, one page of PDF can be as small as 20kb or as large at 72kb per page, depending on the technique that the publisher used to convert the document into a PDF document. Unless you need to keep a copy on your computer for archival purposes, it is usually more practical to print.

## Help

Help is only a click away Adobe Customer Support at http://www.adobe.com/support/products/acrobat.html.

## Advantages and Disadvantages of PDF

This is a great format for distributing large amounts of information in an easy-to-read medium. It can show data as it would appear in print and has all the advantages of print: the familiarity of the medium and very low learning curve to using it, all the supporting reference information is bundled into the title, it's very portable, it is a static record that cannot be changed, and it's a great medium for archiving (printed page lasts longer than the software applications). PDF also allows for capturing the data or image to be placed in another program, no matter how misaligned the data look, it's better than retyping the information. Archiving is a plus and a minus; since every title is on the government server, researchers do not have to keep their own copy in print or on their own computer, but because the titles are kept on the government server you are depending on the government not to delete the information and to make sure that it is viewable with the latest version of the software.

Disadvantages of PDF are that the output is static and it cannot be manipulated. The formatting of the PDF does not make it easy for binding; the left margin is too narrow. However, some printers may have ways of changing margins, so the printed pages can be bound without loss of information. There is also a problem for those people without access to the Internet or the sophistication to load Adobe Acrobat Reader. But over all, the PDF access to the Economic Census is helpful to those organizations and researchers who don't have the patience to learn how to use the data in American FactFinder or on CD-ROM.

## INTERNET

The Internet, World Wide Web, Information Super Highway, or Online—whatever you want to call it—is the current tool of choice for collecting and sharing information. The Census Bureau is taking full advantage of the powers of the Internet. They are using the Web to distribute Economic Census data using two main methods in addition to distributing the PDF reports described above. One of these methods is a set of hypertext drill down tables. The other is American FactFinder.

All of the Census Bureau's Internet resources can be reached through their home page http://www.census.gov, shown in Figure 6.2. The hypertext drill-down tables and other information about the Economic Census are reached by clicking on "Economic Census" in the middle of the page. American FactFinder is reached by clicking on the American FactFinder button on the left-hand side of the page. Please note that the Internet is very dynamic. Any images you see here show what things looked like when this book was being prepared; when you go to these pages they may have a different look and feel to them.

## Economic Census Page

The Economic Census page is the quickest way to a wealth of information about the Economic Censuses. It is divided into several sections. On the left-hand side there are links to

- The "Guide to the Economic Census," which is an excellent source for updated information about coverage and release plans
- The latest results from this and earlier Economic Censuses
- General information about the Economic Census, including sample forms, slide shows for presentations, and a writer's toolkit
- Related sites such as NAICS information, data for the Outlying Areas, the Commodity Flow Survey, and the Survey of Business Owners

The main part of the page has a section dealing with the latest Economic Census (see Figure 6.3). Within this section, you can find links to the data and PDF reports by sector or state. You can also link to the industry and subject series reports. The box contains drill-down links (indicated by the blue arrow pointing down) to data for all sectors.

The sector-specific reports section allows you click on a specific sector and then get a list of all of the reports for that sector. It also provides hypertext drill-down tables for the geographic reports. By clicking on the blue arrow next to any state, you can get a report for that state similar to the one shown in Figure 6.4. To get data for a specific industry within the state either click on the blue down arrow next to the sub-sector or just scroll down the page. Clicking on either the column headers (variable names) or industry descriptions, you can get the official definition of that term. Data for metropolitan areas or counties, if they are available, can be obtained by selecting the area in the pull-down menu boxes in the upper-right-hand corner of the page.

Similarly, the Reports by State option provides a list of all reports and hypertext drill-down tables with data for the selected state. It also contains links to the PDF reports for that state and a PDF map of the state showing the metropolitan area boundaries within the state. Clicking on the blue arrow for any report links to a table showing the basic data for that state from the report. Finally, this page shows the prices for purchasing the print-on-demand versions of the various reports.

The Industry Statistics Sampler is a particularly interesting tool because it is a drill-down table that presents basic data for a given industry from all Census Bureau sources covering that industry. This section allows you to enter a description of the industry you want data for and then brings up a list of all entries in the NAICS manual's index matching that description. Then you can select the specific industry you want data for and it will bring up a page containing the following items:

- The basic data for that industry and all higher NAICS levels it is in (i.e., sector, sub-sector, industry group, NAICS industry, and U.S. Industry).
- A definition of the industry.
- The Bridge Table data.
- Comparative statistics with the previous Economic Census.
- Geographic distribution of the industry by state, ranked by sales. There is also the ability to compare it with other industries within a given state (shown by a blue arrow facing left). Were data for some states are not available due to disclosure restrictions or publication cutoffs, the aggregate of all states not shown separately is presented. Where this aggregate is larger than the top ranking state, the user may have to deal with the fact that the state at the top of the list may not be the largest state after all.
- Links to other Economic Census reports, such as the Source of Receipts report for that sector.
- The 2002 Economic Census Questionnaire.
- Data from other Census Bureau Programs, such as County Business Patterns, Nonemployer Statistics, and any other surveys covering this sector.

Below the data section on the Economic Census page are links to American FactFinder, information on ordering the CD-ROMS, conference schedules related to the Economic Census, and other general information links.

**Figure 6.2**
**Census Bureau Home Page**

# U.S. Census Bureau

United States Department of Commerce

**Hispanic Heritage Month**

**Subjects A to Z**
A B C D E F G H I
J K L M N O P Q
R S T U V W X Y Z

**New on the Site**

**Search**

**American FactFinder**

**Access Tools**

**Jobs@Census**

**Catalog**

Census Bureau Recruits for Hispanic Staff at University of Puerto Rico

**United States Census 2000**

Your Gateway to Census 2000 ·
Summary File 4 - All states are available ·
Summary File 3 (SF 3)

**People** Estimates · 2002 Data Profiles - ACS · Projections
· Income · Poverty · International · Genealogy ·
Housing

**Business** Economic Census · Survey of Business Owners ·
Government · E-Stats · NAICS · Foreign Trade

**Geography** Maps · TIGER · Gazetteer

**Newsroom** Releases · Minority Links · Radio/TV/Multimedia ·
Photos · Health Insurance

ECONOMIC CENSUS
**PAST DUE!**

TIGER/LINE FILES HERE

Population Clocks
U.S. 292,341,320
World 6,323,732,306
14:04 EDT Oct 15, 2003

State&County QuickFacts
Select a state
Go!

Latest Economic Indicators

**Figure 6.3**
**Economic Census Page Data Link Section**

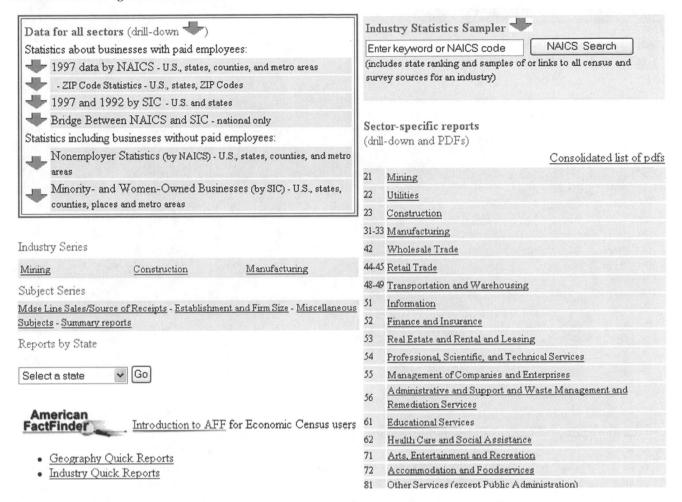

## Advantages and Disadvantages of the Drill-Down Tables

The big advantage is convenience—the convenience of retrieving the data and the low learning curve of point and click to get what you want. The data on the Web is free and the only limits are the bandwidth to upload the page. The obvious disadvantage is the lack of flexibility of the data. You also can't search across different industries. For example, if you want to know every major industry in your MSA, you would not be able to search for establishments that employ over 500 people in your geography.

Most spreadsheet programs have the ability to load html files saved to a local drive. Thus, if the data you want to manipulate appear in an html table like these, you may use your browser's "File—Save As..." functionality to save the file locally and reopen it in the spreadsheet—without going through American FactFinder or CD-ROM.

## American FactFinder

American FactFinder (AFF) is a powerful, though challenging, data delivery system that can be accessed through the Census Bureau's home page. It contains a number of features that are easy to use for the casual data user and others that are targeted towards the advanced user.

The Census Bureau is constantly working to make AFF an even better data source than it already is. This means that several times a year there are significant changes to the system. Many of these system changes are based on feedback from data users. Because of these regular revisions, we cannot do more than describe the system's major features. You will need to

**Figure 6.4**
**Sample Hypertext Drill-Down Table**

## U.S. Census Bureau

| ECONOMIC | 1997 Economic Census: | Select a state ▼ Go |
| CENSUS 1997 | Retail Trade | Arkansas metro areas ▼ Go |
| | Arkansas | Arkansas counties ▼ Go |

### Retail Trade by Subsector

Introductory text includes scope and methodology. Table includes only establishments with payroll. Nonemployers are shown separately. For descriptions of column headings and rows (industries), click on the appropriate underlined element in the table.

| More data | NAICS code | Description | Estab-lish-ments | Sales ($1,000) | Annual payroll ($1,000) | Paid employees |
|---|---|---|---|---|---|---|
| | 44-45 | Retail trade | 12,600 | 21,643,695 | 1,904,412 | 132,335 |
| ⬇ | 441 | Motor vehicle & parts dealers | 1,672 | 6,041,687 | 395,467 | 16,255 |
| ⬇ | 442 | Furniture & home furnishings stores | 674 | 483,811 | 66,803 | 3,592 |
| ⬇ | 443 | Electronics & appliance stores | 440 | 391,114 | 44,251 | 2,432 |
| ⬇ | 444 | Building material & garden equipment & supplies dealers | 1,237 | 2,432,316 | 245,815 | 12,340 |
| ⬇ | 445 | Food & beverage stores | 1,492 | 2,942,513 | 267,451 | 25,232 |
| ⬇ | 446 | Health & personal care stores | 841 | 739,812 | 96,401 | 5,614 |
| ⬇ | 447 | Gasoline stations | 1,843 | 2,286,494 | 139,886 | 13,119 |
| ⬇ | 448 | Clothing & clothing accessories stores | 1,412 | 834,385 | 102,415 | 9,307 |
| ⬇ | 451 | Sporting goods, hobby, book, & music stores | 562 | 374,836 | 42,247 | 3,578 |
| ⬇ | 452 | General merchandise stores | 563 | 3,984,845 | 370,903 | 31,801 |
| ⬇ | 453 | Miscellaneous store retailers | 1,406 | 684,590 | 76,067 | 5,927 |
| ⬇ | 454 | Nonstore retailers | 458 | 447,292 | 56,706 | 3,138 |

read the online tutorial to get a detailed introduction to the system.

There are several major sections to AFF. One is a set of "Fast Access to Information." Another presents data sets ("Getting Detailed Data"). And the third allows the production of maps (accessed by clicking on the "Maps and Geography" button). There is also an internal search capability.

The maps section provides the ability to draw basic maps of the Census Bureau's data. There are two basic types of maps that can be produced—a reference map that allows you to identify where an area is and thematic maps that allow you to view data in a graphic manner. Much more sophisticated maps can be developed using a commercial GIS system. But if you cannot afford one or just want a quick map, AFF's mapping feature might meet your needs.

The workhorse of AFF is in the Data Sets section (accessed through either the "Data Sets" button or within the "Getting Detailed Data" section). In this section you can produce a variety of quick reports or work with detailed statistics.

The Economic Census Industry Quick Reports allow you to look at the basic data and population estimates for a single industry showing all of the states where that industry exists. The Economic Census Geography Quick Reports show the basic data items for all reported industries from the current Economic Census for a single geographic area, which can be the nation, a state, a county, a place, or a metropolitan area. The default Geography Quick Report shows only 2-digit NAICS totals, but more detailed tables can be selected. (ZIP codes are not included here.) These quick reports can be printed or downloaded as either comma and quote delimited (CSV) or tab delimited (LST) files for use in a variety of software programs.

The detailed statistics option gives you the greatest freedom in working with these data sets. Through this option you can select from any of the data sets produced for the Economic Census. A data set usually contains the data shown in one table in the printed reports for all applicable geographic areas. Most of the geographic area reports come from a single data set showing all industries in that sector for all geographic areas. Manufacturing, mining, and construction have additional geographic area tables at the state level only. Through AFF's data sets you can also manipulate multiple geographic areas and choose which variables to display. If you are going to download the data, you should note that AFF has a limit on the number of lines that can be downloaded in a single file. If you wish to download a larger file, you will have to download it in several pieces and combine them on your computer in other software. Currently, the limit is 15,000 lines but the Census Bureau can change that depending on user demand and system resources.

Once you have selected the data set and geographic area, FactFinder shows you the data. You can then refine your request further by focusing in on specific geographic area or industries. You can even limit the data shown by searching on specific values, such as counties and industries with sales greater than $100 million. This is also when you can change which variables are being shown, sort the data, or create ratios or percent changes (depending on the data set).

Once you have the data the way you want it you can print or download it for use in other programs.

When downloading the data you should consider what programs you will use to analyze it. Different programs read the same data in different ways. This can be critical when the data includes numeric-looking codes, such as FIPS codes which use numbers like "01" to represent Alabama. A program like Excel will try to read this as a number and drop the leading zero. If you then try to link this with another file that has the leading zero, you might not get a match. You can reinstate the leading zeroes in Excel by right-clicking on the appropriate column heading, selecting Format Cells, then selecting Custom under Category in the Number tab, and then entering into the "Type" box a string of zeroes equal to the number of characters in the code—2 for a state code, 3 for a county code, etc.

It should be noted that AFF contains only the Geographic Area, Industry, and Subject series datasets from the 1997 Economic Census. Much of the other data is included in the drill-down tables and all of it is included on the CD-ROMs. In contrast, AFF contains all of the datasets from the 2002 Economic Census.

## COMPACT DISC—READ ONLY MEMORY (CD-ROM)

The Economic Census on CD-ROMs is an ideal alternative for heavy users of the data. Unlike the PDF or HTML tables from the Internet, this method gives five distinctive advantages: no Internet access is required, it allows for searching across the different areas or industries, data can be retrieved for only the items desired, data can be easily downloaded and used in statistical programs, and there are some data sets that are only available on the CD-ROM.

The design, software, and content layout of the 2002 Economic Census CD-ROM products were still in the planning stages when this chapter was being written. So very little can be said about their nature. Technology has changed and the Census Bureau will be using DVDs, so all of the data should fit onto one or two discs, where in 1997 it took five CDs.

Regardless of the exact decisions that are made about the 2002 Economic Census CD product, you can be sure that they will allow you to access large amounts of data. You will also be able to choose specific data subjects to include in your tables. Printing and extracting the data will be relatively easy. New features planned for the 2002 Economic Census CDs include the ability to graph and map the data. There are also other assumptions that can be made about the structure of the CD-ROM. It most certainly will be a Windows-based program using normal conventions like point and click and selecting multiple items using the shift or control keys.

Based on the 1997 Economic Census CD-ROMs, you will be able to select the data set you want to use by geographic area, industry, or data subject. Additionally, based on past software, it is reasonable to assume that the 2002 version will

- Present data in a tabular spreadsheet form (rows, columns, fields)
- Allow customized layout, appearance changes, and field effects, so you can change fonts, turn grid lines on/off, and customize report titles
- Manipulate columns—move, resize, create/insert, freeze, hide
- Sort, both ascending and descending, based on one to three data table columns

In summary, the CD-ROMs provide easy access to large amounts of data. They are inexpensive. They do not have limits on the amount of data you can export, unlike American FactFinder. They are one of two sources for data about ZIP codes—the other is the hypertext drill-down table. However, it does take a little time to get used to the software.

While the 1997 Economic Census CD-ROMs included all of the datasets that were issued, American FactFinder and the drill-down tables each contained a few datasets. However, AFF and the drill-down tables generally contained different datasets from each other. Further, the CD-ROMs are the only source for the complete ZIP code, Minority- and Women-Owned Business Enterprises, Business Expenses, and Outlying Areas datasets.

## HOW TO READ A TABLE

Tables are usually one- or two-dimensional representations of the information. In a one-dimensional table, the data variables are generally presented in one column and the data in a second. An example of this is shown in Figure 6.5. These types of tables are most common in reports that show detailed data about one topic, such as the industry reports in manufacturing, mining, and construction. Frequently, these one-dimensional tables will include a wide variety of data about one general topic, such as detailed statistics for manufacturers in Oregon.

You should note that because of the wide variety of data presented in this type of table, the units of measure are shown on each data line—just before the data itself. Thus, there are 5,428 companies in Oregon (this is reported as a number), they paid $7,095,286,000 in annual payroll during 1997 (reported as $1,000), and used 15,278,998,000 kilowatt-hours of purchased electricity (reported as 1,000 kWh).

Usually in a two-dimensional table, you will find the data concepts presented across the top of the table and the industries listed down the side. Looking at Figure 6.6, with a simple glance you can see this is a statistical tool for displaying relationships among data. It can be read horizontally or vertically and depending how you read it, the meaning changes.

Looking at the table in detail, the first line is the title, "Table 1a. Summary Statistics for Firms Subject to Federal Income Tax for the United States: 1997—con." It tells you in general terms what data are contained in the table. The "con." states that this is the continuation of a table from an earlier page. Tables are consistent across all the series. For example, Table 1 in the Geographic Area Series will always contain the Summary Statistics.

The next line is the table's universe, in very small print. This tells you who or what is being counted in this table. In this case it shows "only establishments with payroll." This is telling you that establishments without employees are not included. This would be very important to know if you were trying to draw attention to the importance of your industry. For example, the total of other amusement and recreations services (NAICS 7139) is not just the 47,464 with employees shown in this table, but also includes the 145,698 reported in the separate Nonemployer Statistics, for a total of 193,162. The second line also provides directions on where to find more information about the abbreviations, symbols, and terms.

Then comes the data table itself. Most tables in the Economic Census are easy to read. The Census Bureau has been on the cutting edge of presenting data starting with the *Manual of Tabular Presentation: An Outline of Theory and Practice in the Presentation of Statistical Data in Tables for Publication* (Jenkinson 1949). The basic format uses lines to divide columns and column headers. Indentation is used to show hierarchical relationships. The column headers are clearly stated. *Read* the column headers; they contain important information. These will tell you that the receipts are in thousands of dollars or if the number of paid employees is the actual count on a certain day. Sometimes the headers are divided themselves as in the case of the last two columns. It tells the reader that both columns are shown in percentage of receipts.

You might also see the industries grouped by geographic area. For example in Figure 6.6, the third column shows that there are 47,464 establishments that are classified under other amusement and recreation services. Looking at the data portion of the table one line at a time, the first line tells us that this is a continuation of a table showing totals for the United States. Then it describes the hierarchy of industry sector and sub-sector. The next line starts the progressive hierarchy with the industry group of NAICS 7139. Please note that as digits are added to the NAICS code (in the first column), the indenting increases in the "kind of business" column. A common mistake made in reading the tables is not realizing the data are hierarchical and therefore cumulative. The columns should not be added within the industry group. It's made simple, by giving you the total in the first line. The 47,464 businesses are the total of businesses listed in NAICS 71391, 71392, 71393, 71394, 71395, and 71399. There are only 379 skiing facilities (NAICS 71392) in the United States not 758 (379 plus 379, from NAICS 71392 and 713920).

As stated above it is also critical to pay attention to the indentation of the lines since these show the hierarchy of the data in PDFs. They show which lines can be added together in order to get the appropriate totals. For example, to get the total number of other amusement and recreation services, you would add together the lines for golf courses and country clubs, skiing facilities, marinas, fitness and recreational sports centers, bowling centers, and all other amusement and recreation industries because these are all indented to the same extent under other amusement and recreation services. You would not add the ice skating rinks and roller skating rinks into this total

Figure 6.5
Sample One-Dimensional Table

[For meaning of abbreviations and symbols, see introductory text. For explanation of terms, see appendixes]

| Item | | Value |
|------|------|------|
| **OREGON** | | |
| Companies[1] | number.. | 5 428 |
| | | |
| All establishments | number.. | 5 768 |
| Establishments with 1 to 19 employees | number.. | 4 093 |
| Establishments with 20 to 99 employees | number.. | 1 204 |
| Establishments with 100 employees or more | number.. | 471 |
| | | |
| All employees | number.. | 213 111 |
| Total compensation[2] | $1,000.. | 8 891 591 |
| Annual payroll | $1,000.. | 7 095 286 |
| Total fringe benefits | $1,000.. | 1 796 305 |
| | | |
| Production workers, average for year | number.. | 158 506 |
| Production workers on March 12 | number.. | 153 945 |
| Production workers on May 12 | number.. | 156 585 |
| Production workers on August 12 | number.. | 164 317 |
| Production workers on November 12 | number.. | 159 077 |
| | | |
| Production-worker hours | 1,000.. | 316 808 |
| Production-worker wages | $1,000.. | 4 545 793 |
| | | |
| Total cost of materials | $1,000.. | 22 770 601 |
| Cost of materials, parts, containers, etc., consumed | $1,000.. | 19 948 345 |
| Cost of resales | $1,000.. | 1 387 786 |
| Cost of fuels | $1,000.. | 257 879 |
| Cost of purchased electricity | $1,000.. | 547 579 |
| Cost of contract work | $1,000.. | 629 012 |

| Item | | Value |
|------|------|------|
| **OREGON—Con.** | | |
| Quantity of electricity purchased for heat and power | 1,000 kWh.. | 15 278 998 |
| Quantity of electricity generated less sold for heat and power | 1,000 kWh.. | 681 514 |
| | | |
| Total value of shipments | $1,000.. | 47 665 990 |
| Value of resales | $1,000.. | 1 658 664 |
| | | |
| Value added | $1,000.. | 25 077 180 |
| | | |
| Total inventories, beginning of year | $1,000.. | 5 124 342 |
| Finished goods inventories, beginning of year | $1,000.. | 1 829 981 |
| Work-in-process inventories, beginning of year | $1,000.. | 1 364 488 |
| Materials and supplies inventories, beginning of year | $1,000.. | 1 929 873 |
| | | |
| Total inventories, end of year | $1,000.. | 5 398 261 |
| Finished goods inventories, end of year | $1,000.. | 1 897 536 |
| Work-in-process inventories, end of year | $1,000.. | 1 398 994 |
| Materials and supplies inventories, end of year | $1,000.. | 2 101 731 |
| | | |
| Gross book value of total assets at beginning of year | $1,000.. | 22 006 876 |
| Total capital expenditures (new and used) | $1,000.. | 2 715 770 |
| Capital expenditures for buildings and other structures (new and used) | $1,000.. | 623 652 |
| Capital expenditures for machinery and equipment (new and used) | $1,000.. | 2 092 118 |
| Total retirements[2] | $1,000.. | 869 955 |
| Gross book value of total assets at end of year | $1,000.. | 23 852 691 |
| | | |
| Total depreciation during year[2] | $1,000.. | 1 670 460 |
| | | |
| Total rental payments[2] | $1,000.. | 406 686 |
| Buildings and other structures rental payments[2] | $1,000.. | 203 457 |
| Machinery and equipment rental payments[2] | $1,000.. | 203 229 |

[1]For the census, a company is defined as a business organization consisting of one establishment or more under common ownership or control.
[2]These items are collected in the ASM and estimated for the remaining establishments.

Source: 1997 Economic Census. Manufacturing. Oregon.

Figure 6.6
Sample Two-Dimensional Table: Summary Statistics for Firms Subject to Federal Income Tax for the United States: 1997—Con.

[Includes only establishments with payroll.  For meaning of abbreviations and symbols, see introductory text.  For explanation of terms, see Appendix A]

| NAICS code | Geographic area and kind of business | Establishments (number) | Receipts ($1,000) | Annual payroll ($1,000) | First-quarter payroll ($1,000) | Paid employees for pay period including March 12 (number) | Percent of receipts— From administrative records[1] | Estimated[2] |
|---|---|---|---|---|---|---|---|---|
|  | **UNITED STATES**—Con. |  |  |  |  |  |  |  |
| 71 | **Arts, entertainment, & recreation**—Con. |  |  |  |  |  |  |  |
| 713 | Amusement, gambling, & recreation industries—Con. |  |  |  |  |  |  |  |
| 7139 | Other amusement & recreation services | 47 464 | 27 901 150 | 7 963 355 | 1 771 544 | 656 704 | 24.4 | 8.3 |
| 71391 | Golf courses & country clubs | 8 546 | 8 636 921 | 2 731 863 | 516 430 | 160 118 | 20.6 | 7.1 |
| 713910 | Golf courses & country clubs | 8 546 | 8 636 921 | 2 731 863 | 516 430 | 160 118 | 20.6 | 7.1 |
| 71392 | Skiing facilities | 379 | 1 340 813 | 431 147 | 166 775 | 58 513 | 5.0 | 4.6 |
| 713920 | Skiing facilities | 379 | 1 340 813 | 431 147 | 166 775 | 58 513 | 5.0 | 4.6 |
| 71393 | Marinas | 4 217 | 2 541 481 | 516 589 | 102 145 | 22 765 | 30.6 | 6.5 |
| 713930 | Marinas | 4 217 | 2 541 481 | 516 589 | 102 145 | 22 765 | 30.6 | 6.5 |
| 71394 | Fitness & recreational sports centers | 16 604 | 7 944 954 | 2 405 043 | 562 933 | 256 397 | 24.6 | 10.6 |
| 713940 | Fitness & recreational sports centers | 16 604 | 7 944 954 | 2 405 043 | 562 933 | 256 397 | 24.6 | 10.6 |
| 7139404 | Ice skating rinks | 381 | 298 737 | 78 587 | 19 552 | 8 870 | 20.2 | 7.2 |
| 7139405 | Roller skating rinks | 1 611 | 416 339 | 111 912 | 28 316 | 19 416 | 34.7 | 7.1 |
| 71395 | Bowling centers | 5 590 | 2 820 685 | 821 044 | 213 889 | 88 044 | 22.8 | 6.9 |
| 713950 | Bowling centers | 5 590 | 2 820 685 | 821 044 | 213 889 | 88 044 | 22.8 | 6.9 |
| 71399 | All other amusement & recreation industries | 12 128 | 4 616 296 | 1 057 669 | 209 372 | 70 867 | 34.1 | 9.8 |
| 713990 | All other amusement & recreation industries | 12 128 | 4 616 296 | 1 057 669 | 209 372 | 70 867 | 34.1 | 9.8 |
| 7139901 | Dance studios & halls | 293 | 91 068 | 26 303 | 5 839 | 2 663 | 28.2 | 5.4 |
| 7139902 | Concession operators of amusement devices & rides | 1 072 | 364 054 | 84 290 | 12 688 | 5 967 | 31.5 | 8.9 |
| 7139904 | Miniature golf courses | 1 041 | 307 886 | 72 833 | 12 432 | 5 326 | 29.9 | 4.3 |
| 7139905 | Coin-operated amusement devices (except slot machine operation) | 2 668 | 1 705 888 | 342 156 | 78 275 | 18 907 | 27.7 | 7.8 |

Source: 1997 Economic Census. Arts, Entertainment, and Recreation. United States.

since they are already included in fitness and recreational centers. Industry descriptions are not indented to show hierarchy in AFF, drill-down tables on the Internet, or CD-ROM, so the user must pay careful attention to the length of the NAICS code to indicate category hierarchy.

Remember a table reveals relationships. Vertically, it reflects the hierarchy of a group of industries when reading a two-dimensional table. Horizontally, it provides a description of the industry. So if you want to know about skiing industry you know to read across the table. There are 379 federal-income-tax-paying skiing business with a total of $1,340,813,000 dollars in receipts, an annual payroll of $431,147,000, and with the first quarter (high season for skiing) payroll of $166,775,000. They employed only 58,513 people in that first period up to and including March 12, which would work out to be $2,850 per employee for the first quarter.

The two right-hand columns of this table provide information about the quality of the data in the other columns. In the case of the skiing facilities, they tell us that 5 percent of the total receipts were derived from administrative records and 4.6 percent of the receipts were estimated based on historic company ratios, administrative records, or industry averages. These figures may be used as indicators of data quality. Lower percentages are better. How do you know where the estimated receipts came from? You know that because the footnotes at the bottom of the table provide that information. Footnotes can relate to anything in the table and contain important information.

Going back to Figure 6.6, say you want to compare industries, not look at just one. Reading the table vertically, with an understanding that the data are presented hierarchically would let you do this. If you wanted to compare the receipts from skiing industry with other amusement and recreation services, you would have to first figure out what level of detail would be best, the five-digit NAICS industry or six-digit US industry level. You also have to decide what data subjects you are interested in: establishments, revenue, employee size, or a combination. Maybe by looking at receipts divided by number of employees, you can see which industry is most labor intensive.

## SYMBOLS AND ABBREVIATIONS

Sometimes the Census Bureau needs to avoid publishing a number for any of several reasons. In these cases, they substitute a symbol for the number. Other times, they use abbreviations to save space in a title. This section describes the symbols and abbreviations you can expect to see in the various reports.

All of the reports share the same symbols. The symbol you will see most is "**D**." The **D** means that the data item is being withheld to avoid disclosing data of individual companies. However, the data suppressed at one level are still included in higher-level figures. A scenario where this might happen would be if you ran an online information service (NAICS 514191) and it was the only one in the county you were looking at. The line for 514191 in the reports for this county would have a **D** in the place for revenue and payroll. But it would show a 1 for the number of establishments in the industry in the county and a letter code for the range of employees at the establishment. From there it would get trickier, depending on the number and location of other online information services located elsewhere in the state. If the state had more online providers in the other counties and they had numbers in all the categories, then another county's totals would also be suppressed to prevent you from figuring out the data for the one establishment in the one county by subtraction. By suppressing another county's data, the Census Bureau is still able to provide statewide totals. Even with more than one company in an area you will see **D**, because there may be a dominant establishment and it would be too easy to figure out its payroll and employment. The bottom line is there is no way anyone can figure out the data for an individual company by looking at the Economic Census. Similarly, data for another industry within the county could also be suppressed to avoid getting the data by subtraction.

The next abbreviations you will see frequently are "**N**," "**X**," and "**Z**." When data are not available or it isn't comparable you will see an **N**. This will appear a lot when looking at reports that include numbers from the 1992 Census, because some of the industry classifications just didn't exist then. Similarly, **X** is used when the data are not applicable. When the value in a cell would round to zero, you will see a **Z**. For example, if an industry uses some electricity, but less than 500 kWh in a year, the report would show a **Z** because the standard unit of measure reported is thousands of kilowatt-hours (without any decimal places) and the amount used is less than 0.5 thousands of kWh, which rounds to 0.0 thousands of kWh.

The revised symbol, **r**, is seen in the PDF, American FactFinder, and CD-ROM for data items that have been released earlier with different numbers. The

HTML tables do not use **r** for the revised numbers where the revision occurred before the HTML tables were published. Typically, these revisions are the result of finding that an establishment was placed in the wrong industry or geographic area, or that it was duplicated. As soon as the Bureau got more information they would revise their results. Much to the credit of the Census Bureau's Economic Directorate, they report all of their errors honestly and in a timely manner.

Some of the symbols are specific to certain industry sectors. Finance and insurance (NAICS 52) uses **Q** in place of revenues below the state level, since multi-establishment companies do not report revenues by establishment in these industries. Mostly it is done when a financial institution is a branch and the income from that branch is not counted separately for that establishment. In the Commodity Flow Survey, a **V** represents less than 50 vehicles or .05 percent. In the retail sector, a **Y** is used when disclosure is withheld because of insufficient coverage of merchandise lines. In the few reports that calculate ratios, **F** is used when showing the ratio cannot be calculated correctly for some reason.

Other symbols are related to the statistical quality of the data. The most common is **S,** which signifies that data are being withheld because estimates did not meet the Census Bureau's statistical standards for publication. This means that not enough establishments reported the data for a clean number to be given. In the construction sector, **A** is used when the standard error is 100 percent or more. In infrequent cases when sampling was used to calculate the numbers, you might see **p, q,** or **s** to mean respectively 10 to 19 percent estimated, 20 to 29 percent estimated, and sampling error exceeds 40 percent.

When it comes to reporting employee size for an industry subject to suppression, the Bureau uses lower case letters to show the workforce range. You can estimate the numbers by subtracting the other industries in that sub-sector and see the remaining numbers. The drill-down tables show the range, not the letters:

- a—0 to 19 employees.
- b—20 to 99 employees.
- c—100 to 249 employees.
- e—250 to 499 employees.
- f—500 to 999 employees.
- g—1,000 to 2,499 employees.
- h—2,500 to 4,999 employees.
- i—5,000 to 9,999 employees.
- j—10,000 to 24,999 employees.
- k—25,000 to 49,999 employees.

- l—50,000 to 99,999 employees.
- m—100,000 employees or more.

In the PDF documents, when the products lines of revenue, production, and merchandise are collected, but the respondent did not specify a listed category, they are labeled **nsk,** which stands for "not specified by kind." When using SIC-based reports you might see the abbreviation **nec** in an industry description, to mean "not elsewhere classified."

Some geographic areas also have standard abbreviations. See the terminology chapter (chapter 3) for descriptions of these areas. Abbreviations you can expect to see are

- **CC** is for a consolidated city.
- **IC** is for independent city.
- **MSA** and **MeSA** both stand for Metropolitan Statistical Area. MSA was used in the 1997 Economic Census. MeSA was used in 2002 to avoid confusion with Micropolitan Statistical Areas.
- **MiSA** stands for Micropolitan Statistical Area (2002).
- **PMSA** is for Primary Metropolitan Statistical Area (1997).
- **CMSA** is the abbreviation used for Consolidated Metropolitan Statistical Area. CSA represents a Combined Statistical Area (1997).
- **MD** stands for Metropolitan Division (2002).

## CITING THE ECONOMIC CENSUS

One aspect of research is that researchers keep building on the work of each other. Frequently, this entails going back to a previous researcher's information sources, even if it is just as a starting place to find related information that might be interesting. Therefore, it is important to let your readers know where you are getting your information. Citations are the standard way of giving your readers this information.

Additionally, the people who put your information source together did a substantial amount of work for you. Citations are also a way of thanking those people for their effort.

There are two basic types of citations. The first type tells the reader exactly where you got a specific piece of information. The other type is a more general reference to the sources you used in your research.

The first type of citation is often referred to as in-text citations. These may be footnotes; endnotes; or parenthetic or in-line citations. These citations are tied to specific text within your work and refer to exact locations in the source material.

The second type of citation is often referred to as a bibliography, works cited, or references cited list. These are more general in nature and provide general information about the source document. Usually, these are located at the end of your work, but can be placed at the ends of chapters.

There are numerous standards for each type of citation depending on the exact type of document being cited. Additionally, there are a number of format styles available for citing the same type of document. Some of the more commonly used format styles are the Modern Language Association (MLA), American Psychological Association (APA), University of Chicago Press, Turabian, and Government Documents Round Table (GODORT) of the American Libraries Association (ALA) styles. Additionally, specific fields of study have their own citation standards that are generally limited to their own field; for example, the legal profession generally uses their own style manual. The standards for each of these styles are included in reference books published by the various organizations. As a writer, your choice of format and style should be guided by the expectations or requirements of your audience or publisher.

To assist you in developing citations, we are suggesting some ways to cite the various Economic Census data sources. For the purposes of this section, the style set forth by the Government Documents Round Table (GODORT) of the American Libraries Association (ALA) will be used in the bibliographic (b) listing and the Turabian style will be used in examples for parenthetical references (pr) and footnote (n) styles. Parenthetical references generally include just enough information to find the document in the bibliographic list and the location of the information being cited within the source document, such as the page number.

To fill out a bibliography you will need to know things like author, title, publisher, and publication format. The publication format will determine what your citation will look like. Generally, the information included in a citation includes the author, title, and date and location of publication. Additional information might include the format—especially if this is not a printed document, report number, notes to make finding the source easier, and page numbers—especially for in-text citations.

The examples below are based on the data concerning the key statistics for cosmetology and barber schools (NAICS 611511) in the state of Missouri.

Bibliographic citations are a variation of: Issuing agency. *Title.* (Agency report number; medium). Edition. Place of publication: publisher, date. (Series). (Note: Including additional information such as SuDoc Number, alternate distributors, method of access, etc., can help other users find and use your sources.)

Footnote citations include the tables and page numbers to the citation.

## Printed Materials

Author. *Title.* Place of Publication: Publisher, Date. (Series elements). (Notes).

Since none of the geographic area reports is issued in print, the example used is the *1997 Economic Census. Survey of Minority-Owned Business Enterprises. Summary.*

(b)

U.S. Bureau of the Census. *1997 Economic Census. Survey of Minority-Owned Business Enterprises: Summary.* (EC97CS-7). Washington, DC: Government Printing Office, 2001. (SuDoc: C3.277/3:97-7).

(pr)

(Census, *Summary,* 36)

(n)

[1] "Table 2. Statistics for Minority—Owned Firms by Minority for States: 1997—Con.," p. 36. in U.S. Bureau of the Census. *1997 Economic Census. Survey of Minority-owned Business Enterprises: Summary.* (EC97CS-7). (Washington, DC: Government Printing Office, 2001).

(Note: the table number would not bring you to the data, a page number brings you to the page with the data.)

## PDF Documents

Author. *Title, edition.* Medium. Date of publication/load. Supplier. Available at: [URL]; Accessed: [date retrieved].

The PDF citation is much like the print with the URL and date retrieved in the note section instead of the SuDoc number. The date is the date shown on the cover of the PDF report. You do not have to include a page number in the footnote, as long as you give the table number.

(b)

U.S. Bureau of the Census. *1997 Economic Census, Educational Services, Geographic Area Series: Missouri* (EC97S61A-MO). PDF format. August 1999. Washington: The Bureau. Available: http://www.census.gov/prod/ec97/97s61-mo.PDF; Accessed: July 23, 2003.

(pr)

(Census, Educational Services, *Missouri*)

(n)

[1]"Table 1a: Summary Statistics for Firms Subject to Federal Income Tax for the State: 1997," in U.S. Bureau of the Census. *1997 Economic Census, Educational Services, Geographic Area Series: Missouri.* Available: http://www.census.gov/prod/ec97/97s61-mo.PDF; Accessed: July 23, 2003.

## Hypertext Drill-Down Tables

Author (Agency). *Title, edition.* Medium. Date of publication/load. Supplier. Available at: [URL]; Accessed: [date retrieved].

When citing an item directly off the Internet, the rule of thumb for defining the title is to use the header of the page, without adding the browser name. The publication date is the same as the load date. In the case of the drill-down tables, the publication/load date would be the last modified date found at the bottom of the page, not the released date listed on the referring page. Since some Web pages are long and they do not have page numbers relating to the scrolling, insert phrases such "Data from:..." to let others know that information is coming from a larger page.

This standard works well for "static html" pages. Some long and complicated URLs are generated "on the fly" by programs. Before you cite a complicated URL, make sure you can access it in another session (e.g., open a different browser and paste it in). If not you may have to revert to citing only the system's entry page (as in most American FactFinder tables).

(b)

U.S. Bureau of the Census. *1997 Economic Census: Educational Services—Missouri.* Web page. Last modified February 6, 2001. Washington: The Bureau. Available at: http://www.census.gov/epcd/ec97/mo/MO000_61.HTM; Accessed: July 23, 2003.

(pr)

(Census, *Missouri*)

(n)

[1]"Educational Services by Industry" taken from *1997 Economic Census: Educational Services—Missouri.* Release date February 6, 2001. Available at: http://www.census.gov/epcd/ec97/mo/MO000_61.HTM; Accessed: July 23, 2003.

## American FactFinder

Author (Agency). "Name of data repository/source." (Edition). Data set: name of source of data. Available at: name of software used to generate the extraction/tabulation. URL of the application software's main page; Accessed: Date.

There are two ways to get data out of the American FactFinder through quick reports and self-generated data. The *quick reports* use the same format as the Web page, however, since you can use this data in a spreadsheet the medium is Excel format and you might also include the size of the file.

(b)

U.S. Bureau of the Census. *Cosmetology & Barber Schools: NAICS: 611511, Selected Industry Statistics by State: 1997 and 1992* (Industry Quick Report). Data set: Economic Census, 1997. Available at: American FactFinder. http://factfinder.census.gov; Accessed: July 23, 2003.

(pr)

(Census, *AFF*)

(n)

[1] "*Cosmetology & Barber Schools: NAICS: 611511, Selected Industry Statistics by State: 1997 and 1992*" (Industry Quick Report). Data set based on Economic Census, 1997. Available at: American FactFinder (Census Bureau). http://factfinder.census.gov; Accessed: July 23, 2003.

For a *self-generated report* it is harder to define the author, title, and source. It is good to list the name of the person who generated the data, in case any questions are asked about the source or access method.

(b)

U.S. Bureau of the Census. Data Set: *Economic-Wide Key Statistics: 1997* (Excel File). generated by Jennifer Boettcher; using American FactFinder. http://factfinder.census.gov; Accessed: July 23, 2003.

(pr)

(Census, *AFF*)

(n)

[1]"Sector 61: Educational Services: Geographic Area Series: 1997" (Excel File). Data set: *Economic-Wide Key Statistics.* generated by Jennifer Boettcher; using American FactFinder (Census Bureau). http://factfinder.census.gov; Accessed: July 23, 2003.

**Figure 6.7**
**Map Created with GIS Software**

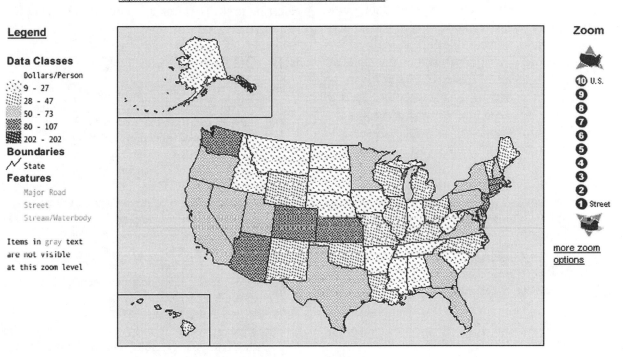

Source: U.S. Bureau of the Census, 1997 Economic Census

## CD-ROM

Author. *Title, edition* (Agency Report Number, Medium). Place of publication: Publisher, Date. (Notes).

The CD-ROM is the second most used media, behind the Internet. It might be necessary to identify a dataset within the title in the parenthetical. The style of the data will depend on how you retrieve the data (PDF reports or generated table). If a choose to get a PDF report printed off the CD-ROM then use the PDF format, but use the disk information instead of a URL.

The examples given here are for those data tables generated from the CD-ROM. The title of the work listed in the endnote should reflect what is listed on the top of the report. If you print out the report, you will have the option to change the report name.

(b)

U.S. Bureau of the Census. *1997 Economic Census* (CD-ROM). ECON97S, Geographic Report Series, Release 1F. Washington, DC: The Bureau, November 2001. (3.277:C 1-E 97-NA 1 F-17-US 1)

(pr)

(Census, Missouri, CD-ROM)

(n)

[1]"Ed (NAICS), MO, 1997" (dBASE format). Data from U.S. Bureau of the Census. *Economic Census* (CD-ROM). Washington, DC: The Bureau.

## Maps

Author or statement of responsibility. *Map Title* (map). Data date if known. Scale; Name of the person who generated map; Name of Software used to generate the map or "Title of the complete Web site." (date generated).

With increases in the flexibility of data come greater ways to use it. Any database that uses a geographic variable will probably be linked with a FIPS code. The FIPS code can then be used in any standard Geographic Information System (GIS) software to generate a map. One way to draw a simple map is to create a thematic map on the American FactFinder Web site (see Figure 6.7). As of the 1997 Census only industry sectors by state or country can be mapped.

(b)

U.S. Bureau of the Census. *Value of Shipments/ Sales/Receipts per Capita for Educational Services (taxable only):1997* (map). Scale undetermined; generated by Jennifer Boettcher; using "American FactFinder, Thematic Maps." http://factfinder. census. gov/servlet/ThematicMapFramesetServlet?_ lang=en. (August 19, 2003).

(pr)

(Census, Map)

(n)

[1]*TM-61–004T Value of Shipment/Sales/Receipts per Capita for Education Services (Taxable only): 1997* (map). Visual scale; American FactFinder. http:// factfinder.census.gov. (August 19, 2003).

## Secondary Sources

When working with another source, you will sometimes recognize tables with data taken from the Economic Census. At a minimum, you should cite the source that you are using. In many situations, you should also indicate that the data came from the Economic Census. Since there are many subtleties involved with these types of citations, you are best off referring to the style manual you are following for the rest of your work.

## BIBLIOGRAPHY

Cheney, Debora, ed. 2002. *The Complete Guide to Citing Government Information Resources: A Manual for Social Science and Business Research.* 3rd ed. Bethesda, MD: Congressional Information Service.

Jenkinson, Bruce Le Roy. 1949. *Manual of Tabular Presentation; an Outline of Theory and Practice in the Presentation of Statistical Data in Tables for Publication.* Washington, DC: Government Printing Office.

Turabian, Kate. 1996. *A Manual for Writers of Term Papers, Theses, and Dissertations.* 6th ed. Chicago: University of Chicago Press.

U.S. Bureau of the Census. 2003. Economic Census. http://www.census.gov/epcd/www/econ97.html (accessed October 10, 2003).

U.S. Bureau of the Census. 2003. Guide to the 2002 Economic Census. http://www.census.gov/epcd/ec02/ guide.html (accessed October 10, 2003).

# PART II
# Selected Industries

# CHAPTER 7
# Agriculture

*Some inquiries having been made of me by important characters, on the state of agriculture in America, Comprehending its several relations, and intended to ascertain the value of our lands, with their yield in the several kinds of grains, grass, etc. The prices and farming stock; the prices of produce, etc. Together with a list of the taxes in the different States, which may in a way affect the farmer; as an object highly interesting to our country, I have determined to enter the most just and satisfactory answers that the best information I can obtain from different parts of the United States will enable me to give.*

*—George Washington (Letter, August 25, 1791, Philadelphia)*

1. Overview and History
2. Conducting the Census

   A. Questionnaire Design
   B. Coverage
   C. Data Collection Procedures
   D. Error Handling Procedures

3. Question: What Is in the Census of Agriculture?
4. Product Distribution

   A. Printed Reports
   B. Census of Agriculture on the Internet
   C. Census of Agriculture on CD-ROM
   D. Special Tabulations

5. Using the Agricultural Census

   A. Government
   B. Business
   C. Farmers
   D. Farm Associations and Other Organizations
   E. Researchers and Scholars

6. Current Surveys and Data
7. Answers: What Is in the Census of Agriculture?
8. Agriculture According to NAICS

## OVERVIEW AND HISTORY

The quest to understand the United States' economy must include agriculture. In fact, the history of the United States can be told through its agricultural roots. To understand those roots, one needs a picture of the nation's farms. This chapter describes how the National Agricultural Statistical Service (NASS) conducts the Census of Agriculture, provides an explanation of the data available in that Census, and explains how to use the different formats the data come in. Examples of data users and a review of surveys that are available to update the census also will be found in this chapter.

In 1790, 90 percent of the population was estimated to be working in agriculture; in 2001 it was only 1.7 percent, according to the Bureau of Labor Statistics. That information and more about what happened in between comes from the civil servants who design the questions, collect data, crunch the numbers, distribute the results, and use the information in decisions. It was estimated in 2003 that there are around 2.1 million farms. The growth and decline in farms are seen in Table 7.1.

The 1810 Population Census contained questions covering manufacturing and farming, but the data collected were inconsistent throughout the nation. But it was not until Martin Van Buren was able to convince the Congress to fund the 1840 Economic Census, including agriculture, mining, commerce, and manufactures that we can say that there was a true agricultural census. This was the first time agricultural production was measured on a standardized basis nationally.

Before the 1840 Census, agricultural statistics were collected by the local agricultural societies and some state censuses. The United States Patent Office was also responsible for early agricultural data. On September 30, 1859, at the Wisconsin State Fair, Abraham Lincoln noted, "Many years ago I saw it stated in a Patent Office Report that eighteen bushels was the average crop of the wheat through the United States." In 1862 Abraham Lincoln created the Department of Agriculture, with responsibility for "Collecting, arranging, publishing, and disseminating, for the benefit to the Nation, statistical and other useful information in regards to agriculture in the widest accept" (*U.S. Commissioner of Agriculture Report, 1862*, 20). However, agricultural data collected in the census was still done by the Census Office, which was a temporary office established for each census until 1910.

**Table 7.1**
**Farms in History**

| Year | Farms (average size in acres) | Year | Farms (average size in acres) |
|------|------|------|------|
| 1997 | 1,911,859 (487) | 1992 | 1,925,300 (491) |
| 1987 | 2,087,759 (462) | 1982 | 2,240,976 (440) |
| 1978 | 2,257,775 (449) | 1974 | 2,314,013 (440) |
| 1969 | 2,730,250 (389) | 1964 | 3,157,857 (352) |
| 1959 | 3,710,503 (303) | 1954 | 4,782,416 (242) |
| 1950 | 5,358,437 (216) | 1945 | 5,859,169 (195) |
| 1940 | 6,102,417 (175) | 1935 | 6,812,000 (155) |
| 1930 | 6,295,000 (157) | 1925 | 6,372,000 (145) |
| 1920 | 6,454,000 (149) | 1910 | 6,366,000 (139) |
| 1900 | 5,740,000 (147) | 1890 | 4,565,000 (137) |
| 1880 | 4,009,000 (134) | 1870 | 2,660,000 (153) |
| 1860 | 2,044,000 (199) | 1850 | 1,449,000 (203) |

Historical data from the agriculture census is available every ten years starting in 1840 through 1950. Historians can use the data to show the changes in the U.S. economy from a country where farms were small, plentiful, and local in their sales to today where farms are fewer, much larger, highly mechanized, and national—even global—in their sales area. Further, by looking at the farms by region and comparing that information with the changing transportation and population distribution patterns over time, a clearer picture of our nation's development comes to light.

Additional mid-decade censuses were conducted in 1925, 1935, and 1945. During the 1954 to 1974 period the census was taken for the years ending in 4 and 9. There was a special census in 1978 so the Congress could finally adjust the data reference years to those ending in 2 and 7 so they coincided with the economic censuses.

One result of the 1997 Appropriations Act was that the responsibility of the Census of Agriculture was transferred from the Census Bureau to the Department of Agriculture's National Agricultural Statistics Service (NASS). For the first time in our nation's history the Agriculture Census was consolidated with the annual, monthly, and weekly surveys conducted by NASS. The 2002 Census of Agriculture was also conducted by NASS.

## CONDUCTING THE CENSUS

As with all data collection efforts, there are a number of issues that need to be resolved in order to ensure that data is collected and reported efficiently and accurately. This section discusses the issues involved with designing the questionnaires, providing accurate and complete coverage, describing how the data were actually collected, and explaining the methods used to minimize data errors. The data reporting methods are discussed in the section on products.

## Questionnaire Design

The Agriculture Census was carried out by a dedicated team of staff, most of whom were transferred from the Census Bureau to NASS during the 1997 Census cycle. While they were still at the Census Bureau, they reviewed and revised the census forms in order to account for changes due to the implementation of NAICS and changes in farming and the needs of data users.

Two forms were used in this census—a short form and a long form. The short form, sent to 75 percent of the farms, asked basic questions on land use; ownership; irrigated land; crop acreage and quantities harvested; livestock and poultry inventories; value of products sold; acres set aside in federal acreage reduction programs; payments for participating in federal farm programs; the amount received from Commodity Credit Corporation loans; number of hired farm workers; number of injuries and deaths; and operator characteristics.

The long forms were sent to the other 25 percent of the recipients. This form covered the basic questions from the short form and included additional questions on production expenses; fertilizer and chemicals use; machinery and equipment inventories; market value of land and buildings; and income from farm-related sources. The resulting data went into the special studies.

The forms were also tailored for various parts of the country to account for thirteen regional differences in crops. All in all, most of the forms used the same questions from previous census forms. A total of 37 different forms were finalized. Once the survey instruments were designed, identifying where they should be sent was the next big step.

## Coverage

There are several aspects involved in defining the coverage of a census. In the Census of Agriculture the major coverage issues are who to include, what products to include, and for which geographic areas.

### Who Is Included in the Agricultural Census?

The coverage of the census starts with the definition of a farm. In this census the term farm is used generically to include ranchers, foresters, fishermen, furriers, nurserymen, and anyone else who produced agricultural products during the census year. To qualify as a farm the value of the products has to be $1,000 or more. The census form was also sent to farms that normally would have sold or produced $1,000 or more, but because of crop failure, abandonment, soil conservation, sale of the land, and other similar reasons had very low income from the farm for the reference year.

## What Is an Agricultural Product?

Historically, agricultural products have been defined according to the SIC system and included the traditional products of farming, forestry, and fishing such as grains, raw milk, shellfish in the shells, or cattle fed for slaughter. This concept does not include flour, wine, or other food products, because they are altered by a process and considered a manufactured product. With NAICS replacing SIC, new products are considered to be agricultural products. However, these changes were not included in the 1997 Census due to the timing of the census transition and approval of the new classification system, but were picked up in the 2002 Census of Agriculture. Services supporting agricultural activities in NAICS sectors are not included in the Census of Agriculture, but the U.S. Departments of Agriculture and Commerce report data about these industries in other reports.

Due to NASS's greater ongoing contact with the farming community and special efforts to increase coverage, described below, the Census of Agriculture represents a greater coverage of establishments, especially women and minority farm operators and farm operations on American Indian reservations, since moving to NASS than when it was conducted by the Census Bureau. NASS reports data by various geographic areas including the nation, states, counties, tribal lands, U.S. territories, congressional districts, and selected ZIP code areas.

## Data Collection Procedures

The first step in conducting a census is to locate the population to be included. For the Census of Agriculture, this means creating a mailing list containing all of the farms, ranches, and similar establishments. In order to create this mailing list, NASS mailed out letters and postcards to farmers, ranchers, local farm organizations, and county agents asking if they knew of any operators who might have been missed in previous agricultural censuses.

All farm operators were required by law to respond to the forms, even if they had not operated the farm in the reference year. The forms were sent out in December of the reference year and were due back in February of the following year. To help the farmer, NASS offered assistance through printed materials, toll-free telephone numbers, and workshops. It should be noted that NASS and other services from USDA routinely have representatives collecting data directly from farmers around the country, so they and the farmers generally have a good rapport with each other, which aids in the data collection effort.

The initial response rate was higher than expected based on the responses collected by the Census Bureau in earlier census years. This may be true for many reasons, including the fact that the reporting burden was decreased through the increased use of administrative records and transferring the census from the Department of Commerce to the Department of Agriculture (USDA). The farmers already had relations with USDA through county agents, financial assistance programs, and using technical reports, which could explain the increased the response rate. They also were familiar with the other statistical reports generated through NASS, so they know the benefits of their reporting.

However, not everyone returned the form by February. This started the usual types of follow-up activities used with most censuses with mail notices, phone calls, and visits. Once the forms were returned to NASS, they were entered into the computer. Then the number crunching began.

## Error Handling Procedures

Any time someone is asked a question there is a possibility of error. When a whole population is asked questions it's called a census and is only prone to nonsampling errors. These include the possibility of incorrect or incomplete responses to the census questionnaire or to the questions posed by an enumerator. To reduce reporting error, each respondent's answers were checked for completeness, reasonableness, and consistency with their other answers. The accuracy of the census is also affected by other nonsampling errors' sources, including incorrect data keying, editing, and imputing for missing data. Various procedures are used to reduce the impact of these errors.

Unlike the Economic Census, the Census of Agriculture did not issue any advance reports. The first data from the Census of Agriculture were included in the "State and County Highlights Table" and "State and County Profiles" issued two years after the reference year. The last set of data was released in the last of the Special Studies reports. The data reported in all of these Census of Agriculture reports remained consistent even if it was found that revisions were needed before all of the reports were released. If data needed to be revised, errata sheets with the revisions were issued.

---

## QUESTION: WHAT IS IN THE CENSUS OF AGRICULTURE?

**Can the following be found in the Census of Agriculture? Answers are at the end of this chapter.**

Bunny farms
Catfish farms
Corn farms
Cotton ginning
Cottage cheese makers
Farm stands
Gender of owner
Grapevine yards
Hiring seasonal workers
Horse stables
International trade
Internet use
Irrigation techniques
Organic production certification
Ostrich farms
Nursery plants
Pecan farms
Pesticide use
Slaughterhouses
Subsidy programs

---

## PRODUCT DISTRIBUTION

The Census of Agriculture includes several report series, also known as volumes. Volume One is the Geographic Area Series including one report for each state, territory, and summary of national statistics. ZIP code data are only available electronically in the Subject Series. Volume Two is the Subject Series that contains the Agricultural Atlas of the United States and Ranking of States and Counties. Volume Three includes the special studies reports: Farm and Ranch Irrigation Survey, Census of Horticultural Specialties, Census of Aquaculture, and Agricultural Economics and Land Ownership Survey.

Unlike the Economic Census, where very few reports are actually printed, the Census of Agriculture used printed reports as a major method of distribution. Other media used are CD-ROMs, the Internet, and custom reports. The printed reports are available in federal depository libraries as a core item, NASS state offices, various state government offices, and are available for purchase through the Government Printing Office.

The Internet increases the availability of the reports to a global audience and offers free access. All of the titles mentioned above are available in PDF format and are on the Internet. Additionally, selected reports can be downloaded in electronic format to be used in spreadsheets or GIS programs. The option to compute the data is a great benefit for researchers who want to combine the data with other factors for analysis.

ZIP Code and Congressional District Tabulations, and special tabulations are only available in electronic formats. Special tabulations are cross-tabulations of the census data produced by NASS on a customized basis for users who are willing to pay the price. Table 7.2 gives the media formats and release dates for the 2002 Census of Agriculture.

## Printed Reports

The Census of Agriculture is divided up into geographic, subject, and special series. Most of the Agriculture Census reports look no different from the comparable reports in earlier censuses. The content changes—as a result of the NASS collecting data—are reflected in the greater coverage of the land used in farming and details on how it is used. The Special Studies Series is also new to the Census of Agriculture.

If agriculture is not your primary interest, but you need some basic agricultural data, there are only three printed titles you need: *Census of Agriculture: United States Summary and State Data*, *Agricultural Atlas of the United States*, and the *Census of Agriculture: Statistical Detail*.

### Volume 1, Geographic Area Series

This series of reports focuses on geographic areas. Which means that each report presents all of the data for a single group of geographic areas, such as a state and its counties. U.S. territories and protectorates

**Table 7.2**
**Scheduled Release Dates for 2002 Census of Agriculture Products**

| Products | Media Formats Offered | Scheduled release Dates (Internet Only) * |
|---|---|---|
| Volume 1. Geographic Area Series | | |
| United States | I, P, C, D | February 2004 |
| State and County | I, P, C, D | February 2004 |
| Puerto Rico | I, P, C, D | February 2004 |
| Guam | I, P | Summer 2003 |
| U.S. Virgin Islands | I, P | Summer 2003 |
| Northern Mariana Islands | I, P | Summer 2003 |
| American Samoa (2003) | I, P | Summer 2004 |
| Specialty Products | | |
|    State and County Highlights | I | Spring 2004 |
|    County Profiles | I | Spring 2004 |
|    Native American | I, P | Fall 2004 |
|    Top Commodities | I | Fall 2004 |
| Volume 2. Subject Series | | |
| Agricultural Atlas | I, P | Summer 2004 |
| Congressional District Ranking | I, P | December 2004 |
| ZIP Code Tabulations of Selected Items | I | December 2004 |
| Congressional District Tabulation | I | December 2004 |
| History | I, P | TA |
| Volume 3. Special Studies | | |
| Farm and Ranch Irrigation Survey (2003) | I, P | December 2004 |
| Census of Horticultural Specialties (2004) | I, P | December 2005 |
| Census of Aquaculture (2005) | I, P | December 2006 |
| I - Internet, P- Printed publication, C- CD-ROM, D - Online Ag Statistics Database * These are INTERNET Release Dates. Release of printed publications and CD-ROMs will follow within a few months after these dates. | | |

(American Samoa, Northern Mariana Islands, Guam, Puerto Rico, and Virgin Islands) are also covered in the Census of Agriculture, in some cases for the first time in 1997. American Indian reservations data was also disaggregated to reflect the different farms in the reservations.

Chapter 1 of the *United States Summary and State Data* contains historical comparisons of national level data in tables 1 through 45. Tables 46 through 52 show data cross-tabulated by several categories, for example, Table 50 "Market Value of Agricultural Products

Sold" shows a cross-tabulation of the value of the crop by revenue of the farm in different states.

In chapter 2, tables 1 through 17 contain general data for all states comparing the previous census with the current reference year data, such as table three "Farm Production Expenses and Poultry—Inventory and Sales." Tables 18 through 39 show only those states reporting production of the agricultural product in the table, for example tables 20 and 36 "Angora Goats—Inventory and Sales" or "Farms Operated by Blacks and Other Races by Tenure." These tables also show the national totals for the previous census. The states are listed alphabetically instead of being ranked. To do the ranking easily, the researcher will have to have to use the data in electronic form that is available via the CD-ROM or refer to the *Ranking of States and Counties* report.

If you are interested in state- and country-level details, use the *Census of Agriculture: Statistical Detail* report. Chapter 1 has aggregated state-level data. This chapter contains historical data in table 1. Tables 2 through 19 deal with farm operational characteristics, such as land use (table 7) and the money spent on petroleum products (table 14). Details on the inventory and sales of specific farm products are shown in tables 20 through 44. Summaries of the characteristics of owners, size of farm, and other farm characteristics are shown in tables 45 to 52 of this chapter.

Chapter 2 has the county-level data. In this chapter, table 1 is the "Summary Highlights," while tables 2 through 12 have information about the operations of the farm and the characteristics of the farmers. The remaining tables through table 39 have crop and livestock data providing the inventory, sales, and production output for each county.

Even if you are limited to *United States Summary and State Data* and *Census of Agriculture: Statistical Detail,* just think of all of the interesting possibilities of exploring U.S. Agriculture. You can read about some of these uses later on in this chapter. However, the other parts of the census are worth looking at, especially if your interest lies in aquaculture, horticulture, irrigation, or policy decisions.

## Volume 2, Subject Series

The reports in this series present data in a number of specialized ways, such as by ZIP code or as maps.

### Agricultural Atlas of the United States

The *Agricultural Atlas of the Unites States* is the graphical counterpart to the *Summary and State Data* report described above. The Atlas proves that a picture is worth a thousand words, or in this case, a thousand data entries. The Atlas contains maps of the United States with states' outlines for nearly every item in the census. The maps are either 7.5 inches by 5 inches or 10 inches by 7.5 inches in color showing a range of shades for the percentage of an item by county or black and white maps with dots representing concentration of the item. The reader can easily see which regions of the country dominate in fattened cattle sold

or expenses for diesel fuel. Another handy feature of the Atlas is the two transparent overlays with the outlines of the counties and states that fit over the maps.

### Ranking of States and Counties

This report ranks the leading states and counties for selected items from the Census of Agriculture. Items ranked include number of farms, value of products sold, inventory of livestock and poultry, and production and acreage of major crops. Most tables show data for the 20 leading states and the 100 leading counties. Also, most tables include the cumulative percent of the United States total, as each leading state or county is ranked.

### ZIP Code and Congressional District Tabulations

Additional data by ZIP Code and Congressional District (as defined at the time of the census) are available as two files on a single CD-ROM, but not in printed form. Presented in these files are agricultural statistics by five-digit postal ZIP Code and current congressional district for all farms in all 50 states. Tables show the total market value of products sold and the number of farms by size for land in farms; cropland harvested; selected crops; and inventory of cattle, calves, hogs, and pigs. Crops vary by state, and tables show number of farms by acres harvested for commodities such as tobacco, cotton, soybeans for beans, peanuts for nuts, and land in orchards. Generally, these data will be shown in less detail than in the geographic area series.

### Volume 3, Special Studies

These are special studies that were done to gather more information about areas of special interest than would normally be found in the agricultural census. The farms included in these studies were selected on the basis of their answers to specific questions on the long form in the Census of Agriculture.

### Farm and Ranch Irrigation Survey

This report displays results from a sample survey of farm and ranch operators who reported using irrigation. It includes data on acres irrigated, yields of specified crops, method of distribution, quantity and source of water used, number and depth of wells, pumps used in moving water, energy use, and expenditures for maintenance and investments for all 50 states, 18 water resource areas, and the United States. Also included are some comparative data from earlier surveys. The first Irrigation Survey was conducted in 1979.

## Census of Horticultural Specialties

The *Census of Horticultural Specialties* includes producers of floriculture, nursery, and other specialty crops such as maple sap gathering, sod, mushrooms, food crops produced under glass (i.e., in green-houses), transplants for commercial production, Christmas tree farms, and seeds. It presents tabulations on the number of establishments, value of sales, type of horticultural products, market channels, and other data items for horticultural operations. The areas covered are the United States and each state. The first *Census of Horticultural Specialties* was conducted in 1889.

## Census of Aquaculture

The *Census of Aquaculture* collected information relating to on-farm aquaculture (the farming of fish) practices, size of operation based on water area, production, sales, method of production, sources of water, point of first sale outlets, cooperative agreements and contracts, and aquaculture distributed for restoration or conservation purposes. This was the first aquaculture census; however, earlier data are available under different programs, such as Catfish Production or Regional Aquaculture Center Compendium. This does not cover commercial fishing activities, such as the collection of fish at sea. To learn more about trends in fishing industries see *Fisheries in the United States,* issued by the National Oceanic and Atmospheric Administration's National Marine Fisheries Service.

## Agricultural Economics and Land Ownership Survey

The *Agricultural Economics and Land Ownership Survey* (AELOS) is a comprehensive survey of farm finances and land ownership. Data are published at the national and state level. Tables 1 through 67 are devoted to land in farms and financial characteristics of farms including expenses, assets, and debt for the farm operator and for the associated landlords. Tables 68 through 103 describe land ownership and related characteristics for both landlords who operate farms as well as landholders who are not farm operators.

Similar historic data can be found back to 1880; earlier titles of this survey are *Survey of Agricultural Finance* and *Farm Finance Survey.*

## Census of Agriculture on the Internet

In many cases, the first, and last, stop in answering a question from the Census of Agricultural can be NASS's Web site on the Internet. Go to the Census of Agriculture portion of the NASS Web site at http://www.nass.usda.gov/census/index.htm and choose your subject. This is a particularly useful option for the occasional user of the Census of Agriculture. (Frequent data users will probably find the printed reports and CD-ROMs more convenient.)

The site is organized along the same lines as the printed reports and covers all volumes of the Census: Geography Area Studies, Subject Studies, and Special Studies. In fact, some of the ZIP Code data that is not released in print can be found on this Web site. The Web page also has the ability to create user-defined queries and reports in the Geographic Area Studies section. You can also download or view the printed reports as PDF files from this Web site.

Understanding what is shown on this Web site is simple. Some Web pages let the user use a map to identify a state or county to drill down to the data or have glossaries, introduction, and other text available in HTML or PDF format. Once you found the table you want, click on its number and the PDF image will appear. To look at the forms used in the Census of Agriculture's data, click the "General Information" link at the bottom of the page. Most of the data shown on the NASS Web site are in Adobe Acrobat's Portable Document Format (PDF). Please note that except for the "Data Queries" link, which takes you to a site at Oregon State University, all of the links lead you to other pages on the NASS Web site.

## PDF Basics

To view the PDF files on the Web you must have the Adobe Acrobat Reader program loaded in your computer. While a brief introduction to working with the Acrobat Reader is provided here, if you want to learn more about working with this program, go to the Formats chapter (chapter 6) of this book.

To search documents in PDF format you have to have an Adobe Reader loaded on your computer. Once the file is loaded into Adobe, click on the binocular icon at the top of the page, or press the Ctrl and F keys at the same time, then type in a single word or

**Figure 7.1**
**Census of Agriculture Web Site**

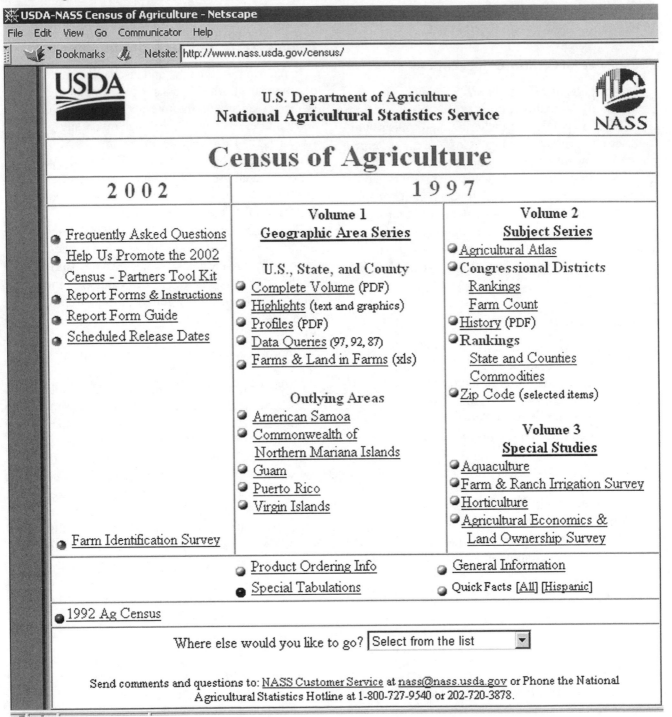

short phrase (it is not case sensitive) and click Find. It will look for those letters in the whole file. Be aware that if you search for the word "rope," you will also get words like grope and Europe. There are options in the search feature to limit the search by just the word, not the letters, and limit by making it case sensitive.

To continue the search, once you click outside of the Find box, use the Find Again icon to the right of the Find icon.

To print a PDF image go to the print icon on the top of the image on the NASS Web page. Note you will only print the current PDF document. Most of the titles are divided into sections, so you will not be able to print out a whole title at once. To see how many pages will print, look at the second box on the lower left of the image.

## Data Queries Basics

Searching with the Data Queries option on the Web site is very similar to searching the Profiles on the CD-ROM described below. However, there is no way to search by data item. Everything is defined by geography. The query will lead you to the Oregon State Libraries where you follow the steps:

1. Click on the Geographic Area button
2. Click on the state desired or select from the list beside the map
3. Click on the county or select multiple counties from the list by using the control key
4. Search for a word or scroll down list and select a table and click on Submit Query button
5. Show results

You can print results or download the HTML coded page. There is no way to download the data for a spreadsheet or statistical package. If you want to manipulate the data you will have to use the CD-ROM. Data on the Oregon State Libraries Web site only has the tables from Volume 1, Geographic Area Series.

## Saving Data for Manipulation

Downloading is very limited in the Internet version of the Census of Agriculture. The only data you download as Excel data files are in the Highlights and Farms & Land in Farms sections.

It is possible to transfer data from PDF images to a downloadable format. To do this, have your PDF image open and click the Text Select Tool icon. Highlight the selection you want and then click on the Copy icon. Open a word processor and choose Edit and select Paste. The words and numbers will be copied onto that page, however not in the same configuration as they appeared in the original page. Once the information is in a word processor you can do what you want with it.

## Census of Agriculture on CD-ROM

In addition to the printed reports and the Internet, the Census of Agriculture is on CD-ROM. While the printed reports and Web allow you to look at the data, the CD-ROMs give you the capability to easily manipulate the data to meet your own needs. Additionally, more data are available on the CD-ROM than in the printed reports or online.

## Data Content

The Census of Agriculture, Geographic Area Series, Volume 1, comes in a three-disc set containing a runtime version of Microsoft Access and the appropriate data files. It also contains the printed reports in Adobe Acrobat Portable Document Format (PDF). The data provided in the set include number of farms; land in farms; land use; irrigation; crops; livestock; poultry; value of farm products sold; hired farm labor; production expenses; and operator characteristics at the national, state, and county level.

Disc 1A has the setup software for extracting and viewing the program. Disc 1B contains the data for every county and state and for national data. There are some selected data from the previous and most current census on the discs for the summary data. Disc 1C has the Adobe Acrobat PDF images from Geographic Area Series for each state and national summary and duplicates what's in the printed books.

An additional report presenting data by ZIP Code and Congressional District (as defined for the Congress in session at the time of the Census of Agriculture) are only available on CD-ROM. This is described above in the section for printed reports.

The booklet that comes with the CDs has instructions for installing the software. Table 7.3 shows the minimum requirements for using these disks.

## Working with the Census of Agriculture Software

To begin searching on the 1997 Census of Agriculture, click on Start on the task bar. Scroll to Programs on the Start Menu. Select AG97. The Entry Screen will appear. There are four options available to you at this point.

"List of Tables" gives you the table of contents for the pre-defined reports. This table of contents only shows which reports are available; you cannot access them from here.

"Access Pre-Defined Reports" allows you to select a topic for a state from a drop down menu and get a pre-defined report.

"Search by Profiles or Data Items" is the most powerful function; it lets you create a query and a report

**Figure 7.2**
**Census of Agriculture CD-ROM Opening Screen**

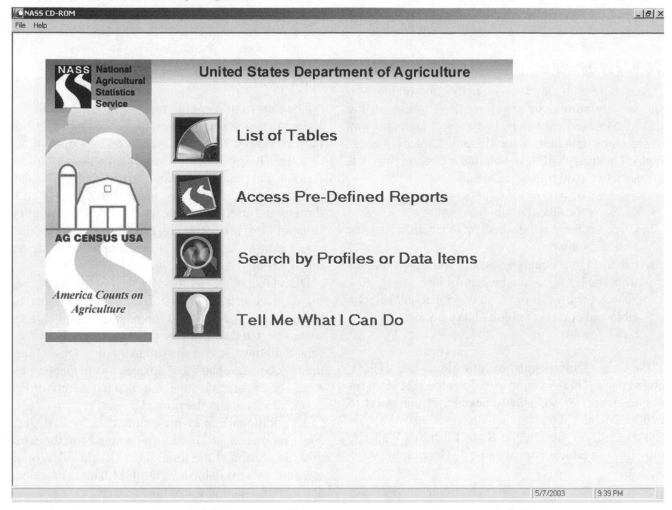

by geography or data items with only those items meeting your criteria.

"Tell Me What I Can Do" links to a Lotus Screen-Can tutorial. The tutorial is strictly visual and contains no audio. If you are reading this book you should not need the tutorial.

## Fundamentals

Moving the cursor in this program uses the standard Windows conventions. It's best if you use the mouse to move to commands. To select a single item, when given an option, just click on your choice with the mouse. To select multiple items in sequence, click on the first item and then scroll down to the last item you want, hold the shift key, and click the mouse again. This will select a range of items. (An alternate method, without using the mouse, is to click on the first item by holding down the Shift and Enter keys at the same time.) Every item in the range should be highlighted. To select various items not in a sequence, every time you scroll over an item that you want to select, click on the item while pressing the Ctrl (control) key.

Depending where you are, help is only a click a way. Help on the tool bar, from the Main Menu is the most complete. For help in the other screens use the Help Menu and choose Contents and Index. The help screen will have three tabs: Contents, Index, and Find. If you don't know how to define what you want, use the Find tab and type a single word that best describes your query. In the "Search by Profiles for Data Items" the Help screens are different depending on where you are in the program. It includes topics like sorting, print-

Table 7.3
**Minimum Computer Requirements for the Census of Agriculture CD-ROM**

| | **Disks 1A and 1B (Database)** | **Disk 1C (PDF version of reports)** |
|---|---|---|
| Processor | Pentium 100 | 386 |
| RAM | 16 MB | 4 MB |
| Operating System | Windows 95 or Windows NT 4.0 | Windows 95 |
| Hard Disk space | 7 MB | 5 MB (Plus 7 MB during installation) |
| Other | SVGA monitor with a resolution of 800 x 600 | Web browser and Adobe Acrobat Reader |

ing, hiding columns, and other related topics. There are no Help screens for "Access Pre-Defined Reports" or "Tell Me What I Can Do."

## Pre-Defined Reports

The Pre-Defined Reports option within the software allows you to quickly and easily access a selection of reports that will meet the needs of many data users. However, you have very limited control over the content of these reports. Generally, you are limited to selecting the geographic area you wish to look at.

It is important to remember that the data for these reports are divided between Discs 1A and 1B. Therefore, it is important to make certain that you have the appropriate disk in the computer.

For example, if you are interested in seeing the racial characteristics of farmers for 1987, 1992, and 1997, you can find this on table 17. However, this table is on Disc 1A, so you need to make certain this disk is in the computer. However, to get county-level pre-defined reports for "County Summary Highlights" or "Market Value of Agricultural Products Sold by NAICS," Disc 1B must be in the drive.

To select a report make sure the correct disk is in the drive, before you start searching. To search, select the "Access Pre-Defined Reports" icon. A Pre-Defined Report screen will appear in the middle of your screen. Select a topic from the drop down box, for example, "County Table 1: County Summary Highlights." Choose a state and select a county. Only one pre-defined report can be selected a time. To select multiple reports, you must use the query screen in "Search by Profiles or Data Items."

Once a report is selected, click on "Get Report." A pre-defined report will appear. In the tool bar across the top are the icons for moving through the report one page at time or jumping to the end of the report. It will

also tell how many pages are in the reports and show the icons for printing or downloading. There is an option to change the size of the image on the screen. Generally, 100% gives the user a good size to read on the computer. Unlike the printed reports, the footnotes to abbreviations are not always obvious. In order to learn what an abbreviation means in a footnote, go to the help screen or if you are in the query screen use the "G" icon. For a complete list of abbreviation definitions used in this census look in chapter 6 of this book.

Once the report is on the screen, click the print icon at the top of the screen. A print window will appear identifying the printer to be used and giving you the option of printing all of the pages or just do selected pages and how many copies to print.

To save the report once it is in the viewer, click on the download icon (the image of an envelope). The first of many download dialog boxes will appear. The first dialog box asks you to decide on which format and destination. In order to save the file in the most flexible format, save it in "Character-Separated Values (CSV)" format and use "Disk File" as the destination. If you want to use data in a specific application, review the options in the first box to find which format will best meet your needs. Once the format and destination have been selected, click OK. If you choose CSV format you will be asked for a separator and delimiter; it is recommended you keep the defaults and click OK. The next box will ask if you want to keep the number and date formats of the report, check both options and click OK. At this point it will ask were the file should go. Choose your drive, directory, and file name. The file type and extension should show the option of your select in the first dialog box. Click on OK. The file should be able to be opened with any spreadsheet or statistical program. Note that files saved in a CSV format will not appear as they appear in the

**Figure 7.3**
**Sample County Profile**

MERCED COUNTY, CA

COUNTY TABLE 1. COUNTY SUMMARY HIGHLIGHTS

| | 1997 | 1992 | 1987 |
|---|---|---|---|
| Farms (number) | 2,831 | 2,879 | 3,048 |
| Land in farms (acres) | 881,696 | 978,831 | 1,049,302 |
| Land in farms - average size of farm (acres) | 311 | 340 | 344 |
| Land in farms - median size of farm (acres) | 42 | N | N |
| | | | |
| Est mkt val land & buildings@1: avg per farm (dollars) | 950,554 | 798,225 | 605,365 |
| Est mkt val land & buildings@1: avg per acre (dollars) | 3,149 | 2,306 | 1,736 |
| Est mkt val machinery & equipment@1: avg per farm (dollars) | 95,876 | 68,802 | 65,472 |
| | | | |
| Farms by size: 1 to 9 acres | 411 | 382 | 449 |
| Farms by size: 10 to 49 acres | 1,074 | 1,160 | 1,231 |
| Farms by size: 50 to 179 acres | 677 | 708 | 723 |
| Farms by size: 180 to 499 acres | 362 | 296 | 319 |
| Farms by size: 500 to 999 acres | 135 | 153 | 147 |
| Farms by size: 1,000 acres or more | 172 | 180 | 179 |
| | | | |
| Total cropland (farms) | 2,485 | 2,522 | 2,661 |
| Total cropland (acres) | 532,327 | 534,318 | 517,026 |
| Total cropland, harvested cropland (farms) | 2,219 | 2,207 | 2,321 |
| Total cropland, harvested cropland (acres) | 434,074 | 417,346 | 382,246 |
| Irrigated land (farms) | 2,411 | 2,409 | 2,543 |
| Irrigated land (acres) | 493,072 | 427,815 | 423,414 |
| | | | |
| Market value of agricultural products sold ($1,000) | 1,273,475 | 907,600 | 792,105 |
| Mkt val of agr prods sold, average per farm (dollars) | 449,832 | 315,248 | 259,877 |
| Mkt val of crops, incl nurs&grnhse crops ($1,000) | 577,894 | 386,256 | 318,278 |
| Mkt val of livestock, poultry, and their prods ($1,000) | 695,581 | 521,344 | 473,827 |
| | | | |
| Farms by value of sales: Less than $2,500 | 443 | 452 | 469 |
| Farms by value of sales: $2,500 to $4,999 | 166 | 194 | 244 |

viewer. To have it look as it appeared on-screen, save the file in Text format and use a word processor to open it.

Opening a new pre-defined report can only be selected one at a time. So you will need to produce a new report each time you want to change either the geography or table that you are looking at.

Since each pre-defined report opens in a new screen, in order to avoid confusion, it is recommended that you close the report you just produced before starting a new one. To request a new pre-defined table go back to the Main Menu and click the Access Pre-Defined Report icon again.

In order to select multiple reports, you must use the query screen in "Search by Profiles or Data Items."

To exit out of a report click the X in the upper right corner of the screen. To exit out of the program click on the X or choose File and select Exit.

## "Search by Profiles or Data Items" Option

This option leads to the workhorse portion of the CD-ROM software. With this option, you can select multiple states, county, and data items within the same table. This query screen provides a space allowing you to form complicated requests and alter the display to only include the items needed. It also provides the ability to sort data. There is also a context sensitive help. If you are not sure what can be done next while creating a query, click on the Help Menus and choose "What is This?" then move your mouse (moving a question mark) over an item and it will tell you what the item contains.

Again, it is important to make certain that you have the correct disk in the computer. To search American Indian Farm Operations on reservations and state-level data use Disc 1A. In order to find county-level data you will need to use Disc 1B.

Using the "list of tables" screen on the main menu will make searching the data easier. It is helpful to remember that states and counties do not have the same tables. Use the index of tables to learn which tables have the data you need. For example, tobacco information for counties is found in tables 1, 2, 12, 13, and 27; for states the tables are 1, 2, 41, 42, and 45. Knowing that a state's table 2 is "Market Value of Agricultural Products Sold and Direct Sales" and that state's table 42 is "Specified Crops by Acres Harvested" will help you decide what table to go to in getting needed data.

To search by geography, the Profiles section is most like the printed reports. The only difference is that you

can be selective in which geography you want. Also the ability to alter the results on the screen is convenient. This is a four-step process:

1. Choose a geography (state, county, or state summary);
2. Choose a table from the upper left pull-down box;
3. Choose the region desired, your selections should appear in the box below the list (remember you can select more than one); and
4. Click "Get Data." The data will load and show in the right side of the screen.

To search by data items click the small bar in the lower left corner marked "Data Items." You can select multiple items from only one table at a time. To get items from different tables you will have to run another search. The search steps are similar to those in searching Profiles. For example, to get the results shown in Figure 7.4

1. Select By State;
2. Select 42 Specific Crops then choose "Tobacco (Farms)," "Tobacco (acres)," and "Tobacco (pounds)" by holding down the Ctrl key and clicking on the items at the same time;
3. Click Get Data; and
4. Highlight the column marked 1997 and select the sort icon with ZA↓, to sort for the data.

To view the results without the selection criteria, you click Get Data; if you no longer need the selection items you can remove them by clicking on the tool bar icon, which looks like an open book. Unlike the printed reports, the footnotes to abbreviations are not always obvious. To learn what any of the letters mean use the G icon.

There are three ways to sort the data: by geography, data item, and date column. The default view is by geography using the Federal Information Processing System (FIPS) code. If a number of items were selected, you can compare items among geographic regions by clicking the Item icon in the tool bar. To rank results, click the year header to highlight the column. Once the column is highlighted select the ascending icon, AZ9, or the descending icon, ZA9, to sort the data in the order you want.

To download, you arrange the results the way you want them, then you can save the data for use in other programs. To do this, click the disc icon or choose File and select Save As.... Then a Save As window will appear where you can decide on the drive, file name, and format. The format choices reflect the popular software packages: Text TXT, Jet Engine MDB, Dbase DBF, Excel XLS, Lotus WK1, and Quattro WB1.

To print the data on the screen, click the printer icon or choose File and select Print. The print preview page will appear, similar to Figure 7.4. To print, click on the printer icon. If you want to change the orientation of the page from portrait to landscape or specify a different printer, then use the printer icon showing a wrench.

### Exiting the Software

To exit the program, go to File and select Exit. It will bring you to the Main Menu, then choose File and select Exit again.

## Special Tabulations

The Census of Agriculture offers the researcher a smorgasbord of opportunities. The tables issued by NASS are based on the most commonly requested combinations of data and these answer nearly all of the questions data users have. However, there are still some questions that need more detail than exists in the standard tables. To meet this need NASS has a program of offering special tabulations on a cost-reimbursable basis to data users.

These special tabulations are customized reports run against the original responses designed to meet the users' needs. They also must meet NASS's standards for publication, including the standards of protecting respondent confidentiality and statistical quality. While every effort is made to determine whether or not a particular table will be able to be released before the tabulation is run, there is always the possibility that when the final product is reviewed, it is found to violate one or more of the release standards. If this is the case, an effort may be made to group data into larger categories that are still useful to the data user and that still meet the publication standards for release.

When should someone request a special tabulation? When what they need is not found in the Census of Agriculture, reports by commodity, or other NASS publications; or when you need to customize a specific report or calculations are based on a statistical model or a specified set of assumptions. For example, you may want to get the farm expenses and income for or-ange growers and compare counties between California and Florida growers for the past 15 years. It is very important to remember, however, that these special tabulations come at a price—the minimum charge is $500.

## USING THE AGRICULTURAL CENSUS

There are a lot of users, researchers, decision makers, and politicians who are dependent on the data provided by the Census of Agriculture. This section provides some examples of how the data have been used in the past. For a more comprehensive list of scholarly uses, review a citation index like the Social Science Citation Index.

One obvious use of the data is to gain an understanding of a geographic area. Other examples are

- How does one county compare to the whole state?
- Which state is supplying the most strawberries to the nation?
- What is the primary crop grown in a county?
- Who uses the most tractor tires?
- Where does honey bee research need to be focused due to decreasing bee colonies?
- To compare how much your farm produces with other farms of the same size raising the same livestock.

### Government

Governments at all levels are concerned about equality. Questions about the racial, educational level, age, and form of organization help them create programs to assist those who may not have the political savvy to save their farm because of unfair competition. Sometimes a picture is worth a thousand words; the census can provide the data to make the pictures.

### Federal

A clear picture of the state of agriculture helps elected officials and government agencies create and evaluate programs needed to help farmers and the businesses supplying them. The federal government is also responsible for the disaster plans for droughts, floods, diseases in food supplies, and ensuring a fair market for food products. The census provides them with the data either directly or by using the data as a baseline for statistical models. They track the trends in the production of food in order to make sure the federally funded technology is focusing in the changing taste of America. The data are also used in macro-

**Figure 7.4**
**Census of Agriculture CD-ROM Sample Data Item Search**

NASS CD-ROM — File  View  Sort  Help

Profiles / Data Items

- By State
- By County
- All Items per County
- State/US Totals (County Data)
- St. Cty. US Total (County Data)

Data Items list:
- Cotton, 3,000 to 4,999 acres, irrigated land
- Cotton, 3,000 to 4,999 acres, irrigated land
- Cotton, 5,000 acres or more (farms)
- Cotton, 5,000 acres or more (acres)
- Cotton, 5,000 acres or more (bales)
- Cotton, 5,000 acres or more, irrigated land
- Cotton, 5,000 acres or more, irrigated land
- Tobacco (farms)
- Tobacco (acres)
- Tobacco (pounds)
- Tobacco, irrigated land (farms)
- Tobacco, irrigated land (acres)
- Tobacco, 0.1 to 0.9 acres (farms)
- Tobacco, 0.1 to 0.9 acres (acres)
- Tobacco, 0.1 to 0.9 acres (pounds)
- Tobacco, 0.1 to 0.9 acres, irrigated land (fa
- Tobacco, 0.1 to 0.9 acres, irrigated land (a
- Tobacco, 1.0 to 1.9 acres (farms)
- Tobacco, 1.0 to 1.9 acres (acres)
- Tobacco, 1.0 to 1.9 acres (pounds)
- Tobacco, 1.0 to 1.9 acres, irrigated land (fa
- Tobacco, 1.0 to 1.9 acres, irrigated land (a
- Tobacco, 2.0 to 2.9 acres (farms)
- Tobacco, 2.0 to 2.9 acres (acres)
- Tobacco, 2.0 to 2.9 acres (pounds)
- Tobacco, 2.0 to 2.9 acres, irrigated land (fa

Get Data

Tobacco (farms)
Tobacco (acres)
Tobacco (pounds)

| Geography | Item | 1997 | 1992 | 1987 |
|---|---|---|---|---|
| UNITED STATES | Tobacco (pounds) | 1,747,702,321 | N | N |
| NORTH CAROLINA | Tobacco (pounds) | 703,559,462 | N | N |
| KENTUCKY | Tobacco (pounds) | 505,257,589 | N | N |
| SOUTH CAROLINA | Tobacco (pounds) | 125,220,334 | N | N |
| VIRGINIA | Tobacco (pounds) | 115,735,107 | N | N |
| TENNESSEE | Tobacco (pounds) | 106,785,282 | N | N |
| GEORGIA | Tobacco (pounds) | 85,789,611 | N | N |
| OHIO | Tobacco (pounds) | 21,629,638 | N | N |
| INDIANA | Tobacco (pounds) | 17,275,291 | N | N |
| PENNSYLVANIA | Tobacco (pounds) | 17,098,232 | N | N |
| FLORIDA | Tobacco (pounds) | 16,191,980 | N | N |
| MARYLAND | Tobacco (pounds) | 11,987,083 | N | N |
| MISSOURI | Tobacco (pounds) | 6,430,795 | N | N |
| WISCONSIN | Tobacco (pounds) | 5,355,466 | N | N |
| CONNECTICUT | Tobacco (pounds) | 4,115,845 | N | N |
| WEST VIRGINIA | Tobacco (pounds) | 2,737,090 | N | N |
| MASSACHUSETTS | Tobacco (pounds) | 1,881,034 | N | N |
| UNITED STATES | Tobacco (acres) | 838,530 | N | N |
| NORTH CAROLINA | Tobacco (acres) | 320,599 | N | N |
| KENTUCKY | Tobacco (acres) | 255,053 | N | N |
| UNITED STATES | Tobacco (farms) | 89,706 | N | N |
| TENNESSEE | Tobacco (acres) | 59,427 | N | N |
| SOUTH CAROLINA | Tobacco (acres) | 54,660 | N | N |
| VIRGINIA | Tobacco (acres) | 54,035 | N | N |
| KENTUCKY | Tobacco (farms) | 44,967 | N | N |
| GEORGIA | Tobacco (acres) | 41,083 | N | N |
| TENNESSEE | Tobacco (farms) | 14,995 | N | N |
| NORTH CAROLINA | Tobacco (farms) | 12,095 | N | N |
| OHIO | Tobacco (acres) | 11,457 | N | N |
| INDIANA | Tobacco (acres) | 8,507 | N | N |
| PENNSYLVANIA | Tobacco (acres) | 7,953 | N | N |
| MARYLAND | Tobacco (acres) | 7,939 | N | N |
| FLORIDA | Tobacco (acres) | 6,881 | N | N |
| VIRGINIA | Tobacco (farms) | 5,870 | N | N |
| OHIO | Tobacco (farms) | 2,811 | N | N |
| MISSOURI | Tobacco (acres) | 2,677 | N | N |
| WISCONSIN | Tobacco (acres) | 2,553 | N | N |
| CONNECTICUT | Tobacco (acres) | 2,529 | N | N |
| INDIANA | Tobacco (farms) | 2,017 | N | N |
| WEST VIRGINIA | Tobacco (acres) | 1,630 | N | N |

153 records

Appendix

5/7/2003   9:57 PM

economic calculations for current statistical series such as the Gross Domestic Product and Producer Price Index.

## States

Some resources, such as land use, water pollution, and public utilities are managed by the state. These governments need to know things like how much fertilizer is being used or how much agricultural land has been used for set asides, woodlands, and wetlands. Even suppliers of public services like electricity or water need to know what to expect when considering privatization and setting of rates for non-residential customers. To keep rates down should the governments subsidize farmers when deregulating utilities?

## Local

Local governments need to have an understanding of their regional strengths and weaknesses. Every five years, the Census provides a picture that they can use to evaluate how their community is changing and adjust the economic development programs, educational direction, tax base, land management, social services, and zoning laws.

## Business

The most obvious use of the data is locating a new business or defining a sales territory. Managers want to know what crops are being raised in an area so they can stock the right equipment. It is not just the location of retailers of equipment and services that are important; these data can also identify the geographic regions where suppliers of their raw material are located. This is important to many food processors because it is often wiser to locate a manufacturing plant near the supplies. This upstream/downstream identification is necessary in logistics.

## Farmers

What if you just bought a new farm and you needed to know basic costs for operating a farm growing an unfamiliar product? You could turn to the Census and the USDA County Agent. You could also identify higher yielding crops or livestock, if you decide to diversify your operation.

## Farm Associations and Other Organizations

Some organizations take the data straight from NASS and push it to their members as soon as it's available, while other groups take the data and use it to evaluate policies and programs affecting their members. It also helps them see trends that may affect their specific interest, for example, increasing or decreasing pesticide use.

## Researchers and Scholars

Researchers are also constantly trying to improve methods and products for farmers. They need a baseline to understand the operations and production of farmers and develop ways to help them. For example, which soil is best used for fish farming?

The Agriculture Census has been taken in some form since 1840. It reflects how America has changed and shows patterns that might predict the future. NASS is trying to keep the time periods between the censuses consistent, so that trends may be easier to identify.

There are many national dialogs that are based on agriculture issues: land degradations, conservation, valuing ecosystems, regional advantages, national competitiveness, urban growth, pricing vs. valuation, laborers rights, equal rights, federally funded programs, nature resources, banking reform, economic growth, public safety, and understanding the past of the country. The Census of Agriculture sheds light on all of these issues.

## CURRENT SURVEYS AND DATA

If you are looking for information about agriculture for time periods other than those covered in the Agriculture Census, hope is far from lost. The National Agricultural Statistical Service provides a wealth of information on a more current basis than the census. It is important, however, to remember that this information is based on surveys rather than a census. Therefore, it is slightly less accurate. (NASS is still very concerned about the statistical reliability of their surveys and is constantly trying to improve that.)

A look at the NASS Web site http://www.usda.gov/nass/ shows a wealth of reports covering every aspect of agriculture. Some of these reports are weekly. Others are monthly, quarterly, or annual in their coverage. Some, such as the report on cotton production, are issued periodically during the appropriate season with an annual summary and a later revision. Many of these reports are only a couple of pages long and contain national and some state data.

There are also many state-level reports issued by the NASS State Offices. (In many cases, these offices are shared with the state's agricultural statistical service.) These reports can also be found on the NASS Web site. But the specific reports vary by state because each state has a different set of significant agricultural products. For example, you will not find a report on rice production in New York State, since rice is far from a significant crop in the state (but it is grown there). You will find, however, detailed information on apple production, since New York is a leading producer of this product.

Detailed directions for obtaining these reports on a regular basis can be found on the last page of any reports. Options for getting them include downloading them from the NASS Web site, having them e-mailed to you; having some reports faxed (though not all are available this way), and purchasing selected reports on a subscription basis from NASS.

Here is a list of some of the more general reports issued by NASS and their individual Web sites. You can access the complete set of reports through the publications page on the NASS Web site http://www.usda.gov/nass/pubs/pubs.htm. They are organized to allow you to access them a number of different ways, such as by title, by commodity, or by state.

Agricultural Marketing Service. *AMS Market News.* [http://www.ams.usda.gov/marketnews.htm].

Economic Research Service. *ERS Calendar.* [http://www.ers.usda.gov/calendar/].

Fisheries Statistics & Economics Division. *Fisheries of the United States.* [http://www.st.nmfs.gov/st1/fus/fus00/].

Foreign Agricultural Service. *Current World Market and Trade Publications.* [http://www.fas.usda.gov/currwmt.html]. Notes: FAS Online

Forest Service. *Timber Sale Program Information Reporting System* (TSPIRS). [http://www.fs.fed.us/land/fm/tspirs/tspirs.htm].

National Agricultural Statistics Service. *Livestock Slaughter Charts.* [http://www.usda.gov/nass/aggraphs/slaughtr.htm].

National Agricultural Statistics Service. *USDA National Agricultural Statistics Service Publications.* [http://www.usda.gov/nass/pubs/pubs.htm].

Office of Chief Economist. *World Agricultural Supply and Demand Estimates.* [http://www.usda.gov/oce/waob/wasde/wasde.htm].

**ANSWERS:**

**What Is in the Census of Agriculture?**

Bunny farms—Yes, NAICS 11293 covers all fur-bearing animals and rabbit production.
Catfish farms—Yes, NAICS 112511 includes finfish farming and fish hatcheries, however, regular commercial fishing is not included.
Corn farm—Yes, NAICS 11115 combines SIC 0115 (Corn) and parts of SIC 0119 (Cash grains, NEC [popcorn farming]).
Cotton ginning—No, NAICS 115111 is a support activities for crop production and falls in the agricultural industry sector, but it does not appear in the Census of Agriculture. The Cotton Ginning Survey (PCG-BB http://usda.mannlib.cornell.edu/reports/nassr/field/pcg-bb/) provides all segments of the cotton industry.
Cottage cheese makers—No, this is a manufactured product.

## ANSWERS (CONTINUED):

### What Is in the Census of Agriculture?

Farm stand—Yes and No, if a farm has generated more than $1,000 at a farm stand, then that farm is included in Census of Agriculture. The products they sell will be included in the tables for those products. Volume 1: part 51, chapter 2, table 3, has a column for Direct Sales, but not by product.

Gender of owner—Yes, operator characteristics is in volume 1, part 51, chapter 2, table 17, of the Geographic Area Series.

Grapevine yards—Yes, NAICS 111332 is for grapevine yards, but does not include data for the process of making wine, which is manufacturing.

Hiring seasonal workers—Yes, operations of the farm are included in the Census. In this case this table is found in volume 1, part 51, chapter 2, table 5.

Horse stables—No, this industry is under NAICS 713990, all other amusement and recreation industries, along with ballrooms, miniature golf, and ping-pong parlors.

International trade—No, however, agricultural international trade can be found in FASOnline.

Internet use—Yes and No, these data were not collected in the 1997 Census, however they are reported in the 2002 Census of Agriculture.

Irrigation techniques—Yes, these data are in the volume three, Farm & Ranch Irrigation Survey, table 4.

Organic production certification—Yes and No, these data were not collected in the 1997 Census, however they are reported in the 2002 Census of Agriculture.

Ostrich farms—Yes and No, these data were not collected in the 1997 Census, however they are reported in the 2002 Census of Agriculture.

Nursery Plants—Yes, this is can be found in volume 3, Census of Horticultural Specialties, tables 13, 32, and others.

Pecan farm—Yes, this would be considered tree nut farming (NAICS 111335).

Pesticide use—Yes, this information is found throughout the Census.

Slaughterhouse—No, Census of Agriculture has feedlots (NAICS 112112) and retail has butcher (NAICS 445210). There are reports from Livestock Slaughter Charts.

Subsidy program—Yes, this information is found throughout the Census.

## AGRICULTURE ACCORDING TO NAICS

The Agriculture, Forestry, Fishing, and Hunting sector comprises establishments primarily engaged in growing crops, raising animals, harvesting timber, and harvesting fish and other animals from a farm, ranch, or their natural habitats. Excluded from the Agriculture, Forestry, Fishing, and Hunting sector are establishments primarily engaged in agricultural research and establishments primarily engaged in administering programs for regulating and conserving land, mineral, wildlife, and forest use. These establishments are classified in Industry 54171, Research and Development in the Physical, Engineering, and Life Sciences, and Industry 92412, Administration of Conservation Programs, respectively. First column lets you know if the 1997 Census of Agriculture includes that industry (see Table 7.4).

## BIBLIOGRAPHY

*U.S. Commissioner of Agriculture Report, 1862.* 1863. Washington, DC: Government Printing Office.

Table 7.4
SIC–NAICS Comparison

| Census[a] | NAICS | NAICSTEXT | COMP[b] | SIC | SICTEXT |
|---|---|---|---|---|---|
|  | 11 | Agriculture, Forestry, Fishing and Hunting |  |  |  |
|  | 111 | Crop Production |  |  |  |
|  | 1111 | Oilseed and Grain Farming |  |  |  |
| Y | 11111 | Soybean Farming | E | 0116 | Soybeans |
| Y | 11112 | Oilseed (except Soybean) Farming | N | 0119 | Cash Grains, NEC (oilseed, except soybean farming) |
| Y | 11113 | Dry Pea and Bean Farming | N | 0119 | Cash Grains, NEC (dry pea and bean farms) |
| Y | 11114 | Wheat Farming | E | 0111 | Wheat |
| Y | 11115 | Corn Farming | R | 0115 | Corn |
|  | 11115 | Corn Farming |  | 0119 | Cash Grains, NEC (popcorn farming) |
| Y | 11116 | Rice Farming | E | 0112 | Rice |
|  | 11119 | Other Grain Farming |  |  |  |
| Y | 111191 | Oilseed and Grain Combination Farming | N | 0119 | Cash Grains, NEC (oilseed and grain combination farms) |
| Y | 111199 | All Other Grain Farming | R | 0119 | Cash Grains, NEC (except popcorn, soybean, and dry pea and bean, and oilseed and grain combination farms) |
|  | 1112 | Vegetable and Melon Farming |  |  |  |
|  | 11121 | Vegetable and Melon Farming |  |  |  |
| Y | 111211 | Potato Farming | E | 0134 | Irish Potatoes |
| Y | 111219 | Other Vegetable (except Potato) and Melon Farming | R | 0161 | Vegetables and Melons |
|  | 111219 | Other Vegetable (except Potato) and Melon Farming |  | 0139 | Field Crops Except Cash Grains (sweet potatoes and yams) |
|  | 1113 | Fruit and Tree Nut Farming |  |  |  |
| Y | 11131 | Orange Groves | N | 0174 | Citrus Fruits (orange groves and farms) |
| Y | 11132 | Citrus (except Orange) Groves | R | 0174 | Citrus Fruits (except, orange groves and farms) |
|  | 11133 | Noncitrus Fruit and Tree Nut Farming |  |  |  |

Table 7.4 (Continued)
SIC–NAICS Comparison

| Census[a] | NAICS | NAICSTEXT | COMP[b] SIC | | SICTEXT |
|---|---|---|---|---|---|
| Y | 111331 | Apple Orchards | N | 0175 | Deciduous Tree Fruits (apple orchards and farms) |
| Y | 111332 | Grape Vineyards | E | 0172 | Grapes |
| Y | 111333 | Strawberry Farming | N | 0171 | Berry Crops (strawberry farms) |
| Y | 111334 | Berry (except Strawberry) Farming | R | 0171 | Berry Crops ( except strawberry farms) |
| Y | 111335 | Tree Nut Farming | E | 0173 | Tree Nuts |
| Y | 111336 | Fruit and Tree Nut Combination Farming | N | 0179 | Fruits and Tree Nuts, NEC (combination farms) |
| Y | 111339 | Other Noncitrus Fruit Farming | R | 0175 | Deciduous Tree Fruits (except apple orchards and farms) |
| | 111339 | Other Noncitrus Fruit Farming | | 0179 | Fruit and Tree Nuts, NEC (except combination farms) |
| | 1114 | Greenhouse, Nursery, and Floriculture Production | | | |
| | 11141 | Food Crops Grown Under Cover | | | |
| Y | 111411 | Mushroom Production | N | 0182 | Food Crops Grown Under Cover (mushrooms, growing of) |
| Y | 111419 | Other Food Crops Grown Under Cover | R | 0182 | Food Crops Grown Under Cover (except mushroom, growing of) |
| | 11142 | Nursery and Floriculture Production | | | |
| Y | 111421 | Nursery and Tree Production | N | 0181 | Ornamental Floriculture and Nursery Products (nursery farming) |
| | 111421 | Nursery and Tree Production | | 0811 | Timber Tracts (short rotation woody crops) |
| Y | 111422 | Floriculture Production | N | 0181 | Ornamental Floriculture and Nursery Products (floriculture farming) |
| | 1119 | Other Crop Farming | | | |
| Y | 11191 | Tobacco Farming | E | 0132 | Tobacco |
| Y | 11192 | Cotton Farming | E | 0131 | Cotton |
| Y | 11193 | Sugarcane Farming | N | 0133 | Sugarcane and Sugar Beets (sugarcane farms) |
| Y | 11194 | Hay Farming | N | 0139 | Field Crops, Except Cash Grains, NEC (hay farms) |
| | 11199 | All Other Crop Farming | | | |

Table 7.4 (Continued)
SIC–NAICS Comparison

| Census[a] | NAICS | NAICTEXT | COMP[b] | SIC | SICTEXT |
|---|---|---|---|---|---|
| Y | 111991 | Sugar Beet Farming | N | 0133 | Sugarcane and Sugar Beets (sugar beet farms) |
| Y | 111992 | Peanut Farming | N | 0139 | Field Crops, Except Cash Grains, NEC (peanut farms) |
| Y | 111998 | All Other Miscellaneous Crop Farming | R | 0139 | Field Crops, Except Cash Grains, NEC (except peanut, sweet potato, yam and hay farms) |
| | 111998 | All Other Miscellaneous Crop Farming | | 0191 | General Farms, Primarily Crop |
| | 111998 | All Other Miscellaneous Crop Farming | | 0831 | Forest Products (maple sap, gathering of) |
| | 111998 | All Other Miscellaneous Crop Farming | | 0919 | Miscellaneous Marine Products (plant aquaculture) |
| | 111998 | All Other Miscellaneous Crop Farming | | 2099 | Food Preparations, NEC (reducing maple sap to maple syrup) |
| | 112 | Animal Production | | | |
| | 1121 | Cattle Ranching and Farming | | | |
| | 11211 | Beef Cattle Ranching and Farming, including Feedlots | | | |
| Y | 112111 | Beef Cattle Ranching and Farming | R | 0212 | Beef Cattle, Except Feedlots |
| | 112111 | Beef Cattle Ranching and Farming | | 0241 | Dairy Farms (dairy heifer replacement farms) |
| Y | 112112 | Cattle Feedlots | E | 0211 | Beef Cattle Feedlots |
| Y | 11212 | Dairy Cattle and Milk Production | R | 0241 | Dairy Farms |
| Y | 11213 | Dual Purpose Cattle Ranching and Farming | L | | Null Set for U.S. |
| | 1122 | Hog and Pig Farming | | | |
| Y | 11221 | Hog and Pig Farming | E | 0213 | Hogs |
| | 1123 | Poultry and Egg Production | | | |
| N | 11231 | Chicken Egg Production | E | 0252 | Chicken Eggs |
| Y | 11232 | Broilers and Other Meat Type Chicken Production | E | 0251 | Broiler, Fryers, and Roaster Chickens |
| Y | 11233 | Turkey Production | E | 0253 | Turkey and Turkey Eggs |
| Y | 11234 | Poultry Hatcheries | E | 0254 | Poultry Hatcheries |

Table 7.4 (Continued)
SIC–NAICS Comparison

| Census[a] | NAICS | NAICSTEXT | COMP[b] | SIC | SICTEXT |
|---|---|---|---|---|---|
| Y | 11239 | Other Poultry Production | E | 0259 | Poultry and Eggs, NEC |
|  | 1124 | Sheep and Goat Farming |  |  |  |
| Y | 11241 | Sheep Farming | N | 0214 | Sheep and Goats (sheep farms) |
| Y | 11242 | Goat Farming | N | 0214 | Sheep and Goats (goat farms) |
|  | 1125 | Animal Aquaculture |  |  |  |
|  | 11251 | Animal Aquaculture |  |  |  |
| Y | 112511 | Finfish Farming and Fish Hatcheries | N | 0273 | Animal Aquaculture (finfish farms) |
|  | 112511 | Finfish Farming and Fish Hatcheries |  | 0921 | Fish Hatcheries and Preserves (finfish hatcheries) |
| Y | 112512 | Shellfish Farming | N | 0273 | Animal Aquaculture (shellfish farms) |
|  | 112512 | Shellfish Farming |  | 0921 | Fish Hatcheries and Preserves (shellfish hatcheries) |
| Y | 112519 | Other Animal Aquaculture | R | 0273 | Animal Aquaculture (except finfish and shellfish) |
|  | 112519 | Other Animal Aquaculture |  | 0279 | Animal Specialties, NEC (alligator and frog production) |
|  | 1129 | Other Animal Production |  |  |  |
| Y | 11291 | Apiculture | N | 0279 | Animal Specialties, NEC (apiculture) |
| Y | 11292 | Horse and Other Equine Production | E | 0272 | Horse and Other Equine |
| Y | 11293 | Fur-Bearing Animal and Rabbit Production | E | 0271 | Fur-Bearing Animals and Rabbits |
| Y | 11299 | All Other Animal Production | R | 0219 | General Livestock, Except Dairy and Poultry |
|  | 11299 | All Other Animal Production |  | 0279 | Animal Specialties, NEC (except apiculture) |
|  | 11299 | All Other Animal Production |  | 0291 | General Farms, Primarily Livestock and Animal Specialties |
|  | 11299 | All Other Animal Production |  |  |  |
|  | 113 | Forestry and Logging |  |  |  |
|  | 1131 | Timber Tract Operations |  |  |  |
| N | 11311 | Timber Tract Operations | R | 0811 | Timber Tracts (long term timber farms) |
|  | 1132 | Forest Nurseries and Gathering of Forest Products |  |  |  |

150

Table 7.4 (Continued)
SIC–NAICS Comparison

| Census[a] | NAICS | NAICSTEXT | COMP[b] | SIC | SICTEXT |
|---|---|---|---|---|---|
| N | 11321 | Forest Nurseries and Gathering of Forest Products | E | 0831 | Forest Nurseries and Gathering of Forest Products (forest products, except gathering of maple sap) |
| | 1133 | Logging | | | |
| N | 11331 | Logging | E | 2411 | Logging |
| | 114 | Fishing, Hunting and Trapping | | | |
| | 1141 | Fishing | | | |
| | 11411 | Fishing | | | |
| N | 114111 | Finfish Fishing | E | 0912 | Finfish |
| N | 114112 | Shellfish Fishing | E | 0913 | Shellfish |
| N | 114119 | Other Marine Fishing | R | 0919 | Miscellaneous Marine Products (except plant aquaculture) |
| | 1142 | Hunting and Trapping | | | |
| N | 11421 | Hunting and Trapping | E | 0971 | Hunting and Trapping, and Game Propagation |
| | 11421 | Hunting and Trapping | | | |
| | 115 | Support Activities for Agriculture and Forestry | | | |
| | 1151 | Support Activities for Crop Production | | | |
| | 11511 | Support Activities for Crop Production | | | |
| N | 115111 | Cotton Ginning | E | 0724 | Cotton Ginning |
| N | 115112 | Soil Preparation, Planting, and Cultivating | R | 0711 | Soil Preparation Services |
| | 115112 | Soil Preparation, Planting, and Cultivating | | 0721 | Crop Planting, Cultivating, and Protecting |
| N | 115113 | Crop Harvesting, Primarily by Machine | E | 0722 | Crop Harvesting, Primarily by Machine |
| N | 115114 | Postharvest Crop Activities (except Cotton Ginning) | R | 0723 | Crop Preparation Services For Market, Except Cotton Ginning (except custom grain grinding) |
| N | 115115 | Farm Labor Contractors and Crew Leaders | E | 0761 | Farm Labor Contractors and Crew Leaders |
| N | 115116 | Farm Management Services | E | 0762 | Farm Management Services |
| | 1152 | Support Activities for Animal Production | | | |

151

Table 7.4 (Continued)
SIC–NAICS Comparison

| Census[a] | NAICS | NAICSTEXT | COMP[b] | SIC | SICTEXT |
|---|---|---|---|---|---|
| N | 11521 | Support Activities for Animal Production | N | 0751 | Livestock Services, Except Veterinary (except custom slaughtering) |
|  | 11521 | Support Activities for Animal Production |  | 0752 | Animal Specialty Services, Except Veterinary (horses and equines services and animal production breeding) |
|  | 11521 | Support Activities for Animal Production |  | 7699 | Repair Services, NEC (farriers) |
|  | 1153 | Support Activities for Forestry |  |  |  |
| N | 11531 | Support Activities for Forestry | E | 0851 | Forestry Services |
|  | 11531 | Support Activities for Forestry |  |  |  |

[a] = found in the 1997 Census of Agriculture; N = Not in the Census.
[b]E = Existing, N = New, R = Revised

152

# CHAPTER 8
# Transportation and Warehousing

Every improvement of the means of locomotion benefits mankind morally and intellectually as well as materially, and not only facilitates the interchange of the various productions of nature and art, but tends to remove national and provincial antipathies, and to bind together all the branches of the great human family.
—*Thomas Babington Macaulay,* The History of England, *5th ed., vol. 1,*
*chapter 3, p. 370 (1849).*

1. Introduction
2. New in 1997 and 2002
3. Geographic and Subject Reports

   A. Transportation and Warehouse Data from the Economic Census
   B. Additional Transportation and Warehousing Information in Other Parts of the Census

4. Vehicle Inventory and Use Survey

   A. Coverage
   B. Procedures
   C. Printable VIUS Reports
   D. Electronic data

5. Commodity Flow Survey

   A. Procedures
   B. Printable CFS Reports
   C. Electronic Data

6. Beyond 20/20 Software

   A. Installation
   B. Starting the Software

      i. Commodity Flow Survey
      ii. Vehicle Inventory and Use Survey

   C. Working with Pre-defined Tables
   D. Summarizing Items
   E. Creating Tables from Microdata

7. Using the Transportation and Warehousing Data from the Economic Census

   A. Cautions
   B. Choosing the Data Presentation Format to Use
   C. How Others Use Transportation Data

8. Additional Transportation and Warehousing Data

   A. Other Census Bureau Data
   B. Bureau of Transportation Statistics Data
   C. Other Sources of Highway and Motor Vehicle Data
   D. Data about Buses and Trains
   E. Data about Boats and Waterways
   F. Aviation Data
   G. Data on Pipelines
   H. Other Related Data

9. NAICS–SIC Crosswalk

## INTRODUCTION

The transportation and warehousing sector covers the movement of goods or people from one location to another. It also includes the storage of those goods. There are three major components of this sector, (1) the movement of goods or people (transportation), (2) the storage of goods (warehousing), and (3) services supporting transportation activities. Examples of transportation related activities include scheduled and charter air services, passenger and freight trains, water transportation, truck transportation, taxi and limousine services, all types of bus transportation services, sightseeing services—including charter fishing services, couriers and messengers, and natural gas and refined petroleum pipelines. Transportation support services include such activities as airport operations, tugboat services, motor vehicle towing, and freight transportation arrangement services. Note that travel agents and other travel arranging services are part of the Administrative and Support and Waste Management and Remediation Services Sector (Sector 56).

It is important to note that large certificated passenger air transportation (i.e., large commercial airlines), rail transportation (i.e., Amtrak), and the United

States Postal Service are outside of the Economic Census's scope.

The geographic areas covered in this sector are limited to the United States, the states and the District of Columbia, and metropolitan areas. There are no data reported for ZIP Codes, economic places, counties, or the outlying territories.

This sector differs from the other sectors included in the Economic Census because in addition to the usual geographic, industry, and subject reports, this sector has a survey covering the different types of vehicles used in business and the way they are used. There is also a survey covering the trips that goods make around the country.

Since there are three distinct parts to the transportation and warehousing data, we will describe them separately. First we describe the geographic and subject reports, which are most like the rest of the Economic Census. Then we will describe the Vehicle Inventory and Use Survey. Finally, the Commodity Flow Survey is discussed.

## NEW IN 1997 AND 2002

Nearly all of the changes affecting this sector occurred as part of the 1997 Economic Census. The only change affecting the data in 2002 is that warehouses, which were previously classified as auxiliary establishments, are now counted in this sector.

As part of the conversion from SICs to NAICS, the transportation and warehousing industries were separated from the communications and public utility industries. However, some parts of this industry come from other SIC sectors. For example, the postal service industry now includes private postal service contractors, which had been classified as business services. As a result of this change and others like it, all businesses involved with the movement of people and goods are now grouped together in this industry.

The major business activity moving into this sector is automotive vehicle towing services. Prominent activities moving from the transportation and warehousing SIC major groups to other sectors are travel agents, tour operators, miniwarehouses, marinas, waste collection, and ambulances.

## GEOGRAPHIC AND SUBJECT REPORTS

The only printed transportation and warehousing data are those found in the *Advance, Bridge, Outlying*

*Area,* and *Minority- and Women-Owned Business* reports. Most of the data is available in PDF form on the census Web site. The CD-ROMs include the same data as the PDF. American FactFinder only has the data from volume one of the CD-ROM. It does not have the SIC code or nonemployer data. For reports released since 2000 there are HTML Web tables and data files in comma delimitated and dBase formats directly for the report's Web page, which means there is no need to use the American Fact Finder or CD-ROMs for some data sets. No rankings or derived measures are in the reports. Tables incorporating ratios or rankings based on the published numbers are no longer included since any user can derive that information from databases on the Internet and CD-ROM.

## Transportation and Warehouse Data from the Economic Census

The movement of goods from one location to another within the country is essential to our national (and global) economy. If goods are not transported, nothing would be where it was needed, so transportation is essential to our economy. In addition to measuring how goods move around this country, this sector also measures the nation's ability to move people and to store goods that are being moved around.

The transportation and warehouse sector (NAICS 48–49) covered by the Economic Census includes a geographic and subject series. Additionally, there are two surveys that help measure the transportation industry in this country.

The geographic reports contain the four key statistics: establishment numbers, employees, payroll, and sales. These are repeated for each industry. Other reports include source of revenues; establishment and firm size by employees and sales; concentration by larger firms, and legal forms of organization. The largest part of the transportation and warehousing data is found in the Geographic Area Series. A separate report is issued for the United States, each state, and the District of Columbia. Each report contains definitions and industry statistics for establishments with employees. These include number of establishments, employees, payroll, sales, and data-quality entries. Each state report presents the basic data items by industry for the state and the metropolitan areas within the state. Data for transportation establishments with no paid employees are published in the separate *Nonemployer Statistics* report. This report is for all sectors, but should be remembered because most other census reports cover only establishments with paid employees. There are nonemployer statistics in transportation for Metropolitan Statistical Areas, each state, the District of Columbia, and the United States.

Special subject reports for transportation and warehousing are collected at a broader geographical level. The *Sources of Revenue* reveals what the establishments in these industries do to earn revenue. Only national data are available in viewable (PDF) reports. Internet and CD-ROM databases contain merchandise line data for states, MSAs, and the area within each state outside any MSA. For example, it shows the different kinds of activities that nonscheduled air transportation engages in to earn money and the relative importance of each activity. Looking at Figure 8.1, we see that 55 percent of the revenues come from charter passenger service followed by 13 percent from domestic airfreight.

*Establishment and Firm Size (including Legal Form of Organization)* presents national data on the number of establishments, sales, payroll, and employment. These industry totals are cross-tabulated by size of establishment, size of firm, and legal form of organization. Establishment data are presented by sales size and employment size; data for firms, by sales size (including concentration by largest firms), by employment size, and by number of establishments operated. Use of this data allows policy makers to see which industries are more monopolistic than others or for pension fund managers to target those industries with a higher concentration of employees instead of those industries with lower employee counts.

The *Miscellaneous Subjects* presents specialized data at the national and state level on purchased transportation by motor freight carriers, revenue-generating equipment for passenger transportation (i.e., number of vehicles by type by industry), cost of arranged transportation by mode of shipping, and construction activities by pipeline establishments.

The *Summary Report* is a compilation of selected tables from the geographic areas, source of revenues, establishment and firm size, and the miscellaneous subjects reports. If you have limited space and are interested in data on the national level, this is the report to print and save.

*Comparative Statistics* have also moved. Statistics from the previous census are no longer shown in the Geographic Area Series; to do a historical comparison between transportation industries you can use two reports: *Bridge Between the NAICS and SIC* and the *Comparative Statistics*. It's best if you use the Web version—they are laid out logically and allow for linking between the two systems.

## Additional Transportation and Warehousing Information in Other Parts of the Census

Other transportation and warehousing data in the Economic Census generally use SIC definitions (SIC 41–47), so be warned when comparing with the Transportation and Warehousing reports. It is critical that you use the Bridge Tables to determine the compatibility between datasets of an industry *and* never make the mistake of comparing SIC transportation related industry groups with the NAICS transportation and warehousing sector. It was calculated that 99.5 percent of the SIC-based arrangement of passenger transportation, n.e.c. (not elsewhere classified) revenues was moved out of this NAICS sector and $356 million of amusement and recreation services, n.e.c. moved in. Along with all the other changes in transportation and warehousing, it's best to use the Bridge Tables at the disaggregated areas.

National transportation and warehousing data are in the *Business Expenses* report. These data are taken for the 1997 Business Expenditures Survey (BES). Tables give detailed operating expenses for the years 1992 and 1997. Items covered are employer costs for programs required by law; payroll including all salaries, wages, commissions, bonuses, and allowances for vacation, holiday, and paid sick leave; employer costs for other fringe benefits; contract labor; depreciation charges; taxes; lease and rental payments; cost of office supplies, stationary, and postage; cost of communication services; cost of fuels and electricity; cost of other utilities; legal services from other firms; accounting services from other firms; data processing and other computer-related services; cost of repair services; and all other operating expenses, such as insurance expense (non-employee), uninsured casualty losses, and bad debt.

The *Women- and Minority-Owned Business* report has transportation and warehousing information down to the SIC three-digit level, industry group. Geographic coverage goes all the way from national to places of 2,500 population. Be aware that the small geographic region has less detail. Comparing between years is not that easy despite the fact that they both use

Figure 8.1
**Sample 1997 Economic Census, Transportation and Warehousing Source of Revenue Report Table**

[Includes only establishments with payroll. For meaning of abbreviations and symbols, see introductory text. For explanation of terms, see Appendix A]

| NAICS code and RL code | Kind of business and source of revenue | Establishments (number) | Revenue[1] ($1,000) | Revenue from specified source of revenue as percent of total revenue[1] | Revenue of establishments reporting sources of revenue as percent of total revenue[1] |
|---|---|---|---|---|---|
| **481112** | **Scheduled freight air transportation**—Con. | | | | |
| 5040 | Domestic air freight | 236 | 1 488 323 | 36.4 | X |
| 5050 | International air freight | 222 | 2 208 817 | 54.0 | X |
| 5060 | Domestic air mail | 20 | 172 064 | 4.2 | X |
| 5090 | Ramp service, parking, tie down, and storage fees | 22 | 4 804 | .1 | X |
| 5100 | Aircraft rental and leasing | 13 | 1 333 | Z | X |
| 5110 | Aircraft maintenance and repair | 24 | 7 940 | .2 | X |
| 5120 | Flight training and instruction | 8 | 574 | Z | X |
| 5130 | Other airport or aircraft services | 9 | 499 | Z | X |
| 9810 | All other operating revenue | 20 | 92 356 | 2.3 | X |
| **4812** | **Nonscheduled air transportation** | **1 800** | **3 964 104** | **100.0** | **74.8** |
| 3100 | Sales of fuels and lubricants | 323 | 99 219 | 2.5 | X |
| 3300 | Sales of new and used aircraft | 78 | 17 907 | .5 | X |
| 3350 | Sales of aircraft parts and supplies | 241 | 47 345 | 1.2 | X |
| 3750 | Sales of other merchandise | 153 | 3 616 | .1 | X |
| 5000 | Scheduled passenger revenue | 38 | 22 252 | .6 | X |
| 5010 | Charter passenger revenue | 1 480 | 2 191 549 | 55.3 | X |
| 5020 | Sightseeing passenger revenue | 147 | 12 301 | .3 | X |
| 5030 | Other passenger revenue | 81 | 22 119 | .6 | X |
| 5040 | Domestic air freight | 339 | 523 875 | 13.2 | X |
| 5050 | International air freight | 183 | 139 773 | 3.5 | X |

SIC. Read the section on the *Minority- and Women-Owned Business* report for more detail.

## VEHICLE INVENTORY AND USE SURVEY

As mentioned above, the Economic Census collects information about the numbers and types of trucks and related vehicles. It also collects information about the characteristics and uses of those vehicles. This is done through the vehicle inventory and use survey. Except for one change in the survey design, the *1997 Vehicle Inventory and Use Survey* (VIUS) is very comparable to the *1992 Truck Inventory and Use Survey* (TIUS).

### Coverage

This survey includes all types of private and commercial trucks registered in the country as of July 1, 1997. In addition to what most people think of as trucks, this survey includes sport utility vehicles (SUVs), station wagons, and minivans. It excludes vehicles owned by governmental entities; ambulances; buses; motor homes, farm tractors, unpowered trailer units (the trailer on tractor trailers); and trucks that have been sold, junked, or wrecked prior to July 1, 1996. Also, some vehicles are excluded because they do not have to be registered in a state. An example of this would be an "off-highway" truck used exclusively on private property.

The geographic coverage is limited to the fifty states, the District of Columbia, and the nation as a whole.

The subject areas covered in this survey include

- How and when the truck was acquired.
- How and when the truck was disposed of.
- The details of the leasing arrangement for the truck, such as the length of the lease and what is covered by the lease.
- The truck's physical characteristics, such as the make; model year; body type; and number, type, and arrangement of the axles.
- The presence of various types of equipment, such as power steering, various types of fuel conservation features, anti-lock brakes, and air conditioning.
- The number and characteristics of trailers pulled during the year.
- The percent of mileage pulling trailers of various types.
- Type, source, and efficiency of fuels.
- Who performed general maintenance on the truck.

- Who performed any major overhauls on the truck.
- Types, distance, and area of trips. The area is defined relative to the truck's home base.
- Mileage based on various types of operations, such as independent, lease to a company, private fleet as a private carrier, or common carrier.
- The types of products carried on percent of mileage basis.
- Types of hazardous materials carried on a percent of mileage basis.

### Procedures

As with most Census Bureau surveys, these data are collected on the basis of a stratified random probability sample. In this case there are two independent samples that are used.

The primary or initial sample contains about 128,000 trucks. These trucks were randomly selected from five strata in each of the 50 states and the District of Columbia. The five strata within each geographic area represent five different types of trucks: (1) pickups; (2) vans, minivans, and panel trucks; (3) light single-unit trucks (gross vehicle weight less than 26,000 pounds); (4) heavy single-unit trucks (gross vehicle weight of 26,000 pounds or more); and (5) truck-tractors.

The one change in coverage that occurred between the 1992 Truck Inventory and Use Survey and the 1997 Vehicle Inventory and Use Survey was the addition of about 3,000 trucks to the sample. This supplemental sample was composed of trucks that were registered in one state, but whose registrant's mailing address was in another state (e.g., a truck registered in Idaho, but the owner receives mail in Oregon). This sample was based on the same five truck-type strata as the initial sample. However, the 51 "states" were grouped into four mutually exclusive classes.

The trucks to be included in these samples were found through the files of active truck registrations maintained by each of the states. An appropriate number of trucks were selected from each of the 275 geography-by-truck strata to provide statistically reliable estimates for each stratum.

A questionnaire was mailed to each registered owner. The type of truck determined which of four questionnaires the owner received. This questionnaire had the make, model year, license number and state of registration, and vehicle identification number preprinted on it so that the owner could identify the specific truck the questionnaire applied to.

Each truck for which a response was received was assigned a weight based on its probability of being selected for the sample and an adjustment factor to account for nonresponse. The total of these weights produced the national and state estimates for the survey.

## Printable VIUS Reports

There are several national and state-specific printable (PDF) documents that were produced as part of the 1997 VIUS. These include a detailed national geographic summary, shorter state summaries, state and national truck trends, and summary tables showing the number of registered drivers for various types of trucks. These reports can be found on the Census Bureau's Web site on the Internet and on the 1997 Vehicle Inventory and Use CD-ROM.

*Vehicle Inventory and Use Survey—Geographic Area Series—United States.* This report presents detailed data on truck types and their usage for the nation as a whole. There are 13 tables presenting data and two additional tables with variability (statistical quality) measures. Most tables show only 1997 data, but two tables (2 and 3) compare 1992 and 1997. Table 1a shows very basic percent distributions comparisons for 1982, 1987, 1992, and 1997.

An example of the data you can find in this report is the percent change in the number of cab forward over engine trucks between 1992 and 1997. You can also find the number of trucks with double trailers that primarily carried farm products or the total number of miles that insulated refrigerated van trucks were driven in 1997.

It is important to note that tables showing the number of trucks report thousands of trucks. So, a table showing that 544.1 medium-size vehicles had general maintenance done by the owner, this is really 544,100 vehicles. Tables showing mileage counts report numbers in millions of miles.

*Vehicle Inventory and Use Survey—Geographic Area Series—State Reports.* These 12-page reports show basic counts of vehicles for 1992 and 1997 and percent change between these two years for many vehicles and operation characteristics. These reports lack the cross-tabulations of these characteristics by vehicle size, truck type, mileage class, and operational range (same state, etc.) that are shown in the national report. Data on truck mileage, which is reported on a national level, are also lacking in these reports.

*Fast Facts.* This is a series of two page summaries providing standardized, computer-generated narra-

tives for the nation and each of the states. The topics covered in these summaries are

- The number of registered trucks
- Types of trucks registered
- Population and licensed drivers per SUV and pickup truck
- Percent of trucks carrying hazardous materials
- Percent of trucks used for personal transportation and operated for business
- Percent of trucks that were leased.

*National summary tables.* Additionally, there are tables in PDF format showing the number of registered drivers per SUV, pickup truck, and minivan in each state.

## Electronic Data

Unlike the other parts of the Economic Census, the only VIUS data available online are the PDF reports described above. There is a wealth of data on the CD-ROM.

The CD-ROM includes both the PDF reports and the data that were used to produce these reports. It also includes software that can be used to look at the data. The Ivation Beyond 20/20 Browser software can be used to view and print tabulations. These tables can also be exported in a variety of formats.

Details about working with the Ivation Beyond 20/20 Browser are included later in this chapter.

## COMMODITY FLOW SURVEY

The *Commodity Flow Survey* (CFS) is a joint statistical activity of the Census Bureau and the Bureau of Transportation Statistics. This survey collects and reports information on the value, weight, mode of transportation, origin and destinations of goods shipped from manufacturing, mining, wholesale, and selected types of retail establishments. This information is used to determine the demands on the national and state transportation systems. It is also used to help forecast future transportation needs.

This survey was conducted for the economic census years between 1963 and 1983. While the data were collected for 1983, they were never developed into public products. It was not conducted again until 1993. The 1997 survey continues this series.

## Procedures

A stratified random sample of about 100,000 manufacturing, mining, wholesale, catalog mail-order houses, and selected auxiliary establishments was selected from a population of around 800,000 such establishments. The strata were defined on the basis of three-digit SIC classification, estimates of the total value of shipments for 1994, auxiliary status, and national transportation analysis region (a grouping of states).

Next, each selected establishment was randomly assigned to one of thirteen groups. Each one of these groups was assigned one week every quarter during 1997 in which to be surveyed about their shipments. Each group was sent a questionnaire for their assigned week, 12 weeks were then skipped, and then they were sent a questionnaire for the next quarter. Therefore, if an establishment was sampled during the first week of the quarter, they would be sampled during the first week of every quarter.

When an establishment received their questionnaire, one of the first questions asked was to identify the total number of outbound shipments (including customer pick-ups) during the one week covered by this questionnaire. Then they were instructed to identify a selection rate based on the number of outbound shipments. This selection rate is shown in Table 8.1. Using this selection rate, they then chose an appropriate sample of their shipments for the rest of the survey. The selection rate was designed to collect between 20 and 40 shipments for each establishment.

The directions for selecting specific shipments were included on the questionnaire. They are shown in Figure 8.2.

Once the shipments were selected, the respondent was asked to provide the following information about each shipment in the sample:

- **Shipment ID Number**—a number, such as invoice or shipment number, that the establishment could use to identify the shipment if there was a question about it.
- **Shipment Date**—the month and day the shipment left the establishment.
- **Shipment Value**—the dollar value of the entire shipment excluding freight charges and excise taxes. Estimates were accepted if the actual value was not readily available.
- **Shipment Weight**—The weight, in pounds, of the total shipments. Estimates were requested if the actual weight was not readily available.
- **Commodity Code**—The Standard Classification of Transported Goods (SCTG) Codes from a manual provided with the questionnaire for the goods included in the shipment. If more than one commod-

**Table 8.1**
**Commodity Flow Survey Selection Rates**

| Number of Shipments during sample week | Selection Rate |
| --- | --- |
| 1 - 40 | 1 |
| 41 - 80 | 2 |
| 81 - 100 | 3 |
| 101 - 200 | 5 |
| 201 - 400 | 10 |
| 401 - 800 | 20 |
| 801 - 1,600 | 40 |
| 1,601 - 3,200 | 80 |
| 3,201 - 6,400 | 160 |
| 6,401 - 12,800 | 320 |
| More than 12,800 | Special directions from the Census Bureau were to be followed. |

ity was included in the shipment, the commodity with the greatest weight was to be reported.

- **Commodity Description**—A brief non-technical description (e.g., electrical transformers or gasoline) of the commodity being shipped. If there was more than one commodity included in the shipment, the commodity with the greatest weight was to be reported.
- **Hazardous Materials Code**—If this was a hazardous material, either the United Nations or North American classification number was to be provided.
- **Containerization**—Did this shipment leave the establishment in an intermodal or stackable container.
- **U.S. Destination**—For shipments to locations within the United States, the city, state, and ZIP code of the buyer or receiver was to be reported. For international shipments by sea or air, the port of exit from the United States was to be reported as the U.S. destination. For land shipments to Canada or Mexico, the border crossing location into those countries was to be reported here.
- **Mode(s) of Transport**—*All* modes of transport used to get the shipment to its U.S. destination were to be reported in. These modes included

**Figure 8.2**
**CFS Shipment Selection Directions**

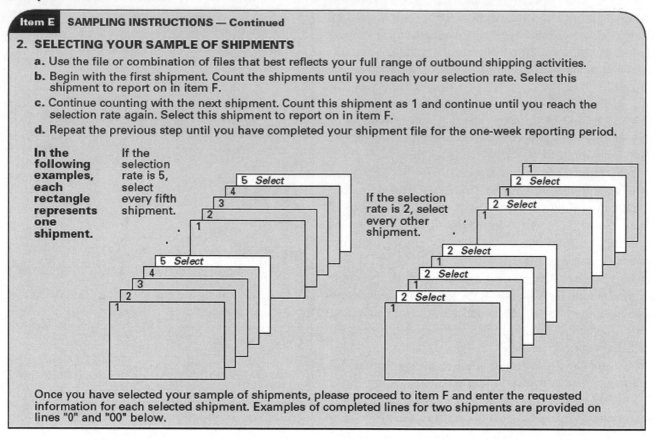

| Item E | SAMPLING INSTRUCTIONS — Continued |

## 2. SELECTING YOUR SAMPLE OF SHIPMENTS

**a.** Use the file or combination of files that best reflects your full range of outbound shipping activities.

**b.** Begin with the first shipment. Count the shipments until you reach your selection rate. Select this shipment to report on in item F.

**c.** Continue counting with the next shipment. Count this shipment as 1 and continue until you reach the selection rate again. Select this shipment to report on in item F.

**d.** Repeat the previous step until you have completed your shipment file for the one-week reporting period.

In the following examples, each rectangle represents one shipment.

If the selection rate is 5, select every fifth shipment.

If the selection rate is 2, select every other shipment.

Once you have selected your sample of shipments, please proceed to item F and enter the requested information for each selected shipment. Examples of completed lines for two shipments are provided on lines "0" and "00" below.

- Parcel delivery, courier, or U.S. Postal Service
- Private truck
- For-hire truck
- Railroad
- Shallow draft vessel (shipping designed for rivers, canals, harbors, the Great Lakes and the Saint Lawrence Seaway, the Intracoastal Waterway, the Inside Passage to Alaska, major bays and inlets, and the ocean close to the shoreline)
- Deep draft vessel (shipping designed primarily for the open ocean)
- Pipeline
- Air
- Other modes
- Unknown

- **Export Shipments**—An indication of whether or not the shipment was intended for export. Exports included shipments to Puerto Rico and U.S. territories and possessions.
- **Foreign Destination**—the city and county of an export shipment's ultimate destination.

- **Export Mode**—The mode of transport, from the same list of options as domestic modes of transport, by which the shipment left the United States.

If any of these data was missing from an individual shipment, the Census Bureau attempted to impute it from other similar shipments. A usable shipment was defined as one containing at least its value, weight, origin ZIP code, and destination ZIP code. If any of these four items was missing and could not be imputed, then the shipment was classified as unusable.

Establishments were also asked to report the total value of shipments during the week covered by the questionnaire and if there were any individual shipments worth more than $2 million.

There were also questions about whether there were more than one shipping site or set of shipping files for the establishment. If the respondent said yes to either of these questions, they were asked if it would be easier to receive a separate questionnaire for each site or file.

During the last quarter of 1997, a sub-sample of about 25,000 establishments was sent a questionnaire with additional questions about the availability and use of various types of on-site shipping facilities, such as rail sidings or docks. They were also asked about the use of company-owned or leased transportation equipment, such as barges, trucks, and rail cars. Finally, they were asked about who generally makes decisions about transportation modes.

In order to represent all shipments of goods within the scope of this survey, each shipment included in the sample was assigned a weight. These weights were based on seven factors involving: (1) the chances of that shipment being selected out of all of the establishment's shipments for that week, (2) the proportion of usable shipments reported by that establishment, (3) the chances of that week being selected for the quarter (usually a factor of 13), (4) the number of quarters that the establishment reported and was in business, (5) an establishment-level adjustment to correct for sampling or non-sampling errors that occur during the sampling of shipments by the respondent, (6) the chances of the establishment being selected for the sample, and (7) an industry-level adjustment to account for changes in the population of establishments between the initial selection of establishments in 1995 and the data collection phase in 1997.

## Printable CFS Reports

The Census Bureau produced individual printable reports (PDF files) for the nation as a whole, the four census regions, the nine census divisions, each of the states, and selected metropolitan areas (MSAs and CMSAs), and remainders of the states containing those metropolitan areas. These files are available on the Census Bureau's Web site and the Commodity Flow Survey CD-ROM.

Most tables in these reports present data for just 1997. Several tables in the national, regional, division, and state reports also show data for 1993 and the change between 1993 and 1997. Nearly all of these tables show the value of the shipments in millions of dollars, the thousands of tons shipped, and the millions of ton-miles shipped. Tables 1 and 2, as described below, also show the average miles per shipment. The specific tables in these reports are shown in Table 8.2.

The data on exports is found in the *1997 Commodity Flow Survey United States Exports*. This report contains the shipment characteristics by

- The mode of transportation used to export goods out of the country
- The mode of transportation used to get the goods to their domestic destination
- The country of destination (Canada, Mexico, all other countries combined)
- Commodity
- Commodity and export mode of transportation
- Selected state of origin (19 states and all other states combined)

The *1997 Commodity Flow Survey, United States, Hazardous Materials* report contains a variety of data on the modes of transportation, type of hazardous material (by hazardous class and UN Numbers), origin, destination, and export status. Many of the tables compare intrastate with interstate transportation.

## Electronic Data

All of the tables from the printed reports are available as ASCII, comma-delimited files on the Census Bureau's Web site. Being ASCII, comma-delimited files, they can easily be imported into most spreadsheets or databases for further analysis.

There are some additional national, state, and hazardous materials data files on the Census Bureau's Web site. These tend to be more detailed tables than those shown in the printed reports, for example, one additional table is titled "Hazardous material shipment characteristics by for-hire truck for intrastate versus interstate for selected commodities." Another table shows information for four-digit commodity for the nation.

The CD-ROM contains the printable reports. It also contains the data—shown in the geographic area reports as pre-defined tables—and the software (Ivation Beyond 20/20 Browser) to read these tables. The software allows these tables to be exported to a variety of other programs. The microdata behind these charts are not accessible to data users. The details of working with the Beyond 20/20 Browser are described below.

## BEYOND 20/20 SOFTWARE

Both the *Commodity Flow Survey* and the *Vehicle Inventory and Use Survey* are available on CD-ROM. These CD-ROMs include the Ivation Beyond 20/20 Browser as the means of accessing the data, PDF reports, and information about these surveys. The CD-ROMs also include version 4.0 of the Adobe Acrobat Reader.

**Table 8.2**
**Tables Included in the Community Flow Survey by Geographic Level (Numbers refer to the table number in the report)**

| Table Content | National | Region / Division | State | Metropolitan Area / Remainder of State |
|---|---|---|---|---|
| Mode of Transportation: 1997 | 1a | 1a | 1a | 1 |
| Mode of transportation: 1997 and 1993 | 1b | 1b | 1b | |
| Mode of transportation: Percent of total 1997 and 1993 | 1c | 1c | 1c | |
| Total modal activity: 1997 (Total ton-miles for each mode without multiple modes) | 2 | 2 | 2 | |
| Inbound shipments by mode of transportation for the area of destination 1997 | | | | 2 |
| Mode of transportation and distance shipped: 1997 | 3 | 3 | 3 | 3 |
| Mode of transportation and the shipment size:1997 | 4 | 4 | 4 | 4 |
| Two-Digit Commodity: 1997 | 5a | 5 | 5 | |
| Commodity group: 1997 | | | | 5 |
| Two-digit commodity: 1997 and 1993 | 5b | | | |
| Two-digit commodity: Percent of total 1997 and 1993 | 5c | | | |
| Three-digit commodity: 1997 | 6 | 6 | | |
| Two-digit commodity and mode of transportation: 1997 | 7 | 7 | 6 | |
| Commodity group and mode of transportation: 1997 | | | | 6 |
| Two-digit commodity and distance shipped: 1997 | 8 | 8 | | |
| Two-digit commodity and shipment size: 1997 | 9 | 9 | | |
| Two-digit commodity and shipment size by distance shipped: 1997 | 10 | 10 | | |
| Area of destination for this area of origin (e.g. Delaware report shows states of destination for shipments from Delaware) | | | 7 | 7 |
| Inbound shipment characteristics for area of origin for this area of destination (e.g. Delaware report shows states of origin for shipments to Delaware) | | | 8 | 8 |

## Installation

The installation of this program is very simple. The basic system requirements are

• Windows 95, 98, or NT4.0
• Pentium 100 MHz (133 or faster is recommended)
• 10 MB RAM (32 MB or more is recommended)
• 800 by 600 or higher SVGA screen resolution
• CD-ROM drive.

If your computer system has at least these minimum requirements and the Windows autorun feature turned on, you simply need to insert the CD-ROM into your CD-ROM drive. Then, depending on which survey you are using, the welcome screen shown in either Figure 8.3 or Figure 8.4 will appear. If these do not appear, you will need to go to the Windows Start Button at the bottom of your screen, click on Run, and Browse until you find Launch.exe on your CD-ROM drive. Then select this program and run it by clicking on OK.

With either of these screens, simply press the Install button to start the installation process. Then simply follow the installation directions provided. It is best to use the default choices provided by the installation software, except that you might need to designate a different CD-ROM drive depending on your computer's arrangement. Like all Windows installations, it is best to have all other Windows programs shut down before starting the installation.

## Starting the Software

Once the software is installed, you need to actually start it. This is done by clicking on the Launch The Software button for the CFS or the Documents/Data button for the VIUS. You can also start the software by finding it on the Windows Start, Programs button.

### Commodity Flow Survey

When you start the CFS program, you will see the screen shown in Figure 8.5.

The buttons on this screen do the following:

**Figure 8.3**
**Commodity Flow Survey Welcome Screen**

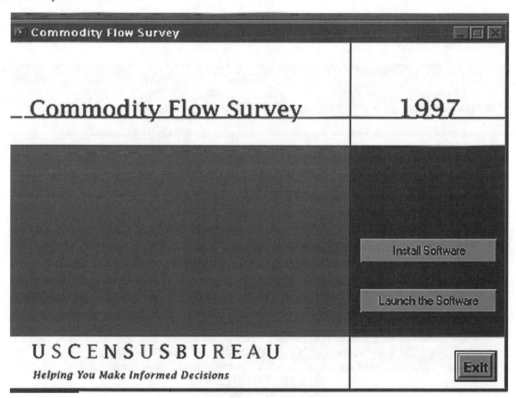

**Figure 8.4**
**Vehicle Inventory and Use Survey Welcome Screen**

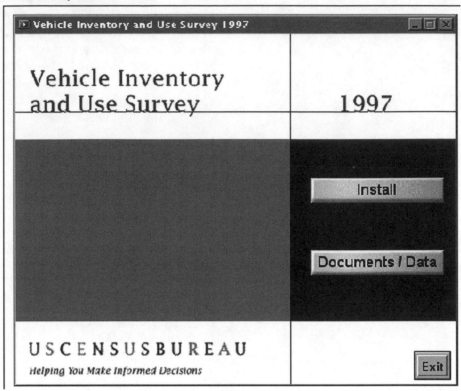

**Figure 8.5**
**Commodity Flow Survey Home Page**

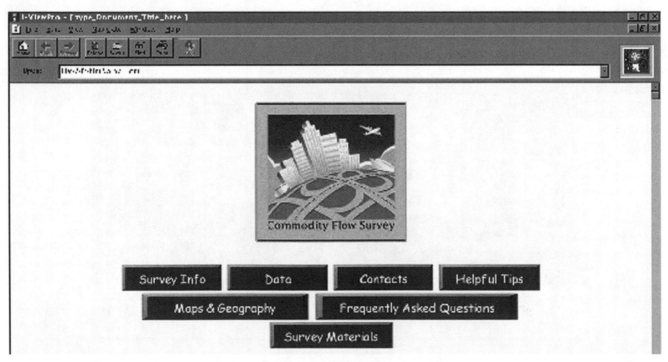

- The Survey Info button provides very important background information about the survey. This includes details about how the data were collected, the statistical reliability of the numbers presented, and explanations of the terms used in this survey.
- The Data button provides access to the PDF reports and the pre-defined data tables included on the CD-ROM.
- The Contacts button provides information on who to contact with questions about this survey. It is probably one of the more useful buttons on this screen.
- The Helpful Tips button opens a 16-page PDF document containing a user's guide to working with the CD-ROM in general and the Ivation 20/20 Browser in detail. This is probably a useful document to look at before using the software.
- The Maps & Geography button links to maps and an ASCII file identifying the counties included in the metropolitan areas shown in this survey's reports.
- The Frequently Asked Questions button provides the answers to 10 questions related to working with the data and files on the CD-ROM.

- The Survey Materials button leads to copies of the questionnaire, instructions for completing the questionnaire, and the commodity coding manual for the survey.

## Vehicle Inventory and Use Survey

Once you have started the VIUS program you will see the screen shown in Figure 8.6. This screen has the following options:

- Microdata File—This gives the user the opportunity to produce custom tabulations of the survey responses.
- PDF Files—This is where the user can access, read, and print the PDF files from the survey.
- Pre-defined Tables—This button provides access to a set of Ivation 20/20 Browser tables that have already been created by the Census Bureau.
- Data Dictionary—Here is where data users can find detailed information about each of the variables included in the microdata or pre-defined tables.

The CD Info button provides the minimum system requirements to work with this CD-ROM.

**Figure 8.6**
**VIUS Home Screen**

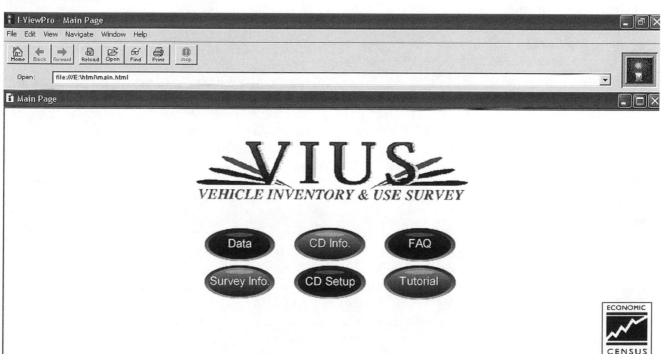

The CD Setup button gives the instructions for installing the software.

The FAQ button provides the answers to about 20 common questions about the survey and software. Many questions have links to more detailed information. It is important to note that some of these links are sites on the Internet and will only work if the computer has Internet access and the URL for the site is still valid.

The Tutorial button provides directions for and access to a series of Lotus ScreenCam formatted tutorials. Some of these tutorials show how to access the data in their various formats. Others provide guidance on working with the Ivation 20/20 software. Data users who are new to working with this survey or the software will probably find these short tutorials very helpful.

## Working with Pre-defined Tables

Accessing the pre-defined tables in either survey is actually very easy. From the home page, you simply click on the Data button and then on the Pre-Defined Tables link. This will open up the Beyond 20/20 Browser and present a dialog box showing a variety of table categories and the specific tables in each category. You can select the table or change categories simply by scrolling through the appropriate list and then clicking on your choice.

Once you click on the table of your choice, it will open up in the Beyond 20/20 Browser window. Selecting the range of operation by body type table from the VIUS resulted in the table shown in Figure 8.7.

From here it is possible to save this table to be used in other programs, such as spreadsheets or databases. This is done through the File, Save As menu choices.

It is possible to sort the data based on one item within a variable (dimension in Beyond 20/20 Browser language). To do this sort, you first click on the item you wish to use as the basis of sorting, then click on the dimension you wish to sort, then choose either the sort button from the toolbar or Dimension, Sort from the menu bar. When the dialog box comes up, you would indicate that you wish to sort the data and the order of the sort (ascending or descending).

For example, if you wanted to find which types of trucks are used most for local transportation, you would first click on the column labeled local. Then you would click on the body type dimension. Following this, you would click on the Dimension, Sort choices on the menu bar. In the dialog box, you would

click on Data and Decreasing. Lastly, you would click OK and your data will be sorted by decreasing number of trucks being used for local transportation.

## Summarizing Items

Data can be summarized in two ways from these tables. The first way is to create a chart from it. The second way is to calculate new items, for example, totals, averages, etc.

To create charts in the Beyond 20/20 Browser, you first select the data items that you are interested in charting and then clicking on the chart button on the toolbar. You can also select View, Chart from the menu bar. Either of these will produce the default chart. You can then change the type of the chart and the way parts of it appear through the Chart Options choices available either on the View menu or by right-clicking your mouse. It should be noted that while this graphing capability exists in the Beyond 20/20 Browser, the graphs are rather basic and much more sophisticated and useful graphs can be produced in other software such as Microsoft Excel.

Calculating new items can be done in the Beyond 20/20 Browser by saving the table to another file with File, Save As (this removes the read-only protection). The new table will be the new active table. Now you can select the items that you wish to combine and then group them together with the Item, Define Group menu options. This opens a dialog box where you name the group and tell the software what to do with it (such as produce a total for the group).

## Creating Tables from Microdata

If none of the pre-defined tables from the *Vehicle Inventory and Use Survey* meet your needs, another option for getting at the data exists. This is to produce your own tables using the microdata (this option does not exist for the *Commodity Flow Survey*).

When developing tables with microdata it is critical to also use the data dictionary. The data dictionary tells you the mnemonic names of the variables that you are interested in and how they are coded.

As an example, assume that you are looking to identify which vehicle makes had airbags in each state. You would first identify the variables that you need for the tables. These would be (1) BASTATE—the vehicle's base state, (2) MAKE—the make of the vehicle, (3) AIRBAG—the presence of airbags. You would also need the EXANF (expansion factor or weight) for the vehicle.

Figure 8.7
VIUS Predefined Table

AREAOP

| BODYTYP | Total | Off-the-road | Local | Short range | Short range-medium | Long range-mediu |
|---|---|---|---|---|---|---|
| Total | 1,044,234,964,209 | 26,180,774,800 | 657,762,135,478 | 172,748,470,760 | 68,171,626,721 | 53,373,302,2 |
| Pickup | 453,720,956,799 | 14,545,582,868 | 308,163,902,751 | 86,169,629,403 | 25,472,897,134 | 10,180,834,8 |
| Panel or van | 71,414,507,072 | 1,724,430,992 | 45,803,989,077 | 12,917,905,415 | 5,597,024,478 | 2,388,909,9 |
| Multistop or step van | 9,428,571,516 | 87,510,338 | 3,697,603,745 | 2,743,419,622 | 1,163,569,615 | 1,293,572,8 |
| Platform with added devices | 3,670,069,588 | 127,746,616 | 2,002,736,195 | 818,888,946 | 300,143,706 | 221,195, |
| Low boy or depressed center | 2,708,600,130 | 60,110,184 | 713,272,965 | 620,948,554 | 366,413,804 | 386,674,4 |
| Basic platform | 22,383,752,028 | 396,795,931 | 6,617,318,805 | 3,480,975,512 | 2,809,564,684 | 4,209,095,7 |
| Livestock truck | 1,037,258,400 | 17,663,006 | 133,202,823 | 189,226,980 | 166,378,442 | 260,853,9 |
| Insulated nonrefrigerated van | 2,575,821,878 | 2,057,117 | 89,161,786 | 146,288,153 | 242,875,096 | 338,759,0 |
| Insulated refrigerated van | 16,362,951,678 | 52,045,120 | 1,020,482,629 | 1,503,595,578 | 1,689,000,655 | 2,344,819,8 |
| Drop-frame van | 2,357,476,119 | 12,050,049 | 274,093,544 | 201,229,490 | 161,073,250 | 560,926,4 |
| Open-top van | 1,032,886,490 | 3,707,183 | 144,749,518 | 376,535,914 | 264,063,259 | 149,019,3 |
| Basic enclosed van | 55,849,393,786 | 263,495,562 | 5,718,326,611 | 6,437,863,114 | 7,812,910,913 | 14,873,908,6 |
| Beverage | 1,244,722,184 | 15,217,767 | 584,464,381 | 478,339,559 | 134,975,132 | 19,944,8 |
| Public utility | 1,668,962,690 | 45,305,203 | 1,145,805,389 | 337,513,943 | 89,725,255 | 38,697,2 |
| Winch or crane | 808,089,583 | 29,690,148 | 444,020,354 | 217,763,396 | 49,807,997 | 42,793,3 |
| Wrecker | 1,737,322,864 | 11,723,148 | 1,296,270,926 | 215,350,996 | 127,935,269 | 35,200,8 |
| Pole or logging | 2,158,759,075 | 71,154,017 | 479,475,131 | 1,016,400,900 | 310,920,775 | 201,766,8 |
| Auto transport | 915,290,723 | 3,848,365 | 105,358,894 | 46,770,170 | 74,289,187 | 267,795,7 |
| Service truck | 2,263,790,759 | 67,389,222 | 1,420,221,222 | 543,331,281 | 154,306,735 | 76,633,4 |
| Yard tractor | 113,834,665 | 33,524,975 | 49,648,373 | 5,734,034 | 22,846,972 | 691,3 |
| Sport utility | 190,521,116,190 | 3,811,623,570 | 140,582,410,191 | 26,288,152,877 | 8,840,252,099 | 6,449,660,4 |
| Station wagon | 24,315,093,686 | 412,434,824 | 17,347,554,142 | 2,928,702,778 | 1,355,571,949 | 1,113,097,9 |
| Minivan | 146,899,610,946 | 3,592,472,901 | 107,638,963,885 | 18,288,308,751 | 7,172,642,521 | 4,966,994,0 |
| Oilfield truck | 440,730,273 | 47,252,606 | 155,073,058 | 109,803,872 | 54,279,628 | 50,874,8 |
| Grain body | 2,772,518,064 | 111,592,929 | 923,984,923 | 587,665,405 | 522,256,145 | 432,263,4 |
| Garbage hauler | 2,306,962,145 | 18,380,795 | 1,463,739,361 | 559,581,327 | 186,120,441 | 62,457,7 |
| Dump truck | 11,369,601,049 | 430,232,464 | 6,220,165,164 | 2,977,658,299 | 957,280,983 | 543,507,4 |
| Tank truck (liquids or gases) | 8,604,563,122 | 148,057,320 | 2,209,101,647 | 1,961,012,917 | 1,565,978,221 | 1,153,909,4 |

Having identified the variables that you are interested in and their mnemonic names, you would then go back to the data page and click on the microdata link. That will open the Beyond 20/20 Browser with the microdata. This will look like Figure 8.8.

Note that the mnemonic names are on the right side of the table. Also, there is room at the top and left of the table to move the mnemonics to be the columns and rows. You should note that you could have up to eight variables (or dimensions) in a table. This is accomplished by nesting the variables under each other. After moving the variables that you are interested in to their positions on the table by left clicking on them with your mouse and dragging them into position, the table now looks like Figure 8.9.

Now that the table shell is set up, two steps remain before the table is done. The first of these is to identify the variable to be used in weighting the results to reflect the entire population. This is done by selecting Data, Set Weight Field from the menu and then choosing the appropriate weight variable in the dialog box. In this example, you would choose EXPANF (as identified above).

The last step in creating the table is to run the tabulation itself. This is done by clicking on the traffic light button on the tool bar. The final table looks like Figure 8.10.

## USING THE TRANSPORTATION AND WAREHOUSING DATA FROM THE ECONOMIC CENSUS

### Cautions

One of the largest problems with using industry sector numbers is that it is easy to forget that the transportation and warehousing industry in the 1997 and 2002 Economic Censuses is not the same as the transportation portion of the Transportation, Communications, and Public Utilities sector reported on in 1992 and earlier Censuses. This may lead to confusion to anyone using the transportation and warehousing numbers. Please make sure when time series data are being used and read the footnotes to the data to see how they handled the break in the industry. Also in order to be fair to (and make life easier for) your readers, be sure to include any comments about changing definitions in your report when you create a time series.

Another pitfall to watch for is whether the data include nonemployer statistics or not. For example, na-

tionally there are 332,535 general trucking establishments generating $106,892,942,000 in revenue; of those, 287,754 of them are nonemployers, however, the establishments with employees provide $88,425,515,000 (or 83 percent) of the income.

## Choosing the Data Presentation Format to Use

The best medium to use when looking for data will depend on several factors. Here we give you some advice on which medium to look at first in different situations. Ultimately, the choice of medium is a personal one, partially dictated by your resources.

If you need one point of data or a few data points, the PDF reports are ideal. One reason this tends to be the choice for finding a few data points is that it is a format that most users are very comfortable with since it approximates the printed volumes of the past. Additionally, they can be used anywhere—once they have been printed. The big down side of this format is that the data must be converted to another format, often by hand, before it can be manipulated.

However, if you want to compare among industries or geographic locations, you can use either American FactFinder or the CD-ROM to select the data. Both of these media allow you to select the data that interest you. You can then either print them from these sources or move them to other software for further analysis.

If you are using the *Commodity Flow Survey* or the *Vehicle Inventory and Use Survey* and are looking for just a few numbers that happen to appear in the PDF reports, then that is probably the best source to use. If you need to manipulate the data and they are already tabulated, then either the ASCII files on the Census Bureau's Web site for the CFS or the pre-defined Beyond 20/20 Browser tables on the CFS or VIUS CD-ROMs are the best choices. Finally, if you are interested in VIUS data tabulations that are not included in any of the above sources, you can try using the microdata and the Beyond 20/20 Browser software on the CD-ROM.

## How Others Use Transportation Data

There are many different uses for the transportation and warehousing data from the census. Most of these involve combining this data with other information. Here are just some examples that can be used.

State governments use the data from the *Commodity Flow Survey* to help determine the amount of goods coming into or leaving the state by mode. By looking at the sources and destinations of goods moving into other

**Figure 8.8**
**Beyond 20/20 Microdata Table Shell**

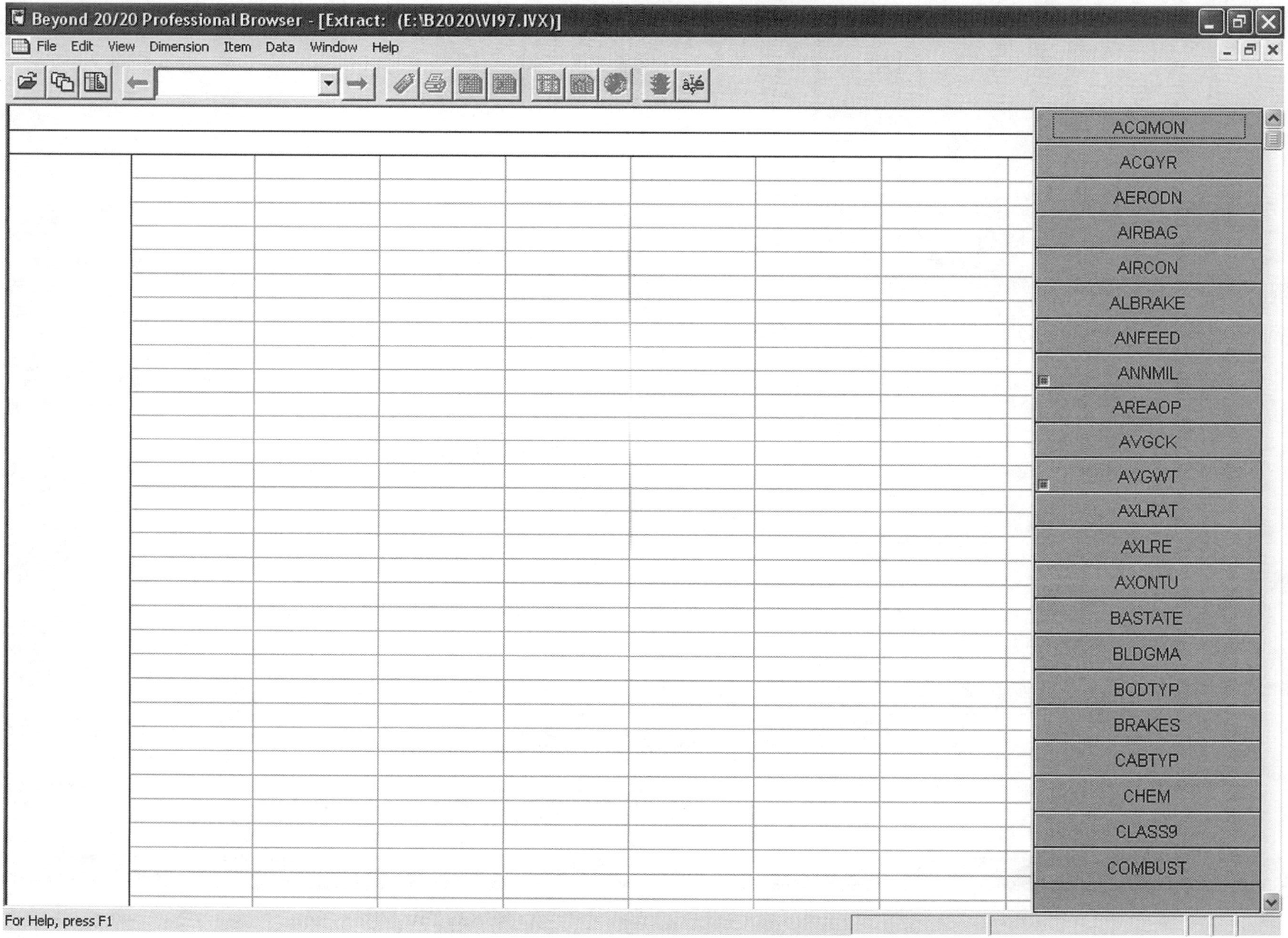

Figure 8.9
Beyond 20/20 Browser after Creating Table Shell for VIUS Microdata

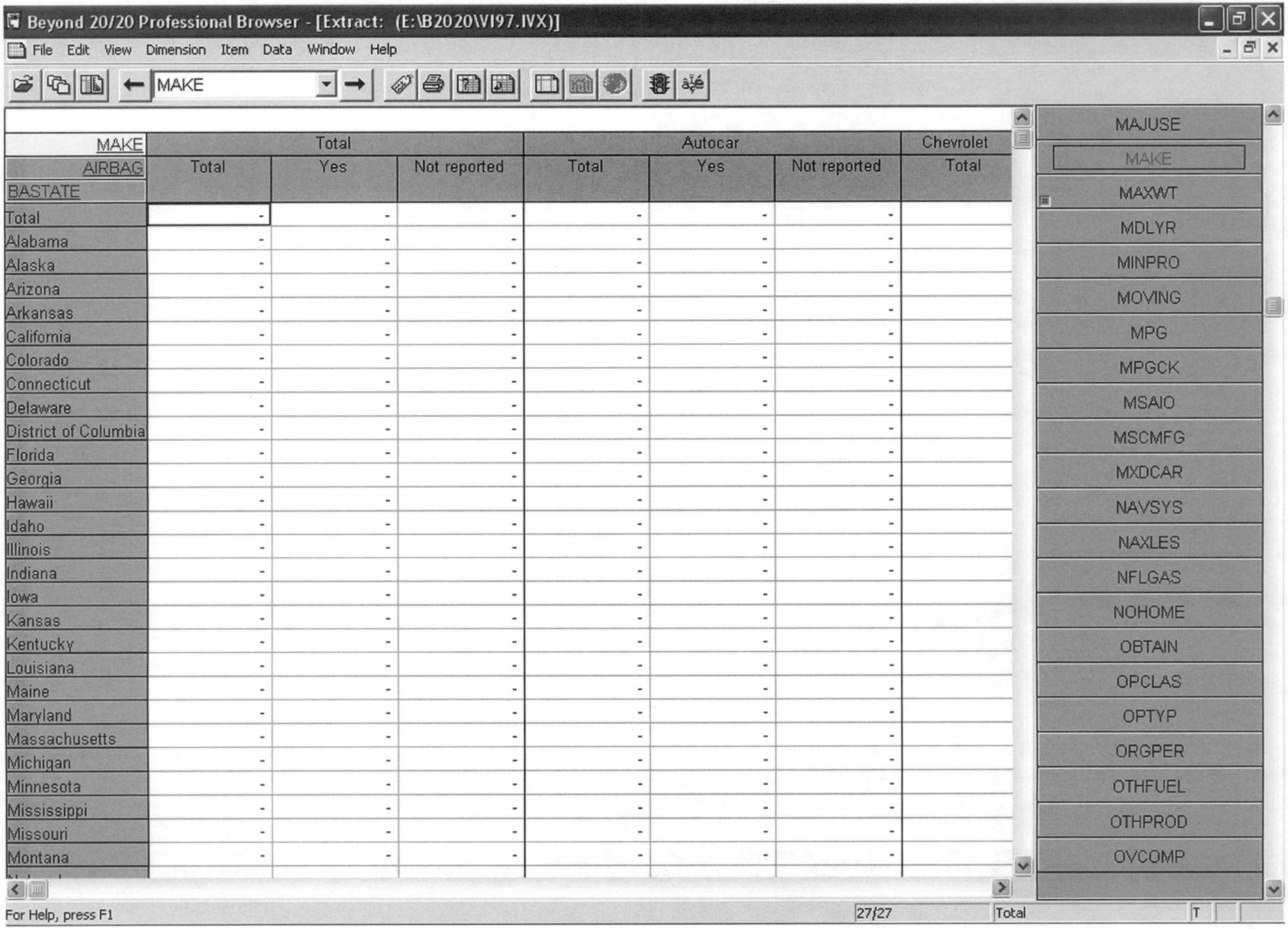

**Figure 8.10**
**Final Table Based on VIUS Microdata**

File   Edit   View   Dimension   Item   Data   Window   Help

MAKE

| MAKE / AIRBAG | Total | | | Autocar | | | Chevrolet | | |
|---|---|---|---|---|---|---|---|---|---|
| BASTATE | Total | Yes | Not reported | Total | Yes | Not reported | Total | Yes | Not repo… |
| Total | 72,800,252 | 17,904,568 | 54,895,684 | 13,050 | 977 | 12,073 | 19,522,414 | 3,322,203 | 16,20… |
| Alabama | 1,414,298 | 329,206 | 1,085,091 | 150 | - | 150 | 450,891 | 55,175 | 39… |
| Alaska | 237,388 | 39,320 | 198,067 | 24 | - | 24 | 61,760 | 8,838 | 5… |
| Arizona | 1,319,194 | 310,705 | 1,008,489 | 101 | - | 101 | 369,020 | 74,057 | 29… |
| Arkansas | 829,662 | 185,524 | 644,138 | 10 | 10 | - | 258,522 | 32,456 | 22… |
| California | 8,504,693 | 1,888,114 | 6,616,579 | 529 | - | 529 | 1,885,929 | 301,541 | 1,58… |
| Colorado | 1,415,385 | 319,588 | 1,095,798 | 43 | - | 43 | 347,593 | 47,982 | 29… |
| Connecticut | 744,738 | 224,700 | 520,037 | 108 | - | 108 | 196,600 | 33,242 | 16… |
| Delaware | 189,009 | 55,820 | 133,190 | 48 | 6 | 42 | 42,288 | 8,404 | 3… |
| District of Columbia | 31,184 | 12,690 | 18,494 | - | - | - | 8,554 | 4,458 | … |
| Florida | 3,181,551 | 1,010,602 | 2,170,949 | 396 | - | 396 | 697,581 | 179,559 | 51… |
| Georgia | 2,218,215 | 627,716 | 1,590,499 | 231 | 56 | 175 | 545,207 | 111,147 | 43… |
| Hawaii | 272,552 | 59,260 | 213,292 | 16 | - | 16 | 43,204 | 8,217 | 3… |
| Idaho | 519,044 | 94,857 | 424,187 | 29 | - | 29 | 145,839 | 20,023 | 12… |
| Illinois | 2,432,889 | 744,470 | 1,688,419 | 169 | - | 169 | 742,721 | 117,468 | 62… |
| Indiana | 1,720,180 | 395,216 | 1,324,964 | 72 | - | 72 | 576,115 | 77,376 | 49… |
| Iowa | 907,163 | 170,863 | 736,299 | - | - | - | 284,804 | 42,787 | 24… |
| Kansas | 1,054,687 | 243,789 | 810,898 | 158 | - | 158 | 317,300 | 43,377 | 27… |
| Kentucky | 1,228,928 | 269,104 | 959,824 | 87 | - | 87 | 363,364 | 49,890 | 31… |
| Louisiana | 1,209,908 | 301,975 | 907,933 | 101 | - | 101 | 350,539 | 88,882 | 26… |
| Maine | 364,879 | 82,523 | 282,356 | 43 | - | 43 | 80,194 | 8,607 | 7… |
| Maryland | 1,129,108 | 348,690 | 780,418 | 258 | - | 258 | 299,008 | 75,011 | 22… |
| Massachusetts | 1,205,850 | 370,889 | 834,961 | 939 | - | 939 | 195,639 | 35,773 | 15… |
| Michigan | 2,586,004 | 869,608 | 1,726,397 | 340 | - | 340 | 724,371 | 164,492 | 55… |
| Minnesota | 1,416,700 | 379,932 | 1,036,768 | 52 | - | 52 | 440,521 | 97,517 | 34… |
| Mississippi | 733,560 | 141,894 | 591,667 | - | - | - | 246,953 | 35,743 | 21… |
| Missouri | 1,537,111 | 375,860 | 1,161,251 | 150 | 50 | 100 | 441,962 | 67,658 | 37… |
| Montana | 395,635 | 58,102 | 337,533 | 41 | - | 41 | 99,178 | 9,417 | 8… |

states and combining this with information about the highway system, it is possible to estimate the amount of goods flowing through the state. For example, the *Commodity Flow Survey's* table on shipment characteristics by destination and mode of transportation indicates that 2.0 billion tons of goods went from New Jersey to Connecticut by truck during 1997. Adding in a basic knowledge of geography, it is clear that these goods traveled through New York State, probably either through Bronx County (along Interstate 95), along Interstate 287 (through Rockland and Westchester Counties and the Tappan Zee Bridge), or along Interstate 87 (the New York State Thruway) and Interstate 84 (through Orange, Dutchess, and Putnam counties). If information about bridge crossings and thruway entrances and exits were available, we would be able to estimate the number of tons going along each of these routes.

A business interested in servicing particular types of equipment, such as truck air brakes could use the *Vehicle Inventory and Use Survey* to identify where there are concentrations of older trucks with air brakes. Based on this information they would be able to identify possible locations in which to establish their business.

An academic looking at productivity in a particular industry at different locations could use the revenues, employment, and payroll information included in the geographic area series. They would use this to define a productivity measure (such as revenues per employee or revenues per payroll dollar). Then this measure would be calculated for different geographic areas and compared.

## ADDITIONAL TRANSPORTATION AND WAREHOUSING DATA

Other reports in the Economic Census with information on transportation and warehousing are limited to three reports: (1) *Bridge Between NAICS and SIC,* (2) *Comparative Statistics,* and (3) *Nonemployer Statistics.* Each of these reports is described in other chapters of this book. It is important to remember that these are limited to the industry statistics.

There is a wealth of transportation related data that is not included in the three components of the Economic Census described in this chapter. There are many other sources for these data. The sources described below are just a few of the major ones. There are likely to be other very specialized sources that can be found through the Internet, bibliographic database searches, and word of mouth.

## Other Census Bureau Data

The Decennial Census of Population and Housing conducted by the U.S. Census Bureau contains information on the number of vehicles available to residents of households throughout the nation. It also contains a wealth of information on commuting patterns, such as mode of travel, starting time, destination, and travel time. The U.S. Bureau of Transportation Statistics contracted with the U.S. Census Bureau for a specialized product from the Population and Housing Census showing data on commuting and demographics by place of work instead of residence. This product is the *Census Transportation Planning Package.* Michael R. Lavin's *Understanding the Census* describes these data products in more detail.

The Census Bureau produces detailed data on exports and imports on a monthly and annual basis. These data include the value and volume of shipments by commodity, port, and destination country. Data are also provided by state of origin and state of shipper where these are known.

Other than the data collected during the various censuses and the data on foreign trade, since 1999 the Census Bureau only collects and distributes data as part of the *Service Annual Survey.* This source provides data on commercial motor freight transportation and public warehousing (NAICS 484, 492, and 493). Between 1982 and 1998, the transportation industries were a separate survey (the *Transportation Annual Survey*). The information reported in these surveys includes operating revenue, sources of the operating revenue, commodity types and weight of shipments handled, distance the shipment was moved, the shipment's country of origin and destination, and an inventory of the vehicle fleet.

## Bureau of Transportation Statistics Data

The U.S. Bureau of Transportation Statistics (BTS) is actually the major source for transportation data in the United States. This agency provides data on most areas of transportation. Their major statistical publication, and a good place to start looking for data, is the annual *National Transportation Statistics.* This report provides many summary statistics that will answer many of the questions commonly asked about transportation.

Through their Web site (www.bts.gov), it is possible to gain access to their data on motor carrier financial and operating statistics, the nationwide personal transportation survey (a major source for information about all types of personal travel), profiles of freight transportation on a state-by-state basis, and data about freight moving by surface means into or from Canada or Mexico.

The BTS also provides extensive data on airlines in the nation. These data get as detailed as monthly data on the consumption and cost of airline fuel by domestic and international travel by scheduled versus non-scheduled airlines. They also have detailed data about on-time performance of the nation's air transportation system. If you are interested in any type of data about the air transportation system in the United States, this is an excellent starting point because it contains many more data series than the couple described here.

Detailed data on major motor carriers (buses) can be found on the BTS Web site. This includes information on key financial data and passengers. These data are reported by individual bus companies.

The BTS Web site is also a portal to many other federal data sources providing transportation data. These other agencies include the Federal Aviation Administration, the United States Coast Guard, the Federal Highway Administration, and the U.S. Army Corps of Engineers.

The Bureau of Transportation Statistics also provides an extensive collection of transportation related research reports. Many of these are available on-line.

Finally, the U.S. Census Bureau, BTS, and their counterparts in Canada (Statistics Canada and Transport Canada) and Mexico (Instituto Mexicano del Transporte and Instituto Nacional de Estadistica, Geografia e Informática) have joined together to produce an extensive report on transportation throughout North America—*North American Transportation in Figures*. This is a good source for comparative statistics for the three nations.

## Other Sources of Highway and Motor Vehicle Data

The Federal Highway Administration (FHA) provides many statistics about the nation's road system. This includes the number of miles of different types of roads in each state and conditions of bridges along these roads. FHA also provides detailed information about the funding of the nation's highway systems. This agency also provides information on fuel consumption.

Statistics on highway accidents are reported by the National Safety Council and the National Highway Traffic Safety Administration. These include information on the types of vehicles involved in the accidents, the number of people killed and injured in accidents, and the involvement of speeding and alcohol with the accident.

The American Automobile Association, Ward's Automotive Reports, and the American Automobile Manufacturers Association all provide data on sales and expenditures of motor vehicles in the United States. ADT Automotive provides information on used passenger car sales. The Recreation Vehicle Industry Association provides annual information on the number and value of recreational vehicles shipped. The Federal Reserve System (the nation's bank) provides information on household leasing of motor vehicles and the characteristics of the people leasing vehicles.

The Texas Transportation Institute prepares an annual report on roadway congestion by urbanized area in the nation. This includes information on daily vehicle miles traveled on the areas' freeways, the annual persons spent in delays, and the costs of these delays.

## Data about Buses and Trains

Data on the nation's mass transit systems can be found through the Federal Transit Administration. Additional data on the nation's passenger transit system can be obtained from the private American Public Transportation Association's annual *Public Transportation Fact Book.*

Extensive data about the freight railroad system in the United States can be obtained from the various publications of the Association of American Railroads.

## Data about Boats and Waterways

Since they are responsible for the nation's waterways, the U.S. Army Corps of Engineers provides detailed information about the quantity and types of goods moved along the nation's internal waterways. These waterways include the nation's rivers, canals, harbors, and ports. Some of these data are available on a monthly basis.

Data on deep sea and ocean shipping can be obtained from various publications of the U.S. Maritime Administration or Lloyd's Register of Shipping.

The United States Coast Guard is responsible for providing information on boating accidents. The Tanker Advisory Center, Inc. provides information about tanker related casualties, deaths, and oil spills.

Data on all types of worldwide shipping accidents and losses can also be obtained from Lloyd's Register of Shipping.

## Aviation Data

Aviation safety data can be obtained from the Federal Aviation Administration (FAA) and the National Transportation Safety Board. Much of these data items are not confidential individual records. Both of these organizations also publish statistical reports. Data on airline fatalities worldwide can be obtained from the International Civil Aviation Organization's annual report, *Civil Aviation Statistics of the World.*

The FAA also provides information about airport activity. Additionally, they provide information about all types of civil aviation including, for example, number of airports, presence of runway lights, number of pilot certificates by type, their own employees by type, and hours flown and fuel consumed.

The Air Transport Association of America provides extensive data on the scheduled airline industry in the United State. This includes information about number of passengers, revenues, operating revenues by source, employees by general function, and cost factors. Information about commuter and regional airlines can be obtained from the Regional Airline Association and AvStat Associates.

Information about the production of aircraft can be obtained from the Aerospace Industries of America.

## Data on Pipelines

Since they are used to transport goods, NAICS includes pipelines within the transportation and warehousing sector. While the Economic Census includes some information about these transportation modes, there are a number of other characteristics that people interested in the petroleum and gas industries have questions about. Data on regulated interstate petroleum pipeline companies can be obtained from Penn-Well Publishing Company's *Oil & Gas Journal.* Data on the interstate natural gas pipeline companies can be found in the U.S. Energy Information Administration's *Statistics of Interstate Natural Gas Pipeline Companies.*

Additional detail about these types of companies can be gathered from their filings with the various federal and state agencies charged with their regulation, such as the Federal Energy Regulatory Commission or the state public utility commissions. However, these data are often not tabulated and can be buried in extensive reports or, even more awkward, in the testimony presented in their various proceedings before these agencies.

## Other Related Data

The U.S. Bureau of Labor Statistics (BLS) provides monthly estimates of employment in the transportation and warehousing industries. (Currently, these data are produced on the basis of SICs. BLS will convert to reporting on a NAICS 2002 basis during 2002.) BLS also provides information on the payroll of establishments in these industries.

The Energy Information Administration provides information about alternative fuel vehicles. This agency also provides information on the characteristics of warehouses in the United States.

The Eno Transportation Foundation, Inc. is a transportation-related think-tank. This group produces an annual report *Transportation in America.* This report includes information on passenger and freight transportation outlys and the volume of freight and passenger traffic.

### NAICS–SIC Crosswalk

As detailed in Table 8.3, this NAICS sector is derived from parts of several SIC divisions.

**Table 8.3**
NAICS-SIC Crosswalk

| NAICS | NAICSTEXT | COMPᵃ | SIC | SICTEXT |
|-------|-----------|-------|-----|---------|
| 48-49 | Transportation and Warehousing | | | |
| 481 | Air Transportation | | | |
| 4811 | Scheduled Air Transportation | | | |
| 48111 | Scheduled Air Transportation | | | |
| 481111 | Scheduled Passenger Air Transportation | N | 4512 | Air Transportation, Scheduled (passenger) |
| 481112 | Scheduled Freight Air Transportation | N | 4512 | Air Transportation, Scheduled (freight) |
| 4812 | Nonscheduled Air Transportation | | | |
| 48121 | Nonscheduled Air Transportation | | | |
| 481211 | Nonscheduled Chartered Passenger Air Transportation | N | 4522 | Air Transportation, Nonscheduled (passenger) |
| 481212 | Nonscheduled Chartered Freight Air Transportation | N | 4522 | Air Transportation, Nonscheduled (freight) |
| 481219 | Other Nonscheduled Air Transportation | N | | Establishments that use general purpose aircraft to provide a variety of specialized flying services |
| 482 | Rail Transportation | | | |
| 4821 | Rail Transportation | | | |
| 48211 | Rail Transportation | | | |
| 482111 | Line-Haul Railroads | E | 4011 | Railroads, Line-Haul Operating |
| 482112 | Short Line Railroads | N | 4013 | Railroad Switching and Terminal Establishments (belt line and logging railroads) |
| 483 | Water Transportation | | | |
| 4831 | Deep Sea, Coastal, and Great Lakes Water Transportation | | | |
| 48311 | Deep Sea, Coastal, and Great Lakes Water Transportation | | | |
| 483111 | Deep Sea Freight Transportation | E | 4412 | Deep Sea Foreign Transportation of Freight |
| 483112 | Deep Sea Passenger Transportation | R | 4481 | Deep Sea Transportation of Passengers, Except by Ferry (deep sea activities) |
| 483113 | Coastal and Great Lakes Freight Transportation | R | 4424 | Deep Sea Domestic Transportation of Freight |
| 483113 | Coastal and Great Lakes Freight Transportation | | 4432 | Freight Transportation on the Great Lakes - St. Lawrence Seaway |

Table 8.3 (Continued)
NAICS–SIC Crosswalk

| NAICS | NAICSTEXT | COMPᵃ | SIC | SICTEXT |
|---|---|---|---|---|
| 483114 | Coastal and Great Lakes Passenger Transportation | R | 4481 | Deep Sea Transportation of Passengers, Except by Ferry (coastal activities) |
| 483114 | Coastal and Great Lakes Passenger Transportation | | 4482 | Ferries (coastal and Great Lakes) |
| 4832 | Inland Water Transportation | | | |
| 48321 | Inland Water Transportation | | | |
| 483211 | Inland Water Freight Transportation | E | 4449 | Water Transportation of Freight, NEC |
| 483212 | Inland Water Passenger Transportation | R | 4482 | Ferries (inland) |
| 483212 | Inland Water Passenger Transportation | | 4489 | Water Transportation of Passengers, NEC (water taxi) |
| 484 | Truck Transportation | | | |
| 4841 | General Freight Trucking | | | |
| 48411 | General Freight Trucking, Local | N | 4212 | Local Trucking without Storage (general freight) |
| 48411 | General Freight Trucking, Local | | 4214 | Local Trucking with Storage (general freight) |
| 48412 | General Freight Trucking, Long-Distance | | | |
| 484121 | General Freight Trucking, Long-Distance, Truckload | N | 4213 | Trucking, Except Local (general freight, truckload) |
| 484122 | General Freight Trucking, Long-Distance, Less Than Truckload | N | 4213 | Trucking, Except Local (general freight, less than truckload) |
| 4842 | Specialized Freight Trucking | | | |
| 48421 | Used Household and Office Goods Moving | N | 4212 | Local Trucking Without Storage (household goods moving) |
| 48421 | Used Household and Office Goods Moving | | 4213 | Trucking, Except Local (household goods moving) |
| 48421 | Used Household and Office Goods Moving | | 4214 | Local Trucking With Storage (household goods moving) |
| 48422 | Specialized Freight (except Used Goods) Trucking, Local | N | 4212 | Local Trucking without Storage (specialized freight) |
| 48422 | Specialized Freight (except Used Goods) Trucking, Local | | 4214 | Local Trucking with Storage (specialized freight) |
| 48423 | Specialized Freight (except Used Goods) Trucking, Long-Distance | N | 4213 | Trucking, Except Local (specialized freight) |
| 485 | Transit and Ground Passenger Transportation | | | |
| 4851 | Urban Transit Systems | | | |
| 48511 | Urban Transit Systems | | | |
| 485111 | Mixed Mode Transit Systems | N | 4111 | Local and Suburban Transit (mixed mode) |

**Table 8.3 (Continued)**
NAICS–SIC Crosswalk

| NAICS | NAICSTEXT | COMP[a] SIC | SIC | SICTEXT |
|---|---|---|---|---|
| 485112 | Commuter Rail Systems | N | 4111 | Local and Suburban Transit (commuter rail) |
| 485113 | Bus and Other Motor Vehicle Transit Systems | N | 4111 | Local and Suburban Transit (bus and motor vehicle) |
| 485119 | Other Urban Transit Systems | N | 4111 | Local and Suburban Transit (other than mixed mode, commuter rail, and bus and motor vehicle) |
| 4852 | Interurban and Rural Bus Transportation | | | |
| 48521 | Interurban and Rural Bus Transportation | E | 4131 | Intercity and Rural Bus Transportation |
| 4853 | Taxi and Limousine Service | | | |
| 48531 | Taxi Service | R | 4121 | Taxicabs |
| 48531 | Taxi Service | | 4899 | Communications Services, NEC (taxi cab dispatch services) |
| 48532 | Limousine Service | N | 4119 | Local Passenger Transportation, NEC (limousine rental with driver and automobile rental with driver) |
| 4854 | School and Employee Bus Transportation | | | |
| 48541 | School and Employee Bus Transportation | R | 4151 | School Buses |
| 48541 | School and Employee Bus Transportation | | 4119 | Local Passenger Transportation, NEC (employee transportation) |
| 4855 | Charter Bus Industry | | | |
| 48551 | Charter Bus Industry | R | 4141 | Local Charter Bus Service |
| 48551 | Charter Bus Industry | | 4142 | Bus Charter Services, Except Local |
| 4859 | Other Transit and Ground Passenger Transportation | | | |
| 48599 | Other Transit and Ground Passenger Transportation | | | |
| 485991 | Special Needs Transportation | N | 4119 | Local Passenger Transportation, NEC (special needs transportation) |
| 485999 | All Other Transit and Ground Passenger Transportation | R | 4111 | Local and Suburban Transit (airport transportation service) |
| 485999 | All Other Transit and Ground Passenger Transportation | | 4119 | Local Passenger Transportation, NEC (hearse rental with driver and carpool and vanpool operation) |
| 486 | Pipeline Transportation | | | |
| 4861 | Pipeline Transportation of Crude Oil | | | |
| 48611 | Pipeline Transportation of Crude Oil | E | 4612 | Crude Petroleum Pipelines |
| 4862 | Pipeline Transportation of Natural Gas | | | |

**Table 8.3 (Continued)**
NAICS–SIC Crosswalk

| NAICS | NAICSTEXT | COMP[a]SIC | SIC | SICTEXT |
|-------|-----------|------------|-----|---------|
| 48621 | Pipeline Transportation of Natural Gas | R | 4922 | Natural Gas Transmission |
| 48621 | Pipeline Transportation of Natural Gas | | 4923 | Natural Gas Transmission and Distribution (transmission) |
| 4869 | Other Pipeline Transportation | | | |
| 48691 | Pipeline Transportation of Refined | E | 4613 | Refined Petroleum Pipelines |
| 48691 | Pipeline Transportation of Refined | E | | |
| 48699 | All Other Pipeline Transportation | | 4619 | Pipelines, NEC |
| 487 | Scenic and Sightseeing Transportation | | | |
| 4871 | Scenic and Sightseeing Transportation, Land | | | |
| 48711 | Scenic and Sightseeing Transportation, Land | N | 4119 | Local Passenger Transportation, NEC (sightseeing buses and cable and cog railways, except scenic |
| 48711 | Scenic and Sightseeing Transportation, Land | | 4789 | Transportation Services, NEC (horse-drawn cabs and carriages) |
| 48711 | Scenic and Sightseeing Transportation, Land | | 7999 | Amusement and Recreation Services, NEC (scenic transport operations, land) |
| 4872 | Scenic and Sightseeing Transportation, Water | | | |
| 48721 | Scenic and Sightseeing Transportation, Water | N | 4489 | Water Transportation of Passengers, NEC (airboats, excursion boats, and sightseeing boats) |
| 48721 | Scenic and Sightseeing Transportation, Water | | 7999 | Amusement and Recreation Services, NEC (charter fishing) |
| 4879 | Scenic and Sightseeing Transportation, Other | | | |
| 48799 | Scenic and Sightseeing Transportation, Other | N | 4522 | Air Transportation, Nonscheduled (sightseeing planes) |
| 48799 | Scenic and Sightseeing Transportation, Other | | 7999 | Amusement and Recreation Services, NEC (aerial tramways, scenic and amusement) |
| 488 | Support Activities for Transportation | | | |
| 4881 | Support Activities for Air Transportation | | | |
| 48811 | Airport Operations | | | |
| 488111 | Air Traffic Control | N | 4581 | Airports, Flying Fields, and Airport Terminal Services (private air traffic control) |
| 488111 | Air Traffic Control | | 9621 | Regulation and Administration of Transportation Programs (government air traffic control) |

178

**Table 8.3 (Continued)**
**NAICS–SIC Crosswalk**

| NAICS | NAICSTEXT | COMP[a] | SIC | SICTEXT |
|---|---|---|---|---|
| 488119 | Other Airport Operations | N | 4581 | Airports, Flying Fields, and Airport Terminal Services (airfreight handling at airports, hangar operations, airport terminal services, aircraft storage, airports, and flying fields) |
| 488119 | Other Airport Operations | | 4959 | Sanitary Services, NEC (vacuuming of runways) |
| 48819 | Other Support Activities for Air Transportation | N | 4581 | Airports, Flying Fields, and Airport Terminal Services (aircraft servicing and repairing) |
| 4882 | Support Activities for Rail Transportation | | | |
| 48821 | Support Activities for Rail Transportation | R | 4013 | Railroad Switching and Terminal Establishments (all but short line railroads) |
| 48821 | Support Activities for Rail Transportation | | 4741 | Rental of Railroad Cars (grain leveling in railroad cars, grain trimming for railroad equipment, precooling of fruits and vegetables in connection with transportation, and railroad car cleaning, icing, ventilating, and heating) |
| 48821 | Support Activities for Rail Transportation | | 4789 | Transportation Services, NEC (car loading and unloading; cleaning of railroad ballasts; dining, parlor, sleeping, and other car operations; and railroad maintenance) |
| 4883 | Support Activities for Water Transportation | | | |
| 48831 | Port and Harbor Operations | N | 4491 | Marine Cargo Handling (dock and pier operations) |
| 48831 | Port and Harbor Operations | | 4499 | Water Transportation Services, NEC (lighthouse and canal operations) |
| 48832 | Marine Cargo Handling | R | 4491 | Marine Cargo Handling (all but dock and pier operations) |
| 48833 | Navigational Services to Shipping | N | 4492 | Towing and Tugboat Services |
| 48833 | Navigational Services to Shipping | | 4499 | Water Transportation Services, NEC (piloting vessels in and out of harbors and marine salvage) |
| 48839 | Other Support Activities for Water Transportation | R | 3731 | Ship Building and Repairing (floating dry docks not associated with a shipyard) |
| 48839 | Other Support Activities for Water Transportation | | 4499 | Water Transportation Services, NEC (all but lighthouse operations, piloting vessels in and out of harbors, boat and ship rental, marine salvage, and canal operations) |
| 48839 | Other Support Activities for Water Transportation | | 4785 | Fixed Facilities and Inspection and Weighing Services for Motor Vehicle Transportation (marine cargo checkers) |

**Table 8.3 (Continued)**
NAICS–SIC Crosswalk

| NAICS | NAICSTEXT | COMP^a | SIC | SICTEXT |
|---|---|---|---|---|
| 48839 | Other Support Activities for Water Transportation | | 7699 | Repair Shops and Related Services, NEC (ship scaling) |
| 48841 | Support Activities for Road Transportation | | | |
| 48841 | Motor Vehicle Towing | N | 7549 | Automotive Services, Except Repair and Carwashes (towing) |
| 48849 | Other Support Activities for Road Transportation | R | 4173 | Terminal and Service Facilities for Motor Vehicle Passenger Transportation |
| 48849 | Other Support Activities for Road Transportation | | 4231 | Terminal and Joint Terminal Maintenance Facilities for Motor Freight Transportation |
| 48849 | Other Support Activities for Road Transportation | | 4785 | Fixed Facilities and Inspection and Weighing Services for Motor Vehicle Transportation (all but marine cargo checkers) |
| 4885 | Freight Transportation Arrangement | | | |
| 48851 | Freight Transportation Arrangement | R | 4731 | Arrangement of Transportation of Freight and Cargo (except freight rate auditors and tariff consultants) |
| 4889 | Other Support Activities for Transportation | | | |
| 48899 | Other Support Activities for Transportation | | | |
| 488991 | Packing and Crating | E | 4783 | Packing and Crating |
| 488999 | All Other Support Activities for Transportation | R | 4729 | Arrangement of Passenger Transportation, NEC (arrangement of carpools and vanpools) |
| 488999 | All Other Support Activities for Transportation | | 4789 | Transportation Services, NEC (pipeline terminals and stockyards for transportation) |
| 491 | Postal Service | | | |
| 4911 | Postal Service | | | |
| 49111 | Postal Service | R | 4311 | United States Postal Service |
| 49111 | Postal Service | | 7389 | Business Services, NEC (post office contract stations) |
| 492 | Couriers and Messengers | | | |
| 4921 | Couriers | | | |
| 49211 | Couriers | R | 4215 | Courier Services, Except by Air (hub and spoke intercity delivery) |
| 49211 | Couriers | | 4513 | Air Courier Services |

**Table 8.3 (Continued)**
NAICS–SIC Crosswalk

| NAICS | NAICSTEXT | COMP[a] | SIC | SICTEXT |
|---|---|---|---|---|
| 4922 | Local Messengers and Local Delivery | | | |
| 49221 | Local Messengers and Local Delivery | N | 4215 | Courier Services, Except by Air (local delivery) |
| 493 | Warehousing and Storage | | | |
| 4931 | Warehousing and Storage | | | |
| 49311 | General Warehousing and Storage | R | 4225 | General Warehousing and Storage (all but self-storage miniwarehouse warehousing) |
| 49311 | General Warehousing and Storage | | 4226 | Special Warehousing and Storage, NEC (warehousing in foreign trade zones) |
| 49312 | Refrigerated Warehousing and Storage | R | 4222 | Refrigerated Warehousing and Storage |
| 49312 | Refrigerated Warehousing and Storage | | 4226 | Special Warehousing and Storage, NEC (fur storage) |
| 49313 | Farm Product Warehousing and Storage | E | 4221 | Farm Product Warehousing and Storage |
| 49319 | Other Warehousing and Storage | R | 4226 | Special Warehousing and Storage, NEC (all but fur storage and warehousing in foreign trade zones) |

[a]E = Existing, N = New, R = Revised

181

# CHAPTER 9
# Manufacturing

*When you automate an industry you modernize it; when you automate a life you primitivize it.*
—*Eric Hoffer (1902–1983), U.S. philosopher,* Reflections on the Human Condition
*(1973)*

1. What Is Manufacturing?
2. NAICS and SIC Manufacturing Definitions
3. Question: Manufacturing Data in the Economic Census
4. Economic Census Reports
   A. Common Data Items
   B. Geographic Area Reports
   C. Industry Reports
   D. Subject Reports
5. Uses of Manufacturing Statistics
   A. Government
   B. Business
   C. Researchers
6. Current Data
7. Answers: Manufacturing Data in the Economic Census
8. NAICS/SIC Tables

Just as agriculture dominated the 1800s, manufacturing was the principle sector of the economy in the twentieth century. The entire Economic Census started with a look at manufacturing in the United States. The 1810 Census included a question on the value of products manufactured in the home. This one question was the first formal look at economic activity in the United States and laid the foundation for the more detailed and extensive look covered in the modern economic censuses.

## WHAT IS MANUFACTURING?

Very simply, manufacturing is the process of transforming a variety of inputs into a different product. Naturally, the Census Bureau doesn't use this simple a definition. They follow the NAICS definition, which is:

The Manufacturing sector comprises establishments engaged in the mechanical, physical, or chemical transformation of materials, substances, or components into new products. The assembling of component parts of manufactured products is considered manufacturing, except in cases where the activity is appropriately classified in Sector 23, Construction.

Establishments in the Manufacturing sector are often described as plants, factories, or mills and characteristically use power-driven machines and materials-handling equipment. However, establishments that transform materials or substances into new products by hand or in the worker's home and those engaged in selling to the general public products made on the same premises from which they are sold, such as bakeries, candy stores, and custom tailors, may also be included in this sector. Manufacturing establishments may process materials or may contract with other establishments to process their materials for them. Both types of establishments are included in manufacturing.

As can be seen, this is a much more specific definition. The NAICS definition implicitly requires that the materials being transformed be physical materials and that they go through some form of mechanical, physical, or chemical transformation or assembly. Thus, the tabulation of responses to the Economic Census questionnaires into statistical reports does not qualify as manufacturing. However, the processes of printing the few reports that appear on paper or producing the compact disks to distribute the data and reports are considered manufacturing activities.

## NAICS AND SIC MANUFACTURING DEFINITIONS

Comparing the manufacturing sector using the NAICS definition with the one that was based on the SIC definition, we see a number of changes; see Figures 9.5 and 9.6 for an indication of the major movement in and out of this sector. Most of these changes involved the movement of establishments from one specific industry within the sector to another industry within the sector. For example, an establishment that makes rubber raincoats for girls is classified in NAICS industry 315232 (Women's and girls' cut and sew suit, coat, and skirt manufacturing). However, the same establishment might have been classified as SIC industry 2385 (Waterproof outer garments) or SIC industry 3069 (Fabricated rubber products, n.e.c.) depending on the source of the rubber used to make the raincoats.

Another group of changes involves the movement of establishments out of manufacturing and into other sectors. The most prominent examples of these establishments are those involved with logging, publishing (but not printing), and auxiliary establishments. For example, the offices involved with editing and marketing this book are now included in the Information sector, but would have been considered manufacturing establishments under the SIC system. However, the plant that put the ink on the paper and bound the paper to make this book is considered a manufacturing facility under both definitions.

Under the SIC scheme of industry definitions, logging was part of manufacturing because it was so closely tied to the various wood products manufacturing industries. However, in NAICS logging was classified with agriculture, fishing, and hunting because these industries involve growing and harvesting renewable resources that become the primary inputs to other industries.

Auxiliary establishments are business locations that provide some form of support to other establishments within their own company. Typically, these are some form of central administrative offices (such as corporate headquarters), backroom operations, warehouses, or research and development facilities. According to the SIC system, these establishments were classified according to the major activity of the company they support. So, for example, General Electric's Corporate Research and Development facility in the Schenectady, New York, area was classified as an auxiliary manufacturing establishment (even though there is no manufacturing beyond some prototype systems done

there). Now, under NAICS, this establishment is classified in the scientific and professional services sector along with research facilities that provide similar services to clients outside their own organization.

In addition to the movement of industries within the manufacturing sector and the transfer of some industries or activities out of the sector into other sectors, there was some movement into manufacturing from other areas. Some of the activities that moved into manufacturing from other sectors are bakeries and candy stores where the candy is made at the store's location. Custom tailors and makers of custom draperies are some other examples of this type of movement. As can be seen from these examples, this type of movement involved establishments that made the products they sold. The logic behind placing these establishments into manufacturing is that if they didn't make the products, they would not have items for sale. Thus, their primary activity is manufacturing these products for sale.

---

### QUESTION: MANUFACTURING DATA IN THE ECONOMIC CENSUS

**Is it manufacturing? Answers can be found at the end of this chapter.**

Analytical laboratory instrument mfg
Bakeries & tortilla mfg
Concrete patio construction
Cost of purchased advertising services
Cotton ginning
Ford Motors Headquarters
LIFO inventory method
Logging
Semi-moist cat food
Tailor
Total capital expenditures
Use of molasses in creation of product

---

## ECONOMIC CENSUS REPORTS

The Economic Census contains a variety of reports on manufacturing. Like nearly all other sectors, there are *Geographic Area* reports that describe the manufacturing sector in any given state or equivalent area. Also, like the other sectors, there are reports on subjects, which provide data on the products produced by manufacturing establishments in the country, the materials consumed in each manufacturing industry, data on how concentrated the activity of a particular industry is between companies, and summaries of the other reports. Additionally, there are reports about each industry in the sector that provide extensive details about the location, products, inputs, and other operations of the industry. Each of these types of reports is described in detail below.

Nonemployer statistics are not included in any of the reports mentioned below. However, if you want an accurate count of the sector, the information about non-employer businesses should not be neglected. There are 666,609 establishments in manufacturing, but the most any report will state is 363,753. The remaining 302,856 are nonemployer businesses—establishments that are usually operated by a sole proprietor who does not take a salary. Of the manufacturing industries only sugar and confectioner product, other food product, apparel, leather and allied product, wood product, clay product, glass product, electrical equipment appliance and components, and miscellaneous manufacturing establishments make up over half of the establishments listed in the nonemployer data. If you think about these industries carefully, you will note that most of the industries can be related to making money from a traditional art. When considering those industry subsectors, try to remember there are artisans creating in the same field. The money generated by artisans is small when compared to the economic contributions to the GDP. Of the $3,854,380,535,000 of receipts for all manufacturing, only .32 percent comes from nonemployer businesses.

## Common Data Items

There are a number of data items that are shown in all of the reports for the manufacturing sector. These include

1. Establishments—the number of establishments in the specified industry within the specified geographic area. This is never suppressed.
2. Establishments with 20 or more employees—the number of establishments meeting this criterion. This is never suppressed.
3. All Employees (Number)—the average number of employees working during the payroll period including the 12th of March. This includes the officers of corporations, but excludes proprietors and partners of unincorporated businesses. These data are subject to suppression, but estimates are shown as ranges represented by letters (e.g., a "c"

represents 100 to 249 employees and an "f" represents 500 to 999 employees).
4. All Employees Payroll ($1,000)—the total payroll, in thousands of dollars, of all employees working at the establishments in this industry. Companies were directed to use the same definition of payroll as required on federal tax forms. This excludes employers' contributions to social security, employees' pension plans, group insurance premiums, and workers' compensation.
5. Production Workers (Number)—the number of workers involved in actually producing the establishment's products and working during the payroll periods including the 12ths of the months of March, May, August, and November. This includes all workers involved with fabricating, processing, assembling, inspecting, receiving, storing, handling, packing, warehousing, shipping (but not delivering), maintenance, repair, janitorial and guard services, product development, auxiliary production for the plant's own use (such as a power plant dedicated to the establishment), record keeping, and other services closely associated with these production operations. These workers are sometimes called blue-collar or pink-collar workers. It includes the people doing the actual work and the first-line supervisors. You can subtract the number of production workers from all employees to find the middle- and top-management at those establishments.
6. Production Workers Hours (1,000)—the actual number of hours, in thousands, that were worked by production workers. This includes overtime counted as the actual hours (there is no adjustment for any overtime premium in the pay). These data are subject of suppression.
7. Production Workers Wages ($1,000)—the total wages paid to production workers. These data are subject to suppression. To find the amount spent on other benefits go to the industry and subject reports.
8. Value added by manufacture ($1,000)—this is an estimate of the economic contribution the industry makes through the process of transforming the raw materials into the finished product. It is derived by subtracting the cost of purchased production inputs (materials, supplies, containers, fuel, purchased electricity, and contract work) from the value of shipments.
9. Cost of materials ($1,000)—this is the total amount actually paid (or payable), including

freight and related charges, for items used in the production process. These items include the cost of parts, components, containers, fuels consumed for heat and power, purchased electricity, contract work, and products bought and sold in the same condition. It doesn't matter if these materials and services were actually purchased from another company, another establishment of the same company, or taken out of inventory.

10. Value of shipments ($1,000)—this is the total value of all products shipped out of the plant. It excludes freight and taxes, but includes the value of the primary products, secondary products (such as scrap material that will be used by another establishment in their products), contract work performed for others related to the products sold (e.g., installation and repair work). Who the customer is doesn't matter—it could be the ultimate customer or another establishment in the same company. This is the variable that represents the establishment's sales or revenues.

11. Total capital expenditures ($1,000)—this represents the total cost of (1) permanent additions and major alterations to manufacturing establishments and (2) machinery and equipment used to replace older machinery and equipment or as an addition to plant capacity. These are included whether they are purchased new or used, as long as the company would normally maintain a depreciation account for the items. It also includes the costs of assets leased from a nonmanufacturing company through a capital lease.

Selected reports contain additional variables. These are described when the specific reports are discussed.

## Geographic Area Reports

Like most of the other sectors, there are *Geographic Area* reports for each state. These reports contain data for the state, metropolitan areas, counties, and places within the state. In order to be shown in this report, an industry needs to have at least 100 employees in the geographic area of interest. For example, Douglass County, Oregon has 2,362 employees working in veneer, plywood, and engineered wood product manufacturing (NAICS 32121), so data are reported for this industry. However, Coos County, Oregon has 897 people working in the wood product manufacturing (NAICS 321) sub-sector, but no more than 100 in any

specific industry, so data are shown for the sub-sector, but not for the specific industries within Coos County.

As shown in Figure 9.1, these tables contain the 11 common data items listed above. In addition to these common items, the industry statistics tables (tables 1 through 4, which are based on geographic levels) have a data column (labeled "E"), which indicates the portion of establishments with data collected from administrative records. These are shown in ranges of 10 percent (e.g., a "1" indicates that data for 10 to 19 percent of the establishments were collected from administrative records). Administrative records were only used to collect data on establishments with fewer than 20 employees.

These reports also have a table that provides more detailed information about the manufacturing sector overall in the state as shown in Figure 9.2. This table includes data on such topics as annual payroll and total fringe benefits, costs of materials broken out into major types, and number of production workers during each of the four reference periods. The *Annual Survey of Manufacturers* updates the data disclosed in this report.

## Industry Reports

*Industry* reports show detailed information about one specific industry, but generally only at the national level. However, there are a couple of tables showing the basic information for selected states in the industry. If you are a manufacturer, at least one of the 480 industry reports is a "must read" for you.

Each industry report includes eight tables. Six of these tables provide data for the United States as a whole. Table 1 provides the common data items plus the number of companies for the industry (as defined in NAICS) and the pieces that come from the various SIC industries much like Bridge Tables, see Figures 9.5 and 9.6. Table 3 provides details about the operations of the industry—this is very similar the table in the geographic area reports, shown in Figure 9.2, but with more details. Table 4 shows the basic data items for establishments grouped by the number of employees so you can see the concentration of the industry in larger or small factories. Table 5 shows these same data items but with the establishments grouped by the primary product class (such as sulfate woodpulp, including soda) they produce. Table 6a (shown in Figure 9.3), provides the number of companies with shipments of $100,000 or more of specific products, the

Figure 9.1
1997 Economic Census, Manufacturing, Geographic Area Report Industry Statistics Sample

[Includes data for industry groups and industries with 100 employees or more. For information on geographic areas followed by * and explanation of terms, see appendixes. For meaning of abbreviations and symbols, see introductory text]

| NAICS code | Geographic area and industry | E[1] | All establishments Total | All establishments With 20 employees or more | All employees Number[2] | All employees Payroll ($1,000) | Production workers Number | Production workers Hours (1,000) | Production workers Wages ($1,000) | Value added by manufacture ($1,000) | Cost of materials ($1,000) | Value of shipments ($1,000) | Total capital expenditures ($1,000) |
|---|---|---|---|---|---|---|---|---|---|---|---|---|---|
| | **OREGON** | | | | | | | | | | | | |
| 31-33 | **Manufacturing** .... | – | **5 768** | **1 675** | **213 111** | **7 095 286** | **158 506** | **316 808** | **4 545 793** | **25 077 180** | **22 770 601** | **47 665 990** | **2 715 770** |
| 311 | Food mfg .............. | 1 | 440 | 159 | 21 567 | 546 661 | 16 760 | 31 106 | 359 436 | 2 036 915 | 2 627 276 | 4 662 101 | 138 198 |
| 3111 | Animal food mfg ....... | 1 | 15 | 4 | 275 | 9 036 | 158 | 320 | 4 205 | 51 212 | 74 507 | 124 997 | 1 271 |
| 31111 | Animal food mfg ....... | 1 | 15 | 4 | 275 | 9 036 | 158 | 320 | 4 205 | 51 212 | 74 507 | 124 997 | 1 271 |
| 311119 | Other animal food mfg . | 1 | 15 | 4 | 275 | 9 036 | 158 | 320 | 4 205 | 51 212 | 74 507 | 124 997 | 1 271 |
| 3112 | Grain & oilseed milling .... | 2 | 15 | 7 | 454 | 15 851 | 357 | 737 | 11 519 | 73 647 | 205 799 | 279 472 | 2 851 |
| 31121 | Flour milling & malt mfg . | – | 7 | 3 | 146 | 5 480 | 104 | 240 | 3 466 | 16 246 | 100 717 | 117 509 | 298 |
| 311211 | Flour milling ......... | – | 5 | 3 | c | D | D | D | D | D | D | D | D |

Figure 9.2
1997 Economic Census, Manufacturing, Geographic Area Report Detailed Statistics Sample

| Item | | Value |
|---|---|---|
| **OREGON** | | |
| Companies[1] | number.. | 5 428 |
| All establishments | number.. | 5 768 |
| Establishments with 1 to 19 employees | number.. | 4 093 |
| Establishments with 20 to 99 employees | number.. | 1 204 |
| Establishments with 100 employees or more | number.. | 471 |
| All employees | number.. | 213 111 |
| Total compensation[2] | $1,000.. | 8 891 591 |
| Annual payroll | $1,000.. | 7 095 286 |
| Total fringe benefits | $1,000.. | 1 796 305 |
| Production workers, average for year | number.. | 158 506 |
| Production workers on March 12 | number.. | 153 945 |
| Production workers on May 12 | number.. | 156 685 |
| Production workers on August 12 | number.. | 164 317 |
| Production workers on November 12 | number.. | 159 077 |
| Production-worker hours | 1,000.. | 316 808 |
| Production-worker wages | $1,000.. | 4 545 793 |
| Total cost of materials | $1,000.. | 22 770 601 |
| Cost of materials, parts, containers, etc., consumed | $1,000.. | 19 948 345 |
| Cost of resales | $1,000.. | 1 387 786 |
| Cost of fuels | $1,000.. | 257 879 |
| Cost of purchased electricity | $1,000.. | 547 579 |
| Cost of contract work | $1,000.. | 629 012 |

| Item | | Value |
|---|---|---|
| **OREGON**—Con. | | |
| Quantity of electricity purchased for heat and power | 1,000 kWh.. | 15 278 998 |
| Quantity of electricity generated less sold for heat and power | 1,000 kWh.. | 681 514 |
| Total value of shipments | $1,000.. | 47 665 990 |
| Value of resales | $1,000.. | 1 658 664 |
| Value added | $1,000.. | 25 077 180 |
| Total inventories, beginning of year | $1,000.. | 5 124 342 |
| Finished goods inventories, beginning of year | $1,000.. | 1 829 981 |
| Work-in-process inventories, beginning of year | $1,000.. | 1 364 488 |
| Materials and supplies inventories, beginning of year | $1,000.. | 1 929 873 |
| Total inventories, end of year | $1,000.. | 5 398 261 |
| Finished goods inventories, end of year | $1,000.. | 1 897 536 |
| Work-in-process inventories, end of year | $1,000.. | 1 398 994 |
| Materials and supplies inventories, end of year | $1,000.. | 2 101 731 |
| Gross book value of total assets at beginning of year | $1,000.. | 22 006 876 |
| Total capital expenditures (new and used) | $1,000.. | 2 715 770 |
| Capital expenditures for buildings and other structures (new and used) | $1,000.. | 623 652 |
| Capital expenditures for machinery and equipment (new and used) | $1,000.. | 2 092 118 |
| Total retirements[2] | $1,000.. | 869 955 |
| Gross book value of total assets at end of year | $1,000.. | 23 852 691 |
| Total depreciation during year[2] | $1,000.. | 1 670 460 |
| Total rental payments[2] | $1,000.. | 406 686 |
| Buildings and other structures rental payments[2] | $1,000.. | 203 457 |
| Machinery and equipment rental payments[2] | $1,000.. | 203 229 |

188

Figure 9.3
1997 Economic Census, Manufacturing, Industry Report Products Statistics Sample

[Includes quantity and value of products of this industry produced by (1) establishments classified in this industry (primary) and (2) establishments classified in other industries (secondary). Transfers of products of this industry from one establishment of a company to another establishment of the same company (interplant transfers) are also included. For meaning of abbreviations and symbols, see introductory text. For explanation of terms, see appendixes]

| NAICS product code | Product | 1997 | | | | 1992 | | | |
|---|---|---|---|---|---|---|---|---|---|
| | | | | Product shipments | | | | Product shipments | |
| | | Number of companies with shipments of $100,000 or more | Quantity of production for all purposes | Quantity | Value ($1,000) | Number of companies with shipments of $100,000 or more | Quantity of production for all purposes | Quantity | Value ($1,000) |
| 322110 | Pulp............................ | N | X | X | 6 127 032 | N | X | X | 6 103 858 |
| 322101 | Special alpha and dissolving woodpulp (sulfite and sulfate for chemical conversion, papermaking, and other uses)............ | N | X | X | 842 210 | N | X | X | 921 469 |
| 3221011 | Special alpha and dissolving woodpulp (sulfite and sulfate for chemical conversion, papermaking, and other uses)............ | N | X | X | 842 210 | N | X | X | N |
| 3221101100 | Special alpha and dissolving woodpulp (sulfite and sulfate for chemical conversion, papermaking, and other uses)........1,000 s tons (dry basis).. | 6 | 1 039.3 | 1 073.2 | 842 210 | 7 | 1 518.8 | 1 498.4 | 921 469 |
| 3221103 | Sulfate woodpulp, including soda............... | N | X | X | 4 487 266 | N | X | X | 4 411 596 |
| 3221031 | Sulfate woodpulp, bleached and semibleached, including soda............1,000 s tons (dry basis).. | N | X | X | 4 487 266 | N | X | X | N |
| 3221103111 | | 28 | 26 982.2 | 9 913.9 | 4 349 929 | 29 | 27 740.5 | 9 628.4 | 4 333 125 |
| 3221103121 | Sulfate woodpulp, unbleached ...........1,000 s tons (dry basis).. | 8 | 25 576.1 | 444.7 | 137 337 | 10 | 22 733.1 | 271.4 | 78 471 |

189

quantity of each product produced regardless of the purpose of producing it, and the quantity and value of the product that is actually shipped for two most recent censuses. The seventh table details the materials consumed by the industry in the reference year and the previous census, showing both the quantity and delivered cost of each type of material.

The remaining two tables (tables 2 and 6b) provide state-level data. Table 2 provides the 11 basic data items for the industry in any state with 100 employees or more and where there is no risk of providing information about an individual company within the state. Table 6b provides the value of product shipments by product class in the two most recent census years for every state with at least $2 million worth of shipments of that product class and no risk of disclosure of the shipments of an individual company.

## Subject Reports

In addition to the usual geographic series and industry reports, the manufacturing sector also has a series of *Subject* reports. Like the other economic sectors covered in the Economic Census, this sector has several *Subject* reports that have been produced. There are four different subject reports in this sector. These include: (1) a general summary, (2) a product summary, (3) a materials consumed summary, and (4) a summary showing how concentrated a particular industry's activities are.

## General Summary

The *General Summary* report is divided into three chapters. Chapter 1 summarizes the industry statistics and the 1997 report contains the following seven tables:

- Table 1–1a shows the 11 basic data items for all manufacturing establishments for every year from 1977 to the current census. The sources used are the economic censuses, for years ending in 2 and 7, and the *Annual Survey of Manufactures* for the other years. It should be noted that the number of establishments is reported *only* for the years ending in 2 and 7. Also, these data are based on the definition of manufacturing in use at the time when the data were collected.
- Table 1–1b shows the number of establishments, employees, payroll, and value of shipments for the

industries that were excluded from manufacturing under the 1987 Standard Industrial Classification, and were included in manufacturing under NAICS, see Figure 9.5.
- Table 1–1c shows the number of establishments, employees, payroll, and value of shipments for the industries that were included in manufacturing under the 1987 Standard Industrial Classification, but were moved elsewhere in NAICS, see Figure 9.6.
- Table 1–1d provides the 11 basic data items plus the number of companies involved in each industry group nationally during 1997.
- Table 1–2 presents the 11 basic data items for selected states in each three-digit sub-sector within manufacturing in 1997.
- Table 1–3 presents the 1997 detailed operational statistics, such as energy usage and rental payments, for each manufacturing sub-sector. Even more detailed data are found in the industry reports.
- Table 1–4 again shows the 11 basic data items, but breaks the sub-sectors down by employment size class. For example, the establishments in Food Manufacturing (NAICS 311) employing 5 to 9 people are grouped together.

The 2002 report will contain variations of many of these tables, but the exact details weren't known when this book was prepared.

In chapter 2 the focus changes from industries to geographic areas. Tables 2–1 and 2–2 show the 11 basic data items for states and metropolitan areas grouped by state, respectively. The detailed operational statistics for each state are shown in table 2–3.

The distribution of the various methods of inventory valuation (LIFO—Last-in-First-Out, etc.) used in each of the sub-sectors is summarized in table 3–1 of the third chapter. Table 3–2 shows the actual inventory values at the start and end of the reference year for each sub-sector broken out by those using LIFO (with additional information on the LIFO reserve and value), other identified inventory methods, and those not identifying the inventory method that they used. Completing this chapter on miscellaneous statistics is table 3–3, which shows the 11 basic data items for each sub-sector broken out by type of company ownership (single- versus multi-establishment companies and corporations versus other types of ownership) and legal form of organization (corporate, individual proprietorships, partnerships, and other or unknown types), as shown in Figure 9.4.

Figure 9.4
1997 Economic Census, Manufacturing, Company Organization and Ownership Type Sample

[For meaning of abbreviations and symbols, see introductory text. For explanation of terms, see appendixes]

| NAICS code | Industry, type of company ownership, and legal form of organization | Com-panies[1] | All establish-ments[2] | All employees | | Production workers | | | Value added by manufacture ($1,000) | Cost of materials ($1,000) | Value of shipments ($1,000) | Total capital expendi-tures ($1,000) |
| --- | --- | --- | --- | --- | --- | --- | --- | --- | --- | --- | --- | --- |
| | | | | Number | Payroll ($1,000) | Number | Hours (1,000) | Wages ($1,000) | | | | |
| 334 | **Computer & electronic product mfg** ......... | **15 492** | **17 435** | **1 691 146** | **72 483 848** | **877 002** | **1 746 314** | **26 117 539** | **252 629 768** | **187 875 131** | **439 381 300** | **24 768 490** |
| | Type of company ownership | | | | | | | | | | | |
| | Single-establishment companies . | 13 543 | 13 543 | 376 252 | 13 792 791 | 218 175 | 418 002 | 5 437 491 | 30 986 610 | 23 603 363 | 54 636 202 | 4 330 653 |
| | Corporate .................. | 12 252 | 12 252 | 351 886 | 12 961 774 | 202 321 | 386 653 | 5 040 309 | 28 496 871 | 21 868 561 | 50 449 548 | 3 462 015 |
| | Noncorporate ............... | 1 291 | 1 291 | 24 366 | 831 017 | 15 854 | 31 349 | 397 182 | 2 489 739 | 1 734 802 | 4 186 654 | 868 638 |
| | Multiestablishment companies ... | 1 949 | 3 892 | 1 314 894 | 58 691 057 | 658 827 | 1 328 312 | 20 680 048 | 221 643 158 | 164 271 768 | 384 745 098 | 20 437 837 |
| | Corporate .................. | 1 877 | 3 738 | 1 274 567 | 56 962 912 | 637 594 | 1 285 823 | 20 027 065 | 216 851 120 | 160 646 586 | 376 475 796 | 20 131 706 |
| | Noncorporate ............... | 72 | 154 | 40 327 | 1 728 145 | 21 233 | 42 489 | 652 983 | 4 792 038 | 3 625 182 | 8 269 302 | 306 131 |
| | Legal form of organization | | | | | | | | | | | |
| | Corporate .................. | 14 129 | 15 990 | 1 626 453 | 69 924 686 | 839 915 | 1 672 476 | 25 067 374 | 245 347 991 | 182 515 147 | 426 925 344 | 23 593 721 |
| | Noncorporate ............... | 1 363 | 1 445 | 64 693 | 2 559 162 | 37 087 | 73 838 | 1 050 165 | 7 281 777 | 5 359 984 | 12 455 956 | 1 174 769 |
| | Individual proprietorships ...... | 765 | 771 | 11 047 | 415 184 | 6 777 | 12 093 | 150 174 | 1 224 302 | 878 034 | 1 985 142 | 103 481 |
| | Partnerships ............... | 368 | 382 | 14 103 | 514 275 | 8 308 | 18 502 | 226 824 | 1 796 748 | 1 865 578 | 3 615 753 | 506 133 |
| | Other and unknown .......... | 230 | 292 | 39 543 | 1 629 703 | 22 002 | 43 243 | 673 167 | 4 260 727 | 2 616 372 | 6 855 061 | 565 155 |

## The Concentration Ratios in Manufacturing

The *Concentration Ratios in Manufacturing* report presents information on the significance of the largest companies (without revealing a company's name) in each industry relative to all companies operating in that industry. For example, it shows that the 50 largest manufacturing companies in the nation (ranked by the value added) accounted for 11.7 percent of all manufacturing employees but 23.0 percent of the value of all manufacturing shipments.

There are three different tables in this report. Table 1 summarizes the share of each of 9 of the 11 basic items (the data on establishments are excluded), accounted for by five classes of companies grouped by their value added (e.g., the 50 largest companies and the 51st to 100th largest companies).

Tables 2 and 3, respectively, show the share of shipments and the share of value added accounted for by the 4, 8, 20, and 50 largest companies in each NAICS industry. It is important to remember that these tables have the companies grouped together because the Census Bureau is prohibited from releasing data about individual companies. These tables show the number of companies involved in each industry, the industry's value of shipments or value added, the percent of the value of shipments or value added represented by each group of companies, and the Herfindahl-Herschmann Index (HHI) for the 50 largest companies. The HHI is calculated by squaring each company's share of the value of shipments or value added and then summing these values. The higher the HHI, the more concentrated the industry is. In this report, the Census Bureau limits the calculation to the 50 largest companies or all companies in the industry if there are fewer than 50 companies. For additional information about the Herfindahl-Herschmann Index see an economic dictionary or encyclopedia. This index is a standard measure of market concentration used in investing and by the U.S. Department of Justice and Federal Trade Commission when evaluating mergers.

## Product Summary

The *Product Summary* report is one of the few reports in the Economic Census to show data by products. This report contains two tables, both of which contain data for 1997 and 1992. The first table shows the number of companies with shipments of $100,000 or more, the quantity produced for all purposes, and the quantity and value of product shipments. The two quantity variables are only shown for very specific products, for example canned-ration type dog food, but not for the broader product categories, such as dog food or canned-ration type and other dog food.

The second table shows the value of product shipments for groups of similar products, such as dog food, for each state with shipments of $2 million or more in 1997. Also, state data would be withheld if publishing it would disclose information about an individual company.

## Materials Summary

The *Materials Summary* report contains just one table, but is made up of many pages. That table shows the delivered cost of the materials purchased by each NAICS industry. Where the materials are specific enough (i.e., a single type of material), the quantity consumed is also shown. Where the industrial definition is the same in the SIC system as in NAICS, the same data are shown for 1992. These data are also in the industry reports, but are limited to the materials used in the specific industry.

## USES OF MANUFACTURING STATISTICS

For some people industry is synonymous with manufacturing. Most early economic models looked at the productivity of manufacturers to define growth. Workplace studies analyzed time and motion usage so products could be produced faster. Historically, manufacturing activity was one of the things that brought a country into the developed world. Being developed meant having smokestacks and new products waiting to be shipped. Look into any textbook about logistics, productivity, economics, or human resources and you will find models, methods, and formulas with an element that is direct or derived from the Economic Census.

Because of the importance of manufacturing in the U.S. economy of the 1930s, the SIC codes were created around the manufacturing sector. With economic development comes the need for and development of accurate, standardized, and consistent reporting of the data needed to measure that development. The United States has this type of clean historical record of manufacturing at the national level going back annually to 1948 with the *Annual Survey of Manufacturers*. Just using that data to benchmark a time series study will give credit to any research. To learn more ways to using manufacturing data use the *Social Science Citation Index*, published by Institute of Scientific Information, and search under the cited reference index for "Cens Man*" or any of the titles listed below.

## Government

All levels of government routinely find uses for the manufacturing data included in the Economic Census.

### Federal

There are many ways that the federal government uses these data. One use of the data is in developing economic models at the national and regional levels. The Bureau of Economic Analysis builds several of these models. Many federal agencies, such as the Federal Reserve System and, even, the Census Bureau use the data to benchmark their surveys in order to make sure they are accurate. Regulatory agencies use the data to help determine the need to modify the regulations affecting a specific industry, for example the Environmental Protection Agency uses the data to monitor the types and amounts of materials being used or produced by industries in order to determine which industries are using materials subject to environmental regulations.

### State and Local

When a state or local government is approached by a company looking to locate a manufacturing establishment in its area, they use the Economic Census's data on manufacturing to better understand the operations and needs of that plant. A review of the industry report will help them understand the employment numbers, revenue generation, geographic distribution of the industry, if the work is seasonal, quality of electric purchased, to what extent and which other services are outsourced, typical size of the establishment, types of products produced, and what materials are consumed in the making of the product. This assists the government officials in deciding if they want to offer incentives because of the high employee level with a typical establishment, if they have a small business that could support a larger plant, or if they could get bragging rights for attracting the new business to their region. The government may identify barriers because they need a larger source of electricity than the current suppliers can handle, because the by-products of the materials consumed may be toxic, or because it's a large workforce with low paying jobs.

### Business

This is a boon for any business that knows how to read the data. The Economic Census provides a great overview of a particular industry and related industries. For example, a fabricated metal manufacturer might be interested not only in the information about other fabricated metal product manufacturers, but also their suppliers and customers, such as forging and stamping, metal windows and doors, nuts and bolts, as well as small arms ammunitions.

Another example would be, if you were a box manufacturer, you can use the analysis of the data to learn which industries used the most boxes when manufacturing their product. The box factory can then develop customized boxes for those industries. The purchase of boxes by MSAs can be used to identify areas where there is a lack of box manufacturers. With that data you could decide if you want to expand into that market.

The data can also be used when considering a merger or acquisition. If you convert the data into ratios you can quickly learn the revenue per company, wages per employee, or how many establishments per company are typical in a specific industry. Like all data there is a lag between the time it is collected and the time it is used, which may make it seem out of date; these ratios tend to be much more stable over time than the actual numbers—especially if the appropriate adjustments are made for inflation.

Manufacturing plants tend to be very fixed in a physical location for long periods of time, but that does not mean they don't invest in the physical plant. The Economic Census, along with the *Annual Survey of Manufacturing*, provides data on the capital expenditures of specific industries. Using this data you can identify which industries are investing in their plant. This will be a sign of growth in that industry.

## Researchers

With the wealth of data about manufacturing that is included in the Economic Census, the research uses are limited only by the researcher's imagination. Anytime you are considering questions related to competition, innovation, comparing industries, comparing manufacturing across industries, integration of industries, operational strategies, industrial concentration, or a host of other topics, the Economic Census should be considered as a source of data.

Even if you are conducting your own survey of manufacturing, it is important to look at the Economic Census. The data found here can be used to measure the reasonableness of the data you are collecting.

## CURRENT DATA

While the Economic Census contains an overwhelming wealth of data on the manufacturing sector, it is still collected just once every five years. In order to respond to the demands for more current data, several organizations provide current data. Since these sources rely on surveys, it is important to note that many of them provide data only for large geographic areas, the manufacturing sector and sub-sectors, or a combination of these rather than the detailed combinations provided in the Economic Census.

Bureau of Labor Statistics. *Labor Productivity and Costs Home Page.*
http://www.bls.gov/lpc/home.htm.

The Major Sector Productivity and Costs program develops quarterly labor productivity measures for the major U.S. economic sectors including the business sector; the nonfarm business sector; nonfinancial corporations; and manufacturing, along with sub-sectors of durable and nondurable goods manufacturing.

Census Bureau. *Annual Capital Expenditures Survey* (ACES).
http://www.census.gov/csd/ace/.

The *Annual Capital Expenditures Survey* (ACES) is part of a comprehensive program designed to provide detailed and timely information on capital investment in new and used structures and equipment by nonfarm businesses. The survey is based on a sample of approximately 46,000 companies with employees and approximately 15,000 companies without employees. Beginning with the 1999 ACES, for companies with employees, capital expenditures data are published for 130 industries comprised primarily of three-digit and selected four-digit industries from NAICS, 1997.

Census Bureau. *Annual Survey of Manufactures* (ASM).
http://www.census.gov/mcd/asmhome.html.

The *Annual Survey of Manufactures* (ASM) provides sample estimates of statistics for all manufacturing establishments with one or more paid employee. The data go back to 1949, but you will need to watch for breaks in the time series due to revisions of the SIC System and the conversion to NAICS. The U.S. Census Bureau conducts the ASM in each of the 4 years between the economic censuses. Among the statistics included in this survey are: employment, payroll, value added by manufacture, cost of materials consumed, value of shipments, detailed capital expenditures, supplemental labor costs, fuels and electric energy used, and inventories by stage of fabrication. Three reports are issued from the *Annual*

*Survey of Manufactures: Statistics for Industry Groups and Industries*—(AS)-1, *Value of Product Shipments*—(AS)-2, and *Geographic Area Statistics*—(AS)-3.

Census Bureau. *E-Stats*—Main Page.
http://www.census.gov/eos/www/ebusiness614.htm.

This *E-Stats* analytic report presents tabulations of responses by more than 38,000 manufacturing plants to 39 detailed questions about e-business process use at their plant. This is a relatively new data series, going back just to 1999.

Census Bureau. *Manufacturers' Shipments, Inventories, and Orders.*
http://www.census.gov/indicator/www/m3/.

The *Manufacturers' Shipments, Inventories, and Orders* (M3) survey provides broad-based, monthly statistical data on economic conditions in the domestic manufacturing sector. The survey measures current industrial activity and provides an indication of future business trends. Data from this report appear in the monthly *The Manufacturing and Trade Inventory and Sales* announcements.

Census Bureau. *Quarterly Financial Report for Manufacturing, Mining, and Trade Corporations.*
http://www.census.gov/prod/www/abs/qfr-mm.html.

These reports present aggregate statistics based upon an extensive sample survey, the report presents estimated statements of income and retained earnings, balance sheets, and related financial and operating ratios for the domestic operations of all manufacturing corporations with assets over $250,000, and corporations in the mining and trade areas with assets over $50 million. Data are classified by industry and by asset size.

*IndustryWeek.* Research & Benchmarking Web page
http://www.industryweek.com/Research/default.asp.

*IndustryWeek* is written for manufacturing executives covering trends, technologies, and management strategies. Most of their special issues are available from their Web site. This is a good place for an overview of the whole industry. There are other trade journals for most industry sub-sectors.

## ANSWERS: MANUFACTURING DATA IN THE ECONOMIC CENSUS

Analytical laboratory instrument mfg.—Yes, for the companies that make the instruments use NAICS 334516, other industry sectors cover those who use the instruments. This category is very broad; it comprises non-medical MRIs, hematology instruments, titrimeters, and a host of other instruments.

Bakeries & tortilla mfg.—Yes, tortillas are a new industry covered in the 1997 NAICS 3118 industry group. If the bakery makes its goods for sale at the same location then that bakery is in the retail sector.

Concrete patio construction—No, this is considered in the construction sector. However, if a company manufacturers pre-cast concrete products, then delivers and installs the product, in that case they are classified as manufacturers.

Cost of purchased advertising services—Yes, the cost of purchased services is found in the third table of the industry report for all manufacturing industries. The amount is shown in $1,000 and reflects only those services that establishments purchase from other companies, in other words the outsourced services.

Cotton ginning—No, cotton ginning is found the agriculture sector and data are collected by the U.S. Department of Agriculture. Read the chapter on the Census of Agriculture (chapter 7) for more details.

Ford Motors Headquarters—No, even though Ford Motor makes cars, the establishment that is its headquarters does not manufacture anything. This place would be in the management of companies and enterprises sector.

LIFO inventory method—Yes, inventory method standardization is the only way to understand the value of inventory across all industries. This is reflected in the third table (1), which describes which inventory method is normal for each sub-sector and in the third table (2), which values actual inventories at the beginning and end of the reference year.

Logging—Yes and No, even though under NAICS logging is now under the agriculture sector, the 1997 Economic Census still had an industry report for logging. However, in 2002 the Economic Census discontinued covering the industry.

Semi-moist cat food—Yes, there is no NAICS code for semi-moist cat food, however this is a product code. The sixth table (a) of the industry report provides the number of companies with shipments of over $100,000, quantity of production for all purposes, and quantity and value of shipments for both the current reference year and last census for easy comparisons. Note this is for companies, not establishments.

Tailor—Yes and No, if the tailor only does alterations then they fall into the repair and maintenance sub-sector. If the tailor creates clothes for personal sale then they are a manufacturer of clothes. However, if they work by themselves, they would not be reflected in any of the manufacturing sector reports, because they would be classified as nonemployers. However, if they have employees working for them then the establishment would be included in apparel sector group.

Total capital expenditures—Yes, this total is shown for all industries in manufacturing. It is one of the eleven variables shown in the geographic area reports, industry reports, and subject reports and updated in the *Annual Survey of Manufacturers*.

Use of molasses in creation of product—Yes, these data are found in the industry reports in the seventh table and in the subject reports, material summary report. So if you are a molasses supplier you can focus on industries in which your product is most heavily used.

## NAICS/SIC TABLES

There are 474 U.S. manufacturing industries identified in 2002 North American Classification Industry Classification Systems. While many NAICS industries were created from pieces of various SIC industries, many others simply represent a renaming and/or renumbering of an old industry. Due to the large number of industries involved here, it is impractical for us to show a table listing all of the changes. Therefore, we have decided to limit ourselves to just those industries, or portions of industries, either moving in or out of the sector. The complete comparison of the NAICS Manufacturing Sector with the SIC Manufacturing Division can be found on the Census Bureau's Web site at http://www.census.gov/epcd naics/frames3.htm or in an appendix in the printed 1997 NAICS manual.

The industries moving out of the sector are shown in the general summary report table called "Selected Industry Statistics for Manufacturing Establishments Not-In-Scope of Manufacturing in the 1987 SIC-Based Classification System: 1997," see Figure 9.5. The next table "Selected Industry Statistics for Non-manufacturing Establishments In-Scope of Manufacturing on the 1987 SIC-Based Classification System: 1997" shows the industries moving into the industry (see Figure 9.6).

Figure 9.5
**Data for NAICS Manufacturing Establishments Counted Elsewhere in the SIC System**

[For meaning of abbreviations and symbols, see introductory text. For explanation of terms, see appendixes]

| NAICS code | SIC-based code | SIC-based description | All establishments[1] | All employees | | Value of shipments ($1,000) |
|---|---|---|---|---|---|---|
| | | | | Number | Payroll | |
| | | **Total** .................... | **22 839** | **153 628** | **3 363 627** | **14 670 791** |
| 311330 | 544110 | Candy, nut, and confectionery stores (pt) ........ | 440 | 3 450 | 48 915 | 195 426 |
| 311340 | 544120 | Candy, nut, and confectionery stores (pt) ........ | 349 | 1 278 | 16 210 | 92 142 |
| 311612 | 514706 | Meat and meat products (pt) ........... | 189 | 3 562 | 105 856 | 1 815 012 |
| 311811 | 546111 | Retail bakeries (pt) ............... | 7 119 | 43 603 | 568 243 | 1 946 153 |
| 313311 | 513105 | Piece goods, notions, and other dry goods (pt) ....... | 559 | 7 526 | 261 011 | 1 755 733 |
| 313312 | 513110 | Piece goods, notions, and other dry goods (pt) ....... | – | – | – | – |
| 314121 | 571401 | Drapery, curtain, and upholstery stores (pt) ....... | 1 085 | 4 492 | 75 735 | 280 167 |
| 315999 | 569921 | Miscellaneous apparel and accessory stores. ...... | 724 | 2 407 | 41 935 | 152 641 |
| 326212 | 753420 | Tire retreading and repair shops (pt) ........ | 750 | 7 855 | 189 995 | 970 615 |
| 334611 | 737991 | Reproduction of software ........... | 123 | 7 868 | 302 863 | 1 209 207 |
| 334612 | 781980 | Services allied to motion picture production (pt) ...... | 251 | 8 956 | 263 056 | 1 624 736 |
| 335312 | 769420 | Armature rewinding shops (pt) ........ | 195 | 3 554 | 111 410 | 450 982 |
| 337110 | 571205 | Furniture stores (pt) .......... | 2 055 | 9 893 | 198 646 | 665 553 |
| 337121 | 571210 | Furniture stores (pt) .......... | 576 | 3 150 | 60 638 | 205 422 |
| 337122 | 571215 | Furniture stores (pt) .......... | 815 | 4 880 | 95 480 | 323 428 |
| 339116 | 807200 | Dental laboratories ............. | 7 609 | 41 154 | 1 023 634 | 2 983 574 |

Figure 9.6
Data for SIC Manufacturing Establishments Counted Elsewhere in NAICS
[For meaning of abbreviations and symbols, see introductory text. For explanation of terms, see appendixes]

| NAICS code | SIC-based code | SIC-based description | All establishments[1] | All employees | | Value of shipments ($1,000) |
|---|---|---|---|---|---|---|
| | | | | Number | Payroll | |
| | | **Total** | **36 870** | **822 958** | **26 960 580** | **130 732 311** |
| 113310 | 241100 | Logging | 13 533 | 83 212 | 2 014 254 | 13 625 734 |
| 511110 | 271100 | Newspapers | 8 773 | 400 818 | 11 729 887 | 41 433 090 |
| 511120 | 272100 | Periodicals | 6 331 | 137 865 | 5 997 490 | 29 972 538 |
| 511130 | 273110 | Book publishing (pt) | 2 689 | 90 170 | 3 655 695 | 22 676 105 |
| 511140 | 274110 | Miscellaneous publishing (pt) | 830 | 33 113 | 1 342 004 | 10 776 279 |
| 511191 | 277160 | Greeting cards (pt) | 111 | 21 047 | 644 046 | 5 395 087 |
| 511199 | 274120 | Miscellaneous publishing (pt) | 2 494 | 44 944 | 1 262 980 | 5 636 247 |
| 512230 | 273115 | Music books: publishing or printing and publishing | 259 | 1 765 | 52 144 | 300 570 |
| 512230 | 274102 | Sheet music publishing | 111 | 570 | 21 165 | 95 388 |
| 811490 | 373210 | Boat repair | 1 739 | 9 454 | 240 915 | 821 273 |

# CHAPTER 10
# Wholesale Trade

The God whom science recognizes must be a God of universal laws exclusively, a God who does a wholesale, not a retail business.

*—William James*

1. What Is Wholesaling?
2. Understanding the New Wholesale NAICS Definition
3. Question: Is It Wholesale?
4. Economic Census Wholesale Data
   A. Available Data Formats
   B. Wholesale Trade Reports
   C. Other Economic Census Wholesale Data Sources
5. Using Economic Census Wholesale Trade Data
   A. Preliminary Advice
   B. Accessing the Data
6. How Others Use These Data
   A. Government
   B. Business
7. Updated Sources
8. Answers: Is It Wholesale?
9. SIC–NAICS Comparison

## WHAT IS WHOLESALING?

Wholesaling covers all of the processes involved with transferring ownership of goods from one business to another. This is most commonly thought of as the middle steps in transferring merchandise from the producer to the retailer. However, it also includes transferring the ownership of materials from the producer to the producer of other products who will use the materials as a manufacturing input through a middleman. For example, if a paper bag manufacturer buys the paper it uses in manufacturing the bags from a middleman instead of directly from the paper mill, that middleman is considered to be a wholesaler. There are several types of transfers of goods that might be involved, but they all involve arranging the transfer of goods from one business to another business or business-to-business (B-to-B) commerce.

Normally, wholesalers operate from a warehouse or an office instead of a storefront. Generally, the customers are reached through telephone, in-person marketing (including trade shows), or specialized advertising. Additionally, either the wholesaler or the customer may initiate contacts. Usually wholesalers and their customers exhibit strong ties between the two parties. It is common for there to be long-term relationships between the wholesaler and the customer.

There are four basic ways that wholesalers operate. One of these ways is to buy the goods themselves and then resell them (with or without taking physical possession of the goods). A second method of wholesaling is to be a sales branch for a manufacturer or mining company. The third method is to act as an agent for a seller who continues to own the goods themselves. The fourth method is to create and maintain an electronic marketplace to arrange the sale of goods.

The first type of wholesaler can be called a merchant wholesaler, distributor, jobber, drop shipper, import/export merchant, broker, various types of grain elevators, or a farm product assembler. The key characteristics of this type of wholesaler are that they actually own the goods that they sell and generally do not make any transformations of the goods, except possibly sorting, repackaging, and labeling the goods for retail sales. While most of these wholesalers take actual possession of the goods and operate some type of warehouse, drop shippers arrange for the goods to be delivered to their customers directly from the supplier.

Manufacturers' sales offices simply sell the products produced by their parent company. These are only recognized as wholesalers if they are separate establishments. If they are physically located in the manufacturing facility, their employees, assets, and activities are counted as part of the manufacturing establishment.

The third type of wholesaler, those selling goods owned by others, include agents and brokers, commission merchants, import and export agents, auction companies, and manufacturer's agents. These businesses arrange for the sales of goods owned by others and usually get paid on a commission basis. In the case of auction companies and commission merchants, they typically have physical possession of the goods on a consignment basis, but do not actually own them.

Electronic markets are a relatively new type of wholesaler. These markets have developed along with the great expansion of the Internet during the past decade. While they exist for other types of goods, they are a common way of selling commodities—especially those whose prices can fluctuate quickly.

In addition to there being four different types of wholesalers, wholesalers of each type may sell or arrange for the sale or purchase of three different classes of goods. The goods in the first group are those designed for resale to either other wholesalers or retailers—typically sold in large quantities and are considered capital expenditures. Capital or durable nonconsumer goods such as manufacturing machinery or farm tractors—typically sold in small quantities make up the second type. The final types of goods handled by wholesalers are materials and supplies used in the production of other goods, such as steel going to an automobile parts supplier or glass bottles going to a baby food manufacturer—again, usually sold in large quantities.

## UNDERSTANDING THE NEW WHOLESALE NAICS DEFINITION

While there is a Wholesale sector in both the SIC system and NAICS, the makeup of these sectors are significantly different. During the transition some establishments have moved out of wholesaling into other sectors, and a few other establishments have moved in. Nearly all of the establishments that moved out of wholesaling moved into retailing. However, a few moved from the SIC wholesaling sector to manufacturing. Only one industry moved into wholesaling namely, prerecorded videotape wholesalers, which previously had been in the SIC industry for motion picture and videotape distribution.

The main conceptual difference between the SIC Wholesale division and the NAICS Wholesale sector is that under the SIC system, establishments were generally classified in this sector if their primary class of customers were other businesses. This meant that businesses such as a Staples or OfficeMax store were usually considered wholesale establishments because sales to other businesses were usually their main source of revenue.

Under NAICS, the method of selling is the primary classification criterion. The classification rule used now is that an establishment is placed into either the wholesale or retail sector based on its primary method of selling—if the primary selling method is through catalogs designed for the business community, small showrooms, etc. from a facility not designed to generate a large walk-in business, then the establishment would be classified as a wholesale business. However, if the primary methods of selling involve a store designed to attract the general public, catalogs aimed at the general public, advertising in the general media, etc. then the establishment would be a retail establishment. Under these rules, the Staples or OfficeMax establishments operating out of stores located and designed to attract the general public would be classified as retail establishments.

Finally, the industries within the Wholesale Sector were redefined between NAICS 1997 and NAICS 2002. The primary purpose of this redefinition was to recognize the new and growing importance of electronic markets as a wholesaling process. In this revision, trade agents and brokers, and wholesale electronic markets were separated out from merchant wholesalers.

---

### QUESTION: IS IT WHOLESALE?

**Answers can be found at the end of this chapter.**

Auction House
Building Materials Supplier
Diamond Broker
Motor Vehicle Parts Jobbers
Office Supply Store
Pawn Shop
Petroleum Bulk Terminal
Tractor Dealer
Trucking Company
Warehouse Club

Generally, the NAICS 2002 subdivisions of the merchant wholesale sub-sector follow the same industrial breakouts as the NAICS 1997 wholesale industry. But the new sub-sectors are not divided other than as business-to-business electronic markets, and wholesale trade agents and brokers.

## ECONOMIC CENSUS WHOLESALE DATA

The economic census covered all wholesalers operating as their own establishments. For example, the sales office for a manufacturer would be counted as a wholesale establishment if this office were physically located at a different address than the manufacturing plant. However, if it was located as an office within the manufacturing plant, it would not be counted here, but its employees would be included in the manufacturing data.

### Available Data Formats

Data from the Wholesale portion of the Economic Census is available in printed, printable (PDF), and electronic data files.

The only printed reports showing wholesale data are those found in the *Advance, Bridge, Outlying Area, and Minority- and Women-Owned Business* reports. Additionally, the 1997 Economic Census contained the *Wholesale Summary* report. Any reports that were printed in earlier censuses, such as the Geographic Area Series, are available as printable (PDF) documents. These reports contain most of the commonly used data.

The CD-ROMs include the same data as the PDF reports with the addition of data at the ZIP code level. The 1997 Economic Census in the American FactFinder only has the data from volume 1 of the CD-ROM. It does not have the SIC code, nonemployers, or ZIP code data.

For reports released since 2000, the Census Bureau provides HTML-formatted tables on the wholesale trade Web page. This means there is no need to use the American FactFinder or CD-ROMs in order to look up a few numbers.

None of the reports on wholesale trade contains rankings or derived measures such as sales per employee. Unlike earlier economic censuses, tables incorporating ratios or rankings based on the published numbers are not included in the reports from this census. The reason for this is that users can easily derive these measures from the data that are available on the Internet and CD-ROM.

## Wholesale Trade Reports

The Economic Census wholesale trade sector (NAICS 42) reports include a geographic and subject series. Reports in both of these series show the seven key statistics: number of establishments, employees, payroll, sales, operating expenses, and inventories at the beginning and the end of the reference year. These figures are repeated for each industry.

The largest part of the Wholesale data is found in the Geographic Area Series. A separate report is issued for the United States, each state, and the District of Columbia. Each report contains definitions and industry statistics for establishments with employees. These include number of establishments, employees, payroll, sales, operating expense, inventory, and data-quality entries. Each state report presents the basic data items by industry for the state, metropolitan area, county, and each place with 2,500 inhabitants or more. In the 1997 Economic Census, these reports provide statistics by the type of wholesaler at the state level. The revision in NAICS for 2002 breaks out the data by wholesaler type into different industries.

Other reports include commodity line sales, establishment and firm size by employees and sales, a miscellaneous subjects report, and a national summary. The 2002 Economic Census also contains industry reports for each of the industries within this sector.

The 1997 Economic Census *Summary Report* contains information on wholesaling at a national level, commodity line sales, concentration of the largest firms, and gross margins and profits for merchant wholesalers. This report really just shows tables from other wholesale trade reports and is the best report to retrieve when you want a national overview of the industry.

Data for wholesale establishments with no paid employees are published in the separate *Nonemployer Statistics* report. While this report covers all sectors it should be remembered when looking for wholesale trade data because nearly half of all wholesale establishments in the country have no employees. Nonemployer statistics on wholesale trade are reported for Metropolitan Statistical Areas, each county, each state, the District of Columbia, and the United States.

The *Commodity Lines Sales* reveals what kinds of commodities wholesalers sell, which lines of merchandise, and in what quantities for the nation as a whole. For example, table 1 of this report, shown in Figure 10.1 displays the different kinds of merchandise sold by automobile and other motor vehicle

Figure 10.1
Commodity Line Sales (first table) Sample

| | | | | | | | | | |
|---|---|---|---|---|---|---|---|---|---|
| | | | | E874212 - Wholesale Trade: Commodity Line Sales: Kind of Business by Commodity Lines for the United States: 1997 | | | | | |
| Geography | 1997 NAICS code | NAICS Industry | Type of Operations | Sector number and code | Commodity Lines | Number of establishments | Sales ($1,000) | Broad Insis for this NAICS(%) | Sales of establishments |
| 10000000000 | 42111 | Automobile and other motor vehic | Wholesale trade | 42_0100 | New and used automobiles, motor | 183 | 9,498,770 | 99.9 | 74.0 |
| 10000000000 | 42111 | Automobile and other motor vehic | Wholesale trade | 42_0120 | Buses, campers, and motor homes | 48 | 193,977 | 99.9 | 92.2 |
| 10000000000 | 42111 | Automobile and other motor vehic | Wholesale trade | 42_0130 | Light trucks and vans (14,000 lb or | 109 | 6,481,909 | 100.0 | 71.4 |
| 10000000000 | 42111 | Automobile and other motor vehic | Wholesale trade | 42_0140 | Medium trucks and tractors (14,001 | 87 | 179,434 | 95.4 | 0.0 |
| 10000000000 | 42111 | Automobile and other motor vehic | Wholesale trade | 42_0150 | Heavy trucks and tractors (over 26,0 | 110 | 626,306 | 98.1 | 92.3 |
| 10000000000 | 42111 | Automobile and other motor vehic | Wholesale trade | 42_0200 | New and rebuilt automotive parts a | 93 | 387,062 | 15.1 | 14.5 |
| 10000000000 | 42111 | Automobile and other motor vehic | Wholesale trade | 42_0240 | Used automotive parts, accessories | 25 | 12,842 | 4.5 | 0.0 |
| 10000000000 | 42111 | Automobile and other motor vehic | Wholesale trade | 42_0300 | Tires and tubes | 15 | 1,924 | 0.9 | 4.8 |
| 10000000000 | 42111 | Automobile and other motor vehic | Wholesale trade | 42_2100 | Construction and mining machinei | 19 | 8,583 | 0.6 | 24.9 |
| 10000000000 | 42111 | Automobile and other motor vehic | Wholesale trade | 42_2200 | Farm machinery, equipment, and | 3 | 8,660 | D | 0.5 |
| 10000000000 | 42111 | Automobile and other motor vehic | Wholesale trade | 42_2320 | General-purpose industrial machin | 13 | 212 | Z | 0.0 |
| 10000000000 | 42111 | Automobile and other motor vehic | Wholesale trade | 42_2540 | Other service establishment equipi | 1 | 4,445 | D | 92.8 |
| 10000000000 | 42111 | Automobile and other motor vehic | Wholesale trade | 42_2620 | Marine machinery, equipment, an | 1 | 175 | D | 0.0 |
| 10000000000 | 42111 | Automobile and other motor vehic | Wholesale trade | 42_2700 | Sporting and recreational goods a | 2 | 634 | D | 0.0 |
| 10000000000 | 42111 | Automobile and other motor vehic | Wholesale trade | 42_5400 | Petroleum products | 5 | 1,508 | Z | 0.0 |
| 10000000000 | 42111 | Automobile and other motor vehic | Wholesale trade | 42_9700 | Service receipts and labor charges | 143 | 187,063 | 11.2 | 56.8 |
| 10000000000 | 42111 | Automobile and other motor vehic | Wholesale trade | 42_9720 | Receipts for service contracts | 9 | 1,411 | 0.3 | 0.0 |
| 10000000000 | 42111 | Automobile and other motor vehic | Wholesale trade | 42_9810 | Miscellaneous commodities | 10 | 34,875 | 5.8 | 92.8 |
| 10000000000 | 42111 | Automobile and other motor vehic | Wholesale trade | 42_9940 | Rental and leasing receipts | 34 | 14,383 | 3.2 | 0.0 |
| 10000000000 | 42111 | Automobile and other motor vehic | Wholesale trade | 42_9980 | Receipts for machine shop job wor | 9 | 3,628 | 32.1 | 0.0 |

wholesalers, including the fact that two of these businesses in 1997 sold $634,000 worth of sporting and recreational goods. Figure 10.2 is a sample of table 2 from this report, showing which kinds of wholesalers sell what types of goods in the country. The table also shows that in addition to 11 light truck and van wholesale establishments, light trucks are sold by one farm machinery and equipment dealer and 107 wholesale establishments of other types. These are important facts for marketers. Additional tables show similar information about the different types of wholesalers (e.g., merchant wholesalers). The viewable (PDF) reports show only national data. Meanwhile, data on 15 selected states and 15 selected metropolitan areas are available on the Internet and CD-ROM databases.

*Establishment and Firm Size (including Legal Form of Organization)* presents national data on the number of establishments, sales, payroll, and employment. These industry totals are cross-tabulated by size of establishment, size of firm, and legal form of organization. Establishment data are presented by sales size and employment size; data for firms, by sales size (including concentration by largest firms), by employment size, and by number of establishments operated. Use of this data allows policy makers to see which industries are more monopolistic than others or allows for pension fund managers to target those industries with a higher concentration of employees instead of those industries with lower employee counts.

The *Miscellaneous Subjects* presents specialized data at the national level on sales by class of customer (such as other wholesalers, governmental bodies, or retailers and repair shops). It also has a table showing the number of employees by their general job function. Two tables in this report provide details about the end-of-year inventories for the beginning and end of the reference year (allowing the user to calculate annual changes in an industry's inventory). Additional tables provide information on the commission of agents, brokers, and commission merchants and the gross profits and gross margins of merchant wholesalers. Finally, a set of tables provides information about the operations of petroleum bulk stations and terminals.

Due to the change in industrial classification, statistics from the previous census are no longer shown in Geographic Area Series reports. In order to make a historical comparison between Wholesale industries you can use two reports: *Bridge Between the NAICS and SIC* and the *Comparative Statistics*. It's best if you use the Web version; they are laid out logically and allow for linking between the two systems. Using both

of these reports together is important because most Economic Census reports show data by NAICS industries, but the *Comparative Statistics* report uses SIC industries. In 1997 the Bridge Report provides the information needed to compare the two systems at the national level.

At the time this is being written, the Census Bureau has not finalized the plans for the Industry series. So, the detailed look of these reports is not known. It should be safe to state, however, that these reports will present detailed national-level data on the operating costs of the establishments within the industry. They are also likely to contain information on products sold, class of customer, and materials purchased.

## Other Economic Census Wholesale Data Sources

The 2002 Census includes most of the following reports in NAICS, but the 1997 Economic Census was different. The wholesale data reported in these 1997 Economic Census products are generally based on SIC definitions (SIC 50–51), so be careful when making comparisons with the Wholesale Trade Sector reports. It is critical that you use the Bridge Tables to determine the compatibility between datasets of an industry and *never* make the mistake of comparing SIC wholesale sector with the NAICS wholesale sector. Nationally, it has been estimated that ten percent of the SIC food service was moved out of NAICS and six percent of wholesale sales moved in. Along with all the other changes in Wholesale, it's best to use the Bridge Tables at the disaggregated areas. It is also important to note that the Bridge Tables compare the SIC and NAICS industries at a national level. The further that you go in looking at small geographic areas, the less reliable the national trends become. Thus, it is best to use the Bridge Tables only at the national level.

The *Business Expenses* report contains data taken for the 1997 Business Expenditures Survey (BES). The tables included in this report give detailed operating expenses for the years 1992 and 1997. Items covered are employer costs for payroll including all salaries, wages, bonuses, and allowances for vacation, holiday, and paid sick leave; employer costs for other fringe benefits; contract labor; depreciation and amortization charges; taxes and license fees; lease and rental payments; cost of office supplies; cost of telephones and other communication services; cost of purchased utilities; advertising services; purchases of packaging and other materials; commissions paid;

**Figure 10.2**
Commodity Line Sales (second table) Sample

| | | | | | | | | | |
|---|---|---|---|---|---|---|---|---|---|
| | | | E97421L4 - Wholesale Trade: Commodity Line Sales: Merchant Wholesalers by Broad Commodity Line and Kind of Business: 1997 | | | | | | |
| Geography | 1997 NAICS code | NAICS Industry | Type of Operations | Sector number and cl code | Commodity Lines | Number of establishments | Sales ($1,000) | Broad in sis for this NAICS(%) | Sales of establishments |
| 100000000 | 42 | Wholesale trade | Merchant whole: | 42_0130 | Light trucks | 119 | 1,014,868 | 100.0 | 74.6 |
| 100000000 | 421 | Wholesale trade, durable goods | Merchant whole: | 42_0130 | Light trucks | 119 | 1,014,868 | 100.0 | 70.5 |
| 100000000 | 4211 | Motor vehicle and motor vehicle parts and supplies wholesalers | Merchant whole: | 42_0130 | Light trucks | 117 | 1,014,828 | 100.0 | 88.0 |
| 100000000 | 42111 | Automobile and other motor vehicle wholesalers | Merchant whole: | 42_0130 | Light trucks | 96 | 1,012,541 | 99.8 | 92.8 |
| 100000000 | 421110 | Automobile and other motor vehicle wholesalers | Merchant whole: | 42_0130 | Light trucks | 96 | 1,012,541 | 99.8 | 92.8 |
| 100000000 | 4211101 | Automobile and motorcycle wholesalers | Merchant whole: | 42_0130 | Light trucks | 45 | 40,105 | 4.0 | 93.0 |
| 100000000 | 4211102 | Bus and recreational vehicle wholesalers | Merchant whole: | 42_0130 | Light trucks | 1 | 104 | Z | 77.7 |
| 100000000 | 4211103 | Light truck and van (14,000 lb or less) wholesalers | Merchant whole: | 42_0130 | Light trucks | 11 | 883,575 | 87.1 | 99.4 |
| 100000000 | 4211104 | Medium truck and tractor (14,001 lb to 26,000 lb) wholesalers | Merchant whole: | 42_0130 | Light trucks | 2 | 827 | D | 62.2 |
| 100000000 | 4211105 | Heavy truck and tractor (over 26,000 lb) wholesalers | Merchant whole: | 42_0130 | Light trucks | 37 | 87,930 | 8.7 | 87.0 |
| 100000000 | 421112 | Motor vehicle supplies and new parts wholesalers | Merchant whole: | 42_0130 | Light trucks | 3 | 1,255 | D | 0.0 |
| 100000000 | 421120 | Motor vehicle supplies and new parts wholesalers | Merchant whole: | 42_0130 | Light trucks | 3 | 1,255 | D | 0.0 |
| 100000000 | 4211202 | Motor vehicle supplies and new parts - jobbers | Merchant whole: | 42_0130 | Light trucks | 3 | 1,255 | D | 0.0 |
| 100000000 | 42114 | Motor vehicle parts (used) wholesalers | Merchant whole: | 42_0130 | Light trucks | 18 | 1,032 | 0.1 | 9.0 |
| 100000000 | 421140 | Motor vehicle parts (used) wholesalers | Merchant whole: | 42_0130 | Light trucks | 18 | 1,032 | 0.1 | 9.0 |
| 100000000 | 4218 | Machinery, equipment, and supplies wholesalers | Merchant whole: | 42_0130 | Light trucks | 2 | 40 | Z | 0.0 |
| 100000000 | 42181 | Construction and mining (except petroleum) machinery and equ | Merchant whole: | 42_0130 | Light trucks | 1 | 35 | Z | 0.0 |
| 100000000 | 421810 | Construction and mining (except petroleum) machinery and equ | Merchant whole: | 42_0130 | Light trucks | 1 | 35 | Z | 0.0 |
| 100000000 | 42182 | Farm and garden machinery and equipment wholesalers | Merchant whole: | 42_0130 | Light trucks | 1 | 5 | N | 0.0 |
| 100000000 | 421820 | Farm and garden machinery and equipment wholesalers | Merchant whole: | 42_0130 | Light trucks | 1 | 5 | N | 0.0 |
| 100000000 | 4218201 | Farm machinery and equipment - farm dealers | Merchant whole: | 42_0130 | Light trucks | 1 | 5 | N | 1.0 |

contract work; purchased repair and maintenance services; purchased legal services; purchased accounting, auditing, and bookkeeping services; data processing and other computer-related services; and all other operating expenses, such as inventory storage and shipping cost, insurance expense (non-employee), uninsured casualty losses, and bad debt. However, it is important to note that this report only provides data on merchant wholesalers and then only at the national level.

The outlying areas of Puerto Rico, Guam, U.S. Virgin Islands, and Northern Marina Islands (NMI) also have wholesale data presented in the Economic Census using SIC definitions. Puerto Rico has the greatest level of detail with reports covering commodity lines and kinds of business by commodity lines. The *Geographic* reports have statistics comparing 1992 with 1997 at the same detail as mainland reports. Puerto Rico data can also be downloaded from the Web site. Guam, U.S. Virgin Islands, and Northern Marina Islands have data by industry and kind of business, legal form of organization, sales and receipts size, employment size, and by industry groups and municipalities/election districts. Northern Mariana Islands includes a table of distribution of establishments by citizenship status of the owner. Guam and U.S. Virgin Islands have additional information on the hotel and motel industry. The nonemployer statistics are not available for the outlying areas.

The *Women- and Minority-Owned Business* report has wholesale information down to the SIC three-digit level, also called industry group. Geographic coverage goes all the way from the nation down to places of 2,500 persons in size. Be aware that the smaller geographic regions have less subject detail than the larger areas. Even though both the 1997 and 1992 *Minority- and Women-Owned Business* reports show data based on SIC industries, other changes make comparisons between these years difficult. Read the sector on *Minority- and Women-Owned Business* for more detail in the reports chapter (chapter 5).

## USING ECONOMIC CENSUS WHOLESALE TRADE DATA

There are innumerable ways to use the Economic Census's wholesale trade data. The next section describes some ways that these data have been used in the past. This section contains some cautions in using these data and information on how to access the data.

## Preliminary Advice

The problem with using industry sector numbers is that it is easy to forget that the wholesale sector as defined by the SIC system and NAICS are not the same thing. Further, the industries within the sector are defined differently in NAICS 1997 and NAICS 2002. This may lead to confusion to anyone using the wholesale trade numbers. When using time series data, please make sure to read the footnotes to the data in order to see how the break in the industry definitions is being handled. Also include all appropriate comments about these breaks in your own reports when you create a time series.

Another pitfall to watch for is whether the data include statistics on nonemployer businesses or not. For example there are 38,071 wholesale establishments in Illinois; of those, 16,120 of them are non-employers and generate sales of $1,181.8 million. However, the 21,951 wholesale establishments with employees generate sales of $275,968.4 million. It is very important to note that the sales figures for the employer and nonemployer wholesalers are not comparable and cannot be combined. The major reason for this is that for wholesale agents and brokers without payroll, the receipts item contains commissions received or earnings and any other sources of receipts. In contrast, for wholesale agents and brokers with payroll, the sales item published in the economic census represents the value of the goods involved in the transactions.

## Accessing the Data

The different methods of distribution of the data are better depending on what your needs are. If you need just a few data items, the PDF reports are ideal. However if you want to compare among industries or geographic locations use the spreadsheet files from the Web page. To search within the wholesale sector or geographic area the American FactFinder offers tools to get what you want. If you are searching for data for an SIC industry, ZIP code, or commodity line data or wish to customize a table, the CD-ROM may be the best or, even, only option. Please remember that you can use any of the more sophisticated access methods for a less sophisticated need. For example, if you are looking for just a few data items, you can use any of the other access methods, but they may take longer than simply looking up the data in hypertext tables.

## HOW OTHERS USE THESE DATA

As with all data produced by the Census Bureau, the data on wholesale trade are employed by many users for a variety of purposes. Here are just a few examples.

## Government

The concentration ratios at the national level show if a few companies are dominating a particular wholesale industry. Agencies such as the Securities and Exchange Commission use these data along with other factors in looking at merger and acquisition decisions according to the Hart-Scott-Rodino Antitrust Improvements Act of 1976. National policy makers can see which wholesale industries are being hit by federally mandated programs and taxes using the *Business Expense Survey.*

Since states are always comparing themselves to the other states, they can use the *Geographic Area* reports. By determining the number of employees in a particular wholesale industry and their payroll, a state can build arguments about why a potential wholesaler should locate in their state (or a county in their state) instead of a different state.

## Business

A manufacturer of restaurant equipment, who had previously marketed his products primarily through restaurant and hotel equipment and supplies wholesalers, was impressed by figures from the *Commodity Line Sales* subject report, showing that these wholesalers provided only two-thirds of the market for this type of product. From this report, he also learned that the other major players in this market were industrial and personal service paper wholesalers and various types of grocery and related products wholesalers. Armed with this additional knowledge, he was able to greatly expand his market.

## UPDATED SOURCES

While the Economic Census has a tremendous amount of data about the wholesale sector, a common complaint about it is that the data are dated. Here are some sources for more recent information about wholesaling. But, the data included in these tend to be much more limited either in terms of subject content, geographic detail, or both.

*Annual Wholesale Trade Report*
URL: http://www.census.gov/svsd/www/whltable.html

This is an annual report that is used to benchmark the monthly survey to a larger sample (6,500 wholesale firms instead of 4,000). In addition to the data included in the monthly survey, this includes information about the purchases, gross margins, and gross profits of wholesalers by NAICS sub-sector. This survey has been conducted since 1978 with a new sample being chosen about every five years. The report is released each spring.

*Monthly Wholesale Trade Report*
URL: http://www.census.gov/svsd/www/mwts.html

This report provides data on the dollar value of wholesale sales, inventories, and inventory/sales ratios for merchant wholesalers at the national level. It's released roughly six weeks after the close of the reference month.

*E-Stats*
URL: http://www.census.gov/estats

Wholesale is only one sector covered in this survey. This survey is an attempt to measure the impacts of e-commerce on business. It includes sales of goods and services over the Internet, an extranet, Electronic Data Interchange (EDI), or other online system. Payment for sales covered by this survey may or may not be made online. The data reported is simply the total sales, total e-commerce sales, e-commerce sales as a percent of total sales for each sub-sector, and the sub-sector's share of the sector's total e-commerce sales.

*Farm Production Expenditures*
URL: http://usda.mannlib.cornell.edu/reports/
    nassr/price/zpe_bb/

This report contains the annual estimates of farm production expenditures by U.S. farm production regions and economic class for major expenses; major input items include feed, farm services, rent, agricultural chemicals, fertilizer, lime and soil conditioners, interest, taxes (real estate and property), labor, fuels, farm supplies and repairs, farm improvements and construction, tractors and self-propelled farm machinery, other farm machinery, seeds and plants, and trucks and autos.

## ANSWERS: IS IT WHOLESALE?

Auction Houses—No, these are included in all other miscellaneous store retailers (except tobacco stores) NAICS 453998. However, livestock and tobacco auction markets are considered wholesalers because they deal with selling items in bulk.

Building Material Supplier—Yes or No—The answer depends on how they sell the materials. If they sell the materials as a wholesaler (large quantities sold to other businesses), then they are considered a wholesaler. Otherwise, they are considered retailers.

Diamond Broker—Yes, they are called gemstones merchant wholesalers, 421940 for 2002 NAICS.

Motor Vehicle Parts Jobbers—Yes, they are in 421120 in 1997 NAICS and 423210 for 2002 NAICS.

Office Supply Store—Yes or No—This is another one that depends on how the supplies are sold. A store like Staples or OfficeMax, which generally sells from a store designed to attract customers off the street, would be considered retail. But, a business that sells primarily to other businesses through a catalog would be considered a wholesaler.

Pawn Shop—No, these are considered to be financial services businesses since they are primarily involved with lending money. (522298)

Petroleum Bulk Terminal—Yes, they are classified as 422710 in the 1997 NAICS and 424710 in the 2002 NAICS.

Tractor Dealer—Yes, businesses primarily involved with the sale of farm or industrial equipment are considered wholesalers.

Trucking Company—No, general freight trucking is classified under 4841 in the transportation sector.

Warehouse Club—No, they are in industry 452910 Warehouse Clubs and Superstores, which is part of the retail sector. This industry comprises establishments known as warehouse clubs, superstores, or supercenters primarily engaged in retailing a general line of groceries in combination with general lines of new merchandise, such as apparel, furniture, and appliances.

## SIC–NAICS Comparison

Table 10.1 shows how the wholesale sector was restructured when NAICS was introduced in 1997 and then revised in 2002.

Table 10.1
SIC–NAICS Comparison

| NAICS 1997 | NAICS 2002 | NAICSTEXT | COMP[a] | SIC | SICTEXT |
|---|---|---|---|---|---|
| 42 | | Wholesale Trade | | | |
| 421 | | Wholesale Trade, Durable Goods | | | |
| 4211 | | Motor Vehicle and Motor Vehicle Parts and Supplies Wholesalers | | | |
| 42111 | 423110 | Automobile and Other Motor Vehicle Wholesalers | E | 5012 | Automobiles and Other Motor Vehicles |
| 42112 | 423120 | Motor Vehicle Supplies and New Parts Wholesalers | R | 5013 | Motor Vehicle Supplies and New Parts (except parts sold via retail methods) |
| 42113 | 423130 | Tire and Tube Wholesalers | R | 5014 | Tires and Tubes (except tires sold via retail method) |
| 42114 | 423140 | Motor Vehicle Parts (Used) Wholesalers | R | 5015 | Motor Vehicle Parts, Used (except sold via retail method) |
| 4212 | | Furniture and Home Furnishing Wholesalers | | | |
| 42121 | 423210 | Furniture Wholesalers | R | 5021 | Furniture (except furniture sold via retail method) |
| 42122 | 423220 | Home Furnishing Wholesalers | R | 5023 | Homefurnishings (except homefurnishings sold via retail method) |
| 4213 | | Lumber and Other Construction Materials Wholesalers | | | |
| 42131 | 423310 | Lumber, Plywood, Millwork, and Wood Panel Wholesalers | E | 5031 | Lumber, Plywood, Millwork, and Wood Panels |
| 42132 | 423320 | Brick, Stone, and Related Construction Material Wholesalers | R | 5032 | Brick, Stone, and Related Construction Materials (except construction materials sold via retail method) |
| 42133 | 423330 | Roofing, Siding, and Insulation Material Wholesalers | E | 5033 | Roofing, Siding, and Insulation Materials |
| 42139 | 423390 | Other Construction Material Wholesalers | R | 5039 | Construction Materials, NEC (sold via wholesale method) |
| 4214 | | Professional and Commercial Equipment and Supplies Wholesalers | | | |
| 42141 | 423410 | Photographic Equipment and Supplies Wholesalers | E | 5043 | Photographic Equipment and Supplies |
| 42142 | 423420 | Office Equipment Wholesalers | R | 5044 | Office Equipment (except sold via retail method) |
| 42143 | 423430 | Computer and Computer Peripheral Equipment and Software Wholesalers | R | 5045 | Computers and Computer Peripherals Equipment and Software (except computers, equipment, and software sold via retail method) |
| 42144 | 423440 | Other Commercial Equipment Wholesalers | E | 5046 | Commercial Equipment, NEC |

Table 10.1 (Continued)
SIC–NAICS Comparison

| NAICS 1997 | NAICS 2002 | NAICSTEXT | COMP[a] | SIC | SICTEXT |
|---|---|---|---|---|---|
| | 423450 | Medical, Dental, and Hospital Equipment and Supplies Wholesalers | R | 5047 | Medical, Dental and Hospital Equipment and Supplies (except medical, dental, and hospital equipment and supplies sold via retail method) |
| | 423460 | Ophthalmic Goods Wholesalers | E | 5048 | Ophthalmic Goods |
| | 423490 | Other Professional Equipment and Supplies Wholesalers | R | 5049 | Professional Equipment and Supplies, NEC (except religious and school supplies sold via retail method) |
| 4215 | | Metal and Mineral (except Petroleum) Wholesalers | | | |
| | 423510 | Metal Service Centers and Offices | E | 5051 | Metals Service Centers and Offices |
| | 423520 | Coal and Other Mineral and Ore Wholesalers | E | 5052 | Coal and Other Mineral and Ores |
| 4216 | | Electrical Goods Wholesalers | | | |
| | 423610 | Electrical Apparatus and Equipment, Wiring Supplies, and Construction Material Wholesalers | R | 5063 | Electrical Apparatus and Equipment, Wiring Supplies and Construction Materials (except electrical supplies sold via retail method) |
| | 423620 | Electrical Appliance, Television, and Radio Set Wholesalers | E | 5064 | Electrical Appliances, Television and Radio Sets |
| | 423690 | Other Electronic Parts and Equipment Wholesalers | E | 5065 | Electronic Parts and Equipment, NEC |
| 4217 | | Hardware, and Plumbing and Heating Equipment and Supplies Wholesalers | | | |
| | 423710 | Hardware Wholesalers | R | 5072 | Hardware (except sold via retail method) |
| | 423720 | Plumbing and Heating Equipment and Supplies (Hydronics) Wholesalers | R | 5074 | Plumbing and Heating Equipment and Supplies (Hydronics) (except plumbing equipment sold via retail method) |
| | 423730 | Warm Air Heating and Air-Conditioning Equipment and Supplies Wholesalers | E | 5075 | Warm Air Heating and Air-Conditioning Equipment and Supplies |
| | 423740 | Refrigeration Equipment and Supplies Wholesalers | E | 5078 | Refrigeration Equipment and Supplies |
| 4218 | | Machinery, Equipment, and Supplies Wholesalers | | | |
| | 423810 | Construction and Mining (except Oil Well) Machinery and Equipment Wholesalers | E | 5082 | Construction and Mining (Except Petroleum) Machinery and Equipment |
| | 423820 | Farm and Garden Machinery and Equipment Wholesalers | R | 5083 | Farm and Garden Machinery and Equipment (except lawn and garden equipment sold via retail method) |
| 42183 | 423830 | Industrial Machinery and Equipment Wholesalers | R | 5084 | Industrial Machinery and Equipment |
| 42183 | | Industrial Machinery and Equipment Wholesalers | | 5085 | Industrial Supplies (fluid power accessories) |

Table 10.1 (Continued)
SIC–NAICS Comparison

| NAICS 1997 | NAICS 2002 | NAICSTEXT | COMP[a] | SIC | SICTEXT |
|---|---|---|---|---|---|
| 42184 | 423840 | Industrial Supplies Wholesalers | R | 5085 | Industrial Supplies (except fluid power accessories) |
| 42185 | 423850 | Service Establishment Equipment and Supplies Wholesalers | R | 5087 | Service Establishment Equipment and Supplies (except sales of the service establishment equipment and supplies sold via retail method) |
| 42186 | 423860 | Transportation Equipment and Supplies (except Motor Vehicle) Wholesalers | R | 5088 | Transportation Equipment and Supplies, Except Motor Vehicles |
| 42186 | | Transportation Equipment and Supplies (except Motor Vehicle) Wholesalers | | 7389 | Business Services, NEC (yacht brokers) |
| 4219 | | Miscellaneous Durable Goods Wholesalers | | | |
| 42191 | 423910 | Sporting and Recreational Goods and Supplies Wholesalers | E | 5091 | Sporting and Recreational Goods and Supplies |
| 42192 | 423920 | Toy and Hobby Goods and Supplies Wholesalers | E | 5092 | Toys and Hobby Goods and Supplies |
| 42193 | 423930 | Recyclable Material Wholesalers | E | 5093 | Scrap and Waste Materials |
| 42194 | 423940 | Jewelry, Watch, Precious Stone, and Precious Metal Wholesalers | E | 5094 | Jewelry, Watches, Precious Stones, and Precious Metals |
| 42199 | 423990 | Other Miscellaneous Durable Goods Wholesalers | R | 5099 | Durable Goods, NEC |
| 42199 | | Other Miscellaneous Durable Goods Wholesalers | | 7822 | Motion Picture and Video Tape Distribution (prerecorded video tapes - distribution) |
| 422 | | Wholesale Trade, Nondurable Goods | | | |
| 4221 | | Paper and Paper Product Wholesalers | | | |
| 42211 | 424110 | Printing and Writing Paper Wholesalers | E | 5111 | Printing and Writing Paper |
| 42212 | 424120 | Stationery and Office Supplies Wholesalers | R | 5112 | Stationery and Office Supplies (except stationery and office supplies sold via retail method) |
| 42213 | 424130 | Industrial and Personal Service Paper Wholesalers | E | 5113 | Industrial and Personal Service Paper |
| 4222 | | Drugs and Druggists' Sundries Wholesalers | | | |
| 42221 | 424210 | Drugs and Druggists' Sundries Wholesalers | E | 5122 | Drugs, Drug Proprietaries, and Druggists' Sundries |
| 4223 | | Apparel, Piece Goods, and Notions Wholesalers | | | |
| 42231 | 424310 | Piece Goods, Notions, and Other Dry Goods Wholesalers | R | 5131 | Piece Goods, Notions, and Other Dry Goods (except piece goods converters) |
| 42232 | 424320 | Men's and Boys' Clothing and Furnishings Wholesalers | E | 5136 | Men's and Boys' Clothing and Furnishings |

Table 10.1 (Continued)
SIC–NAICS Comparison

| NAICS 1997 | NAICS 2002 | NAICSTEXT | COMP[a] | SIC | SICTEXT |
|---|---|---|---|---|---|
| 4442 | | Lawn and Garden Equipment and Supplies Stores | | | |
| 44421 | | Outdoor Power Equipment Stores | N | 5083 | Farm and Garden Machinery and Equipment (Wholesale) (sold via retail method) |
| 44421 | | Outdoor Power Equipment Stores | | 5261 | Retail Nurseries, Lawn and Garden Supply Stores (outdoor power equipment) |
| 44422 | | Nursery and Garden Centers | R | 5191 | Farm Supplies (sold via retail method) |
| 44422 | | Nursery and Garden Centers | | 5193 | Flowers, Nursery Stock, and Florists' Supplies (sold via retail method) |
| 44422 | | Nursery and Garden Centers | | 5261 | Retail Nurseries, Lawn and Garden Supply Stores (except outdoor power equipment) |
| 445 | | Food and Beverage Stores | | | |
| 4451 | | Grocery Stores | | | |
| 44511 | | Supermarkets and Other Grocery (except Convenience) Stores | N | 5411 | Grocery Stores (except convenience stores and grocery stores with substantial general merchandise) |
| 44512 | | Convenience Stores | N | 5411 | Grocery Stores (convenience stores without gas) |
| 4452 | | Specialty Food Stores | | | |
| 44521 | | Meat Markets | R | 5421 | Meat and Fish (Seafood) Markets, Including Freezer Provisioners (meat except freezer provisioners) |
| 44521 | | Meat Markets | | 5499 | Miscellaneous Food Stores (poultry and poultry products) |
| 44522 | | Fish and Seafood Markets | N | 5421 | Meat and Fish (Seafood) Markets, Including Freezer Provisioners (seafood) |
| 44523 | | Fruit and Vegetable Markets | E | 5431 | Fruit and Vegetable Markets |
| 44529 | | Other Specialty Food Stores | | | |
| 445291 | | Baked Goods Stores | R | 5461 | Retail Bakeries (selling only) |
| 445292 | | Confectionery and Nut Stores | E | 5441 | Candy, Nut and Confectionery Stores |

Table 10.1 (Continued)
SIC–NAICS Comparison

| NAICS 1997 | NAICS 2002 | NAICSTEXT | COMP[a] | SIC | SICTEXT |
|---|---|---|---|---|---|
| 4229 | | Miscellaneous Nondurable Goods Wholesalers | | | |
| 42291 | 424910 | Farm Supplies Wholesalers | R | 5191 | Farm Supplies (except lawn and garden supplies sold via retail method) |
| 42292 | 424920 | Book, Periodical, and Newspaper Wholesalers | E | 5192 | Books, Periodicals, and Newspapers |
| 42293 | 424930 | Flower, Nursery Stock, and Florists' Supplies Wholesalers | E | 5193 | Flowers, Nursery Stock, and Florists' Supplies (except nursery stock sold via retail method) |
| 42294 | 424940 | Tobacco and Tobacco Product Wholesalers | E | 5194 | Tobacco and Tobacco Products |
| 42295 | 424950 | Paint, Varnish, and Supplies Wholesalers | E | 5198 | Paints, Varnishes, and Supplies |
| 42299 | 424990 | Other Miscellaneous Nondurable Goods Wholesalers | R | 5199 | Nondurable Goods, NEC (except specialty advertising) |
| 422990 | 425110 | Business to Business Electronic Markets (pt) | N | | new in 2002 |
| 422990 | 425120 | Wholesale Trade Agents and Brokers (pt) | N | | new in 2002 |

[a]E = Existing, N = New, R = Revised, L = Not applicable in the U.S.

212

# CHAPTER 11
# Retail Trade

*After all, the chief business of the American people is business. They are profoundly concerned with producing, buying, selling, investing and prospering in the world.*
*—Calvin Coolidge (1872–1933), U.S. president*

1. What Is Retailing?
   A. Store Retailers
   B. Nonstore Retailers
2. Changing Nature of the Retail Sector
3. Question: Is It Retail?
4. Coverage in the Economic Census
5. Data Availability
   A. Retail Trade Reports from the Economic Census
   B. Additional Retail Information in Other Parts of the Census
6. Using the Retail Data from the Economic Census
7. How Others Use the Economic Census Retail Trade Data
   A. Government
   B. Business
8. Current Data
   A. Other Related Reports
9. Answers: Is It Retail?

## WHAT IS RETAILING?

The retailing process is the final step in the distribution of merchandise where products are sold to the final consumer. Retailers are organized to sell merchandise in small quantities to the general public; these businesses are involved with business-to-consumer (B-to-C) commerce. The Retail Trade sector (NAICS 44–45) is comprised of establishments engaged in retailing merchandise, generally without transformation, and rendering services incidental to the sale of merchandise. This sector has two main types of retailers: store and nonstore retailers.

The buying of goods for resale is a characteristic of retail trade establishments that particularly distinguishes them from establishments in the agriculture, manufacturing, and construction industries. For example, farms that sell their products at or from the point of production are not classified in retail, but rather in agriculture. Similarly, establishments that both manufacture and sell their products to the general public are not classified in retail, but rather in manufacturing. However, establishments that engage in processing activities incidental to retailing are classified in retail. This includes establishments such as optical goods stores that do in-store grinding of lenses, and meat and seafood markets.

Wholesalers are those who engage in the buying of goods for resale and are not usually organized to serve the general public. They typically operate from a warehouse or office and neither the design nor the location of these premises is intended to solicit a high volume of walk-in traffic. Wholesalers supply institutional, industrial, wholesale, and retail clients; their operations are, therefore, generally organized to purchase, sell, and deliver merchandise in larger quantities. Dealers of durable nonconsumer goods, such as farm machinery and heavy-duty trucks, are included in wholesale trade even if they often sell these products in single units.

## Store Retailers

Store retailers operate fixed locations also known as brick and mortar stores. They are located and designed to attract a high volume of walk-in customers and have extensive displays of merchandise and use mass-media advertising to attract customers. They typically sell merchandise to the general public for personal or household consumption, but some also serve business and institutional clients. In addition to retailing merchandise, some types of store retailers are also engaged in the provision of after-sales services, such as home delivery, installation, or repair. As a general rule, establishments engaged in retailing merchandise and providing after-sales services are classified in the retail sector, unless the services take place in a separate establishment.

Examples of store retailers include establishments, such as office supply stores, computer and software stores, building materials dealers, plumbing supply stores, and electrical supply stores. Catalog showrooms, gasoline service stations, automotive dealers, and mobile home dealers are also treated as store retailers because they sell goods to the final consumer from a fixed location usually visited by the customer.

## Nonstore Retailers

Nonstore retailers, like store retailers, are organized to serve the general public, but they use different selling methods. The establishments in this sub-sector reach customers and market merchandise with such methods as soliciting on Web pages, broadcasting of an infomercial, broadcasting and publishing of direct-response advertising, publishing of paper catalogs, door-to-door solicitation, selling from portable stalls (e.g., non-food street vendors), and distribution through vending machines. Establishments engaged in the direct sale (nonstore) of products, such as home heating oil dealers and home delivery newspaper routes are also included.

## CHANGING NATURE OF THE RETAIL SECTOR

While the name of this sector stays the same, the sector known as retail has changed with the change in industrial classification systems. Some establishments have moved out of retailing into other sectors, and other establishments have moved into this sector during the change from the SIC system to NAICS.

The stores making candy or baking and selling what they make on the premises are out of retail and are now classified as manufacturing establishments. Custom tailors and seamstresses are also moved to manufacturing. Custom-made wood furniture and cabinet shops get shifted to their rightful place with the other furniture manufacturers.

Pawnshops, because their main purpose is to give temporary loans while holding merchandise as collat-

eral, are moved into the nondepository credit intermediation industry group.

The biggest single move in 1997 within the retail sector is the industry formerly classified SIC 5812 (eating places) and SIC 5813 (drinking places), now a sector of its own called Accommodation and Food services (NAICS 72).

Coming into the family of the retail sector are all those establishments calling themselves wholesale buying clubs (such as Sam's Club). Their main clientele are off the street consumers and their method of sale is similar to retail; just because the floor is concrete does not make it a wholesaler. Aftermarket sales of automobile accessories and other items are reflected with the new industries for automobile parts and tire stores.

Another big move that may cause confusion is the inclusion of repair shops that are a part of the operations of a retail establishment in the retail sector. When a consumer brings a lamp into a lighting store for repair, that income would be counted under NAICS 442299 (All Other Home Furnishings Stores). However, it is possible to get the revenue of these repair operations by using merchandise line data. This combined with information from the Other Services (except Public Administration) sector will allow you to see a complete picture of the repair industry in an area.

---

### QUESTION: IS IT RETAIL?

**Answers can be found at the end of this chapter.**

Auction House
Bakery Outlet Store
Butcher Shop
Farm Stand
Home Delivery Service
Mobile Home Dealer
Movie Theater
Online Book Store
Pawn Shop
Portable Lunch Wagon
Quick Oil Change
Shoe Repair
Shopping Mall
Steakhouse
Tractor Dealer
Warehouse Club

The family of retail sector expanded in 2002. Two 1997 NAICS industries were split to accommodate the changing nature of retail. Department stores divided into department and discount stores. Electronic shopping and mail-order houses were spun into three new industries: electronic shopping, electronic auctions, and mail-order houses. While these changes created new industries within the retail sector, they did not bring establishments into the sector from other sectors.

## COVERAGE IN THE ECONOMIC CENSUS

Not all retail establishments are included in the Economic Census. Retail outlets on government property operated by that government are excluded from the Economic Census. For example, a gift shop at the Grand Canyon that is contracted by the National Park Services would be counted, but a gift shop in a state park run by the state employees would not. However, state run liquor stores are included. On the other hand, retail businesses on military installations are not counted—no matter who operated it.

Also not counted as separate establishments are those departments in a retail establishment that support a retail establishment, for example warehouses, repair centers, headquarters, and call centers if those are housed in the same facilities. If these auxiliary activities occur in an establishment at a different physical location, it will be counted in the sector reflecting its own activity—such as Transportation and Warehousing for the warehouse mentioned above.

Also if an activity is not owned by the establishment, but is leasing space in the business to provide a service (a relationship referred to as backfilling), it is counted as a separate business. An example of this would be a coffee bar in a bookstore or an auto repair service in a gasoline station.

Retail operations on a farm selling products grown on the farm are not included. This is due to the fact that the revenue from these sales is not considered to be the major source of income for the farm—production of agricultural goods is a farm's major income source. However, farm income generated by a farm's retail activity is counted in the Agriculture Census.

Retail sales occurring in the underground economy are not counted because they cannot be identified. The sale of street drugs is an example of something that would not be counted.

## DATA AVAILABILITY

Data from the retail portion of the Economic Census are available in printed, printable (PDF), and electronic data files. The only printed retail reports are those data found in the *Advance, Bridge, Outlying Area,* and *Minority- and Women-Owned Business* reports. Any reports that were printed in earlier censuses, such as the Geographic Area Series, are available as printable (PDF) documents. These reports contain most of the commonly used data.

The CD-ROMs include the same data as the PDF with the addition of data at the ZIP code level. American FactFinder only has the data from volume 1 of the 1997 CD-ROM. It does not have the SIC code, nonemployers, or ZIP code data. All 2002 data are on American FactFinder.

The Census Bureau also provides HTML-formatted tables and data files of the core items in comma-delimitated and dBase formats on the Web page for retail trade. This means there is no need to use the American FactFinder or CD-ROMs in order to look up a few core numbers.

None of the reports on retail trade contains rankings or derived measures such as sales per employee. Unlike earlier economic censuses, tables incorporating ratios or rankings based on the published numbers are not included in the reports from this census. The reason for this is that users can easily derive these measures from the data that are available on the Internet and CD-ROM.

### Retail Trade Reports from the Economic Census

The Economic Census retail trade sector (NAICS 44–45) reports include a geographic and subject series. Reports in both of these series show the four core statistics: number of establishments, employees, payroll, and sales. These figures are repeated for each industry.

The largest part of the retail data is found in the Geographic Area Series. A separate report is issued for the United States, each state, and the District of Columbia. Each report contains definitions and industry statistics for establishments with employees. These include number of establishments, employees, payroll, sales, and data-quality entries. Each state report presents the basic data items by industry for the state, metropolitan area, county, and each place with 2,500 inhabitants or more. The geographic detail has statistics in geographic areas for counties and places with

350 or more retail establishments. The pre-1997 criterion was 500 or more establishments.

Other reports include merchandise line sales; establishment and firm size by employees and sales; concentration by larger firms; legal forms of organization; floor space by department, convenience, superstore, and grocery stores; and class of customer by industry.

Data for retail establishments with no paid employees are published in the separate *Nonemployer Statistics* report. While this report covers all sectors, it should be remembered when looking for retail trade data because nearly two-thirds of all retail establishments in the country had no employees during 1997. Nonemployer statistics in retail trade are reported for Metropolitan Statistical Areas, each county, each state, the District of Columbia, and the United States.

The ZIP Code Statistics Series includes statistics on sales, annual payroll, and number of employees. Also included for each five-digit ZIP Code are data by retail industry on number of establishments in various sales-size and employment-size groups. Since establishment counts are not considered to be a disclosure of confidential information, data are presented for every kind of business with one or more establishments within a ZIP Code.

The *Merchandise Lines Sales* reveals what kinds of stores sell lines of merchandise and in what quantities. For example, Figure 11.1 shows the different kinds of merchandise sold by radio and television stores. The second table of the report includes what other kinds of stores sell televisions in an area. So, if you were interested in learning where to distribute telephone equipment, you would find that television and electronics stores sold nearly $3 billion worth of telephone equipment. You would also note that these stores accounted for 16.4 percent of all telephone sales and that telephone sales accounted for about 9 percent of all sales in these stores. Clearly, you would want to think about distributing your equipment through these stores. While the viewable (PDF) reports show only national information; data for states, metropolitan areas, and the nonmetropolitan portion of each state are available on the Internet and CD-ROM databases.

*Establishment and Firm Size (including Legal Form of Organization)* presents national data on the number of establishments, sales, payroll, and employment. These industry totals are cross-tabulated by size of establishment, size of firm, and legal form of organization. Establishment data are presented by sales size

and employment size; data for firms, by sales size (including concentration by largest firms), by employment size, and by number of establishments operated. Use of this data allows policy makers to see which industries are more monopolistic than others or for pension fund managers to target those industries with a higher concentration of employees instead of those industries with lower employee counts.

The *Miscellaneous Subjects* presents specialized data at the national and state level on floor space by department, convenience, superstore, and grocery stores and class of customer by all retailers. Class of customers are listed as percentage of sales to general public, to builders and contractors, to retailers and wholesalers for resale, institutional, industrial, commercial, farm users (for use in farm production), and government; and others.

Due to the change in industrial classification in 1997, statistics from the previous census are no longer shown in Geographic Area Series reports. In order to make historical comparison between retail industries you can use two reports: *Bridge Between the NAICS and SIC* and the *Comparative Statistics*. It's best if you use the Web version; they are laid out logically and allow for linking between the two systems. Using both of these reports together is important because most 1997 Economic Census reports show data by NAICS industries, but the *Comparative Statistics* report uses SIC industries. The Bridge report provides the information needed to compare the two systems at the national level. See chapter 5 for more details about these reports.

## Additional Retail Information in Other Parts of the Census

Other retail data reported in the 1997 Economic Census generally uses SIC definitions (SIC 52–59), so be careful when comparing data from these other reports with data taken from the *Retail Trade Sector* reports. Some industry definitions changed again in 2002, so it is critical that you use the Bridge Tables to determine the compatibility of an industry between different Economic Censuses.

Because of the major changes that occurred with the introduction of the NAICS, it is also very important to avoid comparing the SIC retail division with the NAICS retail sector. Nationally, it has been estimated that ten percent of the SIC Retail Trade division consisted of food service establishments that moved

Figure 11.1
Merchandise Lines Sales Sample

| Merchandise line (ML) | Merchandise line (ML) | Merchandise sold in Radio, Television, and other Electronics Store (NAICS 443112) | | | | |
|---|---|---|---|---|---|---|
| | | Number of establishments | Sales of estabs w/line ($1000) | Sales ($1,000) | Ln sls as % of sls of est w/ln | Ln sls as% of tot sls of NAICS |
| 0000 | All merchandise lines | 18,305 | X | 32,168,084 | X | 100.0 |
| 0330 | Audio equipment & musical instruments & supplies (including radios, stereos, CDs, sheet music | 13,819 | 29,282,056 | 8,453,091 | 28.9 | 26.3 |
| 0331 | Audio equip, components, parts, & access (incl radios, stereos, tape recorders & players, CD p | 13,806 | 29,279,654 | 7,192,535 | 24.6 | 22.4 |
| 0370 | Computer hardware, software, & supplies | 9,556 | 25,067,192 | 6,531,370 | 26.1 | 20.3 |
| 0320 | Televisions, video recorders, video cameras, video tapes, etc (including parts & accessories) | 5,528 | 23,916,201 | 6,530,989 | 27.3 | 20.3 |
| 0375 | Computer & peripheral equipment | 9,540 | 25,048,543 | 5,749,742 | 23.0 | 17.9 |
| 0321 | Televisions | 5,377 | 23,815,480 | 3,904,263 | 16.4 | 12.1 |
| 0850 | All other merchandise | 13,035 | 18,706,749 | 3,846,525 | 20.6 | 12.0 |
| 0865 | Telephones | 12,508 | 17,878,571 | 2,931,131 | 16.4 | 9.1 |
| 0300 | Major household appliances (including vacuum cleaners, refrigerators, dehumidifiers, dishwash | 2,126 | 20,404,716 | 2,543,537 | 12.5 | 7.9 |
| 0322 | Video tape recorders & cameras (including video laser disc players) | 4,070 | 22,797,298 | 2,338,658 | 10.3 | 7.3 |
| 9900 | Nonmerchandise receipts, excluding sales & other taxes | 12,886 | 26,578,577 | 1,981,579 | 7.5 | 6.2 |
| 9810 | All other merchandise | 9,671 | 20,679,616 | 1,705,684 | 8.2 | 5.3 |
| 0301 | Kitchen appliances, parts, & accessories (including refrigerators, freezers, dishwashers, microw | 1,900 | 20,043,325 | 1,548,193 | 7.7 | 4.8 |
| 0335 | Records, tapes, & compact discs | 1,701 | 19,436,747 | 1,073,287 | 5.5 | 3.3 |

out of this NAICS sector and six percent of wholesale sales moved into it. Along with all the other changes in retail it's best to use the Bridge Tables at the desegregated areas. It is also important to note that the Bridge Tables compare the SIC and NAICS industries at a national level. The further that you go in looking at small geographic areas, the less reliable the national trends are. The 2002 Bridge Tables are issued to the state level.

As part of the Business Expenditures Survey (BES) the *Business Expenses* report includes national data on the retail sector. This report includes tables giving detailed operating expenses between census years. Items covered are employer costs for programs required by law; payroll including all salaries, wages, commissions, bonuses, and allowances for vacation, holiday, and paid sick leave; employer costs for other fringe benefits; contract labor; depreciation charges; taxes; lease and rental payments; cost of office supplies, stationery, and postage; cost of communication services; cost of fuels and electricity; cost of other utilities; purchases of containers, wrapping, packing, and selling supplies; legal services from other firms; accounting services from other firms; data processing and other computer-related services; cost of repair services; and all other operating expenses, such as inventory storage and shipping costs, insurance expense (nonemployee), uninsured casualty losses, and bad debt.

The outlying areas of Puerto Rico, Guam, U.S. Virgin Islands, and Northern Marina Islands (NMI) also have retail data presented in the Economic Census. Puerto Rico has the greatest level of detail with reports covering merchandise lines and kinds of business by merchandise lines. The geographic reports have statistics comparing the same detail as mainland reports with the additional tables on franchise holders and mall/shopping center location data. Puerto Rico data can also be downloaded from the Web site. Guam, U.S. Virgin Islands, and Northern Marina Islands have data by industry and kind of business, legal form of organization, sales and receipts size, employment size, and by industry groups and municipalities/election districts. Northern Mariana Islands includes a table of distribution of establishments by citizenship status of the owner. Guam and U.S. Virgin Islands have additional information on the hotel and motel industry. The nonemployer statistics are not available for the outlying areas.

The *Survey of Business Owners* has retail information down to the industry group level (three-digit level in SICs and four-digit level in NAICS). Geographic coverage goes all the way from the nation down to places of 2,500 inhabitants or more in size. Be aware that in order to maintain confidentiality, the smaller geographic areas have less subject detail than the larger areas. Even though both the 1997 and 1992 *Minority- and Women-Owned Business* reports show data based on SIC industries, other changes make comparisons between these years difficult. While the 2002 survey keeps these other issues the same, it reports the data based on the 2002 version of NAICS.

## Using the Retail Data from the Economic Census

The problem with using industry sector numbers is that it is easy to forget that the retail industry reported on in the 1992 Economic Census, generally, is not the same industry starting with the 1997 Economic Census. This may lead to confusion to anyone using the retail trade numbers. When using time series data, it is very important to read the footnotes to the data in order to see how the break in the industry definitions is being handled. Also include any comments in your report when you create a time series.

Another pitfall to watch for is whether the data include nonemployer statistics or not. For example there are 1,177 retail establishments generating $1,056,976,000 in Yuma MSA; of those, 721 of them are nonemployers, however, the other employers provide $1,035,665,000 of the income. Additionally, the importance of nonemployer businesses varies greatly with the specific industry.

Choosing between the different data distribution methods depends on your needs. If you need just a few data items, the PDF reports are often ideal. However, if you want to compare among industries or geographic locations, getting spreadsheet files from the HTML drill-down tables or American FactFinder may be best. To search for a variety of data within the retail sector, the American FactFinder and the CD-ROM offer tools to get what you want. If you are searching for the older, ZIP code, merchandise line data; searching across core state data; or wishing to customize a table, use the CD-ROM. Please remember that you can use any of the more sophisticated access methods for a less sophisticated need. For example, if you are looking for just a few establishment counts, you can use any of the other access methods, but they may take longer than simply looking up the data in the PDF report.

## HOW OTHERS USE THE ECONOMIC CENSUS RETAIL TRADE DATA

There are probably as many different uses of the retail trade data as there are users. Here are just a few examples of how some data users have worked with these data.

### Government

The concentration ratios at the national level show if a few companies dominate a particular retail industry. Agencies use this data along with other factors when looking at merger and acquisition decisions according to the Hart-Scott-Rodino Antitrust Improvements Act of 1976. National policy makers can also see which retail industries are being hit by federally mandated programs and taxes using the *Business Expense Survey.*

Since states are always comparing themselves to the other states, they can use the various retail trade reports to get some key standardized information to use in these comparisons. For example, a state economic development agency might map the concentration of automobile dealerships within its region using data from the industry report or the geographic area reports along with GIS software and the FIPS codes available in the CD-ROM or American FactFinder.

When setting up local economic development programs targeted towards Asians, local governments can use the minority-owner data to identify other localities having large proportions of Asian-owned businesses. Then they can look at those other localities for possible examples of what types of programs have worked and which have not.

### Business

Time and convenience are major factors related to shifting spending habits. Lately, people have less time, so they shop on the Internet and closer to home. What does this mean for retailers? By looking at the comparative statistics report you can see that the direct sales had increased 49.2 percent between 1992 and 1997. E-commerce may not be the only reason for the increase; however, this number proves that this industry is growing. Direct sales were divided for 2002 among electronic sales, electronic auctions, and direct-mail houses. So they would have to be added back together in order to extend this time series.

You can also use the CD-ROM or American FactFinder to calculate the location of retail outlets of toy stores by geography and then plot it against the population data of families with young children from the Census of Population. This would allow you to see if there is either an untapped market where you would want to open a new toy store or an excess of toy stores that might be saturating a market.

A major food store chain uses retail trade data from the census as the basis for estimating the total weekly food store sales in the trade area for each of its stores—estimates that allow it to calculate its market share and other measures of performance for each existing store and support evaluations of prospective sites for new stores. Since each store's trade area is defined in terms of census tracts and blocks, areas too small for retail trade statistics to be available, the chain calculates per capita weekly food store sales from retail census data and population estimates for counties, then multiplies this per capita amount by the estimated population of the target trade area to estimate potential food store sales. When the *Monthly Retail Trade* is released they adjust the per capita weekly spending to reflect national changes in food store sales.

An entrepreneur hoping to market an edible stirring straw for mixed drinks looked to the retail trade, and food and accommodation census data for information about his potential customers, including liquor stores, hotels, and restaurants. Using the merchandise line sales data he was able to identify other potential markets for the straw.

The publisher of *Television News,* a magazine designed to be given away free at retail stores, wanted to know the number of retail stores by ZIP Code in order to design sales territories. The ZIP Code data on CD-ROM proved especially useful, since they differentiated stores by sales and employment size. The publisher's sales people had found that owners of small stores were more willing to listen to their pitch than were owners of large stores. Therefore, by combining the information about the preference towards small stores with the data on their locations from the Economic Census, the publisher was able to set more realistic sales territories.

A manufacturer of automobile parts and supplies, who had previously marketed his products primarily through new and used car dealers, was impressed by figures from the *Merchandise Line Sales* subject report, which showed that automobile supply stores, gas stations, and department stores sell far more automobile parts and supplies than do car dealers. Using data from the Geographic Area Series on the geographic distribution of these stores, he developed a new marketing program and increased his sales.

Maria wants to start a bodega on a city corner. In designing her store, she wants to know the common mix of floor space usage in convenience stores, which she finds in the *Miscellaneous Subjects* report. Then, she uses the *Merchandise Line Sales* report to find the product mix that sells in a convenience store. Later on, to see if her store's sales are high or low compared to the average in that city she does a market analysis by looking at how many convenience stores there are in her city and how much they make per store. She also looks at average payroll per employee to see if what she is paying her employees is close to the normal amount for convenience stores in her city.

## CURRENT DATA

*Current Business Report—Monthly Retail Trade*
Print: C 3.138/3
URL: http://www.census.gov/econ/www/re0400.html

This report provides data on the dollar value of retail sales and sales for selected establishments as well as data on the value of end-of-month inventories for some retail firms. It's released roughly six weeks after the close of the reference month. Data for census regions and divisions, and selected states, metropolitan areas and cities were dropped for budget reasons after the publication of the 1996 results.

*Current Business Reports—Annual Benchmark Report for Retail Trade*
Print: C 3.138/3–8:
URL: http://www.census.gov/svsd/www/artstbl.html

Collected annually since 1951 and released in spring, this survey currently samples 22,000 retailers and then is projected nationally. It covers retail companies with one or more establishments that sell merchandise and associated services to final consumers. The data reflect the dollar value of retail sales, sales taxes collected, inventories, method-of-inventory valuation, cost of purchases, per capita sales, gross margins, monthly and year-end inventories, inventory/sales ratios, merchandise purchased, monthly and gross margin/sales ratios, and accounts receivable balances for the United States by kind of business. It also republishes a ten-year time series of monthly data.

*Current Business Reports—Advance Monthly Retail Sales*
Print: C 3.138/4:
URL: http://www.census.gov/svsd/www/advtable.html

Released roughly nine days after the close of each month, this report provides an early look at monthly retail sales and trends by kind-of-business groups at the national level. The figures are based on a subsample of the Census Bureau's retail trade survey sample. The series provides the following: advance estimates for the current month, preliminary or final estimates for the two preceding months, and final estimates for the same two months a year earlier. Both unadjusted figures and data adjusted for seasonal variation are included.

*E-Stats*
URL: http://www.census.gov/eos/www/ebusiness614.htm

Retail is only one sector covered in this survey, which is an attempt to measure the impacts of e-commerce on business. It includes sales of goods and services over the Internet, an extranet, Electronic Data Interchange (EDI), or other online system. Payment for sales covered by this survey may or may not be made online. The data given is also reflected in the *Monthly Retail Trade* surveys.

## Other Related Reports

(See chapter 1 for descriptions of these reports)

*Annual Capital Expenditures*
*Country Business Patterns*
*Employment Situation*
*Quarterly Financial Report for Manufacturing, Mining, and Trade Corporations*
*Statistics of Income Bulletin*

### NAICS–SIC Comparison

Table 11.1 shows the relationships between the SIC, NAICS 1997, and NAICS 2002 breakdowns of the retail sector into specific industries.

## ANSWERS: IS IT RETAIL?

Auction House—Yes, 453998 All other miscellaneous store retailers (except tobacco stores). This industry also includes establishments primarily engaged in retailing a general line of new and used merchandise on an auction basis.

Bakery Outlet Store—Yes, 445291 Baked goods stores. This U.S. industry comprises establishments primarily engaged in retailing baked goods not for immediate consumption and not made on the premises. However, if the outlet is attached to the factory, it is not retail.

Butcher Shop—Yes, 445210 Meat markets. This industry comprises establishments primarily engaged in retailing fresh, frozen, or cured meats and poultry. Delicatessen-type establishments primarily engaged in retailing fresh meat are included in this industry.

Farm Stand—Yes and No, vegetable and fruit stands are in retail, but if the farm stand is part of an operating farm/ranch, the data are not included in the Economic Census, but are included in the Agricultural Census.

Home Delivery Service—No, 492210 Local messengers and local delivery. The industry is in the transporting and warehousing sector; it is comprised of establishments primarily engaged in providing local messenger and delivery services of small items within a single metropolitan or within an urban center. However, if the delivery service is run by the retail outlet, they would be included under that establishment data in the census.

Mobile Home Dealer—Yes, 453930 Manufactured (mobile) home dealers. This industry is comprised of establishments primarily engaged in retailing new and/or used manufactured homes (i.e., mobile homes), parts, and equipment.

Movie Theater—No, 512131 Motion picture theaters (except drive-ins). The Information sector is comprised of establishments primarily engaged in operating motion picture theaters (except drive-ins) and/or exhibiting motion pictures or videos at film festivals, and so forth.

Online Book Store—Yes, 454111 Electronic shopping. This industry is comprised of establishments primarily engaged in retailing all types of merchandise by electronic media, such as interactive television or computer. To find out how many books are sold online, use the *Merchandise Line* report. Regular physical bookstores are at 451211 Book Stores.

Pawn Shop—No, 522298 All other nondepository credit intermediation. This industry in the Finance sector is comprised of establishments primarily engaged in providing nondepository credit (except credit card issuing, sales financing, consumer lending, real estate credit, international trade financing, and secondary market financing). Examples of types of lending in this industry are: short-term inventory credit, agricultural lending (except real estate and sales financing), and consumer cash lending secured by personal property (pawnshop).

Portable Lunch Wagon—No, 722330 Mobile food services. This industry in the food service and accommodation sectors is comprised of establishments primarily engaged in preparing and serving meals and snacks for immediate consumption from motorized vehicles or nonmotorized carts. The establishment is the central location from which the caterer route is serviced, not each vehicle, or cart. Included in this industry are establishments primarily engaged in providing food services from vehicles, such as hot dog carts and ice cream trucks.

Quick Oil Change Business—No, 811191 Automotive oil change and lubrication shops. This U.S. industry in the repair and maintenance sector is comprised of establishments primarily engaged in changing motor oil and lubricating the chassis of automotive vehicles, such as passenger cars, trucks, and vans.

## ANSWERS: IS IT RETAIL? (CONTINUED)

Shoe Repair Shop—No, 81143 Footwear and leather goods repair shops. This industry from the repair and maintenance sector includes establishments primarily engaged in repairing footwear and/or repairing other leather or leather-like goods, such as handbags and briefcases, without retailing new footwear and leather or leather-like goods.

Shopping Mall—No, 531120 Lessors of nonresidential buildings (except miniwarehouses). This industry, which came from the real estate sector, is comprised of establishments primarily engaged in acting as lessors of buildings (except miniwarehouses and self-storage units) that are not used as residences or dwellings. Included in this industry are owner-lessors and establishments renting real estate and then acting as lessors in subleasing it to others. The establishments in this industry may manage the property themselves or have another establishment manage it for them.

Steakhouse—No, 722110 Full-service restaurants. This industry, now a part of the food service and accommodation sector, is comprised of establishments primarily engaged in providing food services to patrons who order and are served while seated (i.e. waiter/waitress service) and pay after eating. These establishments may provide this type of food services to patrons in combination with selling alcoholic beverages, providing takeout services, or presenting live, nontheatrical entertainment.

Tractor Dealer—No, 421830 Industrial machinery and equipment wholesalers. This wholesale industry is comprised of establishments primarily engaged in wholesaling specialized machinery, equipment, and related parts generally used in manufacturing, oil well, and warehousing activities.

Warehouse Club—Yes, 452910 Warehouse clubs and superstores. This industry is comprised of establishments known as warehouse clubs, superstores, or supercenters primarily engaged in retailing a general line of groceries in combination with general lines of new merchandise, such as apparel, furniture, and appliances.

Table 11.1
NAICS-SIC Comparison

| NAICS 1997 | NAICS 2002 | NAICSTEXT | COMP[a] | SIC | SICTEXT |
|---|---|---|---|---|---|
| 44-45 | | Retail Trade | | | |
| 441 | | Motor Vehicle and Parts Dealers | | | |
| 4411 | | Automobile Dealers | | | |
| 44111 | | New Car Dealers | E | 5511 | Motor Vehicle Dealers (New and Used) |
| 44112 | | Used Car Dealers | E | 5521 | Motor Vehicle Dealers (Used Only) |
| 4412 | | Other Motor Vehicle Dealers | | | |
| 44121 | | Recreational Vehicle Dealers | E | 5561 | Recreational Vehicle Dealers |
| 44122 | | Motorcycle, Boat, and Other Motor Vehicle Dealers | | | |
| 441221 | | Motorcycle Dealers | E | 5571 | Motorcycle Dealers |
| 441222 | | Boat Dealers | E | 5551 | Boat Dealers |
| 441229 | | All Other Motor Vehicle Dealers | E | 5599 | Automotive Dealers, NEC |
| 4413 | | Automotive Parts, Accessories, and Tire Stores | | | |
| 44131 | | Automotive Parts and Accessories Stores | N | 5013 | Motor Vehicle Supplies and New Parts (Wholesale) (auto parts sold via retail method) |
| 44131 | | Automotive Parts and Accessories Stores | | 5731 | Radio, Television, and Consumer Electronics Stores (automobile radios) |
| 44131 | | Automotive Parts and Accessories Stores | | 5015 | Motor Vehicle Parts, Used (sold via retail method) |
| 44131 | | Automotive Parts and Accessories Stores | | 5531 | Auto and Home Supply Stores (auto supply stores) |
| 44132 | | Tire Dealers | N | 5014 | Tires and Tubes (Wholesale) (tires and tubes sold via retail method) |
| 44132 | | Tire Dealers | | 5531 | Auto and Home Supply Stores (tires and tubes) |
| 442 | | Furniture and Home Furnishings Stores | | | |
| 4421 | | Furniture Stores | | | |
| 44211 | | Furniture Stores | R | 5021 | Furniture (Wholesale) (sold via the retail method) |
| 44211 | | Furniture Stores | | 5712 | Furniture Stores (except custom furniture and cabinets) |
| 4422 | | Home Furnishings Stores | | | |

Table 11.1 (Continued)
NAICS-SIC Comparison

| NAICS 1997 | NAICS 2002 | NAICSTEXT | COMP[a] | SIC | SICTEXT |
|---|---|---|---|---|---|
| 44221 | | Floor Covering Stores | R | 5023 | Homefurnishings (Wholesale) (floor covering sold via retail method) |
| 44221 | | Floor Covering Stores | | 5713 | Floor Coverings Stores |
| 44229 | | Other Home Furnishings Stores | | | |
| 442291 | | Window Treatment Stores | N | 5714 | Drapery, Curtain, and Upholstery Stores (drapery and curtain stores) |
| 442291 | | Window Treatment Stores | | 5719 | Miscellaneous Homefurnishings Stores (blinds and shades) |
| 442299 | | All Other Home Furnishings Stores | R | 5719 | Miscellaneous Homefurnishings Stores (except pottery and crafts made and sold on site and window furnishings) |
| 442299 | | All Other Home Furnishings Stores | | 7699 | Repair Shops and Related Services, NEC (custom picture framing) |
| 443 | | Electronics and Appliance Stores | | | |
| 4431 | | Electronics and Appliance Stores | | | |
| 44311 | | Appliance, Television, and Other Electronics Stores | | | |
| 443111 | | Household Appliance Stores | R | 5722 | Household Appliance Stores |
| 443111 | | Household Appliance Stores | | 7623 | Refrigeration and Air-Conditioning Service and Repair Shops (retailing new refrigerators from a storefront and repairing refrigerators) |
| 443111 | | Household Appliance Stores | | 7629 | Electrical and Electronic Repair Shops, NEC (retailing new electrical and electronic appliances from a storefront and repairing appliances) |
| 443112 | | Radio, Television, and Other Electronics Stores | R | 5731 | Radio, Television, and Consumer Electronics Stores (except auto radios) |
| 443112 | | Radio, Television, and Other Electronics Stores | | 5999 | Miscellaneous Retail Stores, NEC (typewriters and telephones) |
| 443112 | | Radio, Television, and Other Electronics Stores | | 7622 | Radio and Television Repair Shops (retailing new radios and TVs from a storefront and repairing |

Table 11.1 (Continued)
NAICS-SIC Comparison

| NAICS 1997 | NAICS 2002 | NAICSTEXT | COMP[a] | SIC | SICTEXT |
|---|---|---|---|---|---|
| | | | | | radios and TVs) |
| 44312 | | Computer and Software Stores | R | 5045 | Computers and Computer Peripheral Equipment and Software (sold via retail method) |
| 44312 | | Computer and Software Stores | | 5734 | Computer and Computer Software Stores |
| 44312 | | Computer and Software Stores | | 7378 | Computer Maintenance and Repair (retailing new computers from a storefront and repairing computers) |
| 44313 | | Camera and Photographic Supplies Stores | E | 5946 | Camera and Photographic Supply Stores |
| 444 | | Building Material and Garden Equipment and Supplies Dealers | | | |
| 4441 | | Building Material and Supplies Dealers | | | |
| 44411 | | Home Centers | N | 5211 | Lumber and Other Building Materials Dealers (home center stores) |
| 44412 | | Paint and Wallpaper Stores | R | 5231 | Paint, Glass, and Wallpaper Stores (paint and wallpaper) |
| 44413 | | Hardware Stores | R | 5072 | Hardware (sold via retail method) |
| 44413 | | Hardware Stores | | 5251 | Hardware Stores |
| 44419 | | Other Building Material Dealers | R | 5032 | Brick, Stone, and Related Construction Materials (Wholesale) (sold via retail method) |
| 44419 | | Other Building Material Dealers | | 5039 | Construction Materials, NEC (Wholesale) (glass, sold via retail method) |
| 44419 | | Other Building Material Dealers | | 5063 | Electrical Apparatus and Equipment, Wiring Supplies, and Construction Materials (Wholesale) (sold via retail method) |
| 44419 | | Other Building Material Dealers | | 5074 | Plumbing and Heating Equipment and Supplies (Hydronics, sold via retail method) |
| 44419 | | Other Building Material Dealers | | 5211 | Lumber and Other Building Materials Dealers (except home centers) |
| 44419 | | Other Building Material Dealers | | 5231 | Paint, Glass, and Wallpaper Stores (glass) |

Table 11.1 (Continued)
NAICS-SIC Comparison

| NAICS 1997 | NAICS 2002 | NAICSTEXT | COMP[a] | SIC | SICTEXT |
|---|---|---|---|---|---|
| 4442 | | Lawn and Garden Equipment and Supplies Stores | | | |
| 44421 | | Outdoor Power Equipment Stores | N | 5083 | Farm and Garden Machinery and Equipment (Wholesale) (sold via retail method) |
| 44421 | | Outdoor Power Equipment Stores | | 5261 | Retail Nurseries, Lawn and Garden Supply Stores (outdoor power equipment) |
| 44422 | | Nursery and Garden Centers | R | 5191 | Farm Supplies (sold via retail method) |
| 44422 | | Nursery and Garden Centers | | 5193 | Flowers, Nursery Stock, and Florists' Supplies (sold via retail method) |
| 44422 | | Nursery and Garden Centers | | 5261 | Retail Nurseries, Lawn and Garden Supply Stores (except outdoor power equipment) |
| 445 | | Food and Beverage Stores | | | |
| 4451 | | Grocery Stores | | | |
| 44511 | | Supermarkets and Other Grocery (except Convenience) Stores | N | 5411 | Grocery Stores (except convenience stores and grocery stores with substantial general merchandise) |
| 44512 | | Convenience Stores | N | 5411 | Grocery Stores (convenience stores without gas) |
| 4452 | | Specialty Food Stores | | | |
| 44521 | | Meat Markets | R | 5421 | Meat and Fish (Seafood) Markets, Including Freezer Provisioners (meat except freezer provisioners) |
| 44521 | | Meat Markets | | 5499 | Miscellaneous Food Stores (poultry and poultry products) |
| 44522 | | Fish and Seafood Markets | N | 5421 | Meat and Fish (Seafood) Markets, Including Freezer Provisioners (seafood) |
| 44523 | | Fruit and Vegetable Markets | E | 5431 | Fruit and Vegetable Markets |
| 44529 | | Other Specialty Food Stores | | | |
| 445291 | | Baked Goods Stores | R | 5461 | Retail Bakeries (selling only) |
| 445292 | | Confectionery and Nut Stores | E | 5441 | Candy, Nut and Confectionery Stores |

Table 11.1 (Continued)
NAICS-SIC Comparison

| NAICS 1997 | NAICS 2002 | NAICSTEXT | COMP[a] | SIC | SICTEXT |
|---|---|---|---|---|---|
| 445299 | | All Other Specialty Food Stores | R | 5499 | Miscellaneous Food Stores (except food supplements, poultry stores, and stores with food for immediate consumption) |
| 445299 | | All Other Specialty Food Stores | | 5451 | Dairy Products Stores |
| 4453 | | Beer, Wine, and Liquor Stores | | | |
| 44531 | | Beer, Wine, and Liquor Stores | E | 5921 | Liquor Stores |
| 446 | | Health and Personal Care Stores | | | |
| 4461 | | Health and Personal Care Stores | | | |
| 44611 | | Pharmacies and Drug Stores | E | 5912 | Drug Stores and Proprietary Stores |
| 44612 | | Cosmetics, Beauty Supplies, and Perfume Stores | N | 5087 | Service Establishment Equipment and Supplies (beauty and barber shop equipment and supplies sold via retail method) |
| 44612 | | Cosmetics, Beauty Supplies, and Perfume Stores | | 5999 | Miscellaneous Retail Stores, NEC (cosmetics and perfumes) |
| 44613 | | Optical Goods Stores | R | 5995 | Optical Goods Stores (except labs grinding prescription lenses) |
| 44619 | | Other Health and Personal Care Stores | | | |
| 446191 | | Food (Health) Supplement Stores | N | 5499 | Miscellaneous Food Stores (food supplements) |
| 446199 | | All Other Health and Personal Care Stores | N | 5047 | Medical, Dental, and Hospital Equipment and Supplies (sold via retail method) |
| 446199 | | All Other Health and Personal Care Stores | | 5999 | Miscellaneous Retail Stores, NEC (hearing aids and artificial limbs) |
| 447 | | Gasoline Stations | | | |
| 4471 | | Gasoline Stations | | | |
| 44711 | | Gasoline Stations with Convenience Stores | N | 5541 | Gasoline Service Station (gasoline station with convenience store) |
| 44711 | | Gasoline Stations with Convenience Stores | | 5411 | Grocery Stores (convenience store with gas) |
| 44719 | | Other Gasoline Stations | N | 5541 | Gasoline Service Station (gasoline station without convenience store) |

Table 11.1 (Continued)
NAICS-SIC Comparison

| NAICS 1997 | NAICS 2002 | NAICSTEXT | COMP[a] | SIC | SICTEXT |
|---|---|---|---|---|---|
| 448 | | Clothing and Clothing Accessories Stores | | | |
| 4481 | | Clothing Stores | | | |
| 44811 | | Men's Clothing Stores | R | 5611 | Men's and Boys' Clothing and Accessory Stores (clothing stores) |
| 44812 | | Women's Clothing Stores | E | 5621 | Women's Clothing Stores |
| 44813 | | Children's and Infants' Clothing Stores | E | 5641 | Children's and Infants' Wear Stores |
| 44814 | | Family Clothing Stores | E | 5651 | Family Clothing Stores |
| 44815 | | Clothing Accessories Stores | N | 5611 | Men's and Boys' Clothing and Accessory Stores (accessories) |
| 44815 | | Clothing Accessories Stores | | 5632 | Women's Accessory and Specialty Stores (accessories) |
| 44815 | | Clothing Accessories Stores | | 5699 | Miscellaneous Apparel and Accessory Stores (accessories) |
| 44819 | | Other Clothing Stores | R | 5699 | Miscellaneous Apparel and Accessory Stores (miscellaneous apparel) |
| 44819 | | Other Clothing Stores | | 5632 | Women's Accessory and Specialty Stores (specialty stores) |
| 4482 | | Shoe Stores | | | |
| 44821 | | Shoe Stores | E | 5661 | Shoe Stores |
| 4483 | | Jewelry, Luggage, and Leather Goods Stores | | | |
| 44831 | | Jewelry Stores | R | 5944 | Jewelry Stores |
| 44832 | | Luggage and Leather Goods Stores | E | 5948 | Luggage and Leather Goods Stores |
| 451 | | Sporting Goods, Hobby, Book, and Music Stores | | | |
| 4511 | | Sporting Goods, Hobby, and Musical Instrument Stores | | | |
| 45111 | | Sporting Goods Stores | R | 5941 | Sporting Goods Stores and Bicycle Shops |
| 45111 | | Sporting Goods Stores | | 7699 | Repair Shops and Related Services, NEC (retailing new bicycles from a storefront and repairing |

228

Table 11.1 (Continued)
NAICS-SIC Comparison

| NAICS 1997 | NAICS 2002 | NAICSTEXT | COMP[a] | SIC | SICTEXT |
|---|---|---|---|---|---|
| | | | | | bicycles) |
| 45112 | | Hobby, Toy, and Game Stores | E | 5945 | Hobby, Toy, and Game Stores |
| 45113 | | Sewing, Needlework, and Piece Goods Stores | R | 5714 | Drapery, Curtain, and Upholstery Stores (upholstery materials) |
| 45113 | | Sewing, Needlework, and Piece Goods Stores | | 5949 | Sewing, Needlework, and Piece Goods Stores |
| 45114 | | Musical Instrument and Supplies Stores | E | 5736 | Musical Instruments Stores |
| 4512 | | Book, Periodical, and Music Stores | | | |
| 45121 | | Book Stores and News Dealers | | | |
| 451211 | | Book Stores | E | 5942 | Book Stores |
| 451212 | | News Dealers and Newsstands | E | 5994 | News Dealers and Newsstands |
| 45122 | | Prerecorded Tape, Compact Disc, and Record Stores | E | 5735 | Record and Prerecorded Tape Stores |
| 452 | | General Merchandise Stores | | | |
| 4521 | | Department Stores | | | |
| 45211 | 452111 | Department Stores (except Discount Department Stores) | E | 5311 | Department Stores |
| 45211 | 452112 | Discount Department Stores | N | | New in 2002 |
| 4529 | | Other General Merchandise Stores | | | |
| 45291 | | Warehouse Clubs and Superstores | N | 5399 | Miscellaneous General Merchandise Stores (warehouse clubs and supermarket/general merchandise combination) |
| 45291 | | Warehouse Clubs and Superstores | | 5411 | Grocery Stores (grocery stores and supermarkets selling substantial amounts of nonfood items) |
| 45299 | | All Other General Merchandise Stores | R | 5399 | Miscellaneous General Merchandise Stores (except warehouse club and supermarket/general merchandise combination) |
| 45299 | | All Other General Merchandise Stores | | 5331 | Variety Stores |

Table 11.1 (Continued)
NAICS-SIC Comparison

| NAICS 1997 | NAICS 2002 | NAICSTEXT | COMPa | SIC | SICTEXT |
|---|---|---|---|---|---|
| 45299 | | All Other General Merchandise Stores | | 5531 | Auto and Home Supply Stores (other auto and home supply stores) |
| 453 | | Miscellaneous Store Retailers | | | |
| 4531 | | Florists | | | |
| 45311 | | Florists | E | 5992 | Florists |
| 4532 | | Office Supplies, Stationery, and Gift Stores | | | |
| 45321 | | Office Supplies and Stationery Stores | R | 5044 | Office Equipment (sold via retail method) |
| 45321 | | Office Supplies and Stationery Stores | | 5049 | Professional Equipment and Supplies, NEC (school supplies sold via retail method) |
| 45321 | | Office Supplies and Stationery Stores | | 5112 | Stationery and Office Supplies (sold via retail method) |
| 45321 | | Office Supplies and Stationery Stores | | 5943 | Stationery Stores |
| 45322 | | Gift, Novelty, and Souvenir Stores | E | 5947 | Gift, Novelty, and Souvenir Shops |
| 4533 | | Used Merchandise Stores | | | |
| 45331 | | Used Merchandise Stores | R | 5932 | Used Merchandise Stores (except pawn shops) |
| 4539 | | Other Miscellaneous Store Retailers | | | |
| 45391 | | Pet and Pet Supplies Stores | N | 5999 | Miscellaneous Retail Stores, NEC (pet and pet supplies) |
| 45392 | | Art Dealers | N | 5999 | Miscellaneous Retail Stores, NEC (art dealer) |
| 45393 | | Manufactured (Mobile) Home Dealers | E | 5271 | Mobile Home Dealers |
| 45399 | | All Other Miscellaneous Store Retailers | | | |
| 453991 | | Tobacco Stores | E | 5993 | Tobacco Stores and Stands |
| 453998 | | All Other Miscellaneous Store Retailers (except Tobacco Stores) | R | 5999 | Miscellaneous Retail Stores, NEC (except art, pet and pet supplies, hearing aids, artificial limbs, cosmetics, telephones, typewriters, personal appliances, and rough gems) |
| 454 | | Nonstore Retailers | | | |
| 4541 | | Electronic Shopping and Mail-Order Houses | | | |
| 45411 | 454111 | Electronic Shopping | E | 5961 | Catalog and Mail-Order Houses |

Table 11.1 (Continued)
NAICS-SIC Comparison

| NAICS 1997 | NAICS 2002 | NAICSTEXT | COMPᵃ | SIC | SICTEXT |
|---|---|---|---|---|---|
| 45411 | 454112 | Electronic Auctions | N | | New in 2002 |
| 45411 | 454113 | Mail-Order Houses | N | | New in 2002 |
| 4542 | | Vending Machine Operators | | | |
| | 45421 | Vending Machine Operators | E | 5962 | Automatic Merchandise Machine Operators |
| | 4543 | Direct Selling Establishments | | | |
| | 45431 | Fuel Dealers | | | |
| | 454311 | Heating Oil Dealers | R | 5171 | Petroleum Bulk Stations and Terminals (heating oil sold to final consumer) |
| | 454311 | Heating Oil Dealers | | 5983 | Fuel Oil Dealers |
| | 454312 | Liquefied Petroleum Gas (Bottled Gas) Dealers | R | 5171 | Petroleum Bulk Stations and Terminals (LP gas sold to final consumer) |
| | 454312 | Liquefied Petroleum Gas (Bottled Gas) Dealers | | 5984 | Liquefied Petroleum Gas (Bottled Gas) Dealers |
| | 454319 | Other Fuel Dealers | E | 5989 | Fuel Dealers, NEC |
| | 45439 | Other Direct Selling Establishments | R | 5421 | Meat and Fish (Seafood) Markets, Including Freezer Provisioners (freezer provisioners) |
| | 45439 | Other Direct Selling Establishments | | 5963 | Direct Selling Establishments (except mobile food services) |

ᵃE = Existing, N = New, R = Revised, L = Not applicable in the U.S.

# CHAPTER 12
# Remaining Sectors

We evaluate the services that anyone renders to us according to the value he puts on them, not according to the value they have for us.
—*Friedrich Nietzsche (1844–1900),* Human, All-Too-Human, *"Man Alone With Himself," aphorism 533, "Evaluation of Services Rendered," (1878)*

1. Mining
    A. Geographic Area Reports
    B. Industry and Subject Reports
2. Utilities
    A. Coverage
    B. Geographic Area Series
    C. Industry and Subject Series
3. Construction
    A. Construction Sector Reports
4. Information
5. Financial and Real Estate Services
    A. Finance and Insurance
    B. Real Estate and Rental and Leasing
6. Management of Companies and Enterprises
7. Service Sectors
    A. Sector Definitions and Coverage
    B. Federal Income Tax Status
    C. Miscellaneous Subjects Reports
8. Auxiliaries, Excluding Corporate, Subsidiary, and Regional Managing Offices
9. SIC–NAICS Comparison

The remaining sectors of the Economic Census are, in many ways, like the manufacturing, wholesale, or retail sectors. But each one has its own unique features and limitations. Some of these differences relate to the data presented in the reports and others deal with coverage issues. Rather than spending many words repeating what has been said about the three sectors discussed in detail in the previous chapters, this chapter highlights the similarities and differences for each of the remaining sectors.

## MINING

Under NAICS, the Mining Sector (NAICS Sector 21) covers the extraction of naturally occurring materials from the earth. In addition to the actual extraction of these materials, it also includes closely related activities traditionally performed at the mine site or as part of the mining activity, such as crushing, screening for size, and washing the mined materials. This is essentially the same coverage as the SIC system's Mining Division.

The reports for this sector are closest in design and layout to those in the Manufacturing Sector. But, there are some key differences that are important to understand.

## Geographic Area Reports

As with the manufacturing sector, there are *Geographic Area* reports covering each of the states. (However, due to the small area and small number of establishments, Delaware and the District of Columbia are combined into a single report.) There is an additional geographic area report covering the offshore areas not associated with a specific state. The offshore areas associated with specific states (Alaska, California, Louisiana, and Texas) are reported in those specific geographic series reports.

The geographic detail shown in these reports is limited to the nation (in the U.S. report) and the states. There are no sub-state data available in this sector. Thus, you cannot find the number of mining establishments in a particular county.

These reports provide the same 11 common items as shown in the manufacturing geographic area reports (table 1) and the detailed operating statistics in the second table. They also have a table (third table) showing the number of establishments, employees, payroll, and value added data by the type of operation. The types of operations identified include underground mines, open-pit mines, and other types of mines (including well operations). These operation types are split between establishments with just mines or wells and those with preparation plants. There is also a category for separately operated preparation plants.

## Industry and Subject Reports

The *Industry* reports in this sector are essentially the same as the *Industry* reports in the manufacturing sector. It is useful to note that the mining sector has much more historical comparability than most other sectors. Therefore, it is common to see data for 1992 in the 1997 Economic Census reports.

The largest differences between the manufacturing and mining reports are that the only Subject Series reports for mining are the *Product Summary,* the *General Summary,* and the *Materials Consumed Summary.* Unlike manufacturing, there is no summary report showing the concentration of firms within a specific industry.

Additionally, there is a *Location of Mining* report showing the number of establishments by industry, employment size class, and state. This report is not available as a PDF file, but is available through American FactFinder and on CD-ROM.

As with the *Geographic Area* reports for this sector, the geographic detail is limited to the states and the nation.

## UTILITIES

The utilities sector (NAICS 22) includes establishments that provide electric power, natural gas, steam, water, and sewage removal services. Establishments involved in collecting, treating, and disposing waste materials (like household or commercial trash) are not classified as utilities, but are placed in NAICS subsector 562, Waste management and remediation services.

The electric power utility establishments are generally divided into three types:

• Electric power generation, which is further divided by the source of the electricity (i.e. hydroelectric,

fossil fuel, nuclear power, or other sources). The Economic Census divides these into sub-categories based on the portion of electricity generated from that source.
• Electric bulk power transmission and control—those establishments that operate the high-voltage transmission lines and transformer stations and those establishments controlling the characteristics (e.g. regulating voltage) of electricity in the transmission system.
• Electric power distribution—this includes establishments in several different, but related, activities. One set of these activities includes those establishments involved with operating the lower voltage distribution system of power lines, poles, meters, and wiring. Another set of establishments is involved with arranging the sale of electricity through power distribution systems operated by others.

Natural gas utilities are establishments involved in any aspect of getting gas from the well (after it has been extracted) to the final customer. They might do this by operating a gas distribution system or they could be a marketer buying gas from the well and selling it to a distribution system. They might also be a gas broker or agent arranging the sale of gas over a distribution system operated by another establishment. The Economic Census reports on several subcategories of this industry based on the establishment's specific activities.

Water, sewage, and steam systems are combined into one industry group. The water supply and irrigation systems industry involves all aspects of distributing water used for any purpose. These establishments might be treatment plants or they might operate pumping stations, aqueducts, or distribution mains. For agricultural uses of water, consult the *Farm & Ranch Irrigation Survey Census of Agriculture* from the USDA.

The sewage treatment facilities industry is made up of establishments involved in any or all aspects of treating sewage. These activities include operating the sewer systems (pipes), treating the sewage, or disposing the treated waste.

This industry group is rounded out by the steam and air-conditioning supply industry. The establishments in this industry primarily provide steam, heated air, or cooled air through a system of mains. Under the SIC System, this was part of the Transportation and Public Utilities division. Additionally, the industries within this group were structured differently.

## Coverage

The Economic Census covers all of the privately owned establishments within this sector. However, the establishments owned by governmental agencies are excluded. For example, a power plant owned by Consolidated Edison of New York would be counted, but if the same power plant were owned by the Town of Green Island's power department (a municipal agency) it would not be counted. To find more information about power plants go the Energy Information Administration from the Department of Energy's Web site for current data on plant production, operations, and markets.

The impact of this coverage issue can be significant. There are also municipally owned sewage treatment plants that are not covered in either report. For example, 1997 Economic Census *Geographic Areas* report for the nation indicated that there were 696 sewage treatment facilities in the entire country. However, in 1999 the New York State Department of Environmental Conservation reported that there were 609 wastewater treatment plants serving the general population in the state.

## Geographic Area Series

The industries included in this sector tend to have relatively few, but large, establishments in any one geographic area. Due to the small number of establishments and the need to maintain the confidentiality of the responding businesses, the smallest geographic areas reported in this sector are metropolitan areas. The data reported in the Geographic Area Series reports cover the same basic topics as those in the retail trade geographic area reports.

## Industry and Subject Series

The 2002 Economic Census contains an industry series for utilities for the first time. As in the other sectors, these reports provide details about the operations of each specific industry within the sector.

The Subject Series reports included in this sector are a *Revenue Lines* report, an *Establishment and Firm Size* report, and a *Miscellaneous Subjects* report. The *Revenue Lines* and *Establishment and Firm Size* reports are directly comparable with the *Commodity Line Sales* and *Establishment and Firm Size* reports from the Wholesale Trade Sector, except the Utilities Sector reports present data just of the nation as a whole.

The *Miscellaneous Subjects* report in the Utilities Sector contains four data tables. The first table provides data on the revenues received by class of customer (residential, commercial, industrial, etc.) for each of the three major industry groups of this sector within each of the states and the nation. The second table provides information about energy (electricity and natural gas) exported to Canada and Mexico for the nation as a whole. The third table shows the total cost nationally of electricity purchased by utilities to be resold to their customers.

Finally, the fourth table shows construction activities for the three major groups of utilities in each of the states and the nation. These construction activities are divided between capital expenditures and maintenance and repair expenditures. In each case, these reports show the total dollar amount (in thousands of dollars) and the percent spent for work done by the utilities' own employees. This represents the utilities' expenditures on construction.

## CONSTRUCTION

The NAICS Construction Sector (23) includes establishments primarily engaged in constructing buildings, highways, or utility systems. This work includes new construction, additions, alterations, or maintenance and repairs to existing facilities. This sector also includes establishments that prepare sites for new construction or subdividing land for sale as building sites.

While Canada, Mexico, and the United States were able to agree on what the construction sector was when NAICS 1997 was developed, they were not able to agree on how it should be broken down into specific industries in time to include those in the initial version of NAICS. Instead they agreed to let each of the three countries use their own breakdowns within the sector and to continue working on an agreement for NAICS 2002. Thus, the way establishments were distributed in the sector between the two NAICS versions differs. As a result, comparing data between the 1997 and 2002 Economic Censuses below the sector level needs to be done very carefully and with attention to the information included in the 2002 Economic Census Bridge Tables.

In 1997 this sector was divided into three subsectors: (1) building, developing, and general contracting; (2) heavy construction; and (3) special trade contractors. The 2002 version of NAICS also includes three sub-sectors, but this time they were: (1) construction of buildings, (2) heavy and civil engineering construction, and (3) specialty trade contractors. It is interesting to note that land subdivision was part of the building, developing, and general contracting sub-sector in 1997, but in 2002 it was part of the heavy and civil engineering sub-sector. There were other similar changes between the two NAICS versions.

## Construction Sector Reports

The reports in this sector include a Geographic Area Series, an Industry Series, and a Subject Series containing a geographic area summary and an industry summary. By and large these reports are very similar to the reports included in the manufacturing sector.

The *Geographic Area* reports include the standard tables shown in the Geographic Area Series in the other sectors. They also include information on the average number of construction workers during each quarter of the year. Since many construction companies, especially some specialty trade contractors and heavy construction companies serve large geographic areas, as shown in Figure 12.1, these reports also include information on the geographic location (states) of work being done by establishments based in the state being reported on. Finally, due to the more specialized nature of many construction establishments, there isn't a separate line sales report. Instead, this type of information is contained in tables 7 and 8 of each state's *Geographic Area* series report.

The *Area Summary* subject report includes several tables showing data for the nation and broken down by Census Bureau region. Often these tables, dealing with line sales and the detailed operating characteristics, contain more detailed information than the *Geographic Area* reports.

## INFORMATION

The NAICS Information Sector (51) contains establishments primarily involved in (1) producing and distributing information and cultural products (e.g., book and newspaper publishers or motion picture and video production), (2) providing means for communicating, distributing, or transmitting these products, data, or other messages (e.g., movie theaters, radio and television broadcasting, or telecommunications), and (3) processing data. In the transition from the SIC system to NAICS, this sector was created by taking publishing from the SIC Manufacturing division, telecommu-

nications and broadcasting from the Transportation, Communications, and Utilities (TCU) division, and various information-related activities (e.g., data processing, motion picture production, and libraries) from the Services division. In recognition of the increased importance of the Internet during the 1990s, several new industries were identified in the 2002 version of NAICS that had not been recognized in the 1997 version. Thus, care should be taken when comparing 1997 and 2002 Economic Census data for a number of industries in this sector.

It is important to note that many libraries and archives are excluded from the Economic Census because they are governmental agencies. Additionally, many businesses maintain libraries that are not separate establishments, so they are not counted in this sector, unless operated by an outside vendor.

Like most other sectors, the reports in this sector include a *Source of Receipts* report, an *Establishment and Firm Size* report, a *Summary* report in 1997, and a Geographic Area Series with data down to places within each state. The *Miscellaneous Subjects* report includes five tables. The first table shows, nationally and by state, the receipts establishments in each industry within this sector had from exporting goods and services to foreign countries. Table 2 provides national and state-specific data on the percent of receipts telecommunications and online information service establishments received from noncommercial customers and all other customers. Receipts by class of customer and the number of subscribers of cable and other program distribution services establishments are shown nationally and by state in table 3. Construction expenses, broken down into new construction expenses and maintenance and repair expenses, for broadcasting and telecommunications establishments are summarized by state and nationally in table 4. Library and archive revenues and operating expenses are shown by state in table 5.

Additionally, the 1997 Economic Census included Industry Series reports for the publishing industries in this sector, reflecting the same type of data as in the manufacturing sector's *Industry* reports. This happened because the questionnaires sent to these establishments contained the types of information needed for these reports since they had been in the SIC Manufacturing division. The 2002 reports will continue because all industry sectors will have Industry Series report.

Figure 12.1
Construction Work Location Sample Table

[Thousand dollars unless otherwise noted. This table presents selected statistics for establishments according to the geographic location of construction work. Data are not shown for those geographic locations in which construction work is relatively insignificant. For meaning of abbreviations and symbols, see introductory text. For explanation of terms, see Appendix A]

| Geographic location of construction work | Value of construction work | Relative standard error of estimate (percent) |
|---|---|---|
| Total............................................. | 12 566 710 | 2 |
| **ALABAMA** | | |
| Construction work done in Alabama........................ | 10 371 873 | 2 |
| Construction work done in Florida......................... | 455 569 | 9 |
| Construction work done in Georgia........................ | 517 716 | 3 |
| Construction work done in Kentucky....................... | °180 496 | 40 |
| Construction work done in Louisiana...................... | 75 318 | 3 |
| Construction work done in Mississippi..................... | 200 172 | 7 |
| Construction work done in North Carolina.................. | 99 742 | 6 |
| Construction work done in South Carolina.................. | 117 164 | 1 |
| Construction work done in Tennessee..................... | 245 471 | 3 |
| Construction work done in Texas......................... | 71 945 | 1 |

## FINANCIAL AND REAL ESTATE SERVICES

Under the SIC system these two NAICS sectors were the single Finance, Insurance, and Real Estate (F.I.R.E.) division. With the introduction of NAICS, two sectors were created—Finance and Insurance (NAICS sector 52) and Real Estate and Rental and Leasing (NAICS sector 53). These two sectors include most of the SIC F.I.R.E. division and pieces of the SIC Services and Transportation, Communications, and Utilities divisions.

## Finance and Insurance

The Finance and Insurance sector includes establishments primarily engaged in financial transactions (creating, liquidating, or changing the ownership of financial assets) and/or facilitating these types of transactions. These are the types of activities normally associated with banks (including the Federal Reserve System), security and commodity brokers and exchanges, insurance companies and brokers, and various financial vehicles (e.g., pension funds or real estate investment trusts). Notably, pawnshops moved from the SIC Retail Trade division to this sector.

There are two major coverage issues to note about this sector. The first is that while funds, trusts, and other financial vehicles are part of this sector, only real estate investment trusts (REITs) are included in the Economic Census. The other coverage issue is that data are presented only down to the metropolitan area level of geography.

The reports for this sector include a *Source of Revenue* report, *Establishment and Firm Size* report, a *Summary* report (in 1997, but not in 2002), and a Geographic Area Series that reports data for each of the states and metropolitan areas in the state. Additionally, there is a *Miscellaneous Subjects* report.

The first three tables in the *Miscellaneous Subjects* report deal with the insurance sub-sector showing (1) the number of licensed agents and brokers by state (total, full time, and part time), (2) national administrative expenses of insurance carriers, and (3) the benefits paid to policyholders by insurance carriers. The final table in this report shows the revenue from services exported out of the country by the banking and securities industries for the nation and selected states.

## Real Estate and Rental and Leasing

The Real Estate and Rental and Leasing Sector (53) includes establishments involved in renting, leasing, or allowing the use of real estate, equipment, or patents and trademarks. Establishments providing related services, such as managing real estate for others, arranging real estate transactions for others (brokers, etc.), or appraising real estate are also included here. In the transition from the SIC system to NAICS, title abstract offices and land sub-dividers and developers moved to other sectors. Patent owners and lessors, miniwarehouses, and most rental industries moved into this sector from various SIC divisions. Establishments primarily renting equipment with operators are not counted here, but are counted in different sectors depending on the type of services being provided.

This sector's reports include the standard Geographic Area Series, *Source of Receipts* and *Establishment and Firm Size* reports. The *Miscellaneous Subjects* report in this series contains seven tables. Table 1 shows the number of licensed real estate agents and brokers (total, full time, and part time) in the nation and by state. Table 2 shows the commissions and fees paid to co-brokerage companies nationally. Tables 3a, 3b, and 3c show construction expenditures by building lessors nationally and by state. Total construction expenditures and the percent of work done by their own employees are shown in table 3a, table 3b breaks down the expenditures by building type, and table 3c details the type of construction (e.g., new construction for rent or lease, and additions, alterations, or reconstruction). Table 4 shows the revenues for the industries in the rental and leasing sub-sector by class of client (i.e., individuals, government, and all other) for the nation and each state. Table 5 shows national figures for exported services within the rental and leasing sub-sector.

## MANAGEMENT OF COMPANIES AND ENTERPRISES

The establishments in NAICS Sector 55—Management of Companies and Enterprises—are either (1) establishments holding securities (or other forms of equity) of companies and enterprises for the purpose of influencing the management decisions of those companies (i.e., holding companies) or (2) corporate, subsidiary, or regional managing offices responsible for strategic administration, oversight, and management of other establishments of the same company or enterprise (i.e., headquarters). Under the SIC system, the establishments in this sector were either classified as holding companies in the F.I.R.E. division or auxiliaries scattered through the entire set of SIC divisions.

There are only two reports for this sector. One covers the holding companies and the other presents data on headquarters. Both of these reports show just the basic data items for the nation and each of the states. There are no data for any sub-state areas.

## SERVICE SECTORS

For the most part, the various service sectors defined in NAICS and covered by the Economic Censuses come from various parts of the SIC Services division. However, a number of SIC industries from other divisions have also been included. Additionally, many of the exact industry definitions changed with the implementation of NAICS.

All of these sectors have *Geographic Area* reports presenting data from the national level down to places. The CD-ROMs also contain data by ZIP Code for each of these sectors. *Source of Receipts* and *Establishment and Firm Size* reports are produced for all of these sectors. In 1997 *Summary* reports were also produced for all sectors. *Miscellaneous Subjects* reports are produced for all of these sectors except the Educational Services sector.

Because the reports for these sectors vary slightly from each other and from the retail and wholesale trade sectors, they are being described as a group. The first portion of this section describes how each sector is defined and any coverage issues affecting that sector. Then there is a brief discussion of the way the Census Bureau shows that many of these establishments are exempt from paying federal income taxes. Finally, there is a discussion of the *Miscellaneous Subject* reports in each sector.

### Sector Definitions and Coverage

The *Professional, Scientific, and Technical Services* sector includes all types of services requiring a high degree of expertise and training. The kinds of services included in this sector are legal, accounting, architectural, engineering, specialized design, custom computer services, consulting, research and development, advertising, photographic, translation, veterinary, and similar types of services. In 1997, landscape architec-

ture and veterinary services were excluded from the Economic Census. They are included in the 2002 Census. Due to the specialized and independent nature of many of the industries within this sector, it is important to take a look at the nonemployer data for any industry you are studying. (Overall, nonemployers accounted for 81 percent of all establishments and 12 percent of receipts in this sector in 1997.)

While it sounds like an odd combination of activities, the *Administrative and Support and Waste Management and Remediation Services* sector contains establishments that provide support for the day-to-day operations of other organizations. Examples of these services include telephone call centers, temporary help agencies, travel agencies, court reporting and stenotype services, convention and trade show organizers, waste collection services, and materials recovery facilities. Landscaping services were excluded in the 1997 Economic Census but are included in 2002.

The *Educational Services* sector includes establishments providing all types of instruction and training from elementary schools through colleges and universities, to trade schools, to automobile driving schools, and everything in between. While they are included within the sector, elementary and secondary schools; junior colleges; and colleges, universities, and professional schools are excluded from the Economic Censuses. This is another sector where the nonemployer statistics cannot be ignored since they account for 87 percent of the covered establishments and 16 percent of covered receipts.

The NAICS *Health Care and Social Assistance* sector includes establishments providing these kinds of services to individuals. The kinds of establishments covered by this sector include physicians' offices, family planning centers, medical laboratories, ambulance services, hospitals, nursing care facilities, community food services, temporary shelters, vocational rehabilitation services, and child day care services. Hospitals that are owned and operated by governmental agencies are included in the Economic Censuses.

Establishments involved with the production or promotion of live performances, etc. intended for public viewing; preserving and exhibiting historical, cultural, or educational objects and sites; or operating facilities or providing other services enabling patrons to participate in various recreational activities, hobbies, or leisure interests are all included in the *Arts, Entertainment, and Recreation* sector. Dance companies, sports teams and clubs, artists' managers and agents, independent writers, zoos, amusement and theme parks, and bowling centers are all examples of establishments that are included in this sector.

The *Accommodation and Food Services* sector includes all establishments providing customers with lodging and/or food for immediate consumption. Casino hotels are included in this sector, while casinos without hotels are included in the Arts, Entertainment, and Recreation sector.

The various repair and maintenance services; personal and laundry services; and religious, grantmaking, civic, professional, and similar organizations are included in the *Other Services* (except Public Administration) sector. Private households with employees are also included in this sector. Religious organizations, labor unions, political organizations, and private households are excluded from the Economic Census. Pet care services were excluded from the 1997 Economic Census, but included in 2002. Grantmaking foundations were first included in the 1997 Economic Census. Overall, 82 percent of the establishments and 21 percent of receipts in the industries within this sector that were covered by the 1997 Economic Census were accounted for by nonemployers. In some industries the importance of nonemployers is even greater.

## Federal Income Tax Status

There are many establishments in different industries within these sectors that are exempt from paying federal income taxes since they provide services that benefit members of the community who are in need and cannot afford to pay for these services. These establishments are designed to provide these services without making a profit, but are not run by any local, state, or federal agencies. Examples of these types of community service organizations include a health care clinic serving residents of a community with a high poverty rate at little or no cost to the patient, the American Red Cross, a child day care center sponsored by a community center, and a community theater.

Many data users are interested in the number and size of these tax-exempt organizations. In order to provide users with data on them, the Census Bureau has separated them out into different tables in the following sectors:

• Professional, Scientific, and Technical Services
• Educational Services

• Health Care and Social Assistance
• Arts, Entertainment, and Recreation
• Other Services

The 1997 Economic Census shows separate tables for taxable and tax-exempt establishments. The data for taxable establishments were reported for all geographic levels, but the tax-exempt establishment data were only reported for the nation, states, and metropolitan areas. Additionally, there were no tables showing the combined data for these two types of establishments.

The 2002 Economic Census again shows separate tables for the taxable and tax-exempt establishments. But, they are being reported for counties and places in addition to the higher geographic levels. Also, there are tables showing the totals for taxable and tax-exempt establishments combined.

## Miscellaneous Subjects Reports

Except for Educational Services, all of these sectors have *Miscellaneous Subjects* reports. As described below, the exact content of these reports varies by sector. Most of the tables shown in these reports provide data for each state and the nation. Other tables report only on the nation.

The *Professional, Scientific, and Technical Services* report shows data on the receipts from services exported from the United States by each of the states and a national total. It also shows the receipts by class of client for selected services. A number of tables in the report show data on the number of employees and payroll by occupation and the establishment's legal form of organization (corporation, partnership, etc.), usually for the nation and states.

The *Administrative and Support and Waste Management and Remediation Services* report includes data on exported services and the number of leased employees by industry. (Leased employees differ from temporary agency employees due to the longer nature of the placement and the greater involvement in the hiring decision by the establishment where the employee will be working.) Several tables provide data on the fees received from different client classes that are appropriate to different portions of this sector.

The *Miscellaneous Subjects* report in the *Health Care and Social Assistance* sector focuses on the occupation and legal form of organization for various types of health care facilities from offices of physicians to medical and diagnostic laboratories. These tables are limited to firms that must pay federal income taxes. A similar table is also presented for tax-exempt outpatient care centers. There is also a table showing transferred contributions for tax-exempt firms within the social assistance sub-sector.

There are only two tables in the *Arts, Entertainment, and Recreation* report. The first provides data on exported services by state and for the nation as a whole. The second provides information on other sources of receipts (royalties, etc.) for spectator sports by state and for the nation as a whole.

The *Accommodation and Food services* sector report has a number of tables dealing with various aspects of food services. All of these show data for the nation and each state. The topics include such items as the average cost per meal, seating capacity, sales by time of day, and menu type (cuisine). There are also two tables looking at the accommodation portion of this sector. One deals with the number of guestrooms, the other presents information about guestroom size.

The *Miscellaneous Subjects* report for the Other Services sector shows data on exported services and receipts by class of client for selected industries within this sector. There is also a table showing receipts from labor charges and parts installed for repairs and maintenance services. Finally, there is a table showing transferred contributions for tax-exempt grantmaking and similar organizations.

## AUXILIARIES, EXCLUDING CORPORATE, SUBSIDIARY, AND REGIONAL MANAGING OFFICES

Auxiliary establishments are establishments primarily serving other establishments of the same enterprise. For example, these can be corporate headquarters or research and development facilities that are at a different location than the rest of the company.

Under the SIC system's rules for classifying establishments, Auxiliary establishments were classified in the industry or division of the establishments they served. If they served establishments in more than one division, they were classified in the same division as the enterprise's main revenue source. According to the rules used under NAICS, Auxiliary establishments are classified in the industry that describes their own main revenue source—just like any other establishment.

For example, the main research and development facility of a large manufacturing enterprise would be classified as a manufacturing facility under the SIC rules. However, if this enterprise's main source of rev-

enues was actually from subsidiaries involved with providing credit services related to selling the manufactured products and establishments that are not a part of this enterprise, the same research and development facility would be grouped into the F.I.R.E. division. This would happen even though the facility does not manufacture or finance anything on its own. In comparison, under the NAICS rules, this same establishment would be classified somewhere in the Professional, Scientific, and Technical Services sector, depending on the exact activities it provides.

In the 1997 transition from the SIC system to NAICS, the Census Bureau lacked sufficient information to send these establishments the proper questionnaire for their own activities. So, they were sent a general form that allowed them to be classified into the appropriate industry for future surveys and censuses. While they were considered Auxiliary establishments under the SIC system, headquarters facilities were included in the Management of Companies and Enterprises sector in the 1997 Economic Census.

As a result, the 1997 Economic Census has two reports on Auxiliary establishments. One of these is a single *Geographic Area* report for the nation containing national and statewide data. Figure 12.2 is a sample of this report. It shows the basic data items reported by all establishments and the NAICS industry that the establishments are assigned to.

A *Miscellaneous Subjects* report was also prepared in 1997. This report includes national data by type of Auxiliary on

- Exported services
- Source of funding for research and development services (limited to research and development Auxiliaries)
- Sales to customers outside the Auxiliary's own company
- Value of inventories
- Billings to other establishments of the same company
- Sales by type (e.g., products manufactured at this establishment, professional scientific, and technical services, and equipment repairs)
- Billings by type
- Employment by function (e.g., security, legal, advertising, and repair and maintenance)

Since these reports were produced in the 1997 Economic Census due to the transition from the SIC sys-

Figure 12.2
Auxiliaries—Geographic Area Report Sample

[Includes only establishments with payroll.  For meaning of abbreviations and symbols, see introductory text.  For explanation of terms, see Appendix A]

| NAICS code | Geographic area and kind of business | Establishments (number) | Sales ($1,000) | Annual payroll ($1,000) | First-quarter payroll ($1,000) | Paid employees for pay period including March 12 (number) |
|---|---|---|---|---|---|---|
| | **UNITED STATES** | | | | | |
| | **Auxiliaries, exc corp, subsidiary, & regional managing offices** | r12 930 | r11 275 968 | r33 114 319 | r8 433 810 | r792 370 |
| 484 | Truck transportation | 1 084 | 199 850 | 947 158 | 231 059 | 29 788 |
| 4931 | Warehousing & storage | 4 800 | 4 897 584 | 8 810 858 | 2 122 852 | 332 470 |
| 514210 | Data processing services | 387 | D | 1 806 887 | 469 391 | 40 953 |
| 5411 | Legal services | 68 | D | 98 323 | 25 772 | 1 260 |
| 5412 | Accounting, tax return prep, bookkeeping, & payroll services | 1 285 | 201 410 | 2 194 954 | 550 034 | 48 139 |
| 5417 | Scientific research & development services | 1 048 | 728 053 | 13 185 456 | 3 515 343 | 182 077 |
| 5418 | Advertising & related services | 409 | 260 676 | 954 379 | 218 682 | 16 917 |
| 5613 | Employment services | 196 | 19 870 | 300 550 | 76 900 | 6 456 |
| 56161 | Investigation, guard, & armored car services | 46 | D | 49 043 | 10 343 | 1 355 |
| 5617 | Services to buildings & dwellings | 76 | D | 51 545 | 14 643 | 1 823 |
| 811 | Repair & maintenance | 712 | 143 392 | 900 469 | 224 511 | 24 145 |
| 949999 | Other auxiliary establishments | 2 819 | 2 871 429 | 3 814 697 | 974 280 | 106 987 |

tem to NAICS, they were not produced as part of the 2002 Census.

## SIC–NAICS Comparison

There are about 400 industries identified in the sectors covered in this chapter. Many of these are made up from parts of more than one SIC industry. Also, several of these sectors had changes within them between the 1997 and 2002 versions of NAICS. This would result in an enormous SIC–NAICS comparison table. Therefore, we have chosen not to include one for this chapter. We *strongly* recommend that you take a look at the 1997 and 2002 Bridge Tables to determine any historic comparability issues affecting the specific industries you are studying.

# APPENDIX A
# Acronyms and Initials Used in This Book

| | |
|---|---|
| ACES | Annual Capital Expenditures Survey |
| AELOS | *Agricultural Economics and Land Ownership Survey* |
| ASM | *Annual Survey of Manufactures* |
| BEA | Bureau of Economic Analysis |
| BES | Business Expenditures Survey |
| BIDC | Business and Industry Data Center |
| BLS | Bureau of Labor Statistics |
| B-to-B | Business-to-Business |
| B-to-C | Business-to-Consumer |
| BTS | Bureau of Transportation Statistics |
| CBSA | Core Based Statistical Area |
| CDP | Census Designated Place |
| CES | Center for Economic Studies |
| CES | Current Employment Survey |
| CFR | *Code of Federal Regulations* |
| CFS | *Commodity Flow Survey* |
| CIC | Census Information Center |
| CMSA | Consolidated Metropolitan Statistical Area |
| CRSP | Center for Research in Security Prices |
| CSA | Combined Statistical Area |
| CSAQ | Computerized Self-Administered Questionnaires |
| CSV | Character-Separated Values |
| EDI | Electronic Data Interchange |
| EPCD | Economic Planning and Coordination Division |
| FAA | Federal Aviation Administration |
| FDIUS | *Foreign Direct Investment in the U.S.* |
| FHA | Federal Highway Administration |
| FIPS | Federal Information Processing System |
| FIRE | Finance, Insurance, and Real Estate |
| GDP | Gross Domestic Product |
| GIS | Geographic Information Systems |
| GPO | Government Printing Office |

| | |
|---|---|
| HHI | Herfindahl-Herschmann Index |
| HTSA | *Harmonized Tariff Schedule of the United States Annotated* |
| ISIC | International Standard Industrial Classification |
| LIFO | Last-in-First-Out |
| LRD | Longitudinal Research Database |
| MA | Metropolitan Area |
| MD | Metropolitan Division |
| MeSA | Metropolitan Statistical Area (2000 criteria) |
| MiSA | Micropolitan Statistical Area |
| MSA | Metropolitan Statistical Area (1990 criteria) |
| NAICS | North American Industry Classification System |
| NAPCS | North American Product Classification System |
| NASS | National Agriculture Statistical Service |
| NEC, n.e.c. | Not Elsewhere Classified |
| NECTA | New England City and Town Areas |
| NMI | Northern Mariana Islands |
| OMB | Office of Management and Budget |
| PDF | Portable Document Format |
| PMSA | Primary Metropolitan Statistical Area |
| PSA | Public Service Announcements |
| RDC | Research Data Centers |
| REIT | Real Estate Investment Trusts |
| SBA | Small Business Administration |
| SCTG | Standard Classification of Transported Goods |
| SDC | State Data Center |
| SIC | Standard Industrial Classification |
| SMSA | Standard Metropolitan Statistical Area |
| SOI | *Statistics of Income* |
| SSEL | Standard Statistical Establishment List |

| | | | |
|---|---|---|---|
| TCU | Transportation, Communications, and Utilities | USDA | U.S. Department of Agriculture |
| | | USDIA | *U.S. Direct Investment Abroad* |
| TIUS | *Truck Inventory and Use Survey* | VIUS | *Vehicle Inventory and Use Survey* |
| TSPIRS | Timber Sale Program Information Reporting System | ZCTA | ZIP Code Tabulation Area |
| | | ZIP | Zoned Improvement Plan |

# APPENDIX B
# Sample Questionnaires

As mentioned several times in the main part of this book, the Economic Census uses hundreds of different questionnaires. These questionnaires have much in common with each other and much that is customized to meet the needs of specific industries.

This appendix includes five sample questionnaires providing a flavor of the types of data collected in the Economic Census. The specific questionnaires included here are:

**NC-99023—General Classification Form.** This form was sent to very small single-establishment businesses that the Census Bureau had not previously assigned to a specific NAICS industry. If the Census Bureau had enough information to assign a NAICS industry group to the establishment, a more specialized form was sent. This was the only form sent to these businesses—all other data about them was collected through administrative records.

**MA10000—Manufacturing (pages 1 through 7).** This form was sent to all manufacturing establishments, except those in the *Annual Survey of Manufactures* sample, which were sent a variation on this form. Similar forms were sent to establishments in other sectors. These forms collected the basic information about the establishment.

**Manufacturing (Dairy Products).** This form was sent to establishments in the Dairy Products manufacturing industry group. It was used to collect information specific to this type of industry, such as product and materials consumed data. Similar, industry-specific questionnaires were sent to establishments in other industries.

**NC-99001—Report of Organization.** All establishments received either this report or another similar one in order to collect information about the organization's structure, ownership, and control.

**SBO-1—Survey of Business Owners and Self-Employed Persons.** This was one of two similar questionnaires used to collect information for this survey.

U.S. DEPARTMENT OF COMMERCE
Economics and Statistics Administration
U.S. CENSUS BUREAU

FORM
**NC-99023**

**2002 ECONOMIC CENSUS**

GENERAL CLASSIFICATION REPORT

OMB No. 0607-0884: Approval Expires 7/31/2004

NC-99023

**DUE DATE
30 DAYS AFTER
RECEIPT OF FORM**

An Office of Management and Budget (OMB) control number is printed in the upper right corner of this form. If OMB number is not shown on this questionnaire, this survey is invalid. Public reporting burden for this collection is estimated to take 10 minutes to complete this questionnaire. Send comments regarding this burden estimate or any other aspect of this collection of information, including suggestions for reducing this burden, to: Paperwork Project 0607-0884, Room 3110, Federal Building 3, U.S. Census Bureau, Washington, D.C. 20233-1500. You may e-mail comments to Paperwork@census.gov; use "Paperwork Project 0607-0884" as the subject.

Return your completed form to:

**U.S. Census Bureau
1201 East Tenth Street
Jeffersonville, IN 47134-0001**

*(Please correct any errors in this mailing address.)*

---

**1** EMPLOYER IDENTIFICATION NUMBER

Is the Employer Identification Number (EIN) shown in the mailing address the same as the one used for this establishment on its latest Internal Revenue Service Form 941, Employer's Quarterly Federal Tax Return?

*If this establishment did not file form 941, Go to* **2** .

0021 ☐ Yes      0022 ☐ No - Enter current EIN      0025
                 *(9 digits)* ──────▶

---

**2** PHYSICAL LOCATION

**A.** Is this establishment's physical location the same as shown in the mailing address?
*(P.O. box and rural route addresses are not physical locations.)*

0031 ☐ Yes

0032 ☐ No - Enter physical
            location ──────▶

| 0035 Number and street | | |
|---|---|---|
| 0036 City, town, village, etc. | 0037 State | 0038 ZIP Code |

**B.** Is this establishment physically located inside the legal boundaries of the city, town, village, etc.?

0041 ☐ Yes     0042 ☐ No     0043 ☐ No legal boundaries     0044 ☐ Do not know

**C.** Type of municipality where this establishment is physically located

0051 ☐ City, village, or borough     0052 ☐ Town or township     0053 ☐ Other or do not know

---

**3** LEASED EMPLOYMENT

Did this establishment have any full- or part-time leased employees whose payroll was filed under a leasing company's EIN?

*Exclude:*
• Temporary staffing obtained from a staffing service.
• Contractors, subcontractors, or independent contractors
• Purchased or managed services, such as janitorial, guard, or landscape services
• Professional or technical services purchased from another firm, such as software consulting, computer programming, engineering, or accounting services.

0241 ☐ Yes

0242 ☐ No

---

*PENALTY FOR FAILURE TO REPORT*

*CONTINUE ON PAGE 2*

248

**4** PRINCIPAL BUSINESS OR ACTIVITY

*In the past 12 months, what was this establishment's principal business or activity? Find the Economic Sector (e.g., Service, Retail, Construction, Wholesale, Transportation) that best describes your business or activity. Within that sector, choose ONE description that best fits your PRINCIPAL business or activity. Mark (X) only ONE box.*

**✦ SERVICE**

0700

### HEALTH SERVICES AND SOCIAL ASSISTANCE

- 624 410 00 7 ☐ Child Day Care Service
- 339 116 00 6 ☐ Dental Lab
- 621 410 00 0 ☐ Family Planning Center
- 621 493 00 6 ☐ Freestanding Ambulatory Surgical or Emergency Center
- 621 610 00 5 ☐ Home Health Care Service
- 621 310 00 2 ☐ Office of Chiropractor
- 621 210 00 4 ☐ Office of Dentist
- 621 320 00 1 ☐ Office of Optometrist
- 621 391 00 2 ☐ Office of Podiatrist
- 621 111 00 4 ☐ Office of Physician (MD or DO), Except Mental Health
- 621 112 00 2 ☐ Office of Physician (MD or DO), Mental Health
- 621 420 00 9 ☐ Outpatient Mental Health or Substance Abuse Center
- 623 210 00 2 ☐ Residential Care for the Developmentally Disabled
- 623 312 00 6 ☐ Residential Care for the Elderly - No Health Service Provided
- 623 990 00 9 ☐ Residential Care for Youth or Offenders
- 624 110 00 3 ☐ Social Assistance Service for Children and Youth
- 624 120 00 2 ☐ Social Assistance Service for the Elderly and Disabled
- 624 190 00 5 ☐ Social Assistance Service for Families and All Others
- ☐ Other Health Care and Social Assistance - *Specify* ⬐

*(Specify source of receipts in* **6**.)

### AUTOMOTIVE REPAIR SERVICES AND MAINTENANCE

- 811 112 00 2 ☐ Automotive Exhaust System Repair
- 811 122 00 1 ☐ Automotive Glass Replacement Shop
- 811 191 00 6 ☐ Automotive Oil Change and Lubrication Shop
- 811 113 00 0 ☐ Automotive Transmission Repair Shop
- 811 118 20 7 ☐ Brake, Front End, and Wheel Alignment Shop
- 811 192 00 4 ☐ Carwash
- 811 111 00 4 ☐ General Automotive Repair Shop
- 811 121 10 2 ☐ Paint Or Body Repair Shop
- ☐ Other Automotive Repair Services and Maintenance - *Specify* ⬐

*(Specify source of receipts in* **6**.)

### OTHER REPAIR SERVICES (EXCEPT AUTOMOTIVE)

- 811 412 00 6 ☐ Appliance Repair and Maintenance
- 811 310 90 3 ☐ Commercial, Farming, or Industrial Equipment Repair and Maintenance
- 811 212 30 7 ☐ Computer Repair and Maintenance
- 811 211 00 2 ☐ Consumer Electronics Repair and Maintenance
- 811 420 00 9 ☐ Furniture Repair
- 811 490 40 8 ☐ Garment Repair and Alteration Service
- 811 212 40 6 ☐ Office Machine Repair and Maintenance
- ☐ Other Repair Services (Except Automotive) - *Specify* ⬐

*(Specify source of receipts in* **6**.)

### ACCOMMODATIONS

- 721 191 00 5 ☐ Bed and Breakfast Inn
- 721 120 00 4 ☐ Casino Hotel
- 721 110 00 5 ☐ Hotel (Except Casino Hotel), Motel, or Motor Hotel
- 721 214 00 5 ☐ Overnight Recreation or Vacation Camp (Except Campground)
- 721 310 00 1 ☐ Rooming and Boarding House
- 721 211 00 1 ☐ Trailer Park, RV (Recreational Vehicle) Park, or Campground (Except Residential)
- ☐ Other Traveler Accommodation - *Specify* ⬐

*(Specify source of receipts in* **6**.)

### FOOD SERVICES

- 722 213 40 2 ☐ Bagel Shop
- 722 212 00 8 ☐ Cafeteria
- 722 320 00 9 ☐ Caterer
- 722 213 50 1 ☐ Coffee Shop
- 722 213 60 0 ☐ Cookie Shop
- 722 213 30 3 ☐ Donut Shop
- 722 410 00 8 ☐ Bar, Tavern, Pub, or Other Drinking Place (Alcoholic Beverages)
- 722 310 00 0 ☐ Food Service Contractor
- 722 213 20 4 ☐ Frozen Yogurt Shop
- 722 110 00 4 ☐ Full-Service Restaurant
- 722 213 10 5 ☐ Ice Cream and Soft Serve Shop
- 722 211 00 0 ☐ Limited-Service Restaurant
- 722 213 70 9 ☐ Other Snack and Nonalcoholic Beverage Bar
- ☐ Other Food Service - *Specify* ⬐

*(Specify source of receipts in* **6**.)

*CONTINUE ON PAGE 3*

**4** PRINCIPAL BUSINESS OR ACTIVITY - Continued

✦ **SERVICE** - Continued
OTHER SERVICES

713 120 00 4 ☐ Arcade or Family Fun Center
541 310 00 9 ☐ Architectural Service
812 111 00 3 ☐ Barber Shop
812 112 00 1 ☐ Beauty Shop
561 740 00 2 ☐ Carpet and Upholstery Cleaning Service
541 211 00 9 ☐ Certified Public Accountant (CPA)
813 410 40 4 ☐ Civic or Social Club (Except Scouting Organizations)
812 310 20 9 ☐ Coin-Operated Laundry or Drycleaning
561 440 10 8 ☐ Collection Agency
611 610 10 6 ☐ Dance School
812 191 00 5 ☐ Diet or Weight Reducing Service
812 320 20 8 ☐ Drycleaning Plant
561 330 00 2 ☐ Employee Leasing Service
561 310 00 4 ☐ Employment Placement Agency
541 330 00 7 ☐ Engineering Service
541 620 00 1 ☐ Environmental Consulting Service
561 710 00 5 ☐ Exterminating and Pest Control Service
713 940 90 6 ☐ Fitness Center, Gymnasium, or Athletic Club
812 210 10 2 ☐ Funeral Home
713 910 00 8 ☐ Golf Course or Country Club
541 430 00 5 ☐ Graphic Design Service
541 410 00 7 ☐ Interior Design Service
561 611 00 5 ☐ Investigation Service
561 720 00 4 ☐ Janitorial Service
561 730 00 3 ☐ Landscape Service
541 110 10 2 ☐ Law Office
561 622 00 2 ☐ Locksmith
713 930 00 6 ☐ Marina
512 131 00 4 ☐ Motion Picture Theater (Except Drive-In)
812 113 00 9 ☐ Nail Salon
812 930 00 6 ☐ Parking Lot or Garage
561 439 00 1 ☐ Photocopying and Duplicating Service
812 922 00 3 ☐ Photofinishing, One-Hour
812 921 00 5 ☐ Photofinishing (Except One-Hour)
541 921 00 3 ☐ Photographic Studio, Portrait
561 990 90 4 ☐ Printing Broker
813 990 40 5 ☐ Property Owners' Association
561 621 00 4 ☐ Security Systems Service
511 210 00 7 ☐ Software Publishing
611 620 00 6 ☐ Sports and Recreation Instruction
541 370 00 3 ☐ Surveying or Mapping (Except Geophysical) Service
561 790 20 5 ☐ Swimming Pool Cleaning and Maintenance
561 320 00 3 ☐ Temporary Help Service
541 191 00 3 ☐ Title Abstract and Settlement Office
541 940 00 3 ☐ Veterinarian's Office
532 230 00 0 ☐ Video Tape Rental
              ☐ Other Service - *Specify* ⬈

_____
*(Specify source of receipts in* **6***.)*

✦ **TRANSPORTATION**
TRUCKING

484 230 20 6 ☐ Agricultural Products Trucking, Long-Distance
484 220 20 7 ☐ Agricultural Products Trucking Without Storage, Local
484 220 30 6 ☐ Dump Trucking
484 122 00 7 ☐ General Freight Trucking, LTL, Long-Distance
484 110 20 0 ☐ General Freight Trucking Without Storage, LTL, Local
484 121 00 9 ☐ General Freight Trucking, TL, Long-Distance
484 110 10 1 ☐ General Freight Trucking Without Storage, Local, TL
484 220 40 5 ☐ Specialized Freight (Except Waste) Trucking Without Storage, Local
484 230 30 5 ☐ Specialized Freight (Including Waste) Trucking, Long-Distance
484 210 10 9 ☐ Used Household and Office Goods Moving Without Storage, Local
484 210 20 8 ☐ Used Household and Office Goods Moving, Long-Distance
              ☐ Other Trucking – *Specify* ⬈

_____
*(Specify source of receipts in* **6***.)*

OTHER TRANSPORTATION

488 119 10 8 ☐ Airport Operation and Terminal Service
621 910 00 9 ☐ Ambulance or Rescue Service, Except by Air
488 510 20 7 ☐ Arrangement of Transportation of Freight/Cargo
492 110 20 0 ☐ Courier Service - Air
492 210 00 0 ☐ Local Messenger and Local Delivery
492 110 10 1 ☐ Courier Service (Except Air or Local)
488 510 10 8 ☐ Freight Forwarding
485 320 00 6 ☐ Limousine or Luxury Passenger Rental with Driver
485 410 10 4 ☐ School Bus Service
485 991 00 4 ☐ Special Needs Transportation (Senior Citizen, Handicapped, Infirm)
562 111 00 5 ☐ Solid Waste (Except Hazardous Waste) Collection, Local
562 112 00 3 ☐ Hazardous Waste Collection
485 310 00 7 ☐ Taxicab Service
561 510 00 9 ☐ Travel Agency
488 410 00 2 ☐ Towing Service, Motor Vehicle
493 110 10 0 ☐ Warehousing and Storage, General Merchandise
531 130 00 3 ☐ Self-Storage and Mini-Warehousing
              ☐ Other Transportation - *Specify* ⬈

_____
*(Specify source of receipts in* **6***.)*

*CONTINUE ON PAGE 4*

**4** PRINCIPAL BUSINESS OR ACTIVITY - Continued

### ✦ RETAIL TRADE

441 310 40 6 ☐ Automotive Parts and Accessories Store (Except Used)

441 310 50 5 ☐ Automotive Parts and Accessories Store, Used

445 310 00 6 ☐ Beer, Wine, and Liquor Store

451 110 21 7 ☐ Bicycle Shop

441 110 00 4 ☐ Car Dealer, New and Used

441 120 00 3 ☐ Car Dealer, Used Only

443 120 30 8 ☐ Computer Software Store

443 120 10 0 ☐ Computer Store (Custom Assembly)

443 120 20 9 ☐ Computer Store (Except Custom Assembly)

445 120 00 9 ☐ Convenience Food Store

454 110 50 3 ☐ Electronic Shopping, General Merchandise

454 110 61 0 ☐ Electronic Shopping, Computer Hardware and Software

454 110 62 8 ☐ Electronic Shopping, Pharmacy

454 110 63 6 ☐ Electronic Shopping, Other Specialized Merchandise

454 110 70 1 ☐ Mail-Order House, General Merchandise

454 110 81 8 ☐ Mail-Order House, Computer Hardware and Software

454 110 82 6 ☐ Mail-Order Pharmacy

454 110 83 4 ☐ Mail-Order House, Other Specialized Merchandise

448 140 00 4 ☐ Family Clothing Store

442 210 00 1 ☐ Floor Coverings Store

453 110 00 9 ☐ Florist

442 110 10 2 ☐ Furniture Store

447 110 00 8 ☐ Gasoline Station With Convenience Store

447 190 10 9 ☐ Gasoline Station With No Convenience Store

451 110 10 0 ☐ General-Line Sporting Goods Store

453 220 00 6 ☐ Gift, Novelty, Craft and Souvenir Store

444 130 00 9 ☐ Hardware Store

443 111 00 0 ☐ Household Appliance Store

442 299 00 4 ☐ Houseware and Kitchenware Store

445 210 00 8 ☐ Meat Market

444 220 40 4 ☐ Nursery and Garden Center

444 210 00 9 ☐ Outdoor Power Equipment Store

453 910 00 2 ☐ Pet and Pet Supplies Store

446 110 10 8 ☐ Pharmacy and Drug Store

443 112 40 4 ☐ Radio, TV, and Other Electronics Store

522 298 10 8 ☐ Pawn Shop

453 310 20 3 ☐ Second-Hand Store (Except Pawn Shop)

445 110 00 0 ☐ Supermarket or Grocery Store

441 320 00 9 ☐ Tire Dealer

447 190 20 8 ☐ Truck Stop

442 291 00 1 ☐ Window Treatment Store

448 120 00 6 ☐ Women's Clothing Store

448 210 20 3 ☐ Women's Shoe Store

☐ Other Retail Business - *Specify* ↙

_____

*(Specify source of receipts in* **6**.*)*

### ✦ WHOLESALE TRADE

*Mark (X) only ONE box in part 1 and ONE box in part 2.*

**1.** Kind of Business or Activity

421 430 12 5 ☐ Computers and Peripheral Equipment Sold For End Use

421 430 11 7 ☐ Computers and Peripheral Equipment Sold For Resale

421 610 00 7 ☐ Electrical Apparatus and Equipment

421 940 10 7 ☐ Jewelry, Watches, and Gemstones

422 210 10 4 ☐ General-Line Drugs, Cosmetics, and Toiletries

422 210 20 3 ☐ Specialty-Line Drugs, Cosmetics, and Toiletries

421 910 00 1 ☐ Sporting and Recreational Goods

421 450 10 7 ☐ Surgical, Medical, and Hospital Equipment and Supplies

422 320 00 2 ☐ Men's and Boys' Clothing

422 330 00 1 ☐ Women's, Children's, and Infants' Clothing

☐ Other Wholesale Trade - *Specify* ↙

_____

*(Specify source of receipts in* **6**.*)*

**2.** Type of Operation

0600

11  ☐ Merchant Wholesaler

42  ☐ Broker, Representing Buyers and Sellers

46  ☐ Manufacturers' Agent

49  ☐ Electronic Marketer

☐ Other Type of Operation - *Specify* ↙

_____

*(Specify source of receipts in* **6**.*)*

### ✦ MANUFACTURING

0700

323 112 00 3 ☐ Commercial Flexographic Printing

323 110 00 7 ☐ Commercial Lithographic Printing

323 113 00 1 ☐ Commercial Screen Printing

323 115 00 6 ☐ Digital Printing

323 114 00 9 ☐ Quick Printing

☐ Other Commercial Printing - *Specify* ↙

_____

*(Specify source of receipts in* **6**.*)*

113 310 00 7 ☐ Logging Camp and Logging Contractor

332 710 00 3 ☐ Machine Shop

312 130 00 8 ☐ Winery

☐ Other Manufacturing - *Specify* ↙

_____

*(Specify source of receipts in* **6**.*)*

**CONTINUE ON PAGE 5**

**4** PRINCIPAL BUSINESS OR ACTIVITY - Continued

### ✦ CONSTRUCTION

233 110 00 6 ☐ Land Subdivision

SPECIALTY TRADE CONTRACTOR

235 710 10 0 ☐ Asphalt and Concrete Paving Contractor
235 510 90 6 ☐ Carpentry Finishing Contractor
235 510 10 4 ☐ Carpentry Framing Contractor
235 710 90 2 ☐ Concrete Contractor (Except Paving)
235 420 90 8 ☐ Drywall or Insulation Contractor
235 310 00 0 ☐ Electrical Contractor
235 930 00 5 ☐ Excavation Contractor (Building)
234 990 40 6 ☐ Excavation Contractor (Except Building)
235 520 00 4 ☐ Flooring Contractor
235 920 00 6 ☐ Glass Contractor
235 210 10 1 ☐ Highway and Traffic Line Painting
235 410 00 8 ☐ Masonry, Stone Setting, and Other Stone Work Contractor
235 210 90 3 ☐ Painting and Wall Covering Contractor
235 110 90 5 ☐ Plumbing, Heating, and Air Conditioning (HVAC) Contractor
235 610 10 2 ☐ Roofing Contractor
235 610 90 4 ☐ Sheet Metal Contractor (Except HVAC, Roofing and Siding)
235 610 20 1 ☐ Siding Contractor (Including Gutters and Downspouts)
235 430 00 6 ☐ Tile, Marble, Terrazzo, and Mosaic Contractor
            ☐ Other Specialty Trade Contractor - ↙

_____
*(Specify source of receipts in* **6**.)

HEAVY AND CIVIL ENGINEERING CONSTRUCTION

234 110 00 5 ☐ Highway and Street Construction
234 120 10 3 ☐ Bridge Construction
234 910 90 9 ☐ Oil or Gas Pipelines, Mains and Related Structures Construction
234 930 10 5 ☐ Petrochemical Plants and Refineries Construction
234 920 00 7 ☐ Power and Communication Transmission Line Construction
234 930 20 4 ☐ Power Generation Plants and Power Transformer Stations Construction
234 120 90 5 ☐ Tunnel Construction
234 910 10 7 ☐ Water or Sewer Lines, Mains and Related Structures Construction
            ☐ Other Heavy Construction - *Specify* ↙

_____
*(Specify source of receipts in* **6**.)

### ✦ CONSTRUCTION - Continued

RESIDENTIAL BUILDING CONSTRUCTION

233 210 10 3 ☐ Single Family - General Contractor
233 220 10 2 ☐ Multifamily - General Contractor
233 210 20 2 ☐ Single Family - Operative Builder
233 220 20 1 ☐ Multifamily - Operative Builder
233 210 30 1 ☐ Single Family - Remodeling Contractor
233 220 30 0 ☐ Multifamily - Remodeling Contractor

NONRESIDENTIAL BUILDING CONSTRUCTION

233 310 10 1 ☐ Manufacturing and Industrial Warehouse Construction
233 320 90 2 ☐ Commercial and Institutional Building Construction
            ☐ Other Nonresidential Building Construction - *Specify* ↙

_____
*(Specify source of receipts in* **6**.)

### ✦ FINANCE, INSURANCE & REAL ESTATE

523 991 90 9 ☐ Administrator of Private Estate
813 211 00 0 ☐ Grantmaking Foundation
524 210 00 2 ☐ Insurance Agency and Brokerage
524 291 00 2 ☐ Insurance Claims Adjusting
523 930 00 6 ☐ Investment Advice, Without Portfolio Management
531 110 10 4 ☐ Lessor of Apartment Buildings
531 120 20 2 ☐ Lessor of Manufacturing and Industrial Buildings
531 120 10 3 ☐ Lessor of Professional and Other Buildings
531 120 30 1 ☐ Lessor of Shopping Centers and Retail Stores
531 120 90 5 ☐ Lessor of Other Nonresidential Buildings
531 110 90 6 ☐ Lessor of Other Residential Buildings
522 310 00 2 ☐ Mortgage and Other Loan Brokers
523 920 10 6 ☐ Portfolio Management
531 312 00 7 ☐ Property Management - Nonresidential Real Estate
531 311 00 9 ☐ Property Management - Residential Real Estate
531 210 90 4 ☐ Real Estate Agent or Broker - Nonresidential
531 210 10 2 ☐ Real Estate Agent or Broker - Residential
531 320 00 0 ☐ Real Estate Appraiser
523 120 00 4 ☐ Securities Brokerage
524 292 10 9 ☐ Third-Party Administration - Pension, Health, and Welfare Funds
524 292 90 1 ☐ Third-Party Administration of Insurance Funds
523 991 90 9 ☐ Trustees in Bankruptcy
            ☐ Other Finance, Insurance and Real Estate - *Specify* ↙

_____
*(Specify source of receipts in* **6**.)

**CONTINUE ON PAGE 6**

**4** PRINCIPAL BUSINESS OR ACTIVITY - Continued

✦ **RENTAL AND LEASING SERVICES, EXCEPT REAL ESTATE**

VEHICULAR

532 411 90 7 ☐ Aircraft Rental and Leasing Without Pilot

532 111 00 2 ☐ Car (Passenger) Rental Without Driver

532 112 00 0 ☐ Car (Passenger) Leasing Without Driver

532 411 10 5 ☐ Commercial Vessel Rental and Leasing Without Crew

532 411 20 4 ☐ Railroad Car Rental and Leasing

532 120 20 1 ☐ Truck Leasing Without Driver

532 120 10 2 ☐ Truck Rental Without Driver

532 120 90 4 ☐ Utility Trailer and Recreational Vehicle Rental and Leasing

OTHER, EXCEPT REAL ESTATE

532 310 00 0 ☐ General Rental Center

234 990 30 7 ☐ Crane Rental With Operator

234 990 40 6 ☐ Construction Equipment Rental (Except Crane) With Operator

532 420 90 8 ☐ Computer Rental and Leasing

532 420 10 6 ☐ Office Furniture and Machines (Except Computer Rental and Leasing)

532 210 00 2 ☐ Consumer Electronics and Appliances Rental

532 220 10 0 ☐ Formal Wear Rental

532 292 00 0 ☐ Recreational Goods Rental

532 220 90 2 ☐ Wardrobe Rental

532 291 00 2 ☐ Home Health Equipment Rental

532 490 10 9 ☐ Medical Equipment Rental and Leasing (Except Home Health Equipment)

532 490 20 8 ☐ Industrial Equipment Rental and Leasing

532 412 90 5 ☐ Oilfield and Well Drilling Equipment Rental and Leasing

532 490 30 7 ☐ Motion Picture Equipment Rental and Leasing

☐ Other Rental and Leasing (Except Real Estate) - *Specify* ↗

_____

*(Specify source of receipts in* **6**.)

✦ **OTHER**

813 110 00 4 ☐ Churches and Other Religious Organizations

814 110 00 3 ☐ Private Household (Employing Domestic Help, e.g., Cooks, Maids, Gardeners, etc.)

☐ Crop Production
☐ Animal Production
☐ Agricultural and Forestry Services
☐ Fishing, Hunting, and Trapping
☐ Mineral Extraction
☐ Mineral Service
☐ Other Business or Activity

*Specify below* ↙

_____

*(Specify source of receipts in* **6**.)

**5** CLASS OF CUSTOMER

**A.** Was a box marked under the Retail Trade or Wholesale Trade headings on page 4?

☐ Yes - *Go to line B*      ☐ No - *Go to* **6**

**B.** As a general business practice, did this establishment sell to household consumers and individual users in the past 12 months?

0251 ☐ Yes - *Go to line C*      0252 ☐ No - *Go to line D*

**C.** Were 10 percent or more of your sales to household consumers and individual users in the past 12 months?

0281 ☐ Yes      0282 ☐ No

**D.** Were 75 percent or more of this establishment's sales to retailers/wholesalers for resale in the past 12 months?

0256 ☐ Yes      0257 ☐ No

**E.** Did this establishment require proof of business or professional license from new customers in the past 12 months?

0276 ☐ Yes      0277 ☐ No

**6** DETAIL OF SALES, SHIPMENTS, RECEIPTS, OR REVENUE

List below the principal lines of merchandise sold, specific construction work done, products produced, or services provided and indicate the approximate percentage each was of the total dollar volume of business (e.g., gasoline 85%, auto repairs 10%, oil 5%) in the past 12 months.

| Source | Percent |
|---|---|
|  | % |
|  | % |
|  | % |
|  | % |
|  | % |
|  | % |
| Total → | 100 % |

**7** REMARKS

**8** CERTIFICATION - This report is substantially accurate and was prepared in accordance with the instructions.

| | Name of person to contact regarding this report - *Print or Type* | 0074 | Area code | Number | Extension |
|---|---|---|---|---|---|
| 0072 | | Telephone | | — | |

U.S. DEPARTMENT OF COMMERCE
Economics and Statistics Administration
U.S. CENSUS BUREAU

FORM
**MA-10000**

# 2002 ANNUAL SURVEY OF MANUFACTURES

OMB No. 0607-0899: Approval Expires 09/30/2003

*(Please correct any errors in this mailing address.)*

**YOUR RESPONSE IS REQUIRED BY LAW.** Title 13, United States Code, requires businesses and other organizations that receive this questionnaire to answer the questions and return the report to the U.S. Census Bureau. By the same law, **YOUR CENSUS REPORT IS CONFIDENTIAL.** It may be seen only by persons sworn to uphold the confidentiality of Census Bureau information and may be used only for statistical purposes. Further, copies retained in respondents' files are immune from legal process.

| | | Examples: | |
|---|---|---|---|
| •Use blue or black ink. | •Please center numbers in their respective boxes. | | |
| •Do not use pencil. | •Do not put slashes through 0 or 7. | ☒ | 0 1 2 3 4 5 6 7 8 9 |
| •Place an "X" inside the box. | •Complete only the unshaded portion of each item. | | |

The reporting unit for this form is an establishment. An **establishment** is generally a single physical location where business is conducted or where services or industrial operations are performed. For further clarification, see information sheet(s).

**①  MONTHS IN OPERATION**

| | Mark "X" if None | 2002 Number of months |
|---|---|---|
| Number of months in operation during 2002 *(If none, mark "X" and go to ㉙.)* . . . . . . 0002 | ☐ | |

**②  EMPLOYER IDENTIFICATION NUMBER**

Is the Employer Identification Number (EIN) shown in the mailing address the same as the one used for this establishment on its latest 2002 Internal Revenue Service Form 941, Employer's Quarterly Federal Tax Return?

0021 ☐ Yes    0022 ☐ No - Enter current EIN *(9 digits)* ——————➤ 0025 [    ] - [          ]

**③  PHYSICAL LOCATION**

**A.** Is this establishment's physical location the same as shown in the mailing address?
*(P.O. box and rural route addresses are not physical locations.)*

0031 ☐ Yes

| | 0035 Number and street |
|---|---|
| 0032 ☐ No - Enter physical➔ location | |

| | 0036 City, town, village, etc. | 0037 State | 0038 ZIP Code |
|---|---|---|---|
| | | | - |

**B.** Is this establishment physically located inside the legal boundaries of the city, town, village, etc.?

0041 ☐ Yes    0042 ☐ No    0043 ☐ No legal boundaries    0044 ☐ Do not know

**C.** Type of municipality where this establishment is physically located

0046 ☐ City, village, or borough    0047 ☐ Town or township    0048 ☐ Other or do not know

*PENALTY FOR FAILURE TO REPORT*    *CONTINUE ON PAGE 2*

**Form MA-10000**

| | | | 2002 | | |
|---|---|---|---|---|---|
| *HOW TO REPORT DOLLAR FIGURES* | Dollar figures should be **rounded** to **thousands** of dollars. | Mark "X" if None | $ Bil. | Mil. | Thou. |
| | If a figure is **$1,025,628.79:** Report → ☐ | | | 1 | 0  2  6 |
| | If a value is "0" (or less than $500.00): Report → ☒ | | | | |

**4** SALES, SHIPMENTS, RECEIPTS, OR REVENUE

| | Mark "X" if None | 2002 | | | 2001 |
|---|---|---|---|---|---|
| | | $ Bil. | Mil. | Thou. | $ Thou. |
| **A.** Total value of products shipped and other receipts *(Report detail in* ㉒*.)* . . . . . . . . . . . . . . . . . . . . . . . . . . . . 0100 | ☐ | | | | |

**B.** Value of products exported *(This is a breakout of the value reported on line A.)*

*Report the value of products shipped for export. Include shipments to customers in the Panama Canal Zone, the Commonwealth of Puerto Rico, and U.S. possessions, as well as the value of products shipped to exporters or other wholesalers for export. Also, include the value of products sold to the U.S. Government to be shipped to foreign governments. Exclude products shipped for further manufacture, assembly, or fabrication in the United States..* . 0130    ☐

**C.** Shipments to other domestic plants of your company for further assembly, fabrication, or manufacture *(This is a breakout of the value reported on line A.)*

   **1.** Is this the only establishment of this firm?

     0907 ☐ Yes - *Go to* **5**

     0908 ☐ No - *Go to line C2*

   **2.** Market value of products shipped to other domestic plants of your company for further assembly, fabrication, or manufacture *(This is a breakout of the value reported on line A.)* . . . . . . . . . . . . . . . . . . . . . . . . . . . 0905    ☐

**5** E-COMMERCE SALES, SHIPMENTS, RECEIPTS, OR REVENUE

**A.** Did any of the amount reported in **4**, line A include e-commerce sales, shipments, or receipts? *(E-commerce sales, shipments, or receipts are online orders for products from customers where price and/or terms of the sale are accepted or negotiated over an Internet, Extranet, Electronic Data Interchange (EDI) network, electronic mail, or other online system. Payment may or may not be made online.)*

   0181 ☐ Yes - *Go to line B*    0182 ☐ No - *Go to* **6**

| | 2002 |
|---|---|
| | Percent |

**B.** Percent of total value of products shipped and other receipts reported in **4**, line A using e-commerce *(Report whole percents. Estimates are acceptable.)* . . . . . . . . . . . . . . . . . . . . . . . . . 0109    ☐ %

*CONTINUE ON PAGE 3*

**If not shown, please enter your 11-digit Census File Number (CFN) from the mailing address.**

**6** EMPLOYMENT AND PAYROLL

*Include:*

- *Full- and part-time employees working at this establishment whose payroll was reported on Internal Revenue Service Form 941, Employer's Quarterly Federal Tax Return, and filed under the Employer Identification Number (EIN) shown in the mailing address or corrected in ❷.*

*Exclude:*

- *Full- or part-time leased employees whose payroll was filed under an employee leasing company's EIN.*
- *Temporary staffing obtained from a staffing service.*

*For further clarification, see information sheet(s).*

**A.** Number of employees

| | Mark "X" if None | 2002 Number | 2001 Number |
|---|---|---|---|
| **1.** Number of production workers for pay periods including: | | | |
|     **a.** March 12 . . . . . . . . . . . . . . 0325 | ☐ | | |
|     **b.** May 12 . . . . . . . . . . . . . . 0326 | ☐ | | |
|     **c.** August 12 . . . . . . . . . . . . . 0327 | ☐ | | |
|     **d.** November 12 . . . . . . . . . . . 0328 | ☐ | | |
| **2. Sum lines A1a through A1d** . . . . . . . . . . . . 0329 | ☐ | | |
| **3.** Average annual production workers *(Divide line 2 by 4 - omit fractions.)* . . . . . . . . . . . . . 0335 | ☐ | | |
| **4.** All other employees for pay period including March 12 . . . . . 0336 | ☐ | | |
| **5. TOTAL** *(Sum lines A3 and A4)* . . . . . . . . . . 0337 | ☐ | | |

**B.** Payroll before deductions *(Exclude employer's cost for fringe benefits.)*

| | Mark "X" if None | 2002 $ Mil. | 2002 Thou. | 2001 $ Thou. |
|---|---|---|---|---|
| **1.** Annual payroll | | | | |
|     **a.** Production workers . . . . . . . . . . . . . . . . . 0304 | ☐ | | | |
|     **b.** All other employees . . . . . . . . . . . . . 0305 | ☐ | | | |
|     **c. TOTAL** *(Sum lines B1a and B1b)* . . . . . . . . . . 0300 | ☐ | | | |
| **2.** First quarter payroll *(January-March, 2002)* . . . . . . . . . 0310 | ☐ | | | |
| **C.** Employer's cost for fringe benefits . . . . . . . . . . . . . 0220 | ☐ | | | |

| | Mark "X" if None | 2002 Hours Thou. | 2001 Hours Thou. |
|---|---|---|---|
| **D.** Number of hours worked by production workers *(Annual hours worked by production workers reported on line A1.)* . . . . . . . . 0200 | ☐ | | |

**7** LEASED EMPLOYMENT AND PAYROLL

**A.** Did this establishment have any full- or part-time leased employees whose payroll was filed under an employee leasing company's EIN?

*Exclude:*
- *Temporary staffing obtained from a staffing service.*
- *Contractors, subcontractors, or independent contractors.*
- *Purchased or managed services, such as janitorial, guard, or landscape services.*
- *Professional or technical services purchased from another firm, such as software consulting, computer programming, engineering, or accounting services.*
- *Employees already reported in* **6***.*

*For further clarification, see information sheet(s).*

0241 ☐ Yes - *Go to line B*

0242 ☐ No - *Go to* **10**

**B.** Number of leased employees

| | | Mark "X" if None | 2002 Number |
|---|---|---|---|
| **1.** Number of leased production workers for pay periods including: | | | |
| a. March 12. . . . . . . . . . . . . . . . . 0375 | | ☐ | |
| b. May 12. . . . . . . . . . . . . . . . . 0376 | | ☐ | |
| c. August 12 . . . . . . . . . . . . . . . 0377 | | ☐ | |
| d. November 12. . . . . . . . . . . . . . . 0378 | | ☐ | |
| **2. Sum lines B1a through B1d** . . . . . . . . . 0379 | | ☐ | |
| **3.** Average annual leased production workers *(Divide line 2 by 4 - omit fractions)* . . 0385 | | ☐ | |
| **4.** All other leased employees for pay period including March 12 . . . . . . . . 0386 | | ☐ | |
| **5. TOTAL** *(Sum lines B3 and B4)* . . . . . . . . . . . . 0384 | | ☐ | |

**C.** Payroll for leased employees before deductions
*(Exclude employer's cost for fringe benefits.)*

| | Mark "X" if None | 2002 $ Mil. | Thou. |
|---|---|---|---|
| **1.** Annual payroll for leased employees | | | |
| a. Leased production workers . . . . . . . . . . . 0354 | ☐ | | |
| b. Other leased employees . . . . . . . . . . 0355 | ☐ | | |
| c. **TOTAL** *(Sum lines C1a and C1b)* . . . . . . . . . 0350 | ☐ | | |
| **2.** First quarter payroll for leased employees *(January-March, 2002)*. . . . . . . 0360 | ☐ | | |

**D.** Employer's fringe benefits cost for leased employees *(Include fringe benefits for all leased employees reported on line B.)* . . . . . . . . . . . . . . . . . 0225 ☐

| | Mark "X" if None | 2002 Hours Thou. |
|---|---|---|
| **E.** Number of annual hours worked by leased production workers *(Annual hours worked by leased production workers reported on line B1.)* . . . . . . . 0205 | ☐ | |

**8** - **9** Not Applicable.

*CONTINUE ON PAGE 5*

**Form MA-10000**

| If not shown, please enter your 11-digit Census File Number (CFN) from the mailing address. |
|---|

**10** INVENTORIES

*(Report inventories using generally accepted accounting practices.)*

Were inventories of this establishment subject to the Last-in, First-out (LIFO) method of valuation?

0481 ☐ **Yes** - *Use the sum of the LIFO amount plus the LIFO reserve for completing lines A through F2. If you changed to LIFO for calendar year 2002, specify in the REMARKS section.*

0482 ☐ **No** - *Complete only lines A through E1. Line E1 should equal line D.*

| | Mark "X" if None | End of 2002 | | | Mark "X" if None | End of 2001 | | |
|---|---|---|---|---|---|---|---|---|
| | | $ Bil. | Mil. | Thou. | | $ Bil. | Mil. | Thou. |
| **A.** Finished goods . . . . . . . . . . . . 0461 | ☐ | | | | 0471 ☐ | | | |
| **B.** Work-in-process. . . . . . . . . . 0463 | ☐ | | | | 0473 ☐ | | | |
| **C.** Materials, supplies, fuels, etc. . . . . 0462 | ☐ | | | | 0472 ☐ | | | |
| **D. TOTAL**. . . . . . . . . . . . . . 0460 | ☐ | | | | 0470 ☐ | | | |
| **E.** Of the value on line D report: | | | | | | | | |
|    **1.** Amount not subject to LIFO costing *(Report detail in* **11***.)* . . . 0464 | ☐ | | | | 0474 ☐ | | | |
|    **2.** Amount subject to LIFO costing *(gross)* . . . . . . . . . . . . . . 0465 | ☐ | | | | 0475 ☐ | | | |
| **F.** Of the value on line E2 report: | | | | | | | | |
|    **1.** Amount of LIFO reserve . . . . . 0466 | ☐ | | | | 0476 ☐ | | | |
|    **2.** Amount of LIFO value *(net)*. . . . 0467 | ☐ | | | | 0477 ☐ | | | |

**11** INVENTORY VALUATION

Methods of valuation for inventories not subject to LIFO costing

*(Using the inventory value reported in* **10***, line E1 above at the end of 2002, report the breakdown of that total according to the inventory valuation methods shown.)*

| | Mark "X" if None | 2002 | | |
|---|---|---|---|---|
| | | $ Bil. | Mil. | Thou. |
| **A.** First-in, First-out (FIFO) . . . . . . . . . 0491 | ☐ | | | |
| **B.** Average cost . . . . . . . . . . . . . . . . 0492 | ☐ | | | |
| **C.** Standard cost . . . . . . . . . . . . . . . 0493 | ☐ | | | |
| **D.** Other methods *(Specify)* ⟩ | | | | |
| 0895 [                                        ] 0494 | ☐ | | | |
| **E. TOTAL** *(Sum of lines A through D should equal* **10***, line E1 for end of 2002.)* 0490 | ☐ | | | |

*CONTINUE ON PAGE 6*

**12** ASSETS, CAPITAL EXPENDITURES, RETIREMENTS, AND DEPRECIATION

*(Refer to the instructions on how to report leasing arrangements.)*

| Report the dollar value of assets, capital expenditures, and depreciation | Mark "X" if None | 2002 | | 2001 |
|---|---|---|---|---|
| | | $ Mil. | Thou. | $ Thou. |
| **A.** Gross value of depreciable assets (acquisition costs) at the beginning of the year . . . . . . . . . . . . . . . . . . . 0500 | ☐ | | | Not collected in 2001 |
| **B.** Capital expenditures for new and used depreciable assets in 2002 | | | | |
|     **1.** Capital expenditures for new and used buildings and other structures *(Exclude land.)* . . . . . . . . . . . . . . . . . . 0525 | ☐ | | | |
|     **2.** Capital expenditures for new and used machinery and equipment . . . . . . . . . . . . . . . . . . . . . . . 0530 | ☐ | | | |
|     **3. TOTAL** *(Sum lines B1 and B2)* . . . . . . . . . . . . . . . . 0520 | ☐ | | | |
| **C.** Gross value of depreciable assets sold, retired, scrapped, destroyed, etc. . . . . . . . . . . . . . . . . . . . . . . . . . . . 0510 | ☐ | | | Not collected in 2001 |
| **D.** Gross value of depreciable assets at the end of 2002 *(Sum lines A and B3 minus C)* . . . . . . . . . . . . . . . . . . . 0505 | ☐ | | | Not collected in 2001 |
| **E.** Depreciation charges . . . . . . . . . . . . . . . . . 0540 | ☐ | | | Not collected in 2001 |
| **F.** Breakdown of expenditures for new and used machinery and equipment by type *(Reported on line B2.)* | | | | |
|     **1.** Automobiles, trucks, etc., for highway use . . . . . . . . . . . 0522 | ☐ | | | |
|     **2.** Computers and peripheral data processing equipment . . . . . 0523 | ☐ | | | |
|     **3.** All other expenditures for machinery and equipment . . . . . 0524 | ☐ | | | |
|     **4. TOTAL** *(Sum lines F1 through F3)* . . . . . . . . . . . . . . 0529 | ☐ | | | |

**13** RENTAL PAYMENTS

| | Mark "X" if None | 2002 | |
|---|---|---|---|
| | | $ Mil. | Thou. |
| **A.** Rental payments for buildings and other structures *(Include land.)*. . 0551 | ☐ | | |
| **B.** Rental payments for machinery and equipment. . . . . . . . . . 0552 | ☐ | | |
| **C. TOTAL** *(Sum lines A and B)*. . . . . . . . . . . . . . . . . . 0550 | ☐ | | |

**14** Not Applicable.

*CONTINUE ON PAGE 7*

259

**Form MA-10000**

**If not shown, please enter your 11-digit Census File Number (CFN) from the mailing address.**

**15** SELECTED EXPENSES

**A. Selected production related costs**

| | Mark "X" if None | 2002 | | | 2001 |
|---|---|---|---|---|---|
| | | $ Bil. | Mil. | Thou. | $ Thou. |
| 1. Cost of materials, parts, containers, packaging, etc. used *(Report detail in 16.)* . . . 0421 | ☐ | | | | |
| 2. Cost of products bought and sold as such without further processing *(Report sales in 22.)* . . . 0426 | ☐ | | | | |
| 3. Cost of purchased fuels consumed for heat, power, or the generation of electricity . . . 0430 | ☐ | | | | |
| 4. Cost of purchased electricity *(Report quantity on line B1.)* . . . 0425 | ☐ | | | | |
| 5. Cost of work done for you by others on your materials . 0424 | ☐ | | | | |
| 6. TOTAL *(Sum lines A1 through A5)* . . . 0420 | ☐ | | | | |

**B. Quantity of Electricity**

| | Mark "X" if None | 2002 Kilowatthours | | 2001 Kilowatthours |
|---|---|---|---|---|
| | | Mil. | Thou. | Thou. |
| 1. Purchased electricity *(Quantity comparable to cost reported on line A4.)* . . . 0436 | ☐ | | | |
| 2. Generated electricity *(Gross less generating station use.)* . . . 0437 | ☐ | | | |
| 3. Electricity sold or transferred to other establishments *(Include on lines B1 or B2.)* . . . 0438 | ☐ | | | |

**C. Other expenses paid by this establishment**

| | Mark "X" if None | 2002 $ Mil. | Thou. |
|---|---|---|---|
| 1. Purchased repair and maintenance service for buildings and/or machinery . . . 0394 | ☐ | | |
| 2. Purchased communication services *(telephone, Internet, connectivity, online services, FAX, cellular phones, etc.)* . . . 0402 | ☐ | | |
| 3. Purchased legal services . . . 0403 | ☐ | | |
| 4. Purchased accounting, auditing, and bookkeeping services . . . 0404 | ☐ | | |
| 5. Purchased advertising and promotional services *(advertising, marketing, promotional, or public relations services)* . . . 0405 | ☐ | | |
| 6. Expensed computer hardware and supplies and purchased computer services *(software, data transmission, processing services, web design, expensed computer purchases)* . . . 0406 | ☐ | | |
| 7. Refuse removal services *(including water, sewer, and hazardous waste)* . . . 0407 | ☐ | | |
| 8. Purchased management consulting and administrative services not reported above. . . . 0395 | ☐ | | |
| 9. Taxes and license fees *(excluding income, sales, payroll, and excise taxes)*. . . . 0396 | ☐ | | |
| 10. All other expenses not reported above paid by this establishment *(excluding income taxes, payroll, depreciation, rents, and interest expenses) (Specify)* ➤ 0897 _____ 0397 | ☐ | | |
| 11. TOTAL *(Sum lines C1 through C10)*. . . 0449 | ☐ | | |

U.S. DEPARTMENT OF COMMERCE
Economics and Statistics Administration
U.S. CENSUS BUREAU

FORM

# 2002 ECONOMIC CENSUS

OMB No. 0607-0899: Approval Expires 08/31/2004

## DUE DATE
## FEBRUARY 12, 2003

**Mail** your completed form to:

**U.S. CENSUS BUREAU**
**1201 East 10th Street**
**Jeffersonville, IN 47134-0001**

**Please read** the accompanying information sheet(s) before answering the questions.

**Need help or have questions about filling out this form?**

**Visit** our Web site at www.census.gov/econhelp

**Call** 1-800-233-6136, between 8:00 a.m. and 8:00 p.m., Eastern time, Monday through Friday.

*- OR -*

**Write** to the address above. Include your 11-digit Census File Number (CFN) printed in the mailing address.

*(Please correct any errors in this mailing address.)*

**YOUR RESPONSE IS REQUIRED BY LAW.** Title 13, United States Code, requires businesses and other organizations that receive this questionnaire to answer the questions and return the report to the U.S. Census Bureau. By the same law, **YOUR CENSUS REPORT IS CONFIDENTIAL.** It may be seen only by persons sworn to uphold the confidentiality of Census Bureau information and may be used only for statistical purposes. Further, copies retained in respondents' files are immune from legal process.

- • Use blue or black ink.
- • Do not use pencil.
- • Place an "X" inside the box.
- • Please center numbers in their respective boxes. Examples:
- • Do not put slashes through 0 or 7.

☒  | 0 1 2 3 4 5 6 7 8 9

The reporting unit for this form is an establishment. An **establishment** is generally a single physical location where business is conducted or where services or industrial operations are performed. For further clarification, see information sheet(s).

**1** MONTHS IN OPERATION

| | Mark "X" if None | 2002 Number of months |
|---|---|---|
| Number of months in operation during 2002 *(If none, mark "X" and go to ㉙.)* . . . . . . 0002 | ☐ | |

**2** EMPLOYER IDENTIFICATION NUMBER

Is the Employer Identification Number (EIN) shown in the mailing address the same as the one used for this establishment on its latest 2002 Internal Revenue Service Form 941, Employer's Quarterly Federal Tax Return?

0021 ☐ Yes    0022 ☐ No - Enter current EIN *(9 digits)* ⟶ 0025 | | - | |

**3** PHYSICAL LOCATION

**A.** Is this establishment's physical location the same as shown in the mailing address?
*(P.O. box and rural route addresses are not physical locations.)*

0031 ☐ Yes

0035 Number and street

0032 ☐ No - Enter physical ⟶ location

0036 City, town, village, etc.     | 0037 State | 0038 ZIP Code | - |

**B.** Is this establishment physically located inside the legal boundaries of the city, town, village, etc.?

0041 ☐ Yes    0042 ☐ No    0043 ☐ No legal boundaries    0044 ☐ Do not know

**C.** Type of municipality where this establishment is physically located

0046 ☐ City, village, or borough    0047 ☐ Town or township    0048 ☐ Other or do not know

**PENALTY FOR FAILURE TO REPORT**

**CONTINUE ON PAGE 2**

| | | | | Mark "X" if None | 2002 | | |
|---|---|---|---|---|---|---|---|
| | | | | | $ Bil. | Mil. | Thou. |

*HOW TO REPORT DOLLAR FIGURES*

Dollar figures should be **rounded** to **thousands** of dollars.

If a figure is **$1,025,628.79:**    **Report** ⟶ ☐    | | | 1 | 0 2 6

If a value is "0" (or less than $500.00):   **Report** ⟶ ☒

**4**   SALES, SHIPMENTS, RECEIPTS, OR REVENUE

| | | Mark "X" if None | 2002 | | |
|---|---|---|---|---|---|
| | | | $ Bil. | Mil. | Thou. |

**A.** Total value of products shipped and other receipts *(Report detail in ㉒.)*.   . . .   0100   ☐

**B.** Value of products exported *(This is a breakout of the value reported on line A.)*

Report the value of products shipped for export. Include shipments to customers in the Panama Canal Zone, the Commonwealth of Puerto Rico, and U.S. possessions, as well as the value of products shipped to exporters or other wholesalers for export. Also, include the value of products sold to the U.S. Government to be shipped to foreign governments. Exclude products shipped for further manufacture, assembly, or fabrication in the United States.   . . . . . . . . . . . . . . . . . . . . . . .   0130   ☐

**5**   E-COMMERCE SALES, SHIPMENTS, RECEIPTS, OR REVENUE

**A.** Did any of the amount reported in **4**, line A include e-commerce sales, shipments, or receipts? *(E-commerce sales, shipments, or receipts are online orders for products from customers where price and/or terms of the sale are accepted or negotiated over an Internet, Extranet, Electronic Data Interchange (EDI) network, electronic mail, or other online system. Payment may or may not be made online.)*

0181   ☐   Yes - *Go to line B*     0182   ☐   No - *Go to* **6**

| 2002 |
|---|
| Percent |

**B.** Percent of total value of products shipped and other receipts reported in **4**, line A using e-commerce *(Report whole percents. Estimates are acceptable.)*   . . . . . . . . . . . . . . . . . .   0109   |     % |

*CONTINUE ON PAGE 3*

**6** EMPLOYMENT AND PAYROLL

*Include:*

   • *Full- and part-time employees working at this establishment whose payroll was reported on Internal Revenue Service Form 941, Employer's Quarterly Federal Tax Return, and filed under the Employer Identification Number (EIN) shown in the mailing address or corrected in ❷.*

*Exclude:*

   • *Full- or part-time leased employees whose payroll was filed under an employee leasing company's EIN.*
   • *Temporary staffing obtained from a staffing service.*

*For further clarification, see information sheet(s).*

**A.** Number of employees

| | | Mark "X" if None | 2002 Number |
|---|---|---|---|
| **1.** Number of production workers for pay periods including: | | | |
|    **a.** March 12 . . . . . . . . . . . . . . . . . . . . 0325 | | ☐ | |
|    **b.** May 12 . . . . . . . . . . . . . . . . . . . . . 0326 | | ☐ | |
|    **c.** August 12 . . . . . . . . . . . . . . . . . . . 0327 | | ☐ | |
|    **d.** November 12 . . . . . . . . . . . . . . . . . 0328 | | ☐ | |
| **2. Sum lines A1a through A1d** . . . . . . . . 0329 | | ☐ | |
| **3.** Average annual production workers *(Divide line 2 by 4 - omit fractions.)* . . . . . 0335 | | ☐ | |
| **4.** All other employees for pay period including March 12 . . . . . . . . . . . . 0336 | | ☐ | |
| **5. TOTAL** *(Sum lines A3 and A4)* . . . . . . . 0337 | | ☐ | |

**B.** Payroll before deductions *(Exclude employer's cost for fringe benefits.)*

| | Mark "X" if None | 2002 $ Mil. | Thou. |
|---|---|---|---|
| **1.** Annual payroll | | | |
|    **a.** Production workers . . . . . . . . . . . . . . 0304 | ☐ | | |
|    **b.** All other employees . . . . . . . . . . . . . 0305 | ☐ | | |
|    **c. TOTAL** *(Sum lines B1a and B1b)* . . . . . . 0300 | ☐ | | |
| **2.** First quarter payroll *(January-March, 2002)* . . . . . . 0310 | ☐ | | |
| **C.** Employer's cost for fringe benefits . . . . . . . . . 0220 | ☐ | | |

| | Mark "X" if None | 2002 Hours Thou. |
|---|---|---|
| **D.** Number of annual hours worked by production workers *(Annual hours worked by production workers reported on line A1.)* . . . . . . . . . . . . 0200 | ☐ | |

*CONTINUE ON PAGE 4*

**7** LEASED EMPLOYMENT AND PAYROLL

**A.** Did this establishment have any full- or part-time leased employees whose payroll was filed under an employee leasing company's EIN?

*Exclude:*
- *Temporary staffing obtained from a staffing service.*
- *Contractors, subcontractors, or independent contractors.*
- *Purchased or managed services, such as janitorial, guard, or landscape services.*
- *Professional or technical services purchased from another firm, such as software consulting, computer programming, engineering, or accounting services.*
- *Employees already reported in* **6***.*

*For further clarification, see information sheet(s).*

0241 ☐ Yes - *Go to line B*

0242 ☐ No - *Go to* **10**

**B.** Number of leased employees

| | | | Mark "X" if None | 2002 Number |
|---|---|---|---|---|
| **1.** Number of leased production workers for pay periods including: | | | | |
| | **a.** March 12. . . . . . . . . . . . . . . . . . | 0375 | ☐ | |
| | **b.** May 12. . . . . . . . . . . . . . . . . . . | 0376 | ☐ | |
| | **c.** August 12 . . . . . . . . . . . . . . . . . | 0377 | ☐ | |
| | **d.** November 12. . . . . . . . . . . . . . . | 0378 | ☐ | |
| **2. Sum lines B1a through B1d** . . . . . . . . . . . . . . . . . | | 0379 | ☐ | |
| **3.** Average annual leased production workers *(Divide line 2 by 4 - omit fractions)* . . | | 0385 | ☐ | |
| **4.** All other leased employees for pay period including March 12 . . . . . . . . . . | | 0386 | ☐ | |
| **5. TOTAL** *(Sum lines B3 and B4)* . . . . . . . . . . . . . . . . . . . . . . | | 0384 | ☐ | |

**C.** Payroll for leased employees before deductions *(Exclude employer's cost for fringe benefits.)*

| | | | Mark "X" if None | 2002 $ Mil. | Thou. |
|---|---|---|---|---|---|
| **1.** Annual payroll for leased employees | | | | | |
| | **a.** Leased production workers . . . . . . . . . . . . | 0354 | ☐ | | |
| | **b.** Other leased employees . . . . . . . . . . . . . | 0355 | ☐ | | |
| | **c. TOTAL** *(Sum lines C1a and C1b)* . . . . . . . . . | 0350 | ☐ | | |
| **2.** First quarter payroll for leased employees *(January-March, 2002)*. . . . . . . . | | 0360 | ☐ | | |

**D.** Employer's fringe benefits cost for leased employees *(Include fringe benefits for all leased employees reported on line B.)* . . . . . . . . . . . . . . . . . . . . . . . . . . . . 0225 ☐

| | | | Mark "X" if None | 2002 Hours Thou. |
|---|---|---|---|---|
| **E.** Number of annual hours worked by leased production workers *(Annual hours worked by leased production workers reported on line B1.)* . . . . . . . . . . . . | | 0205 | ☐ | |

**8** – **9** Not Applicable.

*CONTINUE ON PAGE 5*

264

**10** INVENTORIES

*(Report inventories using generally accepted accounting practices.)*

Were inventories of this establishment subject to the Last-in, First-out (LIFO) method of valuation?

0481 ☐ Yes - *Use the sum of the LIFO amount plus the LIFO reserve for completing lines A through F2. If you changed to LIFO for calendar year 2002, specify in the REMARKS section.*

0482 ☐ No - *Complete only lines A through E1. Line E1 should equal line D.*

| | Mark "X" if None | End of 2002 | | | Mark "X" if None | End of 2001 | | |
|---|---|---|---|---|---|---|---|---|
| | | $ Bil. | Mil. | Thou. | | $ Bil. | Mil. | Thou. |
| **A.** Finished goods . . . . . . . . . . . 0461 | ☐ | | | | 0471 ☐ | | | |
| **B.** Work-in-process. . . . . . . . . . 0463 | ☐ | | | | 0473 ☐ | | | |
| **C.** Materials, supplies, fuels, etc. . . . . 0462 | ☐ | | | | 0472 ☐ | | | |
| **D. TOTAL**. . . . . . . . . . . . . 0460 | ☐ | | | | 0470 ☐ | | | |
| **E.** Of the value on line D report: | | | | | | | | |
|   **1.** Amount not subject to LIFO costing . . . . . . . . . . . . 0464 | ☐ | | | | 0474 ☐ | | | |
|   **2.** Amount subject to LIFO costing *(gross)* . . . . . . . . . . . . 0465 | ☐ | | | | 0475 ☐ | | | |
| **F.** Of the value on line E2 report: | | | | | | | | |
|   **1.** Amount of LIFO reserve . . . . . 0466 | ☐ | | | | 0476 ☐ | | | |
|   **2.** Amount of LIFO value *(net)*. . . . 0467 | ☐ | | | | 0477 ☐ | | | |

**11** Not Applicable.

*CONTINUE ON PAGE 6*

**12** ASSETS, CAPITAL EXPENDITURES, RETIREMENTS, AND DEPRECIATION
*(Refer to the instructions on how to report leasing arrangements.)*

Report the dollar value of assets, capital expenditures, and depreciation

| | Mark "X" if None | 2002 $ Mil. | Thou. |
|---|---|---|---|
| **A.** Gross value of depreciable assets (acquisition costs) at the beginning of the year. . . 0500 | ☐ | | |
| **B.** Capital expenditures for new and used depreciable assets in 2002 | | | |
|    **1.** Capital expenditures for new and used buildings and other structures *(Exclude land.)* . . . . . . . . . . . . . . . . . . . . . . . . . . . . 0525 | ☐ | | |
|    **2.** Capital expenditures for new and used machinery and equipment . . . . . . . . 0530 | ☐ | | |
|    **3. TOTAL** *(Sum lines B1 and B2)* . . . . . . . . . . . 0520 | ☐ | | |
| **C.** Gross value of depreciable assets sold, retired, scrapped, destroyed, etc.. . . . . . . 0510 | ☐ | | |
| **D.** Gross value of depreciable assets at the end of 2002 *(Sum lines A and B3 minus C)* . 0505 | ☐ | | |
| **E.** Depreciation charges . . . . . . . . . . . . . . . . . . . . . 0540 | ☐ | | |
| **F.** Breakdown of expenditures for new and used machinery and equipment by type *(Reported on line B2.)* | | | |
|    **1.** Automobiles, trucks, etc., for highway use. . . . . . . . . . . . . . . . 0522 | ☐ | | |
|    **2.** Computers and peripheral data processing equipment . . . . . . . . . . . . 0523 | ☐ | | |
|    **3.** All other expenditures for machinery and equipment . . . . . . . . . . . . 0524 | ☐ | | |
|    **4. TOTAL** *(Sum lines F1 through F3)* . . . . . . . . . . . . . . . . . 0529 | ☐ | | |

**13** RENTAL PAYMENTS

| | Mark "X" if None | 2002 $ Mil. | Thou. |
|---|---|---|---|
| **A.** Rental payments for buildings and other structures *(Include land.)*. . . . . . . . . . 0551 | ☐ | | |
| **B.** Rental payments for machinery and equipment. . . . . . . . . . . . . . . . . 0552 | ☐ | | |
| **C. TOTAL** *(Sum lines A and B)*. . . . . . . . . . . . . . . . . . . . . . 0550 | ☐ | | |

**14** Not Applicable.

*CONTINUE ON PAGE 7*

266

**If not shown, please enter your 11-digit Census File Number (CFN) from the mailing address.** ▶

**15** SELECTED EXPENSES

| | | Mark "X" if None | 2002 | | |
|---|---|---|---|---|---|
| | | | $ Bil. | Mil. | Thou. |
| **A.** Selected production related costs | | | | | |
| **1.** Cost of materials, parts, containers, packaging, etc. used *(Report detail in* **16***.)* . . . . . . . . . . . . . . . . . . . 0421 | | ☐ | | | |
| **2.** Cost of products bought and sold as such without further processing *(Report sales in* **22***.)* . . . . . . . . . . . . . 0426 | | ☐ | | | |
| **3.** Cost of purchased fuels consumed for heat, power, or the generation of electricity . . . . . . . . . . . . . . . . . . 0430 | | ☐ | | | |
| **4.** Cost of purchased electricity *(Report quantity on line B1.)* . . . . . . . . 0425 | | ☐ | | | |
| **5.** Cost of work done for you by others on your materials . . . . . . . . . 0424 | | ☐ | | | |
| **6.** **TOTAL** *(Sum lines A1 through A5).* . . . . . . . . . . . . . . . . . . 0420 | | ☐ | | | |

| | | Mark "X" if None | 2002 | |
|---|---|---|---|---|
| | | | Kilowatthours | |
| | | | Mil. | Thou. |
| **B.** Quantity of Electricity | | | | |
| **1.** Purchased electricity *(Quantity comparable to cost reported on line A4.)* . . . . . 0436 | | ☐ | | |
| **2.** Generated electricity *(Gross less generating station use)* . . . . . . . . . . . . 0437 | | ☐ | | |
| **3.** Electricity sold or transferred to other establishments *(Include on lines B1 or B2.)* . 0438 | | ☐ | | |

**16** DETAILED COST OF MATERIALS, PARTS, AND SUPPLIES

**General -** The materials, parts, and supplies listed below are those commonly consumed in the manufacture, processing, or assembly of the products listed in **22**. Please review the entire list and report separately each item consumed. Leave blank if you do not consume the item. If you use materials, parts, and supplies that are not listed, describe and report them in the "Cost of all other materials . . . " at the end of this section. If you consumed less than $25,000 of a listed material, include the value with "Cost of all other materials . . . " Census material code 009700 99 8.

Report materials, parts, and supplies purchased, transferred from other plants of your company, or withdrawn from inventory.

If quantities are requested, please use the unit of measure specified.

If the information as requested cannot be taken directly from your book records, REASONABLE ESTIMATES ARE ACCEPTABLE.

**Valuation of Materials Consumed -** The value of the materials, etc., consumed should be based on the delivered cost; i.e., the amount paid or payable after discounts and including freight and other direct charges incurred in acquiring the materials.

Materials received from other plants within your company should be reported at their full economic value (the value assigned by the shipping plant, plus the cost of freight and other handling charges).

If purchases or transfers do not differ significantly from the amounts actually put into production, you may report the cost of purchases or transfers. However, if consumption differs significantly from the amounts purchased or transferred, these amounts should be adjusted for changes in the materials and supplies inventories by adding the beginning inventory to the amount purchased or transferred and subtracting ending inventory.

**Contract Work -** Include as materials consumed those you purchased for use by others making products for you under contract. Amounts paid to the companies doing the contract work should be reported in **15**, line A5, and should include freight in and out. On the other hand, materials owned by others but used at this establishment in making products for others under contract or on commission should be excluded.

**Resales -** Cost for products bought and sold or transferred from other establishments of your company and sold without further manufacture, processing, or assembly should be reported in **15**, line A2, not in **16**. The value of these products shipped by this establishment should be reported in **22** under Census product code 000999 8900 6, "Resales."

| Line No. | Materials, parts, and supplies | Census material code | Unit of measure for quantities | Consumption of purchased materials and of materials received from other establishments of your company | | | |
|---|---|---|---|---|---|---|---|
| | | | | Quantity | Cost, including delivery cost (freight-in) | | |
| | | | | | $ Bil. | Mil. | Thou. |
| | 0634 | 0630 | 0636 | 0632 | 0631 | | |
| 1 | Whole milk . . . . . . . . . . . . . . . . . . . . . | 112120 00 1 | hundred-weight | | | | |
| 2 | Fluid skim milk . . . . . . . . . . . . . . . . . . . | 311511 01 8 | | | | | |
| 3 | Cream . . . . . . . . . . . . . . . . . . . . . . . . | 311511 03 4 | | | | | |
| 4 | Butter . . . . . . . . . . . . . . . . . . . . . . . . | 311512 00 8 | | | | | |
| 5 | Condensed and evaporated milk . . . . . . . . | 311514 01 2 | 1000 lb | | | | |
| 6 | Dry milk . . . . . . . . . . . . . . . . . . . . . . . | 311514 07 9 | | | | | |
| 7 | Natural cheese, other than cottage cheese . . . . . | 311513 01 4 | | | | | |
| | Dairy product mixes | | | | | | |
| 8 | Ice cream mix (excluding lowfat and nonfat) . . | 311520 01 9 | | | | | |
| 9 | Ice cream mix, lowfat . . . . . . . . . . . . . . | 311520 05 0 | 1000 gal | | | | |
| 10 | Ice cream mix, nonfat . . . . . . . . . . . . . . | 311520 09 2 | | | | | |
| 11 | Sherbet mix . . . . . . . . . . . . . . . . . . . . | 311520 03 5 | | | | | |
| 12 | Yogurt mix . . . . . . . . . . . . . . . . . . . . | 311520 07 6 | | | | | |
| 13 | Fats and oils, all types (purchased as such) . . . . . | 311000 19 4 | 1000 lb | | | | |

*CONTINUE WITH* **16** *ON PAGE 9*

*CONTINUE ON PAGE 9*

**16** DETAILED COST OF MATERIALS, PARTS, AND SUPPLIES - Continued

| Line No. | Materials, parts, and supplies | Census material code | Unit of measure for quantities | Consumption of purchased materials and of materials received from other establishments of your company | | | |
|---|---|---|---|---|---|---|---|
| | | | | Quantity | Cost, including delivery cost (freight-in) | | |
| | | | | | $ Bil. | Mil. | Thou. |
| | 0634 | 0630 | 0636 | 0632 | 0631 | | |
| | Sweeteners | | | | | | |
| 14 | High fructose corn syrup (HFCS) in terms of solids . . . . . . . . . . . . . . . . . . . . . . | 311221 03 0 | ↕ 1000 lb | | | | |
| 15 | Crystalline fructose (dry fructose) . . . . . . . . | 311221 17 0 | | | | | |
| 16 | Dextrose and corn syrup including corn syrup solids (dry weight) . . . . . . . . . . . . . . . . . | 311221 19 6 | | | | | |
| 17 | Sugar (cane and beet) (in terms of sugar solids) | 311310 03 1 | short tons | | | | |
| 18 | Whey, liquid, concentrated, dried, and modified whey products in terms of solids . . . . . . . . . | 311514 03 8 | ↕ 1000 lb | | | | |
| 19 | Casein and caseinates . . . . . . . . . . . . . | 001900 35 6 | | | | | |
| 20 | Chocolate (compounds, cocoa, chocolate liquor, coatings, chocolate flavoring, etc.) . . . . . . . . | 311320 01 4 | | | | | |
| 21 | Flavorings, excluding chocolate (natural, artificial, imitation, etc.) . . . . . . . . . . . . . . . . . . | 001900 36 4 | | | | | |
| 22 | Plastics resins consumed in the form of granules, pellets, powders, liquids, etc., but excluding sheets, rods, tubes, and other shapes . . . . . . . . . . . | 325211 05 0 | | | | | |
| 23 | Packaging paper and plastics film, coated and laminated . . . . . . . . . . . . . . . . . . . . | 001900 A1 7 | | | | | |
| 24 | Bags (plastics, foil, and coated paper) . . . . . . | 001900 A3 3 | | | | | |
| 25 | Plastics products consumed in the form of sheets, rods, tubes, and other shapes . . . . . . . . . . | 326100 13 8 | | | | | |
| | Containers | | | | | | |
| 26 | Glass containers . . . . . . . . . . . . . . . | 327213 01 3 | | | | | |
| 27 | Plastics containers, excluding bags . . . . . . . | 326100 29 4 | | | | | |
| 28 | Paperboard containers, boxes, and corrugated paperboard . . . . . . . . . . . . . . . . . . | 322210 01 4 | | | | | |

*CONTINUE WITH* **16** *ON PAGE 10*

**CONTINUE ON PAGE 10**

269

## 16 DETAILED COST OF MATERIALS, PARTS, AND SUPPLIES - Continued

| Line No. | Materials, parts, and supplies | Census material code | Unit of measure for quantities | Consumption of purchased materials and of materials received from other establishments of your company | | | |
|---|---|---|---|---|---|---|---|
| | | | | Quantity | Cost, including delivery cost (freight-in) | | |
| | | | | | $ Bil. | Mil. | Thou. |
| | 0634 | 0630 | 0636 | 0632 | 0631 | | |
| 29 | Metal cans, can lids, and ends . . . . . . . . . . . | 332431 01 4 | | | | | |
| 30 | Cost of all other materials and components, parts, containers, and supplies consumed (*Specify the principal materials, etc., included in this value.*) ⬊ | 009700 99 8 | | | | | |
| | | | | | | | |
| | | | | | | | |
| | | | | | | | |
| 31 | TOTAL (*Should equal total reported in* 15 *, line A1*) | 771000 00 7 | | | | | |

## 17 - 21 Not Applicable.

## 22 DETAIL OF SALES, SHIPMENTS, RECEIPTS, OR REVENUE

**General** - The manufactured products and services listed below are generally made in your industry. If you make products that are not listed, describe and report them in the "All other products made in this establishment" section at the end of 22. PLEASE DO NOT COMBINE PRODUCT LINES.

If quantities are requested, please use the unit of measure specified.

If the information as requested cannot be taken directly from your book records, REASONABLE ESTIMATES ARE ACCEPTABLE.

**Valuation of Products** - Report the value of the products shipped and services performed at the net selling value, f.o.b. plant to the customer; i.e., after discounts and allowances, and exclusive of freight charges and excise taxes.

If you transfer products to other establishments within your company, you should assign the full economic value to the transferred products; i.e., include all direct costs of production and a reasonable proportion of all other costs and profits.

**Contract Work** - Report PRODUCTS MADE BY OTHERS FOR YOU FROM YOUR MATERIALS on the specific lines as if they were made in this establishment. On the other hand, do not report on the specific product lines PRODUCTS THAT YOU MADE FROM MATERIALS OWNED BY OTHERS. Report only the amount that you received for "commission or contract receipts" under Census code 000930 0000 8.

**Resales** - Do not report on the specific product lines those PRODUCTS BOUGHT AND SOLD OR TRANSFERRED FROM OTHER ESTABLISHMENTS OF YOUR COMPANY AND SOLD WITHOUT FURTHER MANUFACTURE. Report only a value under Census code 000999 8900 6, "Resales."

**Receiving Stations** - Establishments that do not have bottling or pasteurizing operations but receive fluid milk in bulk and ship it, without processing to bottling or other manufacturing plants of the same company, should report on 2002 Economic Census Form TW-48459 "Trucking and Warehousing (Enterprise Support)." Establishments which are engaged in the business of buying bulk fluid milk and selling it at wholesale, without processing or bottling, should report on 2002 Economic Census Form WH-42213, "Dairy Products."

**Distribution Points (Relay Stations)** - Some plants maintain outlying distribution points (relay stations) to facilitate house-to-house delivery in nearby cities. Such locations should be considered as part of this establishment in preparing this report, provided their primary activity is the distribution of goods to household consumers. Any such locations distributing primarily at wholesale (to retail stores, etc.) should be regarded as manufacturer's sales branches and listed separately on 2002 Economic Census Form WH-42213, "Dairy Products."

*CONTINUE WITH* 22 *ON PAGE 11*

**CONTINUE ON PAGE 11**

## 22 DETAIL OF SALES, SHIPMENTS, RECEIPTS, OR REVENUE - Continued

| Line No. | Products and services *Items correspond to products reported on Current Industrial Reports (CIR) 0734 | Census product code 0730 | Unit of measure for quantities 0736 | Products shipped and other receipts | | | |
|---|---|---|---|---|---|---|---|
| | | | | Quantity 0732 | Value, f.o.b. plant | | |
| | | | | | $ Bil. 0731 | Mil. | Thou. |
| | **Butter (churned in this plant)** *(Report butter churned elsewhere and repackaged in this plant as a resale on line 110.)* | | | | | | |
| 1 | Shipped in consumer packages or containers of more than 3 pounds or in bulk . . . . . . . . . | 311512 0111 3 | | | | | |
| 2 | Shipped in consumer packages or containers (3 pounds or less) . . . . . . . . . . . . . . . . . | 311512 0121 2 | | | | | |
| 3 | Anhydrous milkfat (butteroil) . . . . . . . . . | 311512 0131 1 | | | | | |
| 4 | **Margarine, butter blends and butter substitutes** (Corresponds to CIR form M311N, item code 8300)* | 311225 4100 1 | | | | | |
| | **Natural cheese, except cottage cheese (cheddar, Swiss, Italian, brick, cream, grated, dried, etc.)** *(Report cheese manufactured elsewhere and repackaged in this plant as resale on line 110.)* Natural cheese (excluding lowfat natural cheese) except cottage cheese | | | | | | |
| 5 | Shipped in consumer packages or containers (3 pounds or less) . . . . . . . . . . . . . . | 311513 1111 0 | | | | | |
| 6 | Shipped in consumer packages or containers of more than 3 pounds or in bulk . . . . . . | 311513 1121 9 | | | | | |
| | Lowfat natural cheese, except cottage cheese | | | | | | |
| 7 | Shipped in consumer packages or containers (3 pounds or less) . . . . . . . . . . . . . . | 311513 1131 8 | 1000 lb | | | | |
| 8 | Shipped in packages or containers of more than 3 pounds or in bulk . . . . . . . . . . . | 311513 1141 7 | | | | | |
| | **Process cheese and related products (pasteurized and blended)** Process cheese | | | | | | |
| 9 | Shipped in consumer packages or containers (3 pounds or less) . . . . . . . . . . . . . . | 311513 4111 7 | | | | | |
| 10 | Shipped in consumer packages or containers of more than 3 pounds or in bulk . . . . . . | 311513 4221 4 | | | | | |
| 11 | Cheese food . . . . . . . . . . . . . . . . . | 311513 4231 3 | | | | | |
| 12 | Cheese spread . . . . . . . . . . . . . . . . | 311513 4241 2 | | | | | |
| 13 | Other related cheese products (including flavored cheese dips) . . . . . . . . . . . . . | 311513 4251 1 | | | | | |
| | Cheese substitutes and imitations | | | | | | |
| 14 | Products substituting for natural cheese . . . . | 311513 7111 4 | | | | | |
| 15 | Products substituting for processed cheese or related products . . . . . . . . . . . . . . . . | 311513 7121 3 | | | | | |
| 16 | Raw liquid whey . . . . . . . . . . . . . . . . | 311513 A100 3 | | | | | |

CONTINUE WITH 22 ON PAGE 12

CONTINUE ON PAGE 12

271

## 22 DETAIL OF SALES, SHIPMENTS, RECEIPTS, OR REVENUE - Continued

| Line No. | Products and services *Items correspond to products reported on Current Industrial Reports (CIR) 0734 | Census product code 0730 | Unit of measure for quantities 0736 | Products shipped and other receipts | | | |
|---|---|---|---|---|---|---|---|
| | | | | Quantity 0732 | Value, f.o.b. plant | | |
| | | | | | $ Bil. 0731 | Mil. | Thou. |
| | **Dry milk products and mixtures** *(Report soy base or other substitutes on lines 42-45.)* | | | | | | |
| | Shipped in consumer packages or containers (3 pounds or less) | | | | | | |
| 17 | Nonfat dry milk . . . . . . . . . . . . . | 311514 1111 8 | | | | | |
| 18 | Infants' formula . . . . . . . . . . . . . . | 311514 1221 5 | | | | | |
| 19 | Other dry milk products (instant chocolate milk, weight control products, whole milk powder, malted milk powder, powdered cream, etc.) . . . . . . . . . . . . . . . . . | 311514 1331 2 | | | | | |
| | Shipped in consumer packages or containers of more than 3 pounds or in bulk | | | | | | |
| | Food grade (bakeries, confectioners, meat packers, etc.) | | | | | | |
| 20 | Dry whole milk . . . . . . . . . . . . . | 311514 1441 9 | | | | | |
| 21 | Nonfat dry milk . . . . . . . . . . . . | 311514 1551 5 | 1000 lb | | | | |
| 22 | Dry whey . . . . . . . . . . . . . | 311514 1661 2 | | | | | |
| 23 | Modified dry whey products (whey protein concentrates, etc.) . . . . . . . . . | 311514 1671 1 | | | | | |
| 24 | Lactose . . . . . . . . . . . . . | 311514 1681 0 | | | | | |
| 25 | Other food grade dry milk products . . . | 311514 1791 7 | | | | | |
| 26 | Feed grade (dry milk, dry buttermilk, dry whey, etc.) . . . . . . . . . . . . . . . . | 311514 18A1 3 | | | | | |
| | **Canned milk products (consumer type cans)** *(Report soy base or other substitutes on lines 46 and 47.)* | | | | | | |
| 27 | Evaporated milk . . . . . . . . . . . . . . . | 311514 4111 5 | | | | | |
| 28 | Condensed milk . . . . . . . . . . . . . . | 311514 4121 4 | | | | | |
| 29 | Canned dietary supplements, weight control products . . . . . . . . . . . . . . . . . . . . | 311514 4131 3 | | | | | |
| 30 | Infants' formula, liquid . . . . . . . . . . . | 311514 4241 0 | | | | | |
| 31 | Other canned milk products (including canned whole milk) . . . . . . . . . . . . . . . . . | 311514 4351 7 | | | | | |
| | **Concentrated milk products shipped in bulk (barrels, drums, and tanks)** | | | | | | |
| 32 | Feed grade (including concentrated whey and buttermilk) . . . . . . . . . . . . . . . | 311514 7111 2 | | | | | |

*CONTINUE WITH 22 ON PAGE 13*

*CONTINUE ON PAGE 13*

**22** DETAIL OF SALES, SHIPMENTS, RECEIPTS, OR REVENUE - Continued

| Line No. | Products and services *Items correspond to products reported on Current Industrial Reports (CIR) 0734 | Census product code 0730 | Unit of measure for quantities 0736 | Products shipped and other receipts | | | |
|---|---|---|---|---|---|---|---|
| | | | | Quantity 0732 | Value, f.o.b. plant | | |
| | | | | | $ Bil. 0731 | Mil. | Thou. |
| | Concentrated milk products shipped in bulk (barrels, drums, and tanks) - Continued | | | | | | |
| | Food grade (except all types of ice cream mixes) | | 1000 lb | | | | |
| 33 | Concentrated whey in terms of solids .... | 311514 7121 1 | | | | | |
| 34 | Other food grade concentrated milk products | 311514 7131 0 | | | | | |
| | Ice cream mixes and related products | | | | | | |
| 35 | Ice cream (excluding lowfat and nonfat) ..... | 311514 A111 8 | | | | | |
| 36 | Ice cream, lowfat ................. | 311514 A121 7 | | | | | |
| 37 | Ice cream, nonfat ................ | 311514 A131 6 | 1000 gal | | | | |
| 38 | Sherbet ...................... | 311514 A241 3 | | | | | |
| 39 | Yogurt ...................... | 311514 A251 2 | | | | | |
| 40 | Milkshake .................... | 311514 A261 1 | | | | | |
| 41 | Other mixes ................... | 311514 A271 0 | | | | | |
| | Products that substitute for dairy products | | | | | | |
| | Dry | | | | | | |
| 42 | Coffee whiteners ................ | 311514 D111 5 | 1000 lb | | | | |
| 43 | Infants' formula ............... | 311514 D121 4 | | | | | |
| 44 | Sour cream substitutes ........... | 311514 D131 3 | | | | | |
| 45 | Other dry dairy products substitutes (including whipped topping, etc.) *(Specify product.)* | 311514 D141 2 | | | | | |
| | Canned | | | | | | |
| 46 | Liquid infants' formula ............. | 311514 D151 1 | 1000 lb | | | | |
| 47 | Other canned dairy product substitutes (including dietary supplements and weight control products) ............... | 311514 D161 0 | | | | | |
| | Other | | | | | | |
| | Perishable | | 1000 qt | | | | |
| 48 | Flavored dips ................. | 311511 D111 1 | | | | | |
| 49 | Whipped topping (including pressure can type) ...................... | 311511 D121 0 | 1000 lb | | | | |

CONTINUE WITH **22** ON PAGE 14

CONTINUE ON PAGE 14

273

**22** DETAIL OF SALES, SHIPMENTS, RECEIPTS, OR REVENUE - Continued

| Line No. | Products and services<br>*Items correspond to products reported on Current Industrial Reports (CIR)<br>0734 | Census product code<br>0730 | Unit of measure for quantities<br>0736 | Products shipped and other receipts | | | |
|---|---|---|---|---|---|---|---|
| | | | | Quantity<br>0732 | Value, f.o.b. plant | | |
| | | | | | $ Bil.<br>0731 | Mil. | Thou. |
| | Products that substitute for dairy products - Continued | | | | | | |
| | Other - Continued | | | | | | |
| | Perishable - Continued | | 1000 qt | | | | |
| 50 | Coffee whiteners . . . . . . . . . . . . . . | 311511 D131 9 | | | | | |
| 51 | Flavored milk drinks (chocolate drink, etc.) . . . . . . . . . . . . . | 311511 D151 7 | | | | | |
| 52 | Sour cream substitutes . . . . . . . . . . | 311511 D141 8 | | | | | |
| | Other perishable dairy product substitutes (Specify product.) | | | | | | |
| 53 | | 311511 D161 6 | | | | | |
| | Frozen | | 1000 lb | | | | |
| 54 | Whipped topping . . . . . . . . . . . . . | 311412 4111 2 | | | | | |
| 55 | Other frozen dairy product substitutes (except mellorine and similar frozen desserts) . . . . . . . . . . | 311412 4221 9 | | | | | |
| | Ice cream and ices | | | | | | |
| | Ice cream (including custards) | | | | | | |
| | Ice cream (excluding lowfat and nonfat) | | | | | | |
| 56 | Shipped in bulk (containers 3 gallons or more) . . . . . . . . . . . . . . . . . | 311520 0111 6 | | | | | |
| 57 | Shipped in container sizes (less than 3 gallons) . . . . . . . . . . . . . . . . . | 311520 0221 3 | | | | | |
| 58 | Novelty forms . . . . . . . . . . . . . . | 311520 0331 0 | | | | | |
| | Ice cream, lowfat | | | | | | |
| 59 | Shipped in bulk (containers 3 gallons or more) . . . . . . . . . . . . . . . . . | 311520 0441 7 | 1000 gal | | | | |
| 60 | Shipped in container sizes (less than 3 gallons) . . . . . . . . . . . . . . . . . | 311520 0451 6 | | | | | |
| 61 | Novelty forms . . . . . . . . . . . . . . | 311520 0461 5 | | | | | |
| 62 | Shipped in bulk (containers 3 gallons or more) . . . . . . . . . . . . . . . . . | 311520 0471 4 | | | | | |
| | Ice cream, nonfat | | | | | | |
| 63 | Shipped in container sizes (less than 3 gallons) . . . . . . . . . . . . . . . . . | 311520 0481 3 | | | | | |
| 64 | Novelty forms . . . . . . . . . . . . . . | 311520 0491 2 | | | | | |

CONTINUE WITH **22** ON PAGE 15

*CONTINUE ON PAGE 15*

**22** DETAIL OF SALES, SHIPMENTS, RECEIPTS, OR REVENUE - Continued

| Line No. | Products and services *Items correspond to products reported on Current Industrial Reports (CIR) 0734 | Census product code 0730 | Unit of measure for quantities 0736 | Products shipped and other receipts | | | |
|---|---|---|---|---|---|---|---|
| | | | | Quantity 0732 | Value, f.o.b. plant | | |
| | | | | | $ Bil. 0731 | Mil. | Thou. |
| | Ice cream and ices  - Continued | | | | | | |
| | Frozen yogurt *(Report other yogurt on lines 91 and 92.)* | | | | | | |
| 65 | Regular and lowfat frozen yogurt . . . . . . . | 311520 05A1 7 | | | | | |
| 66 | Nonfat frozen yogurt . . . . . . . . . . . . . | 311520 05B1 6 | | | | | |
| | Sherbet | | | | | | |
| 67 | Shipped in bulk (containers 3 gallons or more) . . . . . . . . . . . . . . . . . . . . . | 311520 05C1 5 | 1000 gal | | | | |
| 68 | All other sizes (including novelty forms) . . | 311520 05D1 4 | | | | | |
| | Ices | | | | | | |
| 69 | Water ices containing no real fruit or fruit juice . . . . . . . . . . . . . . . . . . . . . . | 311520 05E1 3 | | | | | |
| 70 | Ices containing some real fruit or fruit juice | 311520 05F1 2 | | | | | |
| 71 | Mellorine and similar frozen desserts containing fats other than butterfat (including tofu-type) . | 311520 05G1 1 | | | | | |
| 72 | Other frozen desserts (frozen pudding, etc.) . . | 311520 05H1 0 | | | | | |
| | Bulk fluid milk and cream (sales and transfers to other plants and dealers) | | | | | | |
| 73 | Fluid whole milk, bulk sales . . . . . . . . . . . | 311511 1111 4 | | | | | |
| 74 | Fluid skim milk, bulk sales . . . . . . . . . . . . | 311511 1221 1 | 1000 lb | | | | |
| 75 | Fluid cream and buttermilk, bulk sales . . . . . . | 311511 1231 0 | | | | | |
| 76 | Other bulk fluid milk and cream (eggnog, lowfat, etc.) . . . . . . . . . . . . . . . . . . . . | 311511 1241 9 | | | | | |
| | Packaged fluid milk and related products (including cartons, bottles, cans, and dispenser cans) | | | | | | |
| | Fluid whole milk | | | | | | |
| 77 | Except U.H.T. . . . . . . . . . . . . . . . . . . | 311511 5111 0 | | | | | |
| 78 | U.H.T. . . . . . . . . . . . . . . . . . . . . . . | 311511 6111 9 | | | | | |
| | Lowfat milk | | | | | | |
| 79 | Except U.H.T. . . . . . . . . . . . . . . . . . | 311511 5211 8 | 1000 qt | | | | |
| 80 | U.H.T. . . . . . . . . . . . . . . . . . . . . . . | 311511 6211 7 | | | | | |
| | Skim milk | | | | | | |
| 81 | Except U.H.T. . . . . . . . . . . . . . . . . . | 311511 5311 6 | | | | | |
| 82 | U.H.T. . . . . . . . . . . . . . . . . . . . . . . | 311511 6311 5 | | | | | |

CONTINUE WITH **22** ON PAGE 16

*CONTINUE ON PAGE 16*

275

**22** DETAIL OF SALES, SHIPMENTS, RECEIPTS, OR REVENUE - Continued

| Line No. | Products and services *Items correspond to products reported on Current Industrial Reports (CIR) 0734 | Census product code 0730 | Unit of measure for quantities 0736 | Quantity 0732 | Value, f.o.b. plant $ Bil. 0731 | Mil. | Thou. |
|---|---|---|---|---|---|---|---|
| | Packaged fluid milk and related products (including cartons, bottles, cans, and dispenser cans) - Continued | | | | | | |
| 83 | Heavy cream (whipping cream containing 36 percent butterfat or more) . . . . . . . . . . . . | 311511 5441 1 | 1000 qt | | | | |
| 84 | Light cream (coffee cream containing less than 36 percent butterfat) . . . . . . . . . . . . . . | 311511 5451 0 | | | | | |
| 85 | Sour cream, unflavored (Report flavored dips on line 93.) . . . . . . . . . . | 311511 5461 9 | | | | | |
| 86 | Half and half . . . . . . . . . | 311511 5471 8 | | | | | |
| 87 | Whipped topping, butterfat base . . . . . . . . | 311511 5481 7 | | | | | |
| | Cottage cheese (including bakers' cheese, pot cheese, farmers' cheese) | | | | | | |
| 88 | Creamed in this plant from purchased curd . . | 311511 7131 6 | 1000 lb | | | | |
| 89 | Manufactured and creamed in this plant . . . . | 311511 7111 8 | | | | | |
| 90 | Manufactured in this plant and sold as curd . . | 311511 7121 7 | | | | | |
| | Yogurt, except frozen (Report frozen yogurt on lines 65 and 66.) | | | | | | |
| 91 | Regular and lowfat yogurt, except frozen . . . . | 311511 A111 4 | | | | | |
| 92 | Nonfat yogurt, except frozen . . . . . . . . . . | 311511 A121 3 | | | | | |
| | Other packaged milk products, nec | | | | | | |
| 93 | Flavored sour cream dips . . . . . . . . . . . . | 311511 G111 8 | 1000 qt | | | | |
| 94 | Flavored milks (chocolate milk, etc.) . . . . . . | 311511 G121 7 | | | | | |
| 95 | Other milk products (eggnog, buttermilk, acidophilus milk, reconstituted milk, etc.) . . . . | 311511 G131 6 | | | | | |
| 96 | Canned orange juice, single strength, all sizes . . . | 311421 J111 7 | | | | | |
| | Fresh fruit juices and nectars Single strength | | | | | | |
| 97 | Orange . . . . . . . . . . . . . . . . . . . . . . | 311421 M111 4 | 1000 gal | | | | |
| | Other (Specify kind.) ⌐ | | | | | | |
| 98 | | 311421 M121 3 | | | | | |

*CONTINUE WITH* **23** *ON PAGE 17*

*CONTINUE ON PAGE 17*

276

**If not shown, please enter your 11-digit Census File Number (CFN) from the mailing address.** ▶

**㉒ DETAIL OF SALES, SHIPMENTS, RECEIPTS, OR REVENUE - Continued**

| Line No. | Products and services *Items correspond to products reported on Current Industrial Reports (CIR) 0734 | Census product code 0730 | Unit of measure for quantities 0736 | Products shipped and other receipts | | | |
|---|---|---|---|---|---|---|---|
| | | | | Quantity 0732 | Value, f.o.b. plant | | |
| | | | | | $ Bil. 0731 | Mil. | Thou. |
| | Fruit drinks, cocktails, and ades, containing some real juice (with added sugar, citric acid, etc.) | | | | | | |
| 99 | 16.9 oz (1/2 liter) containers or less . . . . . . . . | 312111 A111 2 | 1000 gal | | | | |
| 100 | Other size containers (cartons, bottles, cans, etc.) . . . . . . . . . . . . . . . . . . . . . . . . . | 312111 A221 9 | | | | | |
| 101 | Concentrates . . . . . . . . . . . . . . . . . . . . | 312111 A331 6 | | | | | |
| | All other products made in this establishment - *Specify and report each product with sales value of $50,000 or more that cannot be assigned to one of the "listed products and services". For all remaining products, write "Other" and report a single total value.* | | | | | | |
| 102 | | 18 | | | | | |
| 103 | | 26 | | | | | |
| 104 | | 34 | | | | | |
| 105 | | 42 | | | | | |
| 106 | | 59 | | | | | |
| 107 | | 67 | | | | | |
| | Contract work - Receipts for work done for others on their materials *(Specify products worked on and kind of work.)*↗ | | | | | | |
| 108 | | 000930 0000 8 | | | | | |
| 109 | Miscellaneous receipts (including receipts for repair work, scrap, refuse, etc.) . . . . . . . . . . . . . . | 000999 8000 5 | | | | | |
| 110 | Resales - Sales of products bought and sold without further manufacture, processing, or assembly (The cost of such items should be reported in ⑮, line A2.) . . . . . . . . . . . | 000999 8900 6 | | | | | |
| 111 | **TOTAL** *(Should equal ❹, line A)* . . . . . . . . . . | 770000 0000 8 | | | | | |

**㉓-㉗ Not Applicable.**

*CONTINUE ON PAGE 18*

**28** ESTABLISHMENT ACTIVITIES

A. Indicate activities that were performed by this establishment or were performed for this establishment by another company during 2002.
*(Mark "X" ALL that apply.)*

| | This activity was performed - | | | |
|---|---|---|---|---|
| | By this establishment | By another establishment of this company | By another company | Not at all |
| 1. Product design/engineering | 0921 ☐ | 8071 ☐ | 0941 ☐ | 0961 ☐ |
| 2. Order fulfillment | | | | |
| a. Bundling or kitting (combining multiple items into a prepackaged product) | 0923 ☐ | 8072 ☐ | 0943 ☐ | 0963 ☐ |
| b. Pick and pack (taking goods from inventory and packaging them to fill orders) | 0924 ☐ | 8073 ☐ | 0944 ☐ | 0964 ☐ |
| c. Warehousing of finished products | 0925 ☐ | 8074 ☐ | 0945 ☐ | 0965 ☐ |
| d. Breaking bulk (reducing large shipments into smaller portions for customers) | 0926 ☐ | 8075 ☐ | 0946 ☐ | 0966 ☐ |
| e. Local delivery (within a city, town, or other local area, including adjoining towns and suburban areas) | 0927 ☐ | 8076 ☐ | 0947 ☐ | 0967 ☐ |
| f. Long distance delivery (beyond local areas and commercial zones) | 0928 ☐ | 8077 ☐ | 0948 ☐ | 0968 ☐ |
| g. Processing of returned merchandise | 0932 ☐ | 8078 ☐ | 0952 ☐ | 0972 ☐ |

B. During 2002 did this establishment:

1. Manage inventory owned by this establishment AND held at this location? ... 0936 ☐ Yes  0937 ☐ No

2. Manage inventory owned by this establishment BUT held at a customer's location? ... 0956 ☐ Yes  0957 ☐ No

3. Manage inventory owned by another company BUT held at this location? ... 0976 ☐ Yes  0977 ☐ No

4. Manage inventory owned by another company AND held somewhere other than at this location? ... 0994 ☐ Yes  0995 ☐ No

5. Contract with another firm for any of your production using materials owned by this location? ... 8041 ☐ Yes  8042 ☐ No

6. Send any partially completed products to a foreign facility for processing that were then returned to this establishment for completion? ... 8044 ☐ Yes  8045 ☐ No

7. Manufacture products for a government to their specifications? ... 8047 ☐ Yes  8048 ☐ No

8. Manufacture products for another business to their specifications? ... 8016 ☐ Yes  8017 ☐ No

9. Manufacture products for a final retail customer to their specifications? ... 8060 ☐ Yes  8062 ☐ No

*CONTINUE ON PAGE 19*

278

**If not shown, please enter your 11-digit Census File Number (CFN) from the mailing address.**

**29** OPERATIONAL STATUS

Activity that best describes this establishment's status at the end of 2002
*(Mark "X" only ONE box.)*

0011 ☐ In operation

0012 ☐ Under construction, development, or exploration

0013 ☐ Temporarily or seasonally inactive

0014 ☐ Ceased operation - *Give date at right* ⟶

0015 ☐ Sold or leased to another operator - *Give date at right AND enter new name and mailing address below* ⤵

0018

| Month | Day | Year |
|-------|-----|------|
|       |     |      |
|       |     |      |

| 0060 Name of new owner or operator | 0061 Employer Identification Number |
|---|---|
|  | Enter EIN of new owner *(9 digits)* ⟶ |

| 0062 Mailing address (number and street, P.O. Box, etc.) |
|---|
|  |

| 0063 City, town, village, etc. | 0064 State | 0065 ZIP Code |
|---|---|---|
|  |  |  |

Remarks *(Please use this space for any explanations that may be essential in understanding your reported data.)*

**30** CERTIFICATION - This report is substantially accurate and was prepared in accordance with the instructions.

Is the time period covered by this report a calendar year?

0078 ☐ Yes    0079 ☐ No - Enter time period covered ⟶

| FROM 0070 | Month | Year | TO 0071 | Month | Year |
|---|---|---|---|---|---|
|  |  |  |  |  |  |

| 0072 Name of person to contact regarding this report | 0073 Title |
|---|---|
|  |  |

| Telephone 0074 | Area code | Number | Extension | Fax 0075 | Area code | Number |
|---|---|---|---|---|---|---|
|  |  |  |  |  |  |  |

| 0076 Internet e-mail address | Date completed 0069 | Month | Day | Year |
|---|---|---|---|---|
|  |  |  |  |  |

## Thank you for completing your 2002 Economic Census form.

### *PLEASE PHOTOCOPY THIS FORM FOR YOUR RECORDS AND RETURN THE ORIGINAL.*

U.S. DEPARTMENT OF COMMERCE
Economics and Statistics Administration
U.S. CENSUS BUREAU

FORM
## NC-99001

# 2002 REPORT OF ORGANIZATION

OMB No. 0607-0444: Approval Expires 11/30/2003

**DUE DATE**
**FEBRUARY 12, 2003**

*Mail* your completed form to:

**U.S. CENSUS BUREAU**
**1201 East 10th Street**
**Jeffersonville, IN 47134-0001**

*Need help or have questions about filling out this form?*

*Visit* our Web site at
www.census.gov/econhelp

*Call* 1-800-233-6136, between
8:00 a.m. and 8:00 p.m., Eastern
time, Monday through Friday.

*- OR -*

*Write* to the address above.
Include your 11-digit Census File
Number (CFN) printed in the
mailing address.

NC-99001

*(Please correct any errors in this mailing address.)*

**1** CERTIFICATION - This report is substantially accurate and was prepared in accordance with the instructions.

0072 Name of person to contact regarding this report

0073 Title

6071 Mailing address if different from above address *(Number and street, P.O. box, etc.)*

6072 City, town, village, etc.

6073 State

6074 ZIP Code

| | Area code | Number | Extension | | | Area code | Number |
|---|---|---|---|---|---|---|---|
| Telephone 0074 | | - | | Fax 0075 | | | - |

0076 Internet e-mail address

Date completed 0069

| Month | Day | Year |
|---|---|---|
| | | |

280

**2** COMPANY OWNERSHIP OR CONTROL - DOMESTIC

**A.** Does another domestic company hold more than 50 percent of the voting stock of your company **or** have the power to control the management and policies of your company?

0008 ☐ Yes - *Enter the following information on the owning or controlling company* ⌐

0009 ☐ No - *Go to* **3**

| 0080 Name of owning or controlling company | Enter Employer Identification Number (EIN) of owning or controlling company *(9 digits)* → | - |
|---|---|---|
| 0082 Home office address *(Number and street)* | | |

| 0083 City, town, village, etc. | 0084 State | 0085 ZIP Code - |
|---|---|---|

**B.** Percent of voting stock held by owning **or** controlling company *(Mark "X" only ONE box.)*

0027 ☐ Less than 50%     0028 ☐ 50%     0029 ☐ More than 50%

**3** COMPANY OWNERSHIP OR CONTROL - FOREIGN

Does a foreign entity (company, individual, government, etc.) own directly or indirectly 10 percent or more of the voting stock or other equity rights of your company?

6101 ☐ Yes - *Enter the following information on the owning entity and go to* **4** ⌐

| 6103 Name of foreign beneficial owner |
|---|
| 6104 Home office address *(Number and street)* |

| 6105 City | 6106 Country |
|---|---|

Percent ownership (direct and indirect) *(Mark "X only ONE box.)* →

6111 ☐ 10-24%     6113 ☐ 50%     6115 ☐ 100%
6112 ☐ 25-49%     6114 ☐ 51-99%

6102 ☐ No - Does a foreign entity own or control 10 percent or more of any U.S. corporation of which you are the majority owner?

6121 ☐ Yes - *Provide the name, mailing address, and Employer Identification Number (EIN) of subsidiaries in which a foreign entity has a 10 percent or more direct ownership interest on a separate sheet of paper. Be sure to enter the item number, your company's name and address, and Census File Number in the upper right corner of each additional sheet. Then go to* **4**.

6122 ☐ No - *Go to* **4**

**4** FOREIGN AFFILIATES

Does this company alone, or with its domestic affiliates, own 10 percent or more of the voting stock of an incorporated foreign business enterprise, or an equivalent interest in an unincorporated business enterprise, including ownership or real estate?

6126 ☐ Yes

6127 ☐ No

U.S. DEPARTMENT OF COMMERCE
Economics and Statistics Administration
U.S. CENSUS BUREAU

FORM **SBO-1**
(12-20-2002)

# 2002 SURVEY OF BUSINESS OWNERS AND SELF-EMPLOYED PERSONS

In correspondence or telephone calls pertaining to this report, please refer to the first 11 digits of the Identification Number (ID) shown in the label below.

SBO-1

## DUE DATE:
**30 days after receipt of form**

*Mail* the completed form in the return envelope. If you did not receive a return envelope, mail to:

**U.S. Census Bureau
1201 East 10th Street
Jeffersonville, IN
47134-0001**

*Need help or have questions about filling out this form?*

*Visit* our web site at
www.census.gov/csd/sbo

*Call* 1-800-233-6132,
8:00 a.m. to 8:00 p.m.,
Eastern time, Monday through Friday,
- OR -
*Write* to the address above.

*Please correct errors in name, address, and ZIP Code. ENTER street and number if not shown.*

The **purpose** of this survey is to collect statistics on businesses and their individual owners.

**INSTRUCTIONS** – Please read the accompanying information sheet(s) and complete the following questions for the self-employment activity or business activity of the person(s) or business named in the mailing label even if the business has been sold, reorganized, or discontinued.

Examples:

x ｜1 2｜

• **Use blue or black ink.** • **Place an "X" inside the box.** • **Center numbers in boxes.** • **Do not put slashes through 0 or 7.**

---

Print name of person completing this form

Telephone number *(Include Area Code)*

(          )

**1** In 2002, which of the following described the ownership of the business activity named in the mailing label? *Mark X all that apply.*

☐ Alaska Native Regional or Village Corporation
☐ American Indian tribal entity
☐ Foreign-owned
☐ Limited Liability Company (LLC)
☐ Membership/cooperative
☐ Nonprofit
☐ Owned by another organization
☐ Partnership or Limited Liability Partnership (LLP)
☐ Privately held corporation
☐ Publicly held corporation
☐ Other – *Specify* ↙

**2** In 2002, did any individual own 10% or more of the rights, claims, interests, or stock in this business?

☐ Yes – *Go to* **3**
☐ No – *Go to* **36** *on Page 4.*

**3** For those individuals owning the largest percentages in the business in 2002, please list the **percentage owned** by each person and his or her **position title(s).** *If more than 3 persons owned the business equally, select any 3.*

|  | Percentage | Position Title |
|---|---|---|
| *Owner 1:* | % | |
| *Owner 2:* | % | |
| *Owner 3:* | % | |

**4** In 2002, what was *Owner 1's* primary function(s) in this business? *Mark X all that apply.*

☐ Producing this business's goods/services
☐ Managing day-to-day operations
☐ Financial control with the authority to sign loans, leases, and contracts
☐ None of the above

**5** In 2002, what was the average number of hours per week that *Owner 1* spent managing or working in this business?

☐ None
☐ Less than 20 hours
☐ 20–39 hours
☐ 40 hours
☐ 41–59 hours
☐ 60 hours or more

001014

**6** In 2002, did this business provide *Owner 1's* primary source of personal income?

☐ Yes ☐ No

**7** In 2002, did *Owner 1* have a disability which prevented or limited the amount of time spent managing or working in this business?

☐ Yes ☐ No

**8 a.** Is *Owner 1* a veteran of any branch of the U.S. military service including the Coast Guard?

☐ Yes ☐ No – *Go to* **9**

**b.** (If Yes) Was *Owner 1* disabled as the result of injury incurred or aggravated during active military service?

☐ Yes ☐ No

**9** What is the sex of *Owner 1* ?

☐ Male ☐ Female

**10** What was *Owner 1's* age as of December 31, 2002?

☐ Under 25 ☐ 35–44 ☐ 55–64

☐ 25–34 ☐ 45–54 ☐ 65 or over

☞ **NOTE: Please answer BOTH questions** **11** **and** **12** .

**11** Is *Owner 1 Spanish/Hispanic/Latino?* Mark X the *"No"* box if **not** Spanish/Hispanic/Latino.

☐ No ☐ Yes, Cuban

☐ Yes, Mexican, Mexican American, Chicano

☐ Yes, Other Spanish/Hispanic/ Latino – *Specify* ↘

☐ Yes, Puerto Rican

[          ]

**12** What is *Owner 1's* race? *Mark X one or more races* to indicate what this person considers himself/herself to be.

☐ White

☐ Black, African American, or Negro

☐ American Indian or Alaska Native – *Specify name of enrolled or principal tribe* ↘

[          ]

☐ Asian Indian ☐ Korean

☐ Chinese ☐ Vietnamese

☐ Filipino ☐ Other Asian – *Specify* ↘

☐ Japanese

[          ]

☐ Native Hawaiian ☐ Guamanian or Chamorro

☐ Samoan

☐ Other Pacific Islander – *Specify* ↘

[          ]

**13** What was the highest degree or level of school *Owner 1* completed before establishing, purchasing or acquiring this business? *Mark X ONE box only for the highest level completed or degree received.*

☐ Less than high school graduate

☐ High school graduate – Diploma or GED

☐ Technical, trade, or vocational school

☐ Some college, but no degree

☐ Associate Degree

☐ Bachelor's Degree

☐ Master's, Doctorate, or Professional Degree

**14** Was there more than **1** owner listed in **3** on page 1?

☐ Yes ☐ No – *Go to* **36** *on page 4.*

> **Please answer the following questions about *Owner 2* listed in** **3** **on page 1.**

**15** In 2002, what was *Owner 2's* primary function(s) in this business? *Mark X all that apply.*

☐ Producing this business's goods/services

☐ Managing day-to-day operations

☐ Financial control with the authority to sign loans, leases, and contracts

☐ None of the above

**16** In 2002, what was the average number of hours per week that *Owner 2* spent managing or working in this business?

☐ None ☐ 40 hours

☐ Less than 20 hours ☐ 41–59 hours

☐ 20–39 hours ☐ 60 hours or more

**17** In 2002, did this business provide *Owner 2's* primary source of personal income?

☐ Yes ☐ No

**18** In 2002, did *Owner 2* have a disability which prevented or limited the amount of time spent managing or working in this business?

☐ Yes ☐ No

**19 a.** Is *Owner 2* a veteran of any branch of the U.S. military service including the Coast Guard?

☐ Yes ☐ No – *Go to* **20**

**b.** (If Yes) Was *Owner 2* disabled as the result of injury incurred or aggravated during active military service?

☐ Yes ☐ No

**20** What is the sex of *Owner 2* ?

☐ Male ☐ Female

283

**21** What was *Owner 2's* age as of December 31, 2002?

☐ Under 25  ☐ 35–44  ☐ 55–64

☐ 25–34  ☐ 45–54  ☐ 65 or over

☞**NOTE: Please answer BOTH questions 22 and 23.**

**22** Is *Owner 2 Spanish/Hispanic/Latino?* Mark X the *"No"* box if *not* Spanish/Hispanic/Latino.

☐ No

☐ Yes, Mexican, Mexican American, Chicano

☐ Yes, Puerto Rican

☐ Yes, Cuban

☐ Yes, Other Spanish/Hispanic/ Latino – *Specify* ↘

_____

**23** What is *Owner 2's* race? *Mark X one or more races* to indicate what this person considers himself/herself to be.

☐ White

☐ Black, African American, or Negro

☐ American Indian or Alaska Native – *Specify name of enrolled or principal tribe* ↘

_____

☐ Asian Indian  ☐ Korean

☐ Chinese  ☐ Vietnamese

☐ Filipino  ☐ Other Asian – *Specify* ↘

☐ Japanese

_____

☐ Native Hawaiian  ☐ Guamanian or Chamorro

☐ Samoan

☐ Other Pacific Islander – *Specify* ↘

_____

**24** What was the highest degree or level of school *Owner 2* completed before establishing, purchasing or acquiring this business? *Mark X ONE box only for the highest level completed or degree received.*

☐ Less than high school graduate

☐ High school graduate – Diploma or GED

☐ Technical, trade, or vocational school

☐ Some college, but no degree

☐ Associate Degree

☐ Bachelor's Degree

☐ Master's, Doctorate, or Professional Degree

**25** Were there more than **2** owners listed in ❸ on page 1?

☐ Yes  ☐ No – *Go to* **36** *on page 4.*

---

**Please answer the following questions about *Owner 3* listed in ❸ on page 1.**

**26** In 2002, what was *Owner 3's* primary function(s) in this business? *Mark X all that apply.*

☐ Producing this business's goods/services

☐ Managing day-to-day operations

☐ Financial control with the authority to sign loans, leases, and contracts

☐ None of the above

**27** In 2002, what was the average number of hours per week that *Owner 3* spent managing or working in this business?

☐ None  ☐ 40 hours

☐ Less than 20 hours  ☐ 41–59 hours

☐ 20–39 hours  ☐ 60 hours or more

**28** In 2002, did this business provide *Owner 3's* primary source of personal income?

☐ Yes  ☐ No

**29** In 2002, did *Owner 3* have a disability which prevented or limited the amount of time spent managing or working in this business?

☐ Yes  ☐ No

**30** a. Is *Owner 3* a veteran of any branch of the U.S. military service including the Coast Guard?

☐ Yes  ☐ No – *Go to* **31**

b. (If Yes) Was *Owner 3* disabled as the result of injury incurred or aggravated during active military service?

☐ Yes  ☐ No

**31** What is the sex of *Owner 3*?

☐ Male  ☐ Female

**32** What was *Owner 3's* age as of December 31, 2002?

☐ Under 25  ☐ 35–44  ☐ 55–64

☐ 25–34  ☐ 45–54  ☐ 65 or over

☞**NOTE: Please answer BOTH questions 33 and 34.**

**33** Is *Owner 3 Spanish/Hispanic/Latino?* Mark X the *"No"* box if *not* Spanish/Hispanic/Latino.

☐ No

☐ Yes, Mexican, Mexican American, Chicano

☐ Yes, Puerto Rican

☐ Yes, Cuban

☐ Yes, Other Spanish/Hispanic/ Latino – *Specify* ↘

_____

001038　

284

**34** What is **Owner 3's** race? *Mark **X** one or more races* to indicate what this person considers himself/herself to be.

- [ ] White
- [ ] Black, African American, or Negro
- [ ] American Indian or Alaska Native – *Specify name of enrolled or principal tribe* ↘

[ ]

- [ ] Asian Indian
- [ ] Chinese
- [ ] Filipino
- [ ] Japanese
- [ ] Korean
- [ ] Vietnamese
- [ ] Other Asian – *Specify* ↘

[ ]

- [ ] Native Hawaiian
- [ ] Samoan
- [ ] Guamanian or Chamorro
- [ ] Other Pacific Islander – *Specify* ↘

[ ]

**35** What was the highest degree or level of school **Owner 3** completed before establishing, purchasing or acquiring this business? *Mark **X** ONE box only for the highest level completed or degree received.*

- [ ] Less than high school graduate
- [ ] High school graduate – Diploma or GED
- [ ] Technical, trade, or vocational school
- [ ] Some college, but no degree
- [ ] Associate Degree
- [ ] Bachelor's Degree
- [ ] Master's, Doctorate, or Professional Degree

> **Please answer the following questions about the self-employment activity or business activity of the person(s) or business named in the mailing label on page 1.**

**36** In what year was this business originally established?

Year [ ][ ][ ][ ]      [ ] Don't know

**37** When was the business originally established, purchased or acquired by the owner(s) listed in **3** on page 1? *If different years, select the earliest. If no owners listed, go to* **38**.

- [ ] Before 1980
- [ ] 1980–1989
- [ ] 1990–1996
- [ ] 1997
- [ ] 1998
- [ ] 1999
- [ ] 2000
- [ ] 2001
- [ ] 2002

**38** During 2002, was this business operated primarily from somebody's home?

- [ ] Yes
- [ ] No

**39** During 2002, was this business owned exclusively by members of the same family? *(Family refers to spouses, parents/guardians, brothers, sisters, or close relatives.)*

- [ ] Yes
- [ ] No
- [ ] Only one owner

**40** During 2002, was this business operated as a franchise?

- [ ] Yes
- [ ] No

**41** What was the source(s) of capital used to start or acquire this business? *Mark **X** all that apply.*

- [ ] Personal/family savings of owner(s)
- [ ] Personal/family assets other than savings of owner(s)
- [ ] Personal/business credit card of owner(s)
- [ ] Business loan from federal, state or local government
- [ ] Government-guaranteed business loan from a bank or financial institution
- [ ] Business loan from a bank or financial institution
- [ ] Outside investor
- [ ] None needed

**42** During 2002, were any of the following sources used to finance expansion or capital improvements for this business? *Mark **X** all that apply.*

- [ ] Personal/family savings of owner(s)
- [ ] Personal/family assets other than savings of owner(s)
- [ ] Personal/business credit card of owner(s)
- [ ] Business loan from federal, state or local government
- [ ] Government-guaranteed business loan from a bank or financial institution
- [ ] Business loan from a bank or financial institution
- [ ] Outside investor
- [ ] None needed

**43** Which of the following types of customers accounted for 10% or more of this business's total sales of goods/services during 2002? *Mark **X** all that apply.*

- [ ] Federal government
- [ ] State and local government (including school districts, transportation authorities, etc.)
- [ ] Export sales of goods/services
- [ ] Other businesses and/or organizations (excluding export sales)
- [ ] Household consumers and individual users (excluding export sales)
- [ ] All others

**44** During 2002, were any of the following types of workers used by this business?

| | Yes | No |
|---|---|---|
| Full- and part-time paid employees reported on this business's IRS Form 941 . . . . . . . | [ ] | [ ] |
| Paid day laborers . . . . . . . . . . . . . . . . . . | [ ] | [ ] |
| Temporary staffing obtained from a temporary help service . . . . . . . . . . . . . | [ ] | [ ] |
| Leased employees from a leasing service or a professional employer organization . . . . | [ ] | [ ] |
| Contractors, subcontractors, independent contractors or outside consultants . . . . . . | [ ] | [ ] |

**THANK YOU.**
*Please return this form in the enclosed envelope.*

001045

285

# APPENDIX C
# Regional Federal Depository Libraries

In looking at this list of Regional Federal Depository Libraries, please note that some states are served by libraries in nearby states.

## ALABAMA

Amelia Gayle Gorgas Library
Box 870266
University of Alabama
Tuscaloosa, AL 35487-0266
(205) 348-6047

Auburn University at Montgomery Library
7440 East Drive
P.O. Box 244023
Montgomery, AL 36124-4023
(334) 244-3211

## ALASKA

Served by Washington State Library

## AMERICAN SAMOA

Served by the University of Hawaii

## ARIZONA

Arizona State Library, Archives and Public Records
1700 West Washington
State Capitol, Third Floor
Phoenix, AZ 85007
(602) 542-3701

## ARKANSAS

Arkansas State Library
One Capitol Mall
Little Rock, AR 72201-1081
(501) 682-2326

## CALIFORNIA

California State Library
914 Capitol Mall
Sacramento, CA 95814
(916) 654-0243

## COLORADO

Denver Public Library
10 West 14th Avenue Parkway
Denver, CO 80204-2731
(720) 865-1728

Norlin Library
University of Colorado
1720 Pleasant Street
Boulder, CO 80309-0184
(303) 492-4375

## CONNECTICUT

Connecticut State Library
231 Capitol Avenue
Hartford, CT 06106
(860) 757-6599

## DELAWARE

Served by the University of Maryland

## DISTRICT OF COLUMBIA

Served by the University of Maryland

# FLORIDA

George A. Smathers Library
241 Library West
University of Florida
Gainesville, FL 32611-2048
(352) 392-0366

# GEORGIA

Ilah Dunlap Little Memorial Library
University of Georgia
265 South Jackson Street
Athens, GA 30602-1641
(706) 542-0664

# GUAM

Served by the University of Hawaii

# HAWAII

Hamilton Library
University of Hawaii, Manoa
2550 The Mall
Honolulu, HI 96822-2274
(808) 956-8230

# IDAHO

University of Idaho Library
Rayburn Street
Moscow, ID 83844-2353
(208) 885-6344

# ILLINOIS

Illinois State Library
300 South 2nd Street
Springfield, IL 62701-1796
(217) 524-4200

# INDIANA

Indiana State Library
140 North Senate Avenue
Indianapolis, IN 46204-2296
(317) 232-3686

# IOWA

University of Iowa
University Libraries
Washington & Madison Streets
Iowa City, IA 52242-1420
(319) 335-5925

# KANSAS

Anschutz Library
University of Kansas
1301 Hoch Auditoria Drive
Lawrence, KS 66045-2800
(785) 864-4593

# KENTUCKY

University of Kentucky
William T. Young Library
500 South Limestone
Lexington, KY 40506-0456
(859) 257-0500 ext. 2141

# LOUISIANA

Prescott Memorial Library
Louisiana Tech University
Ruston, LA 71272-0046
(318) 257-4989

Troy H. Middleton Library
Louisiana State University, Baton Rouge
Baton Rouge, LA 70803-3312
(225) 578-7021

# MAINE

Raymond H. Fogler Library
University of Maine, Orono
Orono, ME 04469-5729
(207) 581-1680

# MARYLAND

McKeldin Library
University of Maryland, College Park
College Park, MD 20742-7011
(301) 405-9169

# MASSACHUSETTS

Boston Public Library
700 Boylston Street
Boston, MA 02116
(617) 536-5400 ext. 2226

# MICHIGAN

Detroit Public Library
5201 Woodward Avenue
Detroit, MI 48202-4007
(313) 833-1025

Library of Michigan
702 West Kalamazoo Street
P.O. Box 30007
Lansing, Ml 48909-7507
(517) 373-9489

## MICRONESIA

Served by the University of Hawaii

## MINNESOTA

Wilson Library
University of Minnesota
309 19th Avenue South
Minneapolis, MN 55455-0414
(612) 626-7520

## MISSISSIPPI

J. D. Williams Library
University of Mississippi
University, MS 38677-9793
(662) 915-7986

## MISSOURI

Elmer Ellis Library
University of Missouri, Columbia
Lowry Mall
Columbia, MO 65201-5149
(573) 884-8123

## MONTANA

Mansfield Library
University of Montana (MMLA01)
32 Campus Drive
Missoula, MT 59812-9936
(406) 243-6700

## NEBRASKA

D. L. Love Library
University of Nebraska, Lincoln
13th & R Streets
Lincoln, NE 68588-0410
(402) 472-4473

## NEVADA

University Library/322
1664 North Virginia Street
University of Nevada, Reno
Reno, NV 89557-0044
(775) 784-6500 ext. 256

## NEW HAMPSHIRE

Served by the University of Maine

## NEW JERSEY

U.S. Documents Division
Newark Public Library
5 Washington Street
Newark, NJ 07101-0630
(973) 733-7812

## NEW MEXICO

New Mexico State Library
1209 Camino Carlos Rey
Santa Fe, NM 87505-9860
(505) 476-9717

Zimmerman Library
University of New Mexico
Albuquerque, NM 87131-1466
(505) 277-7180

## NEW YORK

New York State Library
Cultural Education Center
Empire State Plaza
Albany, NY 12230-0001
(518) 486-5755

## NORTH CAROLINA

Davis Library, CB #3912
University of North Carolina, Chapel Hill
Chapel Hill, NC 27514-8890
(919) 962-1151

## NORTH DAKOTA

North Dakota State University Libraries
1201 Albrecht Boulevard
Fargo, ND 58105-5599
(701) 231-8863
  in cooperation with
Chester Fritz Library
University of North Dakota
Centennial & University Avenue
Grand Forks, ND 58202-9000
(701) 777-3316

## OHIO

State Library of Ohio
65 South Front Street
Columbus, OH 43215-4163
(614) 644-1971

## OKLAHOMA

Edmon Low Library
Oklahoma State University
Stillwater, OK 74078-1071
(405) 744-6546

Oklahoma Department of Libraries
200 Northeast 18th Street
Oklahoma City, OK 73105-3298
(405) 522-3327

## OREGON

Branford Price Millar Library
Portland State University
951 SW Hall
Portland, OR 97207-1151
(503) 725-4126

## PENNSYLVANIA

State Library of Pennsylvania
Walnut Street & Commonwealth Avenue
Harrisburg, PA 17105-1601
(717) 787-2327

## PUERTO RICO

Served by the University of Florida

## RHODE ISLAND

Served by the Connecticut State Library

## SOUTH CAROLINA

Robert Muldrow Cooper Library
Clemson University
Palmetto Boulevard
P.O. Box 343001
Clemson, SC 29634-3001
(864) 656-5168
   in cooperation with
Thomas Cooper Library
University of South Carolina
1322 Greene Street
Columbia, SC 29208
(803) 777-1775

## SOUTH DAKOTA

Served by the University of Minnesota

## TENNESSEE

University of Memphis Libraries
126 Ned R. McWherter Library
Memphis, TN 38152-1000
(901) 678-4566

## TEXAS

Texas State Library & Archives Commission
1201 Brazos Street
Austin, TX 78711-2927
(512) 463-5455

Texas Tech University Library
18th & Boston
Lubbock, TX 79409-0002
(806) 742-2238 ext. 280

## UTAH

Merrill Library
Utah State University
University Hill
Logan, UT 84321
(435) 797-2683

## VERMONT

Served by the University of Maine

## VIRGIN ISLANDS

Served by the University of Florida

## VIRGINIA

Alderman Library
University of Virginia
160 McCormick Road
P.O. Box 400154
Charlottesville, VA 22904-4154
(804) 924-4963

## WASHINGTON

Washington State Library
Joel M. Pritchard Library
415 15th Street SW
P.O. Box 42460
Olympia, WA 98504-2460
(360) 704-5225

## WEST VIRGINIA

West Virginia University
Charles C. Wise, Jr. Library
1549 University Avenue
Morgantown, WV 26506-6069
(304) 293-4040 ext. 4037

## WISCONSIN

Milwaukee Public Library
814 West Wisconsin Avenue
Milwaukee, WI 53233-2385
(414) 286-2167

State Historical Society of Wisconsin Library
816 State Street
Madison, WI 53706-1488
(608) 261-2460

## WYOMING

Served by University of Colorado, Boulder

# APPENDIX D
# State Data Center/Business and Industry Data Center Lead Agencies

These are the State Data Center (SDC) lead agencies in each state. A + indicates that this agency is the Business and Industry Data Center (BIDC) lead agency within the state. Where there is only one agency listed for a state and it has a +, it is the lead agency for both programs within that state. While every state listed participates in the SDC program, only some of them participate in the BIDC program.

## ALABAMA

Center for Business and Economic Research
University of Alabama
149 Bidgood Hall, Box 870221
Tuscaloosa, AL 35487-0221
(205) 348-6191

## ALASKA

Census & Geographic Information
Network Research & Analysis
Alaska Department of Labor
P.O. Box 25504
Juneau, AK 99802-5504
(907) 465-2437

## AMERICAN SAMOA

Department of Commerce
Statistics Division
Pago Pago, AS 96799
011-684-633-5155

## ARIZONA

+Arizona Department of Economic Security
DES 0452
First Floor, Northeast Wing
1789 West Jefferson St.
Phoenix, AZ 85007
(602) 542-5984

## ARKANSAS

State Data Center
Univ. of Arkansas-Little Rock
2801 South University
Little Rock, AR 72204
(501) 569-8530

## CALIFORNIA

State Census Data Center
Department of Finance
915 L Street, 8th floor
Sacramento, CA 95814
(916) 323-4086

## COLORADO

Division of Local Government
Colorado Department of Local Affairs
1313 Sherman Street, Room 521
Denver, CO 80203
(303) 866-3120

## CONNECTICUT

Office of Policy and Management
Policy Development & Planning Division
450 Capitol Avenue—MS#52ASP
Hartford, CT 06106-1308
(860) 418-6352

## DELAWARE

+Delaware Economic Development Office
99 Kings Highway
P.O. Box 1401
Dover, DE 19901
(302) 739-4271

## DISTRICT OF COLUMBIA

Data Services Division
Mayor's Office of Planning
801 N. Capitol Street NE, Ste. 500
Washington, DC 20002
(202) 442-7632

## FLORIDA

+Agency for Workforce Innovation
Labor Market Statistics
State Census Data Center
MSC G-020
107 E. Madison Street
Tallahassee, FL 32399-4111
(850) 488-1048

## GEORGIA

Office of Planning and Budget
270 Washington Street
Atlanta, GA 30334
(404) 656-6505

## GUAM

Bureau of Statistics and Plans
P.O. Box 2950
Hagatna, Guam 96932
011-1671-472-4201/3

## HAWAII

Hawaii State Data Center
Department of Business, Economic Development, &
 Tourism
250 South Hotel Street, 4th Floor
Honolulu, HI 96813
P.O. Box 2359
Honolulu, HI 96804
(808) 586-2493

## IDAHO

Idaho Department of Commerce
700 West State Street
Boise, ID 83720
(208) 334-2470

## ILLINOIS

Illinois Dept. of Commerce and Community Affairs
Div. of Policy Development, Planning and Research
620 East Adams Street
Springfield, IL 62701
(217) 782-1381

+Illinois Department of Commerce and Community
 Affairs
620 East Adams Street
Springfield, IL 62701
(217) 785-7545

## INDIANA

+Indiana Business Research Center
801 West Michigan
B.S. 4015I
Indianapolis, IN 46202-5151
(317) 274-2205

Indiana State Library
Indiana State Data Center
140 North Senate Avenue
Indianapolis, IN 46204
(317) 232-3733

## KANSAS

State Library of Kansas
300 SW 10th Ave, Room 343N
State Capitol Building
Topeka, KS 66612-1593
(785) 296-3296

## KENTUCKY

+University of Louisville
Urban Studies Institute
College of Business & Public Administration
Louisville, KY 40292
(502) 852-7990

## LOUISIANA

Office of Electronic Services
P.O. Box 94095 (zip for mail address 70804)
1201 N. 3rd St., Suite 2-130
Baton Rouge, LA 70802
(225) 219-5987

## MAINE

+Maine State Planning Office
184 State Street
Augusta, ME 04333
(207) 287-1475

## MARYLAND

+Maryland Department of Planning
301 West Preston Street
Baltimore, MD 21201
(410) 767-4450

## MASSACHUSETTS

University of Massachusetts Donahue Institute
University of Massachusetts
220 Middlesex House Box 35520
Amherst, MA 01003
(413) 545-0176

## MICHIGAN

Library Development & Data Services
Library of Michigan
702 West Kalamazoo Street
Lansing, MI 48909
(517) 373-2548

## MINNESOTA

State Demographer's Office
Minnesota Planning
300 Centennial Office Building
658 Cedar Street
St. Paul, MN 55155
(651) 296-4886

## MISSISSIPPI

Center for Population Studies
The University of Mississippi
Bondurant Bldg., Room 3W
University, MS 38677
(662) 915-7288

+Division of Research and Information Systems
Department of Economic and Community Development
1200 Walter Sillas Building
P.O. Box 849
Jackson, MS 39205
(601) 359-3593

## MISSOURI

Missouri State Library
600 W. Main Street
P.O. Box 387
Jefferson City, MO 65102
(573) 751-2679

+Small Business Research Information Center
University of Missouri-Rolla
104 Nagogami Terrace
Rolla, MO 65409-1340
(573) 341-6484

## MONTANA

+Census and Economic Information Center
Montana Depart of Commerce
P.O. Box 200505
301 S. Park
Helena, MT 59620-0505
(406) 841-2739

## NEBRASKA

Center for Public Affairs Research
Nebraska State Data Center
Peter Kiewit Conference Center, # 232
University of Nebraska at Omaha
Omaha, NE 68182-0001
(402) 554-2134

## NEVADA

Nevada State Library & Archives
100 N. Stewart Street
Carson City, NV 89710
(775) 684-3326

## NEW HAMPSHIRE

Office of State Planning
57 Regional Drive
Concord, NH 03301
(603) 271-2155

## NEW JERSEY

+New Jersey State Data Center
Division of Labor Market and Demographic Research
New Jersey Department of Labor, P.O. Box 388
Trenton, NJ 08625-0388
(609) 984-2595

## NEW MEXICO

New Mexico Economic Development Department
1100 St. Francis Drive
P.O. Box 20003
Santa Fe, NM 87504-5003
(505) 827-0264

+Bureau of Business and Economic Research
University of New Mexico
1920 Lomas NE
Albuquerque, NM 87131-6021
(505) 277-6626

## NEW YORK

+New York State Data Center
Empire State Development
30 S. Pearl Street
Albany, NY 12245
(518) 292-5300

## NORTH CAROLINA

+North Carolina Office of State Budget and Management
20320 Mail Service Center
Raleigh, NC 27699-0321
(919) 733-3270

## NORTH DAKOTA

North Dakota State Data Center
North Dakota State University
P.O. Box 5636
IACC 424
Fargo, ND 58105
(701) 231-8621

## NORTHERN MARIANA ISLANDS

Department of Commerce
Central Statistics Division
Caller Box 10007, Donnie Hill Apts.
Saipan, Mariana Islands 96950
011-670-664-3033

## OHIO

+Office of Strategic Research
Ohio Department of Development
P.O. Box 1001 (zip for using P.O. Box is 43266-0101)
77 South High Street, 27th Floor
Columbus, OH 43215
(614) 466-2116

## OKLAHOMA

+Oklahoma State Data Center
Oklahoma Department of Commerce
900 N. Stiles Avenue
Oklahoma City, OK 73104
P.O. Box 26980 (Mailing address)
Oklahoma City, OK 73126-0980
(405) 815-5184

## OREGON

Center for Population Research and Census
Portland State University
506 SW Mill
570J Urban
Portland, OR 97201
(503) 725-8887, ext. 5159

## PENNSYLVANIA

+Pennsylvania State Data Center
Institute of State and Regional Affairs
Penn State Harrisburg
777 West Harrisburg Pike
Middletown, PA 17057-4898
(717) 948-6336

## PUERTO RICO

Puerto Rico Planning Board
Minillas Governmental Center
North Building, 14th Floor
De Eiego Avenue Pda 22
P.O. Box 411119
Santurce, PR 00940-1119
(787) 728-4430

## RHODE ISLAND

Rhode Island Department of Admin.
Statewide Planning Program
One Capitol Hill
Providence, RI 02908-5873
(401) 222-6183

## SOUTH CAROLINA

Office of Research and Statistical
South Carolina Budget and Control Board
Rembert Dennis Bldg., Room 425
Columbia, SC 29201
(803) 734-3780

## SOUTH DAKOTA

Business Research Bureau
School of Business
University of South Dakota
414 East Clark Street
Vermillion, SD 57069
(605) 677-5287

## TENNESSEE

University of Tennessee-Knoxville
Center for Business and Economic Research
100 Glocker Hall
Business Building
Knoxville, TN 37996-4170
(865) 974-5441

## TEXAS

Texas State Data Center
Institute for Demographic and Socioeconomic
    Research (IDSER)
University of Texas at San Antonio
College of Business
6900 North Loop 1604 West
San Antonio, TX 78249-0704
(979) 845-5115

## UTAH

+Office of Planning & Budget
Capitol Complex, East Building, Suite 210
P.O. Box 142210
Salt Lake City, UT 84114
(801) 538-1038

## VERMONT

Center for Rural Studies
207 Morril Hall—UVM
Burlington, VT 05405
(802) 656-3021

## VIRGIN ISLANDS

University of the Virgin Islands
Eastern Caribbean Center
No. 2 John Brewer's Bay
Charlotte Amalie
St. Thomas, VI 00802
(340) 693-1027

## VIRGINIA

+Virginia Employment Commission
703 East Main Street
Richmond, VA 23219
(804) 786-7496

## WASHINGTON

+Office of Financial Management
Forecasting Division
450 Insurance Bldg., Box 43113
Olympia, WA 98504-3113
(360) 902-0592

## WEST VIRGINIA

+Bureau of Business & Economic Research
West Virginia University
P.O. Box 6025
Morgantown, WV 26506
(304) 293-7832

West Virginia Development Office
Capitol Complex
Building 6, Room 620
Charleston, WV 25305-0311
(304) 558-4010

## WISCONSIN

+Applied Population Laboratory
Department of Rural Sociology
University of Wisconsin
1450 Linden Drive
316 AG Hall
Madison, WI 53706
(608) 265-9545

Department of Administration
Demographic Services Center
P.O. Box 8944
101 E Wilson Street St., 4th Floor
Madison, WI 53702
(608) 266-1927

**WYOMING**

Department of Admin. and Information
Economic Analysis Division
Emerson Building 327E
Cheyenne, WY 82002-0060
(307) 777-7504

# APPENDIX E
# Census Bureau Regional Offices

The Census Bureau has regional offices in 12 cities around the country. Each of these offices has several people responsible for answering data questions from the public. Please note that California, New Jersey, and New York are served by more than one regional office.

Atlanta (AL, FL, GA)
101 Marietta Street, NW
Suite 3200
Atlanta, GA 30303-2700
Phone: 404-730-3833
TDD: 404-730-3964

Boston (CT, MA, ME, NH, NY [part], RI, VT,
    Puerto Rico)
4 Copley Place, Suite 301
P.O. Box 9108
Boston, MA 02117-9108
Phone: 617-424-4501
TDD: 617-424-0565

Charlotte (KY, NC, SC, TN, VA)
901 Center Park Drive
Suite 106
Charlotte, NC 28217-2935
Phone: 704-424-6430
TDD: 704-344-6114

Chicago (IL, IN, WI)
2255 Enterprise Drive
Suite 5501
Westchester, IL 60154
Phone: 708-562-1350
TDD: 708-562-1791

Dallas (LA, MS, TX)
8585 N. Stemmons Fwy

Suite 800 S
Dallas, TX 75247-3836
Phone: 214-253-4481
TDD: 214-253-4434

Denver (AZ, CO, MT, NE, ND, NM, NV, SD, UT,
    WY)
6900 W. Jefferson Avenue
Suite 100
Lakewood, CO 80235-2032
Phone: 303-969-7750
TDD: 303-969-6769

Detroit (MI, OH, WV)
1395 Brewery Park Blvd.
Detroit, MI 48207
Phone: 313-259-1875
TDD: 313-259-5169

Kansas City (AR, IA, KS, MN, MO, OK)
1211 North 8th Street
Kansas City, KS 66101-2129
Phone: 913-551-6711
TDD: 913-551-5839

Los Angeles (southern CA, HI)
15350 Sherman Way
Suite 300
Van Nuys, CA 91406-4224
Phone: 818-904-6339
TDD: 1-800-992-3529

New York (NY [part], NJ [part])
395 Hudson St
Suite 800
New York, NY 10014
Phone: (212) 584-3440
TDD: (212) 478-4793

Philadelphia (DE, DC, MD, NJ [part], PA)
1601 Market Street
21st Floor
Philadelphia, PA 19103-2395
Phone: 215-656-7578
TDD: 215-656-7578

Seattle (northern CA, AK, ID, OR, WA)
700 5th Avenue
Suite 5100
Seattle, WA 98104-5018
Phone: 206-553-5835
TDD: 206-553-5859

# Index

1810 Census, xiii, 4, 17–18, 129
1820 Census, 18
1840 Census, 4, 18, 129
1850 Census, 18
1860 Census, 18
1870 Census, 18
1880 Census, 18
1890 Census, 18
1902 (key date), 18
1905 Census, 4, 18–19
1910 Census, 19
1917–1918 Special Economic Censuses, 19
1920 Census, 19
1930 Census, 4
1940 Census, 19
1947 Census of Manufactures, 19
1948 (key date), 19
1953–1955 (key dates), 19–20
1954 Economic Censuses, 4, 20
1958 Economic Censuses, 4
1963 Economic Censuses, 4
1967 Economic Censuses, 4, 20
1977 Economic Censuses, 4
1987 Economic Censuses, 4
1992 Economic Censuses, 5
1997 Economic Census, 5–6, 20; specific sectors, 130, 154, 203, 235, 236, 238, 239, 240, 241
2002 Economic Census, 6–7, 20, 83; specific sectors, 130, 131, 154, 203, 235, 236, 238, 239, 240

a (symbol), 122
A (symbol), 122
Abbreviations, 121–22
Accessing data, 203
Accommodations and Food Services, 59
*Accommodations and Food Services* (report), 240–41
*Accountant's Guide to the 1997 Economic Census,* 31, 32
Acrobat Reader, 111–12, 135–37. *See also* PDF
Administrative and Support and Waste Management and Remediation Services, 58, 153

*Administrative and Support and Waste Management and Remediation Services* (report), 239–40
Administrative records, 4, 32, 33, 35, 40, 96, 99
Adobe Acrobat, 111–12, 135. *See also* PDF
*Advance Report,* 15, 73
*Agricultural Atlas of the United States,* 134
*Agricultural Economics and Land Ownership Survey,* 135
Agricultural product, 131
Agricultural services, 8
Agriculture Census, 5, 7, 8. *See also specific censuses*
Agriculture, Forestry, Fishing and Hunting, 54–55
American FactFinder, 115–17, 124, 201
American Samoa, 8
*Annual Capital Expenditures Survey,* 21, 194
*Annual Statement Studies,* 24
*Annual Survey of Manufactures,* 19, 186, 194
*Annual Wholesale Trade Report,* 206
Aquaculture, 135
*Area Summary* (construction), 236
*Area Wage Surveys,* 23
Arts, Entertainment, and Recreation, 59, 239–40
*Arts, Entertainment, and Recreation* (report), 241
Authorization, 4, 15, 17–18, 19, 20, 130
Auxiliary establishments, 6, 43, 59–60
*Auxiliary establishments* (report), 241–43
Aviation, 174

b (symbol), 122
*Beige book,* 24
Beyond 20/20, 158, 161–68
Boats, 173–74
Boroughs, 47, 76
*Bridge Between NAICS and SIC,* 15, 16, 86–89, 203, 216
Bridge Tables, 6, 64–67, 243

Budget, 8
Bureau of Economic Analysis (BEA), 60
Bureau of Labor Statistics (BLS), 22–23, 60, 194
Bureau of Transportation Statistics (BTS), 172–73
Buses, 173
Business and Industry Data Center (BIDC), 31, 50
Businesses, xiii, 42–43
*Business Expenditures Survey,* 91–92, 155
*Business Expenses,* 15, 155, 203–5, 218
Business register, 32, 36
Business research, xiii
Business size classes, 43. *See also* Large companies; Medium size business; Small business
Business uses of Economic Census data, 17, 144, 206, 219–20

c (symbol), 122
Capital expenditures, 45
Cautions, 168, 205, 218
CC (symbol), 122
CD-ROM, xiv–xv, 37, 117, 125–26, 137–43
Census, 3, 40
Census advisory committees, 27
Census Bureau, 18, 21–22, 50, 60, 194
Census designated place (CDP), 47
Census employees, 18
Census Information Center (CIC), 50
*Census of Aquaculture,* 135
*Census of Governments,* 7
*Census of Horticultural Specialties,* 135
*Census of Outlying Areas,* 15–16, 103–4, 205
*Census Product Update,* 21
*Census Transportation Planning Package,* 172
Center for Economic Studies, 106–7
Characteristics of Business Owners Survey, 7, 8, 15, 98–101, 218. See also *Minority-owned Business Survey; Women-owned Business Survey*

Cities, 47
Citing economic census data, 122–26
*Civil Aviation Statistics of the World,*
174
Class of customer, 46
CMSA (Consolidated Metropolitan
Statistical Area), 48, 122
Combined statistical area (CSA), 48
Commercial activities, 4
*Commodity Flow Survey (CFS),* 16,
104–5, 158–61, 163–65
*Commodity Flow Survey, United States,
Exports,* 161
*Commodity Flow Survey, United States,
Hazardous Materials,* 161
Commodity lines, 42
*Commodity Line Sales,* 14, 77–79,
201–3. See also *Merchandise Line
Sales; Source of Receipts; Source of
Revenues*
Communications, 5. *See also* Utilities
Company, 4, 40, 98–99
Company headquarters, 6
Company statistics, 46
Company Statistics Division, 27
*Comparative Statistics,* 15, 16, 86,
87–89, 203, 216
*Compensation & Working Conditions,*
22
Complementary disclosure, 20
Computerized Self-administered
Questionnaires (CSAQ), 20
*Concentration Ratios in Manufacturing,*
79, 192
Confidentiality, 18, 19, 20, 98
Congressional Affairs Office, 31
*Congressional District Atlas,* 134
Consolidated cities, 47
Consolidated Metropolitan Statistical
Area (CMSA), 48, 122
Construction, 4, 55, 235–36
Content, 99, 159–61, 185. *See also
specific reports; specific sectors*
Content determination, 27–28
Core Based Statistical Area (CBSA), 7,
47–48, 76
Core business statistics, 14–15
Core data, 44–45
Corporations, 22
Counties, 47, 76
*County Business Patterns,* 21
Coverage, 3, 4, 18; specific sectors and
surveys, 97, 98–99, 130–31,
153–54, 157, 201, 215, 235
CSAQ (Computer Self-Administered
Questionnaires), 20
*Current Business Reports–Advance
Monthly Retail Sales,* 220

*Current Business Reports–Annual
Benchmark Report for Retail Trade,*
220
*Current Business Reports–Monthly
Retail Trade,* 220
Current data, 21–24, 144–45, 193–94,
220
*Current Employment Series,* 67
Current industrial survey, 19
Current surveys, 19, 144–45
Customer Liaison Office, 31

D (symbol), 121
Data, 69; access, 10–11, 113;
availability, 5, 6, 10–13, 131,
215–18; collection, 4, 18, 19, 20,
28–37, 99–100; content, 13, 99,
137, 159–61, 185–86, 201–5 (*see
also specific reports; specific
sectors*); dissemination, xiv–xv, 20;
intermediaries, 50; quality, 49–50,
101; queries, 137; tables, 118–21
Date entry, 36
Data processing, 18, 19
Decennial Census, 18, 172
Demographic data, 39–40
DocuPrint, 20, 33
Domestic help, 8
Drill-down tables, 113–15, 124
DVD, xiv–xv. *See also* CD-ROM;
Products

e (symbol), 122
e-commerce, 7, 20, 38
*E-commerce Statistics,* 15
*Economic Census of Puerto Rico and
the Island Areas,* 101–4
Economic census Web site, 113–15
Economic data defined, 39
*Economic Indicators,* 23
Economic places, 47, 76
Economic Planning and Coordination
Division (EPCD), 27, 30
*Economic Report of the President,* 23
Economy-wide series, 14–16
*Economy-wide Statistics,* 83–86
Editing and imputation, 97
Educational Services, 58
*Educational Services* (report), 239
Electronic computing, 20
Electronic filing, 35, 38
Employers, 42
Employment, 44
*Employment and Earnings,* 22
*Employment, Hours, & Earnings, United
States,* 22
*Employment Situation,* 22–23
Enterprise, 40

Enterprise statistics, 46
Error handling, 131–32
Establishment, 4, 40
*Establishment and Firm Size (including
Legal Form of Organization),* 14,
79, 203, 216, 235, 236, 238, 239
*E-Stats,* 194, 206, 220
Excluded data, 7–8
Exports, 161
Extract software, 6, 16

f (symbol), 122
F (symbol), 122
Farm, 130–31
*Farm and Ranch Irrigation Survey,*
134–35
Farm associations, 144
Farmers, 144
Farming, 18
*Farm Production Expenditures,* 206
Federal Depository Library Program, 16,
50
Federal Highway Administration, 173
Federal income tax status, 240. *See also*
Taxable establishments; Tax-exempt
establishments
*Federal Register,* 23
Federal Reserve System, 24
Finance and Insurance, 5, 57, 238
Financial services, 238
F.I.R.E. (Finance, Insurance, and Real
Estate), 20. *See also* Finance and
Insurance; Real Estate and Rental
and Leasing
Firm, 40. *See also* Establishment
Fisheries, 8
Fishing, 18
Food Services, 216–18
Forestry, 8
Formats available, xiv

g (symbol), 122
*General Summary,* 190, 234
Geographic areas defined, 46–49
Geographic Area Series, 13–14, 75–76;
specific sectors, 132–34, 158, 186,
201, 205, 215–16, 233–34, 235,
236, 238, 239, 241
Geographic coverage, 97
Goods producing sectors, 41
Go software, 6, 16
Government, 5, 7, 16–17, 143–44, 206,
219
Government Printing Office's Federal
Depository Library Program,
16, 50
Guam, 103, 205
*Guide to the Economic Census,* 113

h (symbol), 122
Harmonized system, 42
*Harmonized Tariff Schedule of the
    United States Annotated,* 42
Hawkes, Albert W. (senator), 19
Hazardous materials, 161
Health Care and Social Assistance, 58,
    239–41
Hefindahl-Herschmann Index, 79, 190
Highway data, 173
Historical comparability, 101
Historical data, 5, 16, 22, 89–91
*Historical Statistics of the United States:
    Colonial Times to 1970,* 22
History, 4–5, 17–21, 129–30
Hospitals, 7, 13
Household production, 18
HTML tables, 113–15

i (symbol), 122
IC (symbol), 122
Independent cities, 47, 76
Industrial classification, xiv, 40–41, 52,
    53–54
Industry, 4; norms, 17; report series,
    generally, 7, 13, 38, 73–75; report
    series, specific sectors, 186–90, 203,
    234, 235, 236; Statistics Sampler,
    113
*Industry Surveys,* 24
*Industry Week,* 194
Information, 57, 236
Insurance, 238
Integration, 4, 5, 20, 30
Internal Revenue Service, 23–24, 32
International Standard Industrial
    Classification (ISIC), 41
Internet, xiv–xv, 37, 112–17, 135–37

j (symbol), 122

k (symbol), 122

l (symbol), 122
Labor organizations, 8
*Labor Productivity and Costs,* 194
Landscape architecture, 8
Landscaping services, 8
Large companies, 30, 34, 43. *See also*
    Business size classes; Medium size
    business; Small business
Leased employees, 20, 38
Leasing, 238
Legal forms of organization, 14, 79, 203,
    216, 235, 236, 238, 239
Legislation, 4, 15, 17–18, 19, 20, 130
Lisboa Associates, 30–31
*Location of Manufacturing Plants,* 83

*Location of Mining Operations,* 83, 234
Longitudinal Research Database, 106–7

m (symbol), 122
Mail handling procedures, 35–36
Mail responses, 35–36
Management of Companies and
    Enterprises, 58
*Management of Companies and
    Enterprises* (report), 238–39
Mandatory response, 19, 30
*Manufacturers' Shipments, Inventories,
    and Orders,* 192
Manufacturing, 4, 18, 55–56, 183–84
Manufacturing and Construction
    Division (MCD), 27
*Manufacturing and Trade Inventory and
    Sales,* 192
Maps, 126
Marketing Services Office (MSO), 31
Marketing uses, 17
Materials consumed, 13, 45–46, 73, 192,
    234
*Materials Consumed Summary,* 234
*Materials Summary,* 190
MD (Metropolitan Division), 48, 122
Media, 154, 169
Medium size business, 34, 43. *See also*
    Business size classes; Large
    companies; Small business
Merchandise lines, 42
*Merchandise Line Sales,* 14, 77–79, 216.
    See also *Commodity Line Sales;
    Source of Receipts; Source of
    Revenues*
MeSA (Metropolitan Statistical Area), 7,
    47–48, 122
Metropolitan Areas, 47, 76
Metropolitan Division (MD), 48, 122
Metropolitan Statistical Area (MeSA or
    MSA), 7, 47–48, 122
Microdata, 166–68
Microfilm, 36
Micropolitan Statistical Areas (MiSA),
    7, 48, 122
Mining, 4, 18, 55, 233–34
*Minority-owned Business Survey,* 7, 15,
    155–57, 218. See also *Survey of
    Business Owners and Self-employed
    Persons; Women-owned Business
    Survey*
MiSA (Micropolitan Statistical Areas),
    7, 48, 122
*Miscellaneous Subjects,* 14, 83; specific
    sectors, 203, 216, 235, 236, 238,
    240, 241
Missing data, 49–50, 161
*Monthly Labor Review,* 23

*Monthly Wholesale Trade Report,* 206
Motor vehicle data, 173
MSA (Metropolitan Statistical Area), 7,
    47–48, 122
Multi-establishment companies, 32,
    33–34, 36
Municipal utilities, 235

N (symbol), 121
NAICS (North American Industry
    Classification System), xiv, 4, 6–7,
    20, 41, 51–52, 54–62 (*see also*
    Standard Industrial Classification
    System); NAICS-SIC comparison,
    63–64, 146–51, 196–98, 207–11,
    220, 223–30, 243; NAICS-SIC
    conversion, 6, 16, 67, 154, 184,
    200–201, 214–15, 218
National Agricultural Statistical Service
    (NASS), 7, 8, 129–32, 144
*National Transportation Statistics,* 172
NEC (symbol), 122
New England City and Town Areas
    (NECTAs), 48
Non-employers, 13, 43, 183
*Nonemployer Statistics,* 15, 92–98,
    154–55, 201, 216
Nonresponse follow-up, 8, 33–34
Nonstore retailers, 214
North American Industry Classification
    System. *See* NAICS
North American Product Classification
    System (NAPCS), 7, 42
*North American Transportation in
    Figures,* 173
Northern Mariana Islands, 104, 205
nsk (symbol), 122

Occupation, 4, 18
*Occupational Compensation Survey,* 23
*Occupational Outlook,* 22
Office of Management and Budget
    (OMB), 27–28
*Oil & Gas Journal,* 174
Organizational uses, 144
Origins of the Economic Census, 4
Other Services (except Public
    Administration), 59
*Other Services (except Public
    Administration)* (report), 240, 241
Outlying areas, 101–4, 132–33, 205, 218

p (symbol), 122
Parishes, 47, 76
Payroll, 44
PDF (Portable Document Format), 37,
    110–12, 123–24, 135–37, 158, 161
Personal services, 240

Pet care, 8
Pipelines, 174
Places, 47, 76
PMSA (Primary Metropolitan Statistical Area), 48, 122
Political organizations, 8
Population and Housing Census, xiii, 172
Post-enumeration survey, 19
*PPI Detailed Report,* 23
Predefined reports, 139–41
Press kits, 31–32
Primary Metropolitan Statistical Area (PMSA), 48, 122
Printable reports. *See* Acrobat Reader; Adobe Acrobat; PDF
Printed reports, 123, 132–35
Print format, 110
Print-on-demand service, 110
Private sector uses, 17
Procedures, 35–36, 38, 130–32, 157–58, 158–61
*Producer Price Index (PPI),* 23
Product classification, 7, 38, 41–42
Products (census), 13, 29, 37–38, 100–101, 132–43. *See also specific reports; specific sectors*
Products sold, 41
Product statistics, 73
*Product Summary,* 192, 234
Professional, Scientific, and Technical Services, 58
*Professional, Scientific, and Technical Services* (report), 239–40
Promotion, 28–29, 30–31
Public Administration, 59
Public Information Office, 31
Public Service Announcements (PSAs), 31
*Public Transportation Fact Book,* 173
Publication process, 37
Publicity materials, 31–32
Puerto Rico, 103, 205

q (symbol), 122
Q (symbol), 122
Quality assurance, 36–37
*Quarterly Financial Report for Manufacturing, Mining, and Trade Corporations,* 22, 194
Questionnaires, 20, 28, 32, 33, 35–37, 130

r (symbol), 121–22
Railroads, 8
*Rankings of States and Counties,* 134
Real estate, 5, 238

Real Estate and Rental and Leasing, 57–58
*Real Estate and Rental and Leasing* (report), 238
Receipts, 44
Reference years, 4
Regional depository libraries, 16, 50
Regions, 76
Related surveys, 14–16
Relative standard error, 50
Religious organizations, 8
Remediation services, 239
Rental and leasing, 238
Repair services, 240
Report availability, 71–73. *See also specific reports*
Reports, 71–72, 184–92, 201–3, 215–16, 236
Research and development facilities, 6
Research Data Centers, 106
Research uses, 144
Response promotion, 28–29
Retail, 4, 213–14, 216–18
*Revenue lines,* 14, 42, 235. See also *Commodity Line Sales; Merchandise Line Sales*
Robert Morris Associates, 24

s (symbol), 122
S (symbol), 122
Sales, 44–45
Sample, 40
Sampling, 19, 32–33
Sampling error, 50
Seasonal jobs, 44
Secondary sources, 126
Sectors, 41
*Service Annual Survey,* 172
Service producing sectors, 41
Services, 4, 239–41
Service Sector Statistics Division, 27
SIC (Standard Industrial Classification) System, xiv, 4, 6, 19, 41, 192, 203–5, 216–18 (*see also* NAICS); SIC-NAICS comparison, 63–64, 146–51, 196–98, 207–11, 220, 223–30, 243; SIC-NAICS conversion, 6, 16, 67, 154, 184, 200–201, 214–15, 218
Single-establishment companies, 32, 33
Size of business, 43. *See also* Large companies; Medium size business; Small business
Small business, 17, 43
*Social Science Citation Index,* 192
Social Security Administration, 19, 32
Software, 7, 137–43. *See also specific programs*

*SOI (Statistics of Income) Bulletin,* 23–24
*Source of Receipts,* 14, 42, 77–79, 236, 238, 239. See also *Commodity Line Sales; Merchandise Line Sales*
*Source of Revenues,* 14, 77–79, 238. See also *Commodity Line Sales; Merchandise Line Sales*
Special requests, 106–7
Special studies, 134–35
Special tabulations, 11, 106, 143
SSEL (Standard Statistical Establishment List), 32, 36
Standard & Poors, 24
Standard error, 50
Standard Statistical Establishment List (SSEL), 32, 36
Standard Industrial Classification System, xiv, 4, 6, 19, 41, 192, 203–5, 216–18. *See also* NAICS; SIC
Standard Statistical Establishment List, 32, 36
*State Data,* 132–34
State Data Center (SDC), 31, 50
States, 46–47, 76
*Statistical Abstract of the United States,* 22
Statistical atlas, 18
Statistical consultants, 18
*Statistical Detail,* 134
*Statistical Service,* 24
*Statistics of Income Bulletin,* 24
*Statistics of Income, Corporation Income Tax Returns,* 24
*Statistics of Interstate Natural Gas Pipeline Companies,* 174
*Stat-USA,* 24
Store retailers, 213–14
Subject content, 157
Subject reports, 14, 77–83, 134, 190–92, 234, 235
*Summary of Commentary on Current Economic Conditions (Beige Book),* 24
Summary reports, 7, 14, 38, 83; specific sectors, 201, 236, 238
Supply chain, 20, 38
Support for Economic Census, xiii
Survey, 3
*Survey of Business Owners and Self-employed Persons,* 7, 8, 15, 98–101, 218. See also *Minority-owned Business Survey; Women-owned Business Survey*
*Survey of Current Business,* 24
Symbols, 121–22, 185

Tabulation procedures, 37
Taxable establishments, 43, 240
Tax-exempt establishments, 7, 13, 43, 240
Time series, 62–67, 87, 89–91
Timing of Economic Census, 4, 20
Topics added in 2002, 38
Towns, 47
Townships, 47
Trade associations, 17
Trains, 173
Transportation, 4–5, 153
Transportation and warehousing, 56–57, 154, 155, 168–80. *See also* Information; Utilities
*Transportation Annual Survey,* 172
Transportation, Communications, and Utilities, 20
*Transportation in America,* 174
*Truck Inventory and Use Survey,* 105. See also *Vehicle Inventory and Use Survey*

Underground economy, 7
United States, 46

*United States Code Title 13,* 4, 15, 98. *See also* Authorization
*United States Summary,* 133–34
UNIVAC I, 20
Updated sources, 21–24, 206
User conferences, 38
Users, xiii
Uses, xiii, 3, 100, 104, 143–44, 192–93, 206
U.S. Virgin Islands, 104, 205
Utilities, 5, 55, 234–35

V (symbol) 122
Value added by manufacturing, 44–45
Value of shipments, 44
*Vehicle Inventory and Use Survey (VIUS),* 16, 105–6, 157–58, 165–66, 166–68
Veterinary services, 8
Villages, 47
Virgin Islands, 104, 205

Warehouses, 6
Warehousing, 153. *See also* Transportation and warehousing

Waste management services, 239. *See also* Administrative and Support and Waste Management and Remediation Services
Waterways, 173–74
Watkins, Ralph J., 20
*Watkins Commission Report,* xiii, 20
Wholesale trade, 4, 56, 200–201
*Women-owned Business Survey,* 7, 15, 155–57, 205 See also *Minority-owned Business Survey; Survey of Business Owners and Self-employed Persons*
World War II, 4, 19

X (symbol), 121

Y (symbol), 122
"Your Response if Required by Law," 8–10, 30

z (symbol), 121
ZIP code, 11, 15, 21, 48–49, 77–78, 134, 216
*ZIP Code Business Patterns,* 21
ZIP Code Tabulation Areas (ZCTAs), 49

**About the Authors**

JENNIFER C. BOETTCHER is the Business Reference Librarian at Georgetown University. She is also an adjunct professor at the Catholic University of America in the School of Library and Information Science and is the co-author of *Key Business Sources of the U.S. Government.*

LEONARD M. GAINES is a program research specialist with Empire State Development, where he has worked for about 20 years as the New York State Data Center Program's specialist on the Census Bureau's economic data. He is also an adjunct faculty member at the State University of New York, Empire State College's Center for Distance Learning, where he teaches several quantitative courses.